21世纪英语专业系列教材
·新世纪翻译系列教程·

Advanced English Contract Writing and Translation

高级合同写作与翻译

李克兴 著

北京大学出版社
PEKING UNIVERSITY PRESS

图书在版编目(CIP)数据

高级合同写作与翻译 / 李克兴著. —北京：北京大学出版社，2016.9
（21世纪英语专业系列教材·新世纪翻译系列教程）
ISBN 978-7-301-26128-6

Ⅰ.①高… Ⅱ.①李… Ⅲ.①英语–合同–写作②英语–合同–翻译 Ⅳ.①H315

中国版本图书馆CIP数据核字(2015)第175366号

书　　　名	高级合同写作与翻译
	GAOJI HETONG XIEZUO YU FANYI
著作责任者	李克兴　著
责 任 编 辑	郝妮娜
标 准 书 号	ISBN 978-7-301-26128-6
出 版 发 行	北京大学出版社
地　　　址	北京市海淀区成府路205号　100871
网　　　址	http://www.pup.cn　新浪微博：@北京大学出版社
电 子 信 箱	bdhnn 2011@126.com
电　　　话	邮购部 62752015　发行部 62750672　编辑部 62759634
印 刷 者	北京大学印刷厂
经 销 者	新华书店
	787毫米×1092毫米　16开本　20.5印张　650千字
	2016年9月第1版　2018年5月第2次印刷
定　　　价	58.00元

未经许可，不得以任何方式复制或抄袭本书之部分或全部内容。
版权所有，侵权必究
举报电话：010-62752024　电子信箱：fd@pup.pku.edu.cn
图书如有印装质量问题，请与出版部联系，电话：010-62756370

前　言

与英文合同打交道的主要有两种人员：从事日常合同草拟工作的从业人员，即律师，以及从法律角度研究合同文本的研究者。但这两类人员对当代合同语言的发展趋势都不够重视，因为前者已经习惯于自己的语言风格，后者只关注合同的法律观点。所以现今在各大律师事务所使用和流传的各类英文模式合同（在网上公开售卖的除外）虽然内容全面，但语言晦涩难懂，风格陈旧，用词与时代脱节。这往往让正在学习合同写作的后辈仍然有些无所适从。以下一段是2014年5月份由香港一家律师楼草拟的住房销售合约的序言条款：

THIS AGREEMENT FOR SALE AND PURCHASE made the day of Two Thousand and Fourteen

BETWEEN The party whose name and address or registered office and description are set out in Part I of this First Schedule hereto ("the Vendor") of the one part and the party whose name and address or registered office and description are set out in Part I of the First Schedule hereto ("the Purchaser") of the other part.

WHEREBY IT IS AGREED between the parties hereto as follows：

1. The Vendor shall sell and the Purchaser shall purchase ALL THOSE the premises more particularly described in the Second Schedule hereto ("the Property") and all rights of way (if any) privileges easements and appurtenances thereto belonging or appertaining or therewith at any time used held occupied or enjoyed AND the Vendor shall sell a legal estate in the Property in so far as the Vendor's interest in the Property is a legal estate and an equitable interest in the Property in so far as the Vendor's interest in the Property is an equitable interest (as the case may be) and all the estate right interest property claim and demand whatsoever of the Vendor therein and thereto for the residue of the term of years created by the Government Lease or Conditions (as the case may be) absolutely subject to the payment of the Government rent reserved by and the performance and observance of the covenants conditions and provisos contained in the Government Lease or Conditions in respect of the Property subject to all rights of way easements rights and privileges (if any) to which the same are subject.

合约的当事人之一是作者的同事，她看后根本不知所云。难道是当事人语言水平太低？或是律师的专业知识太深奥以至普通人无法理解？可是，当事人是在美国名牌大学取得语言学博士、一辈子从事英语教学和传媒研究的大学教授。这不得不令作者对当今英美世界法律语言的交流功用和写作风格再度提出质疑。如果这是科技界对某项重大科技成果的表述语言，这项成果会有多大的"普世价值"？

其实，以上这种房产买卖每天都在我们的日常生活中发生，稍有经验的房地产经纪或有一定炒房经历的普通市民对其中的奥秘都了如指掌。只是买卖合约由习惯了典型"师爷语言"风格的律师起草,任何简单的事务就会变得异常复杂;任何普通人都能明白的道理就会变得高深莫测。

　　为此,本书拟从法律英语风格角度对当代法律英文、尤其是英文合同的写作提出一些异议和建议。虽然任何研究者个人都没有资格对某个领域的写作实践提出任何规范,但纵观法律英文和合同语言最近几十年的发展,通过对各类合同做历时和共时比较,我们不妨把行内有识之士的共识和该领域的一些有目共睹的变化做些梳理与归纳,详列于此,以供学习法律英文,尤其是合同写作的学子以及整日忙于合同制作的从业人员参考。当然,如果读者认为这些细节变化已成趋势,而本书分析和提出的建议又是合情合理的,那么将这些建议作为合同及同类性质的法律文本的写作规范又有何妨?

目 录

第一章　英文合同语言的风格(上):句子层面的问题 …………………………… 1
第二章　英文合同语言的风格(下):词汇层面的问题 …………………………… 11
第三章　英文合同写作的技术细节(上) …………………………………………… 20
第四章　英文合同写作的技术细节(下) …………………………………………… 29
第五章　合同中的 shall 及其他情态动词的使用问题 …………………………… 40
第六章　合同序言条款的写作和翻译 ……………………………………………… 42
第七章　定义及解释条款的写作和翻译 …………………………………………… 56
第八章　合同语言与文本条款写作和翻译 ………………………………………… 73
第九章　不可抗力条款的写作、翻译和研究 ……………………………………… 81
第十章　保证条款的写作、翻译和研究 …………………………………………… 98
第十一章　责任及义务条款的写作和翻译 ………………………………………… 118
第十二章　知识产权条款的写作和翻译 …………………………………………… 131
第十三章　保密条款的写作和翻译 ………………………………………………… 142
第十四章　合同期限及终止条款的写作、翻译和研究 …………………………… 157
第十五章　违约条款的写作和翻译 ………………………………………………… 175
第十六章　仲裁条款的写作、翻译和研究(上) …………………………………… 184
第十七章　仲裁条款的写作、翻译和研究(下) …………………………………… 199
第十八章　诉讼地选择条款的写作、翻译和研究 ………………………………… 212
第十九章　转让条款的写作、翻译和研究 ………………………………………… 222
第二十章　法律选择条款的起草、翻译和研究 …………………………………… 233
第二十一章　通知条款的写作、翻译和研究 ……………………………………… 243
第二十二章　弃权条款的写作、翻译和研究 ……………………………………… 258
第二十三章　可分割性条款的写作、翻译和研究 ………………………………… 269
第二十四章　合同变更条款的写作和翻译 ………………………………………… 280

第二十五章　完整协议/最终协议条款的写作和翻译 …………………………… 286
第二十六章　合同附件的写作、翻译和研究 ………………………………………… 291
第二十七章　标准通用合同条款汇总 …………………………………………………… 299
参考文献 ……………………………………………………………………………………………… 320

第一章
英文合同语言的风格(上):句子层面的问题

用简明英文(plain English)写作法律文书,是英美以及一切英联邦国家最近几十年的共同倡导和实践,也是对撰写合同的法律从业人员的最大挑战。其重要性不言而喻:

(1) 任何读者都较容易读懂用简明语言写成的法律文件;
(2) 阅读的速度更快;理解更准确,确定所需信息的位置和获取信息的速度更快;
(3) 任何读者,如果不是别有用心,也更喜欢简明的语言,不希望用复杂艰涩的文字去表达可以用简明语言就能表达清楚的事物;
(4) 用简明语言写作,词不达意或出错的机会较少;
(5) 用简明语言写成的法律文件容易更新(语言风格上较容易保持一致);
(6) 能用简明语言写作法律文件的人员容易培养,因此,制作该类文本的成本也较低。(李克兴,2010)

虽然目前各国在这方面仍然阻力重重,取得的成果也未能如愿,但无可否认:与几十年以前的文本相比,如今的英文合同句子短了,使用拉丁词、古旧词的频率低了,只有律师看得懂的师爷式表达方式少了,尤其是在与民众日常法律活动相关的商务领域(如房屋租赁、信用卡申请、贷款、租车、普通货物买卖),法律文书的英文已经简明了许多、比较接近普通英文了。就合同语言而言,简明英文有哪些特点和具体要求? 笔者认为:

(1) 合同的语言应当是在英美国家受过高等教育的非法律专业的人士(layman,如公司的业务主管)都能看得懂的语言。
(2) 如果合同的有关方并非来自美国,英文合同一般要用英式英文撰写(包括拼写),因为以前英联邦国家和地区(包括新加坡、马来西亚、马耳他、澳大利亚、新西兰、南非以及中国香港,等等)仍然在使用英式英文;由于地缘关系,英式英文对欧盟各国的影响更大,在欧洲更加流行。根据语言从众的规律,写作合同时提倡使用英式英文。
(3) 放弃典型的师爷式语言(lawyerisms or legalese),减少、避免以至消除(当然不指望根除)各种"吸血鬼"(vampire)表达方式[①]。

前面两点非常简单,是一般的认识问题,认识到了,赞同此观点的,很容易做到。第(3)点,极为复杂,其中的问题早已存在数百年,要矫枉纠正,实非易事;而绝大部分需要用英文写作或翻译法律文本的人士,至今对师爷语言认识不足,难以辨别良莠,甚至还模仿不良文风。故不妨在此"详篇大论",以便能明辨是非、判断优劣,或至少起到一些"以儆效尤"或"立此存照"的作用。所以,本文的重点基本上就落在介绍、分析、讨论各种"吸血鬼"表达方式以

[①] 在法律写作领域,把各种不良写作风格称为"吸血鬼"的表达方式的主要见 Brody 等人的著作,详见参考文献 Brody 等人的 *Legal Drafting* 的第 99 页。其实早在其 *Plain English for Lawyers*(1985) 一书中,Richard Wydick 已经把这类师爷式语言称之为"吸血鬼"表达方式。

及各种行之有效的改进措施上,从而达至改进文风,落实用"简明英语"写作合同以及其他法律文书的理念。

师爷语言风格与"吸血鬼"表达方式

所谓师爷语言风格指用典型的传统法律语言撰写法律文书的风格。这类文书是受过良好教育的普通人读不懂或者读得似懂非懂的,但一读便知:"喔,这是律师写的"——所以称之为师爷风格。它涉及的主要是文风问题。具体则体现在大量的"吸血鬼"表达方式上。既然是"吸血鬼",本来应该予以消灭或根除,但由于问题早已根深蒂固,而英美法律界也积重难返,因此想消灭它们,近期内是不可能的,故只能提倡减少和避免使用。首先,我们来认识法律文本、尤其是合同文本中的各种"吸血鬼"。

所谓"吸血鬼"指传说中那青面獠牙、靠吸取人体中最宝贵的血液为生的魔鬼。语言中的"吸血鬼"指干扰读者直接、快速、准确获取文本信息的各种表达方式。法律文本中的"吸血鬼"主要指各种会将文本的重要信息掩埋的法律文体所独有的不良表达方式,尤其是隐藏句子中的、被文本作者的写作习惯所扭曲的行为动作的表达方式。这种方式有些体现在句子层面,有些则以各种独特的词汇或短语形式出现。对这类"吸血鬼",有些我们提倡避免,有些则建议慎用,有些则要减少或因人(读者)而异地使用。首先,我们讨论句子层面的"吸血鬼"。

一、避免使用长条款和长句

最近,中国政法大学魏蘅老师做了一项对比研究:语料为 6 个原创英文合同,共计 95 882 词;11 个中文合同的英译本,共计 26 248 词。研究的合同样本几乎都是以"拿来主义"方式而随机取样。但 6 个英文原创合同却有九万五千多词,平均每个合同有一万六千词;而 11 个中文合同的译文居然不到三万个英文词,平均每个合同只有 2 386 个词,文本长度几乎只有英文合同的七分之一。虽然这些数据不能从统计学角度证明中英文合同一定有任何重大差别,但英文合同文风拖沓、用词累赘、句子冗长的特点是显而易见的。

由于传统和精英主义作祟,英美国家我行我素的律师们总是把法律条文(article or provision)或合同条款(clause or provision)写得复杂冗长,高深莫测。但凡是长条款、长句,读者一概不喜欢。不被喜欢的条款或句子被认真阅读的可能性越低,被真正读懂的机会就更低;如此一来,写作文本的初衷就难以实现。而长条款往往是由长句构成的,句子越长,读者越感到头痛,即使耐着性子阅读,也有很大可能不得要领,或在其中迷失。以引言中的那个房产买卖合约的序言条款为例,一个条款两句话就有 272 个词,其中的第二句足足有 200 个词。其实,要是用以下简明的书面英文去表达,只需要 79 个词可以把同样的概念表达得清清楚楚:

> This agreement is made on _____ , 2014, between _____ , the Seller, address:_____ and _____ , the Buyer, address: _____
>
> The Seller now owns the following described real estate, located at _____ _____ .
>
> For valuable consideration, the Seller agrees to sell and the Buyer agrees to buy this property for the following price and on the following terms:

1. The Seller shall sell this property including it appurtenances to the Buyer, free from all claims, liabilities, and indebtedness, unless noted in this agreement.

以下我们再通过对比一段用传统方式写成的合同条款与用简明英文写成的版本,来发现传统合同文本中的问题以及可能解决这些问题的措施。例如:

Version A:

If the proposed Insured has or acquires actual knowledge of any defect, lien, encumbrance, adverse claim or other matter affecting the estate or interest or mortgage thereon covered by this Commitment other than those shown on Schedule B hereof, and shall fail to disclose such knowledge to the Company in writing, the Company shall be relieved from liability for any loss or damage resulting from any act of reliance hereon to the extent the Company is prejudiced by failure to so disclose such knowledge. If the proposed Insured shall disclose such knowledge of any such defect, lien, encumbrance, adverse claim or other matter, the Company at its option may amend Schedule B of this Commitment accordingly, but such amendment shall not relieve the Company from liability previously incurred pursuant to Paragraph 3 of these Conditions and Stipulations. (Brody, 1994:114)

Version B:

If you know of any legal defects (including lien) affecting the title to your property, you must tell us in writing. If you tell us about a defect, we cannot pay you for a loss that the defect causes, but we will still pay you for any other covered loss you have. If you do not tell us, we will not pay you for any loss you have that we could have avoided if we had known about the defect. (Brody, 1994:114)

这是保险公司的一份保单条款的两种写法。两个版本所传达的信息几乎完全相同。但A版本用了个137个词,而B版本只用了80个词。现代的用户读者(要咬文嚼字打官司的律师除外)很少有人会有耐心读完A版本,而且绝大部分人也读不懂,或者读到后面忘了前面,无法将冗长的词语信息消化从而准确获得该条款或句子所包含的主题信息。

为何A版本的条款如此不堪卒读?除了最主要的句子太长的原因之外,还有以下原因:
(1) 用了不少古旧词(thereon,hereon,hereof,pursuant to);
(2) 使用冗长的名词化动词造句(has or acquires actual knowledge of vs knows; disclose such knowledge of vs tell);
(3) 使用被动语态(be relieved,is prejudiced)的表达方式;
(4) 使用了大量的近义词(has or acquires,defect,lien,encumbrance,adverse claim or other matter;the estate or interest or mortgage;loss or damage);
(5) 滥用shall (shall fail to disclose,shall disclose);
(6) 用冷冰冰的第三人称称呼客户和自家公司(the proposed Insured,the Company),无端端地拉远与读者的距离。

其中A版本的第一句用了84个词只讲述一件简单的事:如果受保人知道产权有问题,他应该怎么做;而其中的产权问题居然用了30个词去修饰(knowledge 后面的 of any defect,lien,encumbrance,adverse claim or other matter affecting the estate or interest or mortgage thereon covered by this Commitment other than those shown on Schedule B hereof 均为其修饰词)。

英美国家的学术期刊对文章的格式,句子的长度,标题的字数甚至词性,都有明确的规定。合同写作领域虽然无此严格规定,但有专门教授合同写作的网站最近建议合同的句子一般不超过 17 个单词[1],有些法律写作权威工具书建议每句平均长度为 20 个词[2],而有些则建议 25 词[3]。虽然这些不是绝对标准,任何人也不可以硬性规定句子该多长或由多少字构成(主要是根据需要),但用简明英文写合同,句子应当尽可能短,能用 10 个词把意思表达清楚的,决不用 11 个词;写作时,作者心中一定要有读者,不能随心所欲把自己习惯的、得心应手的、尤其是一些可以从旧式模块文本中拷贝得来的而又专属律师使用的表达方式或短语都塞进句子。在将法律文本的长句变为短句时,有一些常用的技巧,简介如下。长句例句如:

a. Following years of erosion by juries and courts, almost unanimous criticism by legal scholars, and, perhaps most influential, the rise of alternative no-fault systems for dealing with injuries, the common law doctrine of contributory negligence has been abandoned in a large number of jurisdictions. (Brody, 1994:124)

这个句子非常难懂,因为是一个把若干相关概念都编织在一起的长句。如果仔细分析,该长句包含四层主要意思:(1)很多司法管辖区放弃了"共同过失"(contributory negligence)这个普通法原则;(2)这个原则因为种种原因而受到削弱;(3)对这个原则影响最大可能是"无过错"制度(no-fault systems)的出现;以及(4)"无过错"制度成了处理伤害(dealing with injuries)的一种替代方式。根据这四层意思,可以将该句写成非常容易懂的四个短句:

b. A large number of jurisdictions has abandoned the common law doctrine of contributory negligence. The doctrine had been eroded by courts, juries, and the almost unanimous criticism of legal scholars. The most important influence, however, may have been the rise of no-fault systems. These systems provided an alternative for dealing with injuries.

很明显,将长句变成短句的方法不难归纳为以下四个步骤:(1) 分析句子的核心概念(core idea),(2) 用一个短句去表达一个核心概念,(3) 以逻辑的方式(事情发生的先后顺序或前因后果)将所表达的核心概念联结在一起;(4) 如有必要,加入适当的连词使各短句之间前后照应,产生连贯。

不过,通过分析以上两个长例句,还可以发现被动语态的使用也是造成句子冗长的主要原因之一(第一个例句有 the Company shall be relieved from..., the Company is prejudiced by...;第二个例句有 ...contributory negligence has been abandoned)。

---

[1] www.weagree.com/weblog? topic=18.
[2] Bryan A. Garner, *A Dictionary of Modern Legal Usage*, 2nd ed., 1995.
[3] Robert C. Dick, *Legal Drafting in Plain English*, 3rd ed., 1995.

二、提倡使用主动语态,减少被动语态的表达方式

尽管在法律和科技文体中,不可避免地要使用较多的被动语态和非人性化的表达方式,但还是应该尽量避免使用如"It is agreed and acknowledged",以及"... by [ABC]"的句式。凡是从事英文语言教学的人员,无论是英美国家的中学英语教师[①],还是教授法律专业学生写作的大学英文教授,都规劝学生少用、慎用甚至避免使用被动语态。(Le Clercq,2000:47—48;Brody,1994:95—97;Adams,2001:3;Faulk & Mehler,1996:6)但到了大学法学院,几乎所有的英文写作规矩都给颠覆了,被动语态成了准律师们写作的常态。这种不良倾向必须引起从事法律英语教学人员的警惕。

实用文体的作者一般都希望读者把注意力放在文本的内容而不是形式上,都希望读者一目了然他所要传达的信息,而不是费尽心机去解读句子的结构。英语读者最熟悉的句子、也是最容易读懂的句子结构是由主、谓、宾构成的。例如:

The defendant(主语) struck(谓语动词) the plaintiff(宾语). (Brody,1994:94—95)

如果该句以被动形式表达"The plaintiff was struck by the defendant",其所提供的信息虽然与以主动形式出现的上句所传达的信息是相同的,但被动形式不是读者所预期的表达方式。

几乎所有读者在阅读一个句子时都期待该句子有一个主题,都会本能地寻找句子的行为者(一般都是句子的主语),而且都期待句子的主题(theme/subject)与句子语法上的主语(subject)是相同的。

如上例的"被告打了原告",自然呈现和读者期待的主题是"被告打人",而不是原告被谁打了。所以,以主动形式表达,让主题中的主语或行为者与句子语法上的主语保持一致,是符合读者预期的,是合理的、高效的、符合逻辑的表达方式。所以,作者处理主谓宾的方式直接关系到读者接受信息的效果。

这一特点在英汉两种语言中是相同的。具体而言,当作者确定用主动语态表达信息后,一般要遵循以下按顺序排列的规矩:

    a. 确定句子中的行为者(主语);
    b. 确保行为者是句子中的主语;
    c. 用主动形式的动词来表示行为;
    d. 让行为动词紧跟主语;
    e. 尽可能地将主语与行为动词安置在句首位置;
    f. 让修饰词紧靠被修饰词。(Brody,1994:95)

如果描述行为的句子没有出现行为者,这个句子本身就有严重的信息缺失。如果行为者是以"by... sb."形式出现的,句子必然结构松散,并且拖沓冗长。试看以下两个对比的句子:

The term "cosmic detachment" is issued by Richard Wydick to explain abstract

---

[①] 就被动语态的使用而言,LeClercq 在书中写道:The passive was condemned by high school teachers, grudgingly overlooked by professors, and relied on completely by law students creating memoranda. 而另一本教科书则写道:"... and generally one should avoid using the passive voice."(Adams,2001:3);Faulk & Mebler 在其 *The Element of Legal Writing* 中论述:Active voice verbs carry meaning with more vigor and exactness than passive voice verbs. (Faulk & Mebler,1996:6—7)

legal style. (14 words)

　　Richard Wydick describes abstract legal style as "cosmic detachment." (9 words) (LeClercq,2000:47)

　　如果省去其中的行为者,句子的模糊性则增加。例如:The pedestrian was hit twice. 该被动句的意思模糊,究竟谁撞了行人,用何种工具撞击的,不得而知。而采用主动句式,提供的信息比前句多而且更清晰:The defendant's car hit the pedestrian twice——谁的车,撞了谁,撞了多少次,清清楚楚,一目了然。

　　此外,使用被动语态还容易错误地强调信息。例如:In Jabrowski the defendant's plane was flown low over the plaintiff's land during the crop-dusting operation. 究竟谁对谁干了什么? 句子重点是什么呢? 不清楚。而在主动句 In Jabrowski the pilot flew his plane low over the plaintiff's land during the crop-dusting operation (LeClercq,2000:47-48)中,读者清晰可知"飞行员在原告的土地上把飞机飞得太低"。所以,表达主题的句子由主动语态的主谓宾句式构成是最简明、经济、有效的。

　　但这并不是说被动语态在法律文本中可以禁绝。在以下条件下,采用被动语态的表达方式仍然是合理的:

　　(1) 行为人完全不重要或不可知,或者作者要强调的是行为受体(a person or a thing receiving the action)的状态。如:

　　　　a. Goods were stolen during the transit.
　　　　b. Toxins were found in the river.

　　在 a 句中,陈述货物在运输过程中被偷,但谁偷并不重要,而且可能根本就不可知。b 句只是陈述河流中发现了污染物,至于是谁发现的并不重要。这两个句子的重点并不是放在行为者身上,主题是两个事实:货物被偷以及河流被污染,所以采用被动语态是合适的。

　　(2) 事件或消息的性质完全负面,或需要强调的是结果或后果,而不是行为的本身。如:

　　　　The company was suited several times during the past year. (LeClercq,2000:47-48)

　　　　Johnson was struck and killed in a car accident.

　　此两句强调的都是不幸的事实,至于"被谁告上法庭"或"被谁撞死"并不是作者要表达的重点,所以被动语态用得顺理成章。

　　(3) 最后一种状况属于委婉的表达方式,如有意不让行为者"抛头露面"。例如,法官庭审时决定将面前的罪犯判处死刑,他决不会直面亲为,把自己的判决用主动语态表达出来,因为用主动语态,该有关表述一般会是这样的:

　　　　I have decided that you should die. (Brody,1994:97)

　　很显然,这一主动语态的表述方式太直接、也太无情,尽管这是一个无情的决定。任何一个法官都不想如此直白地告诉被告人是我决定让你去死的。而此时被动语态就派上了用场:

　　　　I have decided that you should be executed. 或者 The death penalty shall be imposed. (Brody,1994:97)

这样的表述语气上就显得较为委婉(第二句似乎与做出该决定的法官毫无关系)。所以,当法律文本的作者决定采用被动语态时,应该都有特殊的考虑;而总体上被动语态应少用、慎用。

三、避免使用累赘句式

所谓累赘句式指法律文本、尤其是合同文本常见的在表达上特别笨拙、内容上纯属多余、造成句子结构臃肿的句式(tautology style),主要体现在律师写作的习惯性"废话"上。由于律师的社会地位和专业定位,对于这类废话很少有人提出质疑或不敢质疑;例如,"The Parties agree that...","Service Provider understands and agrees...","it is acknowledged that..."以及诸如此类的句子开场白,在合同文件中这类句子连篇累牍或随处可见,但有谁敢认定句子有何不妥?

如果说 They arrived one after the other in succession 或者 He sits alone by himself 句子中的累赘是明显的、直接的,那么,以上句子的累赘是隐含的、间接的。其实在大多数情况下,合同内这类句子后面跟的都是法律义务条款,如"Seller shall..."("卖方应做……");因此其前面的"各方同意/理解/确认……"都是多余的。如果各方不同意,不理解,不确认,接着的义务或协议就不成立。任何义务或协议都是在双方自愿、同意的前提下达成的(所以才叫 agreement),否则就是非法的"霸王条款"。我们对比以下例句:

A.

(1) The buyer and seller agree that the sales price shall be $157,937.00.

(2) The buyer and seller agree that the earnest money of $15,000 will be held in an interest bearing account.

(3) The buyer and seller further agree that the seller will execute a warranty deed.

(4) The buyer and seller further agree that time is the essence of this contract...

B.

The buyer and seller agree as follows:

(1) The sales price shall be $157,937.00;

(2) The earnest money of $15,000 will be held in an interest bearing account;

(3) The seller will execute a warranty deed;

(4) Time is the essence of this contract... (Brody,1994:120-121)

A 段包含了四个重复的短语(The buyer and seller agree that),类似的表述在合同中早已见怪不怪。B 段就比较简明:省去了其中三个,意思却与 A 段毫无二致。

另外,句子中一些习惯性短语,如"during the term of this Agreement",也是造成句子结构冗长、语言啰嗦的一种表达方式。《合同起草》一书的作者 Ken Adams 指出:*During the term of this agreement* seems an innocuous enough phrase, but more often than not it's redundant. 原因何在?合同中的义务、禁令一般都是在合同有效期内才有效的,因此重复如此冗长的短语,只是重复一个各方已知的事实,并不会为合同增添任何有效的限制。

例如,<u>During the term of this agreement</u>, the [The] Company shall pay Jones an automobile expense allowance of $1,000 per month, grossed up for income tax purposes, and reimburse Jones for all gasoline and maintenance expenses incurred by him in operating his automobile.

其中画线的有关短语,完全多余,应当删除:公司不会在合同期过后仍然支付费用给 John。如果要超出合同有效期限,则需要具体的日期,例如:During the term of this agreement and five years thereafter (after its expiration), the Recipient shall not, and shall cause each of its Representatives not to, disclose any Confidential Information except as contemplated in this agreement①。

累赘句式还包括在完全没有必要的情况下使用较长的短语去表达一个极短的普通词就可以表达的意思。例如,根据笔者的研究,in the event that... 通常用来表达一个重大的、罕有的而且往往是不幸的条件——"In the event that② the Standing Committee of the National People's Congress decides to declare a state of war or, by reason of turmoil within the Hong Kong Special Administrative Region which endangers national unity or security and is beyond the control of the government of the Region, decides that the Region is in a state of emergency, the Central People's Government may issue an order applying the relevant national laws in the Region.(香港《基本法》第18条)",但是很多法律文本的作者用该"漫长的"短语仅仅表达一个 if 的意思:In the event that Joint Life Coverage has been selected by you...。这一层意思其实用 If you have selected Joint Life Coverage... (Faulk & Mebler,1996:9),就可以表达得清清楚楚。

此外,凡使用以下左边一栏短语造句的,所造的句子必然累赘,故须力求避免;而右边一栏则是相应的可以取而代之的简明英文用词:

due to the fact that	because
in all likelihood	probably
in order to	to
in regards to	regarding
in the event that	if
in/with respect of	for/about/regarding
in/with reference to	for/about/regarding
notwithstanding the fact that	although
provided, however that	if
the time at which	when
until such time as	until
with respect of	for/about/regarding

四、提倡使用"次级句式"的定语从句,减少使用"主流句式"的条件状语从句

在研究法律文本的句式结构时,笔者曾经发现几乎44%左右的立法文本的句子主要是

---

① http://www.adamsdrafting.com/during-the-term-of-this-agreement/.
② 本书画线词语或句子均为作者所加,以引起读者重视,下同。

由"Where/if 为引导词的条件句＋法律主体＋情态动词(shall,must,may)＋法律行为主句"的句式构成的(李克兴,2013)。如：

Where any director knowingly and wilfully contravenes, or permits or authorizes the contravention of this section, he shall be liable to imprisonment and a fine.

任何董事如明知而故意违反本条，或准许或授权他人违反本条，可处监禁及罚款。①

该类句式之所以被称之为"主流句式"(primary sentence pattern)，是因为其在文本中的超高比例；而另外在立法文本中占句子总量10%—20%左右(该比例因文本性质不同而有所差异)的句式是由"A/Any/Every legal subject（如 person/company/director）＋who（定语从句，如 does something）＋情态动词（shall/may/must）＋法律行为(legal action)"的句式构成的，之所以称之为"次级句式"(secondary sentence pattern)是因为其在法律文本中比例非常高，但又次于"主流句式"的缘故。(李克兴,2013)如：

Any director who knowingly and wilfully contravenes, or permits or authorizes the contravention of this section shall be liable to imprisonment and a fine.

其实，从简明英文的写作要求来看，这第二种次级句式对于表达特定法律概念而言(尤其是"任何人做某事，即属犯罪/违法/须受到某种处罚"之类的概念)是一种更简明、更高效的表达方式。虽然"主流句式"与"次级句式"在立法文本中功用基本相同，都同样表述法律条件与法律行为，但"次级句式"表达更直接，重心更突出，具有主位化(thematize)的功能，能让读者一目了然法律主体及其行为，抓住句子所要表达的核心思想(主位思想)；而"主流句式"往往会拉长句子，分散读者注意力，因为它是由各有一套主谓宾结构的两个句子构成的。读者通常在阅读文本的过程中，需要获取更多信息，了解两个主语的行为，确定两者的关系之后，才可以真正理解文本。

所以，在合同文本的写作过程中，如果要表达的法律行为的条件中的行为人，与法律行为的主体同属一人(或一公司)，笔者应采用更直接的"次级句式"的表达方式，即"如你做出某种行为(内地法律为"的"句式)，你就会有何种后果"。例如：

<u>Any defendant who is fined and fails to pay the fine promptly</u> may be searched.

但是，遗憾的是：在中国以往的法律翻译实践中，笔者观察到法律翻译人员似乎根本没有掌握这类"次级句式"，更谈不上该句式的应用；"主流句式"，尤其是用 Where 引导的条件句，则到了被滥用的程度。试看以下例句：

Article 41 <u>Where</u> a limited liability company has a board of directors, its shareholders meeting shall be convened by the board of directors and presided over by the chairman of the board. <u>Where</u> the chairman of the board is unable to or does not perform his function, the meeting shall be presided over by a vice-chairman. <u>Where</u> the vice-chairman is unable to or does not perform his function, the meeting shall be presided over by a director jointly nominated by more than half of the directors. <u>Where</u> a limited liability company does not form a board of directors, the shareholders

---

① 香港法律第227章:《裁判官条例》;translate. legislation. gov. hk/.

meetings shall be convened and presided over by the executive director. *Where* the board of directors or executive director cannot or does not perform its function, the shareholders meeting shall be convened and presided over by the board of supervisors or the supervisor in the absence of a board of supervisors. *Where* the board of supervisors or supervisor cannot or does not perform its function, the meeting shall be convened and presided over by shareholders representing more than one-tenth of the voting rights. (*The Company Law of the People's Republic of China*)

Article 28 Each shareholder shall make in full the amount of the capital contribution subscribed for under the articles of association of the company. *Where* a shareholder makes its capital contribution in currency, it shall deposit the full amount of such capital contribution in currency in the bank account opened by the limited liability company to be established. *Where* a shareholder makes its capital contribution in the form of non-currency property, the property rights therein shall be transferred in accordance with legally prescribed procedures.

Shareholders failing to make full capital contributions they have subscribed for in accordance with the preceding paragraph shall, they shall, in addition to making the contributions in full, be liable for breach of contract towards the shareholders who have made full capital contributions.

(*The Company Law of the People's Republic of China*)

特别是较前一条的公司法条款,一个语段中居然用六个用 Where 引导的条件句,似乎英文中就没有别的句型表达方式似的。

以 1997 版的《中华人民共和国刑法》译本为例,在该法律的 452 条译文中,其中 207 条(典型的中文句式为:"以暴力、胁迫或者其他手段强奸妇女的,处三年以上十年以下有期徒刑。")是完全可以用本文讨论的"次级句式"表达的(该句可译为:Any person who rapes a woman by violence, coercion or other means, shall be sentenced to not less than three years and not more than 10 years of fixed-term imprisonment.)。遗憾的是,中国的广大法律译者还没有认识这类简明直接"次级句式"。

不过,应当指出:当要表达的法律行为发生之条件中的行为人,与法律行为的主体不同属一人(或一公司)时,仍然应当采用"主流"的条件句+主句的表达形式,即"如你做出某种行为,其他人可以对你采取某种法律行动"。例如:

Where a defendant is fined and the same is not forthwith paid, the magistrate may order the defendant to be searched. (Laws of Hong Kong, Cap. 227, Laws of Hong Kong, *Magistrates Ordinance*)

凡被告人被判处罚款,但没有随即缴付罚款,裁判官可命令搜查被告人。[①]

以上是实践"简明英文"写作所涉及的句子层面的问题。而在词汇或短语层面上的问题,更是不胜枚举。在下一篇,我们接续分析,但重点会转移到词汇层面的"吸血鬼"表达方式之上。

---

① 香港法律第 32 章:《公司条例》;translate. legislation. gov. hk/.

第二章
英文合同语言的风格(下):词汇层面的问题

法律英文中词汇层面的"吸血鬼"类别更是不胜枚举。这类"吸血鬼"语言弊端在分析法律英文语篇和介绍法律英语语言特征的各类论文和专著中常有论述。① 但这些著作往往只把它们当作法律英语的特征来介绍、阐释,对其在今日合同及其他法律文本写作中的应用,鲜有作者表明自己的立场,更少有作者系统提出应对措施,以至读者、用者一如既往地应用,让当代的合同语言(尤其是立法语言)仍然充斥大量的与时代潮流脱节、受过良好教育的普通读者读不懂或似懂非懂的词语。本章旨在系统介绍、评估这类词汇层面的"吸血鬼",并提出相应的"防治"或"治疗"措施。

一、避免使用古旧词

公认的古旧词主要指在日常英文、尤其是口语中已经消踪匿迹几百年、一般以 here-,there- 以及 where- 为词根的副词,在法律界通常称之为古旧词(archaic words)。主要有:

aforementioned	undersigned
herein	so as
heretofore	whereas
thereon	hereinafter
aforesaid	thereafter
hereunder	wherefore
thereto	hereinabove
forthwith	thereas
herewith	whereto
hereto	hereinbefore
theretofore	thereby
hereafter	whereupon
notwithstanding	hereof
thereupon	thereof
hereby	witnesseth
pursuant to	whereby

这类词在以往的法律文本中大量使用,其主要目的一般有两个:a. 为了避免用词的重

---

① 在法律写作领域,把各种不良写作风格称为"吸血鬼"的表达方式主要见 Brody 等人的著作,详见参考文献 Brody 等人的 *Legal Drafting* 的第 99 页。其实早在其 *Plain English for Lawyers*(1985)一书中,Richard Wydick 已经把这类师爷式语言称之为"吸血鬼"表达方式。

复,以及 b. 制作出"古色古香"、只有律师专业人士才能懂的"精英语言"文本。但在提倡用"简明英语"写作的时代,它的合理性受到极大怀疑。在当代合同写作实践中,我们建议以四条原则去处理古旧词:

(1) 反对使用:因为这类词汇已经在普通现代人的词汇(尤其是口语中)里消失几百年了。时代在进步,语言在发展,政府在反对,这种词汇阻碍交流,业界不应该反其道而行之。但你反不反对,业界习以为常,还是有大批人照用。因此,考虑到现状,提出第二条原则;

(2) 读者理解和认可原则:如果文本的目标读者是法律专业人士,尤其是老一辈法律专业人士,可以"投其所好",适当使用(但绝不能连篇累牍地滥用);但如果主流读者是非法律专业(公司的业务主管,尤其是普通民众)应尽可能避免使用。总之,在用词上尽可能让主流目标读者明白,得到他们的认可;

(3) 用词经济原则:由于这类古旧词基本上都是由一个副词加一个或多个介词构成的(如 thereafter, hereinafter),所以即便目标读者是法律专业人士,使用该类词时如果只能避免重复两到三个词,还是不应该使用(因为该类词本身就是由两个或三个词构成的),如果用了 hereinabove, heretobefore,而两词分别所表达的只是 the above 与 previously 的意思,那使用就不符合用词经济的原则,就是得不偿失,因为在法律文本中适当重复前述之词无伤大雅;

(4) 以及用词可重复原则:英文法律文本以往大量使用以 here, there, where 为词根的古旧词,其中一个原因是为了避免重复,避免重提前面已经罗列的事项。但在法律写作中,最高的准则是表达的精确性,为了达到精确表达的目的,用相同的词汇表达相同的法律概念是天经地义的:"... exactness often demands repeating the same term to express the same idea. Where that is true, never be afraid of using the same word over and over again. Many more sentences are spoiled by trying to avoid repetition than by repetition."(Weihofen, 2000)

但具体而言,在什么情况下,古旧词的使用才是可以接受的?可以这样说,如果使用一个古旧词能够避免重复至少三个以上的词汇,该古旧词的使用至少是经济的,从增进文本简洁性这一获益角度而论是可以接受的。例如:

> Article 206 Where the company engages in any business activities unrelated to the liquidation, it shall be warned by the company registration authority and its income derived therefrom shall be confiscated.[①]

在这段条文中,古旧词 therefrom 的使用使作者省去了"from engaging in any business activities unrelated to the liquidation"这么一个冗长的短语。如按照普通英文的表达方式,将该句重写成"Where the company engages in any business activities unrelated to the liquidation, it shall be warned by the company registration authority and its income derived from engaging in such business activities shall be confiscated."它的意思才完整、正确、清晰。但相比较而言,用了 therefrom 这个古旧词,该句就显得特别简洁,而且也不给读者带来太多的理解上的困惑。

二、避免动词名词化,慎用抽象词

(1) 名词化(nominalisation)主要有两种基本转化方式,一种是将形容词变成名词,如由

[①] *The Company Law of the People's Republic of China*, www.china.org.cn/english/government/207344.htm

applicable 转化为 applicability、由 careless 转化为 carelessness；另一种是将动词转化为名词,如将 fail 转化为 failure、investigate 转化为 investigation 以及将 move 转化为 movement。

合同写作中应尽量避免的主要是律师作者所习惯的将动词转化为名词的表达方式。英美流行的对法律界语言的其中一句讽刺语是：Lawyer will never pay you, but they will make a payment to you. 名词化的表达方式不但让文本深深地打上了"律师制作"的烙印,更主要的是无端端地拉长了句子,使表达方式拖沓,句子的后续连接困难,句子的核心信息被掩盖以及造成读者理解上的困惑。又如：

The executor effectuated a division of the property.（Brody,1994:99）

读者期望读到的是用动词直接表述行为的句子。本来是简简单单的句子 The executor divided the property. 到了律师笔下就被抽象成上句那样,普通读者对其含义当然是一头雾水。其主要原因是其中的动词 divide 被名词化为 division,再配上一个实际意义"虚无缥缈"的律师专用动词"effectuate",句子就变得又长又难懂了,真像被"吸血鬼"吸干了血液的僵尸句。一个句子里一个主要动词被名词化就可以把句子变得如此干瘪抽象,如果有若干个动词被名词化,又该是一种什么样的情形呢？比较下面两句,读者自然会对这类僵尸句的弊端有更深入的了解：

The amendment of any part of this contract may not be a valid modification unless supportable by express written documentation bearing the signatures of both parties.

The parties may amend any part of this contract only if they both sign a written document that expressly modifies the contract.（Brody,1994:99）

仅仅就句子长度而言,以基本动词(即根动词)形式表达的第二句显然就比第一句短很多,意思清晰上更不可相提并论。所以,要避免名词化的表达方式,恢复使用根动词。

同时,让句子基本保持主谓宾结构；让谓语动词尽可能靠近主语；让宾语尽可能靠近谓语动词；让修饰词尽可能靠近被修饰的词。

(2) 减少使用多音节的抽象词,提倡使用根词。

以上论及的是动词名词化问题,它会拉长句子——因为动词名词化之后在使用时仍然需要有行为动词去执行这些名词,否则句子语法上会出问题。同时,含有名词化词汇的句子意思必然抽象。意思抽象的内容,不论是词汇,还是句子,都会增加读者理解的难度。这跟长句难懂的道理一样。

不过,造成句子意思抽象、难懂不只是动词名词化,还有一个明显的原因是使用音节太多的词汇。音节多寡,与传递信息的效果有直接关系：凡音节越多的词汇,词义越抽象,意思越飘忽,传达的信息越不可捉摸,往往会使句子失去鲜活的生命。

例如：concept 和 conceptualisation 都表达相同的概念,但多音节的以 -tion 结尾的长词 conceptualisation 就比根词 concept 抽象得多、难懂得多。

有法律写作网站建议使用最长不超过五个音节的单词(www.weagree.com)(如 prioritise 为五个音节；generalisibility 为八个音节)。这恐怕难以做到,但在有选择的情况下,应该选用根词(root word)。根词音节都较少。

凡以 -bility,-tion,-sion,-ness,-ment,-ture,-ance,-ence,-ing,-al（Brody,1994:99）结尾或作后缀的词,皆非根词,均属于多音节的抽象词,故在使用时应该特别谨慎。

三、避免使用近义词、配对词、迂腐词

(1) 近义词:造成前文长句(即第一章中的 Version A)之长的另一个明显原因是作者使用了大量的近义词和配对词。在 Version A 的例句中,有问题的产权用了足足 30 个修饰词去表达,其中大部分是近义词和配对词(has or acquires actual knowledge of any defect, lien, encumbrance, adverse claim or other matter affecting the estate or interest or mortgage...)。

尽管律师必须想得比客户周到,要把一切可能发生的事物都包括在合同条款中,事实上这往往是不可能办到的。如果律师觉得已经穷尽了一切可能的事物而最终与此相关的合同纠纷还是发生了,并且最终闹上了法庭,在此情况下,法庭判决往往会对主张因其需要而详尽罗列这些内容的合同方不利,因为法官会认为撰写合同的律师已经穷尽了必须包括的所有内容(Brody,1994:73),而不在此列的内容则应予排除(根据 *Black's Law Dictionary*,6th ed., 1990):"When certain persons or things are specified in a law, contract, or will, an intention to exclude all others from its operation may be inferred."),但事实上"漏网之鱼"一定存在,智者千虑,必有一失,撰写人想得最周到,也难免百密一疏。

所以,所有这类既啰唆又富有争议的写法弊大于利,应予放弃,或采取更明智的"故意模糊"(intentional vagueness)的方法去处理(见上文 Version B 的"any legal defects (including lien) affecting the title to your property")。Brody 等认为:

"... vague language carries a core meaning with undefined limits. Precise language, on the other hand, has a sharper limits... For example, if you were drafting a will for someone who wanted to leave property to her grandchildren, you could choose varying levels of precision: Vague: I give my grandchildren...; Precise: I give John Rogers and Sally Smith...",这个例子中的"grandchildren"意思较含糊,包括在立遗嘱时尚未出生的孙辈子女;而指名道姓的精确版则排除任何其他的孙辈子女。(Brody,1994:66—67)

就上文的产权问题而言,Version A 的表述就过于清晰:"any defect, lien, encumbrance, adverse claim or other matter affecting the estate or interest or mortgage thereon covered by this Commitment other than those shown on Schedule B hereof;而 Version B 用较模糊的方式去表示(any legal defects (including lien) affecting the title to your property")(Brody:122),后一种说法更具包容性,其所包含的可能会影响产权的缺陷事项甚至比前者更多更广,因而其法律上的争议性更少。

(2) 配对词:法律语言中特有的配对词(legal pair)、三联词(triplets)是合同文本中另一类"吸血鬼"。这类词的特点是将原本可以用一个词就能把意思表达清楚的概念用两个、甚至三个词去表达。如说到某一合同方对某项不动产拥有利益,传统上律师会说:"a party's right, title, and interest in any particular property",但其实只用一个 interest 已经可以把意思表达得无可争议。而在合同的管辖法律条款中,传统的合同都会这样写:

"This Agreement shall in all respects be interpreted, construed and governed by and in accordance with the laws of the State of New York" (Adams,2001:101).

在该条款中属于三联词的 interpreted, construed and governed 只需要保留一个 governed, 意思就已经非常到位; 而 in all respects 几乎是律师信手拈来、毫无意义的多余词。同样, 在合同的保证条款中, 说到合同一方的陈述是正确时, 一定会连用三个词, 如"... representations are true, correct, and complete"。其实, 难道有可能陈述是"真实的"但却是"错误的"？或者是"不真实的"但却是"准确的"？

这些词几乎在由律师起草的任何性质的法律文本上都比比皆是。例如: <u>Any controversy, dispute or claim</u> between Seller [GREC] and Purchaser [GRU] <u>arising out of or relating to</u> this Agreement, or the breach thereof, shall be settled <u>finally and conclusively</u> by arbitration according to the Rules of the American Arbitration Association then in effect, unless the parties mutually otherwise agree... The <u>costs and expenses</u> of arbitration shall be paid as awarded by the arbitrators; otherwise <u>costs and expenses</u> shall be shared equally...①

INDEMNIFICATION. You agree to <u>indemnify, defend and hold harmless</u> KZR, its **partners, officers, directors, employees, shareholders, agents, contractors and attorneys** <u>from and against any and all</u> <u>losses, expenses, damages and costs</u>, including reasonable attorneys' fees, resulting from your use of the Website.②

从以上两段引文可以看出近义词(黑体词)与配对词(画线词)在法律文书中的使用已经到了何等泛滥的程度。这些词读起来朗朗上口,用起来得心应手(因为是一串一串的,用了一个就会像接龙一样蹦出第二个),所以合同的撰写人员往往不忍心放弃,能想到的都塞进合同文本。但它们却像依附在句子结构中的"吸血鬼",把句子的生命、也就是实质意思给削弱了。

实用文体作文的目的是有效传递思想,而不是那些累赘的形式。一个词能把意思说明白,再多用一个词,其中一个就是赘词。所以作者在撰写合同调词遣句时要时刻警惕这些词的蹦出,要学会忍痛割爱。

各类教科书上常有罗列的配对词有:

  make, declare, and publish
  free and clear
  true and correct
  part and parcel
  vacate, surrender, and deliver possession
  sole and exclusive
  right, title, and interest
  fair and reasonable
  loss or damage

还有一些非典型的律师专用配对词:

  among and between

---

① https://www.gru.com/.../Demand%20For%20Arbitration%20pdf.
② kleinzelman.com/disclaimer.html.

agree and covenant
any and all
by and between
adjust, amend or otherwise modify
confirm and represent
if and to the extent

总之,这类词难以穷尽,但如果文本中的两个或三个词意思非常相近而文本的上下文已出现过这类典型的配对词,那么这类近义的词组大致上也都属于同类性质。例如:

a. The Disclosing Party hereby *represents and warrants* that it has the <u>right and authority</u> to disclose the Confidential Information to the Receiving Party in accordance with *terms and conditions* herein.

披露方向接受方陈述及保证,他有权向接受方披露本协议项下的保密信息。(范文祥,2007:100)

b. The <u>rules and regulations</u> contained in this lease <u>are</u> hereby <u>made a part of and incorporated into</u> this lease and Tenant shall observe the same. Failure to <u>keep and observe</u> said rules will constitute a material breach of the terms of this lease in the same manner as if contained herein as covenants, and a failure to observe the same shall be of the same effect. Tenant shall <u>keep and observe</u> such further <u>rules and regulations</u> as may be required by Landlord or its agent from time to time which Landlord may deem necessary for the <u>proper and orderly</u> care of the building of which the Premises are a part. (李克兴,2007)①

在以上例句 a 中,represents and warrants 与 terms and conditions 几乎是众所周知的典型的法律配对词,由此作者撰写合同的用词风格已经显而易见,所以另外一组词——<u>right and authority</u>,也就八九不离十是属于同类性质。按照简明英文的写作原则,只要用一个 right 就能将意思表达清楚;而在翻译时,也只需翻译其中一个词的意思即可。

在例句 b 中,作者用了六组配对词:rules and regulations, are... made a part of and incorporated into, keep and observe, keep and observe, rules and regulations, proper and orderly,即使读者以前从来没有碰到过 are... made a part of and incorporated into 以及 <u>keep and observe</u> 之类的词组,不能确定该两组词是否属于配对词,但从该条款的总体文风或用词倾向上,读者已经不难判断该两组词的性质和该条款的"师爷"写作风格了。

(3) 迂腐词:所谓迂腐词指一些普通人非常陌生、而传统型律师(年青一代法律人未必意识到)却时常用来装点门面(说得难听点)或提升行业文字档次的冷僻词、文绉绉的书面词。主要有(右栏是可以取而代之的普通词):

cease　　　　　　　　　　stop
commence　　　　　　　　begin
contiguous　　　　　　　　next

---

① 同类的租约措辞见 http://case.edu/realestate/residentrentals/docs/ResidentialSampleLease.pdf.

donate	give
effectuate	cause or carry out
elucidate	explain
endeavour	try
evince	show
expedite	hurry
expenditure	spend
expire	end or die
feasible	possible
indicate	show
peruse	read
prior to	before
procure	get or obtain
renumerate	pay
subsequent	after
terminate	end
utilize	use

（4）长串词：本身属于短语，但并非普通英文中的常用短语，一般只在法律文本中出现，而且的确是由一长串小词构成的，在上文论述第三种"吸血鬼"句式时，笔者已经指出该类词是构成法律英文中累赘句式的主要"元凶"，在此不妨再次列出常见的长串词（右栏为简明英文中的替换词）：

due to the fact that	because
in all likelihood	probably
in order to	to
in regards to	regarding
in/with respect of	for/about/regarding
in/with reference to	for/about/regarding
notwithstanding the fact that	although
provided, however that	if, but
the time at which	when
until such time as	until
with respect of	for/about/regarding

从词性上讲，这类词基本上都是连词和介词。在简明英文写作中，用一个词、尤其是短词就能表达意思的，不要去用这类长串词，不要让读者把注意力消耗在阅读无谓的词语上。例如：

The Covenantor hereby undertakes to procure that the Customer will comply with all the Customer's obligations to you, the beneficiaries of this deed, (jointly and severally) but should the Customer default in the payment when due of any payment or default in complying with any other obligation, the Covenantor will, without the need for any demand, make immediate payment or performance thereof as the case may be, at the place, in the funds and currency and/or in the manner required of the Customer and without any withholding or deduction whatsoever PROVIDED ALWAYS HOWEVER that no time for limitation of liability in respect of this Deed shall begin to run in favour of the Covenantor unless and until one or both of you shall have made demand on the Covenantor, and if more than one demand is made, then only from the date and to the extent of each demand respectively.

以上这个由四个词组成的长串词组,其实可以用一个 but 取而代之。

(5) 正式词:有些这类词虽然不属于典型的冷僻词,也并非十分书卷气,但对于某些类型读者而言,仍然太正式,语域(register)过高,因为无论是写作还是翻译,调词遣句都要考虑到读者群的水准或接受程度。如果合同文本读者是"普通大众"或普通消费者(如不需要咨询律师便可以签订的简单合同条款、信用卡条款、租车协议、民用住房租约等),则要尽可能避免使用这类正式词。这类词主要有(Brody,1994:115):

acquire	indebtedness	amendment
indemnity	promise	institute
promisor	promulgate	determine
purport	discharge	mortgagor
reside	preceding	resolve
holder	prejudice	sole
in arrears	proceed	

这类高语域词的数量可以相当可观,内容更可以因人而异:不同性质合同的撰写人最好要根据不同的客户群的背景编制一套自己应予警惕使用的词汇表,如果文本的阅读对象是法律专业人士(法官、律师),不但这类正式词,就是古旧词、常用的拉丁词甚至以下一节将要讨论的法律专业的行话、术语,也不在禁忌之列。读者认可的原则,无论如何都是语言使用的一个主要标准。

但是,相比那些由一个短小的英文动词为根词(如 do, put, take, catch)、另加一个或两个介词(如 in, into, up, with) 构成的词组,使用以上这类正式词并不是坏事,至少这类语域高的正式词在词义上比较专一。例如:catch 根词意思是"抓住",catch up 就是"达到/赶上",而 catch up with 除了与前者同义("赶上")外,还有"捕获"的意思,如 The law caught up with him yesterday. (昨天他被捉拿归案。)

对于母语并非英语的作者来说,这些短语动词尤其令人头痛,因为变成介词短语后,该短语的意思跟原根词的意思相比一般都已发生了根本性的变化,作者和读者往往得根据语境来确定意思。所以,在有词义专一的正式"单"词可以取代的情况下,应该舍弃使用。例如在以下例子中(Enquist & Oates,2005:308),后一个句子中的动词就较少有歧义性,是首选用汇:

The brief must be *turned in* by 5:00 pm.	The brief must be *submitted* by 5:00 pm.
The protester *handed out* leaflets.	The protester *distributed* leaflets.
The attorney *put off* the meeting.	The attorney *postponed* the meeting.
Firefighter *put out* the blaze.	Firefighters *extinguished* the blaze.

四、避免使用行话和术语

避免使用法律行业专用的行话(jargon,如绝大部分的拉丁词)和术语(terms of art)[①]。同时更要避免客户行业的行话。最不要使用的是连自己都吃不准意思的行话或术语。行话和术语的使用同样会使合同语言背离简明英语的发展趋势,造成读者理解上的困难。只有在权衡利弊得失之后,在非常有必要的情况下,才使用这类词汇。

---

① 详见李克兴:《法律翻译:理论与实践》,北京:北京大学出版社,2007年。

第三章
英文合同写作的技术细节(上)

以上阐述的涉及合同及同类性质法律文本写作的风格问题,无论是对付句子层面的"吸血鬼"还是词汇层面的"吸血鬼",相对说来,都还比较宏观,概括性的对策是用简明英文写作。接续论述的主要是英文合同的具体写作细节问题。没有多年参与各类合同制作的经验,不太可能会碰到如此之多的问题;不对各类合同做高屋建瓴的细致的对比研究,更不可能知悉业界制作各类合同的基本规范。虽然法律界在这方面没有明文的写作规定,但读者如善于观察和归纳,也可以逐渐悟出业界约定俗成的做法以及这些做法的合理性。在此巨细无遗地罗列,希望能为合同及同类法律文本的写作提供实用的指引。

一、减少写入交互参考以及避免标题与内容不符

减少将不必要的交互参考(cross-reference)写入条文(如 Paragraph 3 of these Conditions and Stipulations),因为合同格式或编号稍有变更,这类交互参考指引就会"牛头不对马嘴",让读者不知所云。此外,交互参考往往让读者眼花缭乱,阅读时需要上下搜索,甚为不便。例如:

Survival: Upon the expiration or termination of this Agreement, the obligations of the parties to each other shall come to an end, except that the provisions of Section 14.2.1(regarding non-competition and non-solicitation) shall survive.

不如干脆写成

... except that the non-competition and non-solicitation clause shall survive.

英美法庭认为合同不可执行(除合同内容违法或缺乏常识之外)还有几个文字格式上的原因:

(a) 合同内交互参考指引出错:如条款标明参阅 3.5.1 节,而 3.5.1 节并不存在或其内容与有关的条款指引毫无关系;以及

(b) 标题与内容不符(会误导合同的有关方)。

二、关于定义

对一些关键词进行界定,是法律文本(包括立法文本和合同文本)写作的一个很重要的特征。需要界定的词汇首先必须是非常重要的概念,必须是反复出现的词汇,必须是可能有不同解读的、容易产生歧义的词汇。如果不是非常重要,如果不会在合同中重复使用两次以上的词,一般不要列入定义词行列(对这类一次性出现的重要词汇只需要在有关的下文加以

描述或阐释即可)。否则,文本撰写人的工作量就会很大。此外,如果不是反复出现的,界定的价值也就不是很大;如果目标读者对这些词汇没有歧义,那么界定就是多余的。

界定或下定义的目的是为了让作者与文本的读者就有关词汇的含义达成一个共识,成为读者所熟悉的词汇。一旦对有关词汇下过定义,作者就要"以身作则",自觉使用、不可再用其他同义词或近义词来取代,否则,定义词不但会"词同虚设",而且还会使读者倍感困惑。例如,一旦作者对"earnest money"作过定义词,在下文表达该概念时就不可以用"deposit"或"down payment"等同义或近义词。每一个词,即便在普通人理解中是毫无疑义的同义词,从法律意义上讲都是有区别的。所以,要表达不同理念,必须用不同的词汇。

合同的定义部分一般都放在引言/序言(Recital)条款之后。在定义部分还可以回过头来对在引言条款中出现过的重要词汇加以定义。具体如何写作和翻译定义条款,本书第七章将进行最详尽的论述。

三、使用单数名词

虽然在较正规的合同条款的词汇定义部分都会有"单数就是复数,复数就是单数"的界定,但在具体写作时,如没有特殊需要,一般须使用单数名词。如一份买卖合同中的买方和卖方,不必写成"The Buyers"和"The Sellers",写成"Buyer"和"Seller"即可(连定冠词 The 都可以省去),而且事实上签署这份买卖合同的买主和卖主往往都只有一个,所以需要摈弃以往名不副实、总是以复数形式的写法。

同样,在"incurring any loss or losses"这个短语中,其中的"losses"已完全没有必要。在尽可能使用单数名词的同时,还要在文本中自始至终保持该风格的一致;也不使用在单数名词之后加(s)的做法,如 buyer(s)and seller(s)。以往曾有合同方因违反合同条款而苦于无借口开脱责任,设法在名词单复数上钻空子[如争辩说合同方没有造成多项损失(losses),因此无须为一项损失(loss)负责],为自己的违约行为辩护。但他们几乎都输了官司。如今"单数就是复数,复数就是单数"几乎是英美法律界的共识。

四、使用带性别特征词汇的问题

虽然在法律或合同条文中,定义部分都会就性别问题做出诸如此类的声明。例如:

"He" includes "he" and "she". /"His" includes "his" and "her". /"Him" includes "him" and "her". 以及 Unless the context otherwise requires in this AGREEMENT, the masculine gender shall include the female gender and vice versa and any gender shall include the other genders.

但在实际写作中,仍然会有性别用词的困惑,尤其是对在非英语母语环境中生活的作者而言,因为他们当年在学校学到的一些基本词汇在以后数十年的社会和文化演变中可能已经发生很大改变,其中一个很重要的影响因素是"女权运动"。例如,chairman,policeman,postman,stewardess,mankind 等词,如今都被认为带有明显的性别歧视色彩,可以取而代之的分别是 chair(chairperson),police officer,postal worker(carrier),flight attendant,human race。

但是,撰写法律文书必然会用到带有明显性别特征的 he,him 或 she,her。例如,An

attorney will often write a letter to the client in order to keep him informed. 其实法律文书的写作不怕用词重复，为了减少歧义，适当重复前述之词未尝不可。所以，可以将上句改写为：An attorney will often write a letter to the client in order to keep the client informed. (Charrow, 1986:44)

第二种常用的避开带性别特征的 he/she 是使用复数第三人称代词(they/their)，甚至第二人称的 you。例如，不用这样的句子 The student should bring her torts book to class. 而是用 Students should bring their torts books to class. 不用 A lawyer must pass the state bar exam if he wants to practice law. 而是用 You must pass the state bar exam if you want to practice law.

我们还须注意到这一惯例：在当前英文合同或立法文本的写作中，单数的 he 已经约定俗成地指代 she 或 they，his 指代 her 或 their。偶尔读者还会见到 s/he 的写法。虽然该新造词别出心裁，可以指代 he 或 she，但仍然没有被接纳为主流用法，况且，与其配套的所有格究竟是用 his 还是 her、宾格是 him 还是 her，尚未有定论，故在正式程度较高的法律或合同文本中不应使用 s/he。

五、关于段落的长度

法律文本段落的长度，根据文本性质不同有所差异。一般而言，合同文本的段落最短，法律条文的段落稍长，诉讼文件的段落最长。但不管是哪种性质的法律文本，很少有超过由五个以上独立句子组成的段落。在现代的法律文本中，短段，尤其是一句一段、一句一条款的构成越来越多。

但这并不是说法律文本的段落句子越少越好。法律文本的段落长短或段内句子多寡主要取决于各段的写作意图。作者通常都会在一个段落内说明一个次级主题（而在一个较长的条款内则阐述一个完整的主题）。如果有必要，一段可以由五个句子组成，也可以由两个或三个句子组成。例如：

ATTORNEY FEES: In the event action is brought by any party to enforce any terms of this agreement or to recover possession of the premises, the prevailing party shall recover from the other party reasonable attorney fees.

It is acknowledged, between the parties, that jury trials significantly increase the costs of any litigation between the parties. It is also acknowledged that jury trials require a longer length of time to adjudicate the controversy. On this basis, all parties waive their rights to have any matter settled by jury trial. (www.lectlaw.com/forms/f091.htm)

以上是一份租约中的有关律师费的条款，由两段组成。第一段是典型的一句一段。第二段则由三个中等长度的句子组成，其中第一句阐述双方的共识：由陪审团审理双方的诉讼会大幅增加诉讼费；第二句是双方的第二个共识：由陪审团解决纠纷耗时太长。基于这两大原因，第三句表示双方愿意放弃以陪审团方式解决纠纷的权利。

这三个句子的内容密切相关，属于同一个主题，所以，放在条款的同一段落中阐述非常合理（尽管原文很啰嗦，有若干属于典型的"吸血鬼"表达方式，如"It is acknowledged, between the parties")。由此可见,决定一段中应该有几个句子的关键是主题内容的相关性。为了表达一个主题,应该将内容相关的句子放在同一个语段。

但是,在现代法律文本中,不管文本属于何种性质,超过八句以上的段落,几乎已经绝迹,因为法律文本的句子本身就较长,在一个由多句组成的段落中,包括若干个由大约20字构成、属于中等长度句子的可能性非常低。因为由八个句子组成的段落,其版面长度一般都已超过一整个页面。

一个占整整一个页面的段落,对读者——无论是谁,即便是自己也习惯于写长句的律师或其他法律专业人员,阅读时都会有心理负担(Enquist & Oates,2005:39),甚至足以让他们产生憎恶感,因为要消化这类长段,抓住其中的要点,他们也都会被逼阅读多遍。

所以,法律文本的段落,切忌超过八句,一般以五句以下为宜。不过,即使在同一类别的合同文本中,段落的长短也可根据读者以及合同性质的不同而有所不同:复杂的专业合同,如融资贷款合同或担保书、公司尤其是跨国公司的兼并合同、大额保单(航空器、远洋船舶)等,段落可以稍长,句子数量可以适当增加,因为这类合同的读者主要是法律专业人士;而普通买卖合同、住宅租约等,段落较短,每段句子数量以两到三句为宜。

关于短段:在非合同性质的文本中,特别短、只有一两句的段落,一般起一个承前启后的过渡作用,尤其是当作者想表达两个完全不同的概念时,在两个长段中夹杂一个只有一两句的短段,往往能将比较不同的思想或主题自然地连接起来(Enquist & Oates,2005:41)。

短段的另一个用途是让读者在阅读长段的过程中有一个"喘息"的机会,也就是说只有一两句的短段通常夹杂在其前段与后段都属于比较长的段落中间。

最后一个用途是:段落长短不一,错落有致,版面上比较美观,往往能比长度比较划一的段落更能收到正面的版面效果,从而不知不觉地受到读者的青睐。

六、例外状语:将例外、限制以及限定状语集中表达,放在主条款的前部

作为条件笼统称之为例外状语的句子成分,在合同条款或法律条文中的比例非常之高。如果合同条款中的例外(exceptions)、限制(limitations)以及限定(qualifications)的内容比较简短,一般应将其放在条款的开始部分,紧接其后的才是表述义务或主要原则的内容。如上文第四部分的例句,把 Unless the context otherwise requires in this AGREEMENT 放在句首。又如:

a. <u>Except as herein provided</u>, full possession of said premises free of all tenants and occupants is to be delivered at the time of the delivery of the deed.

b. <u>Unless stated to the contrary in an Order</u>, the Buyer shall not be obliged to accept delivery by instalments.

以上两句的例外状语均放在主句之前。

在写作条件句的时候,必须注意到,很多英美国家的老牌律师,时常会用错时态,这主要是由于他们习惯于照搬旧式的合同模块,懒得更新而将错就错。他们会在没有必要的情况

下,在条件句部分使用将来时态或滥用 shall 这个情态动词。① 如果读者想系统了解和掌握条件句的写作,建议读者阅读北京大学出版社 2013 年出版的《高级法律翻译与写作》一书,其中有三章是专门论述条件句写作的,可以说这是迄今为止最全面的关于法律文本中条件句写作的论述,虽然其论述可能不是最权威的(因为那些奴性十足的学术评估部门只重视文章是否发表在洋人杂志上),但其关于条件句的研究是最踏实的,有充足数据支持;其先前发表在《中国翻译》上有关法律文本条件句写作和翻译的专论(李克兴:2008;2013),也从未有学者对其观点提出过任何异议,其有关论文和专著已经成为各政法院校和翻译专业的主要教材。

在此需要补充的是:在合同条款的条件句中,条件部分的行为动词一般都用一般现在时态,因为合同都是为将来制订的,极少追溯往事,所以条件部分用一般现在时态、主句部分的行为用强制性的将来时态(即 shall/will+verb,当然还有表示权利或许可的情态动词 may)是天经地义的。但是,在诉讼类或其他法律文本中,尽管主流条件句仍然按以上的常规方式表述,例如:

> If the court applies(一般现在时态)the Reed test, it will find(将来时态)that the element is met. 以及 The prosecutor will charge(将来时态)the defendant with arson unless she has(一般现在时态)an alibi.

但是,条件部分用过去时态也不是没有可能的。例如:

> If the witness saw(过去时态)the defendant's car at the accident scene, he would have also seen the defendant. 以及 The jury might ignore its instructions if it believed(过去时态)the police fabricated the evidence.

对这类条件部分使用过去时态的句子,主句表达的是一种"可能"(possible)、但一般"不会发生"(unlikely to happen)的事件或行为。

此外,以下情形也有可能:

> If the defendant had spoken(过去分词时态)to Mr Torres, he would have apologized(过去完成时态)to him, not threatened to him. 以及 The tenants could have complained(过去完成时态)to the building superintendent if he had been accessible(过去分词时态).

这种句式就是普通英文语法书中介绍的虚拟语态。但普通语法书所用的例句往往比较简单,例如 If I were you, I might try apologizing to him. 虚拟语态的句子在法律性质的实用文本中出现的频率极低,在律师的辩护词中也只是偶尔见到,补充收录于此,是为了让读者对法律文本中条件句的类型有一个较全面的认识。

七、数字与时间以及合同条款编号的表达

数字在合同中有极为关键的作用,几乎所有合同指标都是以数字方式来表达的。万一

---

① 笔者发现一份 2014 年签订的香港房地产买卖合约主要条款与 20 世纪 80 年代出现在合同参考书中的地产买卖合约的主要条款几乎完全相同。

出错,后果往往极为严重。故传统上重要数字都用一目了然的阿拉伯数字和难以涂改的英文拼写方式作双重表述。但如今需要对数字作双重表述的做法(除了支票上的金额)越来越不流行,而且在一些近乎天文数字的表述中,也只有用阿拉伯数字表述才是切实可行的。

但是,根据大部分律师行的规矩,十以内(包括十)数字一般用英文字母组成的单词去表达,十以上的才用阿拉伯数字;不过,百分比、价格、时间、年份和日期(不包括月份)一概用阿拉伯数字表达,超过三位数的数字一定要每隔三位数加一个逗号(",")。例如:

within ten days,
finish in 11months,
count for 9 percent,
at 12:30 a.m.,
between 8 and 17,
for the minimum amount of £5,000 or HK＄70,000,and

If despite the BUYER's diligent efforts a commitment for such loan cannot be obtained on or before 2,January,2014, the BUYER may terminate this agreement by written notice.

The 2012 exports amounted to 19 percent of our total exports of milk powder, butter, and cheese for that year. This contrasts sharply with the 406 million NZ dollars of dairy products we sold to China in 2008 (just 4.6 percent of our total exports of milk powder, butter, and cheese). Logs, wood, and wood articles came second, with 1.1 billion NZ dollars in exports to China in 2012, up by 867 million NZ dollars from 2008.①

当然,如果合同的另一方来自美国,就日期表达而言,可以写成 January 2,2014;虽然,不少合同模块会将该日期写成 this 2nd day of January,2014,作为法律文件的起草者,应该清晰地认识到这是旧式表达方式,太啰嗦、太正式,在简明英文时代已经过时。而另一种表达方式——1/2/2014,虽然简明,却太随便,在普通书信及电邮中勉强可以接受,不过其含义也颇具歧义性,会因读者的语言环境而有不同解读,因为这种表达形式在美国指 2014 年 1 月 2 日,而在英国则指 2014 年 2 月 1 日。

合同条款的编号一般也采用阿拉伯数字,如:1. PARTIES AND MAILING ADDRESSE...;24. WARRANTIES AND REPRESENTATIONS. 但各条款内的细则编号,如果肯定没有更细化的编号,可采用斜体的(a)(b)(c);但如果某些条款之下有更细化的编号,则须继续采用阿拉伯数字,如:

4 Delivery
4.1 The goods shall be delivered to...
4.2 Where a date for delivery of goods is specified...
4.5 Unless agreed by the Buyer to the contrary:
4.5.1 The goods shall be delivered...
4.5.2 The Supplier shall insure the goods for an amount...

---

① 见 fta.mofcom.gov.cn/english/index.shtml

4.6 Where a "goods received note"... (Brody,1994)

八、常用副词和介词在句子中的位置

除有意图的模糊表达之外,合同条款要写得精确无误,消除一切可能的歧义。用词模棱两可,会让合同无端生出歧义,甚至使条款无法实施。作为非母语作者,我们特别容易对一些副词和介词在句子中的位置摆放问题掉以轻心。例如:

Employees only may use this restroom.

由于其中副词 only 位置摆放不妥,读者可能搞不清到底"顾客不可以使用该洗手间",还是"顾客不可以使用其他洗手间";此处的 only 似乎既可以修饰其前面的 employees,也可以是修饰其后面的"may use this restroom"。如果将副词 only 在位置上做些调整,则歧义顿时消解:Only employees may use this restroom. 或者:Employees may use only this restroom.

作者在使用以下副词时,需要特别注意其位置:almost,hardly,nearly,even,just,only,exactly,merely,simply——一般而言,这些副词作修饰词使用时需要置放在离其最近的所修饰之词的前面(而不是后面)。

相反,以下介词则一般需要置放在离其最近的所修饰之词的后面(而不是前面):between,during,regarding,by,except,to,concerning,for,upon,despite,in,with。位置摆放得不对,同样会使合同内容的意思含糊不清,解释模棱两可。例如:

No cheques may be cashed by cashier without prior approval.

究竟是 cashier(出纳)还是 cheques(支票)需要得到批准? 如果是这个 cashier 需要得到事先批准才能去兑现支票的话,这个句子应该这样写:

No cheques without prior approval may be cashed by cashiers.

当然,如果用主动语态(这也是本文提倡的可以提高合同写作精确性的措施之一)表述,那么歧义就很容易消除:Cashier may cash only previously approved cheques. (Brody,1994:75—76)

如前所述,在英文句子中,副词应放在动词(或具有动词性质的分词)之前。该句的两个副词(only,previously)均修饰离其最近的过去分词 approved。

九、or,and 以及特殊连词 and/or 的用法及建议

这是一个汉语中原本没有对应词的连接词。近年往往被翻译成"和/或"。但在英文中,即使是地道的语言高手也未必会用。首先,"and/or"是法律文本撰写人、尤其是律师惯用的体现"师爷"风格的用词,任何法律文本的教科书都反对使用。(Brody,1994:79)

and/or 究竟是什么意思? 逻辑上可以这样解释:如果是"X and/or Y",意思为"X 或 Y,或 X 以及 Y(即两者)"。

但在实际使用上,并没有那么简单,因为 or 本身是英文中一个具有争议性质的连词。如果母亲告诉孩子,You may have "ice cream or cake",孩子只能二选一,不能兼得。如果母

亲告诉孩子，You may go outside to "roller-skate or ride bike"，孩子可以二选一，也可以两者兼做。所以该词的常规用法有时存在"不可理喻"的歧义性。其歧义性同样存在于以下句子中。通过分析以下银行贷款中的条款，我们可以真正领会并学会如何正确使用该连词，避免造成歧义。

1. If a debtor fails to make a payment when due, the bank may:
   (1) sell the collateral or
   (2) assess late fees of 5% of the amount missed.

银行可以出售债务人（debtor）的担保品（collateral），是否还可以向债务人收取相当于未付贷款额5%的迟付金（late fees）？根据上文规定，债务人认为银行只可以采取其中的一项措施，而银行则认为可以"双管齐下"。问题在于其中的 or 是一个可以作模棱两可解释的词汇。

如果明确规定银行只可以采取其中一项措施的，上句应该写成：

2. If a debtor fails to make a payment when due, the bank may either:
   (1) sell the collateral or
   (2) assess late fees of 5% of the amount missed.

如果允许银行可以同时采取两项措施的，应写成：

3. If a debtor fails to make a payment when due, the bank may:
   (1) sell the collateral,
   (2) assess late fees of 5% of the amount missed, or
   (3) both.

如果有两个以上选择，而只允许银行选择其中一项措施的，可以这样写：

4. If a debtor fails to make a payment when due, the bank may only pursue one of the following options:
   (1) sell the collateral,
   (2) assess late fees of 5% of the amount missed, or
   (3) declare the full amount of the indebtedness due and payable immediately.

如果允许银行采取其中一项或多项或全部措施的，可以这样写：

5. If a debtor fails to make a payment when due, the bank may exercise one or more of the following options:
   (1) sell the collateral,
   (2) assess late fees of 5% of the amount missed, or
   (3) declare the full amount of the indebtedness due and payable immediately.

and 通常指在一项选择之外再加上另一项选择。在普通英文中，如父母对孩子说，"Put on your socks and shoes,"遵命的孩子是既要着袜、也要穿鞋。但有时该词也同样模棱两可，例如：

6. If a debtor fails to make a payment when due, the bank may:
   (1) sell the collateral,

(2) assess late fees of 5% of the amount missed, and

(3) declare the full amount of the indebtedness due and payable immediately.
(Brody,1994:77—78)

既然银行有权行使这三项措施的全部,它当然也有权只行使其中的一项,而且债务人也会非常乐意银行这样做。在此情形中,语境和逻辑都告诉我们,and 与 or 意思相同。但有时语境并不能帮上什么忙,例如:

7. Retired and disabled people are entitled to government surplus food.

读完这个带有 and 连接词的规定,到底有权利享受政府剩余食品的人士必须是退休同时又是残疾人士?还是只要退休或者残疾就可以享受?读者从以上例句的字面上得不到答案。and 给你的同样是一个"模棱两可"的选择,读者只能靠语境和逻辑做适当的推理,才可确定该 and 究竟是二选一,还是必须符合其所连接的两项要求,即既是退休人士又患有残疾。

法律文本的写作原则上是要把意思写得清清楚楚的,否则,法律条文或合同条款就不具备可执行性(unenforceable)。所以,要避免给读者这类模棱两可的解读,作者不妨多用一两个词,例如:

Only people who are both retired and disabled are entitled to government surplus food.

达到这两项要求才有资格享受政府的剩余食品。

或者:

Either retired people or disabled people are entitled to government surplus food.
只需达到其中一项要求便有资格。(Brody,1994:78)

小结:如前所述,在现行的法律文本中,and/or 不但用法混乱,歧义多多,而且非常容易将两个不可能组合在一起的事物"拉郎配",因此应尽力避免使用 and/or[①]。如果所有列出的项目都必须包括在内的,不妨用"X or Y or both",或者加个"only"、"all"或"together"——所用的"or"或"and"就不会再有歧义了。此外,如果要连接三项或三项以上的事物,还可以用"one or more of…","any or all(of)…"的短语去表述。例如:

This Agreement may be executed in <u>one or more</u> counterparts with each such counterpart deemed to be an original hereof and all of such counterparts deemed to be one and the same Agreement.

本协议可签署生效一份或多份副本,每份副本视为协议原本,所有此类副本视为完全一致的协议。[②]

This Agreement supersedes <u>any or all</u> prior agreements, written or oral, between Party A and Party B, and constitutes the complete agreement between the parties.

本协议替代甲方和乙方之间以前的所有书面或是口头的协议。[③]

[①] Adams, Brody, www.weagree.com

[②] 见 www.contractstandards.com/contract-structure/…/counterparts

[③] 见 http://dict.cn/This%20Agreement%20supersedes%20any%20and%20all%20prior%20agreements

第四章 英文合同写作的技术细节（下）

一、合同标题、封面、目录的问题

英文合同标题是越短越好，合同签署各方的名字不出现在合同标题中，标题一般全部用大写字母，个别情况也接受首字母大写的书写方式。如 PREFERRED STOCK PURCHASE AGREEMENT，或者 Preferred Stock Purchase Agreement。

封面须单独一页，可以简单也可以复杂；简单一点的，只需包括三项：合同名称，签署方名称以及合同期即可（如：PREFERRED STOCK PURCHASE AGREEMENT，Between ABC & XYZ，2014 to 2015）。复杂一点的，可以包括合同编号，制作人单位名称（一般为律师行名称）等。各项内容的文字一律置中排列。

篇幅较短的合同，一般不需要目录（Table of Content）。但二十页以上的一般都要有目录和封面。合同目录有一定技术含量：内容不仅包括大标题，还包括小标题（非合同类法律文件，如诉讼文件也是如此），还要有页码，它基本上是正文中标题的汇总，目录中的标题字体跟正文标题相同，但不应该有画线。如果有小标题，在排版格式上应该每次一级缩进两个字母的位置，具体可参阅正规教材书籍的目录格式。

此外，目录一定要等到所有正文内容和合同附件全部定稿后才去编制，否则可能会因对标题内容或页码的小小改动而"方寸大乱"。

二、关于注释

合同写作不同于学术论文，不能引经据典，所以合同内的任何内容，不得加注脚或以尾注形式加以说明。如有此必要，可以在引言条款（introductory clause, recital, preamble）或引言之后的定义部分（definition）进行说明或做出界定。如在引言条款中，可以说明该公司业务性质、在何处成立、公司负责人是谁、甚至公司的前身叫什么名，如今跟哪一家公司合并或被收购而成为某某母公司之子公司等，均可在引言条款中作出交代。例如：

1. This XXX Agreement (hereinafter referred to as Agreement) is made and entered into in Hong Kong, China, as the day 10th, January, 2004 by and between:

ABC Company Limited, established and existing under the law of Hong Kong Special Administrative Region of the PRC, whose registered office is at 12/F Kim Wo Plaza, Causeway Bay, Hong Kong (hereinafter referred to as Party A); and

XYZ Co, established and existing under the law of the PRC, having its headquarter domiciled in Beijing (hereinafter referred to as Party B).

Party A and Party B may be referred to as a Party individually or Parties collectively.

2. Contract of Employment

ABCD Company (hereinafter referred to as the "Company"), a corporation duly organized and existing under and by virtue of the laws of the People Republic of China with office address at, represented by its President and Chief Executive Officer, XXX (name), hereinafter referred to as the "Employer".

and

_____, a Chinese citizen of 33 years of age with address at, and personal ID (_____) hereinafter referred to as the "Employee".

Withnesseth that:

Whereas, the Company is in need of a programmer and the Employee possesses the necessary education and professional skills in accordance with the standards and/or qualifications set by the Company;

Whereas, the Employee has applied for the position and fully agreed to the terms and conditions stated herein;

Now, Therefore, for in consideration of the forgoing, the parties freely and voluntarily enter into the Agreement under the following terms and conditions:①

三、机构名、专有名、文件名的表述

该三类名称，如未在合同中专门加以定义，一律用斜体表述，如：

International Chamber of Commerce；REACH，*Good Manufacturing Practices*，IFRS，*the U.S. Export Administration*，WHO，WTO.

四、采用人性化的称呼

关于合同各方称呼问题，前文已有述及，此处再做些补充：绝大部分合同中所用的人称是第三人称，或者称作甲方(Party A)和乙方(Party B)。这是一种冷冰冰的表达方式。根据最近几十年合同语言的发展趋势，如果合同中的双方是公司与客户的关系（如本文开篇的保险条款），建议采用"you-approach"，即将双方称呼改为"you"与"we"。这样的表达更亲切，能无形中缩短与客户的距离、增进与客户的关系。

最后几个技术细节问题主要值得非以英语为母语的法律文本作者的特别注意。

五、动名词和不定式的用法

英文中的动名词(gerund)和不定式(infinitive)谁都会用。但究竟有哪些规律、两者在

---

① 在此笔者不对范例条款的语言风格做任何评论，所以以上语段中保留了许多陈旧的表达方式（主要是画线的词语）；有关通用条款语言风格的讨论详见第六章至最后一章。

用法上有何差异,或者说哪些动词后面该跟动名词、哪些该跟不定式？在普通英文中,这些问题很少有人会提出,但能真正搞得清楚的几乎没有多少人,在法律英文学者中能搞清这些问题的人更少。不以英语为母语的学者或 ESL(English as Second Language)的学者(不仅仅是学生)更是一头雾水。以下简单回答以上问题,但在回答这个些问题之前,必须了解基本上已被语法学家和语言使用者忘掉的 Bolinger 原则:①

Bolinger 原则:已故的哈佛大学语言学教授 Bolinger 在这方面的主要发现是:

有些动词之后跟动名词或不定式,句子的语义变化不大或几乎没有变化。如:

I like camping in the mountains. (It's so peaceful here.)——*more immediate, vivid*(比较直接、生动);

I like to camp in the mountains. (It's so peaceful there.)——*more remote, abstract*(比较遥远、抽象);

Helen started doing her homework at 8 p.m. (and she finished at 11 p.m.)——*suggests that she continued after starting*(暗示她自开始之后就一直在做作业);

Helen started to do her homework at 8 p.m. (but the phone rang and interrupted her work). ——*abstract, no emphasis on continuing nature*(抽象,并不强调她开始之后一直继续做作业的过程)。

These days, investing in financials is not a good idea.

These days, to invest in financials is not a good idea.

When to fly is to soar.

When flying is soaring.

Interesting doesn't mean to have many interests.

Interesting doesn't mean having many interests.

以上最后三对句子的意思几乎无任何变化。

但有些动词(如 *remember*, *forget*, *try*)跟动名词或跟不定式,句子的语义会有极大变化。例如:

I remember locking the door. (remembering occurred after locking——是锁了门之后才记起的)

I remembered to lock the door. (remembering occurred before locking——是在锁门之前就记得的)

I tried closing the window, but that didn't help. I still felt cold.

I tried to close the window, but I couldn't. It was stuck. ②

Bolinger 规律的核心是:不定式主要用以表达"假设性的、将来的以及尚未完成的"行为;动名词主要用以表达"真实的、生动的、已经完成的"行为。以下用与法律事务相关的例子加以说明:

---

① 本节的例句,除注明出处的外,均来自 Enne Enquist, Laurel Currie Oates, *Just Writing: Grammar, Punctuation, and Style for the Legal Writer* (2nd Edition), 301—307。

② http://koreamosaic.net/elp/extras/general/Bolinger.pdf

The defendant wants to enter a plea of not guilty. (该不定式句子表示一个未完成或将来要做的行为或动作。)

The defendant admits hitting the pedestrian. (该动名词句子表示一个过去的已经完成的行为或动作。)

The neighbours hope to obtain an easement. (该不定式句子表示一个将来的行为。)

His responsibilities include hiring employees. (该动名词句表示一个真实而不是假设的行为。(Enquist & Oates,2005:301)

以上四个句子的用法均符合上文阐述的、Bolinger 教授提出的原则。但这一原则并非是放之四海而皆准的。据 Enquist 等的统计,英语中大约有四分之一左右的动词是不受该规律支配的。譬如,anticipate, consider, delay, envision, imagine, keep, mind, postpone, recommend, risk, suggest, understand 等之后所跟的动名词,以及 claim, fail, get, have, hire, manage, teach, tell 之后所跟的不定式,其所表达的意思与 Bolinger 原则不符。

例如,在 Her attorney will recommend accepting the offer 的句子中,其中动词 recommend+动名词 accepting,仍然如不定式结构一样表达的是一个将来的行为。而在下一个句子中 The officer managed to distract the gunman,managed 之后的不定式 to distract 表示的不是将来的行为,而是过去的行为。不过,少数动词的用法不受 Bolinger 原则的支配,并不能否定该原则适用于大部分含有该类动词的句式,所以它对 ESL 作者仍然有很大的参考价值。

1. 以下是美国法律写作专家为法律专业的 ESL 作者提供适用 Bolinger 原则的词汇表。其惯常用法是"动词+动名词"(verb+verb-ing),即不能与动词不定式连用:

acknowledge	keep
admit	keep on
advocate	miss
anticipate	necessitate
appreciate	postpone
approve	practice
avoid	put off
begrudge	delay
cannot help	deny
complete	detest
condemn	disclaim
consider	discuss
contemplate	dislike
defend	enjoy
defer	entail
involve	escape
justify	evade

facilitate	mind
finish	resent
get through	resist
give up	resume
imagine	resume
renounce	risk
report	sanction
quit	shirk
recall	suggest
recollect	tolerate
recommend	understand
relinquish	visualize
relish	withhold
mention	witness

在使用以上这些动词时,应该明白其后所跟的动名词,表示"过去的""真实的"行为。例如:The defendant admits <u>knowing</u> the victim, but he denies <u>killing</u> him. 两个画线的、起限定作用的动名词均指过去的真实行为。

2. 但下列动词一般只跟动词不定式("verb ＋to verb"),与以上只跟动名词的动词不同。

agree *	appear
arrange	learn
ask	manage
attempt	need
bother	offer
care	plan
claim	prepare
condescend	pretend *
consent	promise *
decide *	refuse
demand	say
deserve	seem
desire	struggle
endeavour	swear
expect	tend
fall	threaten
happen	venture
have	volunteer
hesitate	want
hope *	wait
know how	wish

例如：Management plans to offer them a contract with a five percent salary increase. 其中的不定式"to offer"指"将来会提供"，不过以上带有 * 记号的动词，还可以跟宾语从句，且其句子语义与用不定式的表达方式相同。例如：将 The mediator hoped that the negotiation deadline would be extended 与 The mediator hoped to extend the negotiation deadline 做比较，两个句子的语义并无实质性的差异。

3. 以下动词可以跟动名词["动词＋动名词"(verb＋verb-ing)]，也可以跟不定式["动词＋动词不定式"(verb＋to verb)]，而其意思相差些微或无差别：

abhor	disdain
afford	dread
attempt	endure
bear	go
begin	hate
cannot bear	intend
cannot stand	like
cease	love
choose	neglect
commence	propose
continue	scorn
decline	start

例如：

Landowners continue to assert their rights.
Landowners continue asserting their rights.

以上两句的语义在本质上并无差别。不过，也有少数动词，尽管用法上与上列动词相同，可以跟动名词，也可以跟不定式，但句子的语义会有重大差别。例如：forget, prefer, regret, remember, sense, stop, try。其差别在以下实例中可见一斑：

Mrs Warren remembered locking the safe.
Mrs Warren remembered to lock the safe.

第一句指 Warren 女士记起锁上了保险柜这件事（即行为发生后记得的事情——符合 Bolinger 原则）。而第二句指她并没有忘记去锁上保险柜（即行为发生前记得事情——同样符合 Bolinger 原则）。

此外，还有一个系列的跟不定式的动词可以在动词与不定式之间加上宾语——在这种情况下，该宾语就是不定式所执行的行为的主语。这些动词有：

advise	oblige
allow	order
appoint	permit
authorize	persuade
cause	remind

challenge	request
command	require
convince	select
encourage	teach
forbid	tell
force	tempt
get	train
hire	trust
instruct	urge
invite	warn

例如：Opposing counsel will advise her client to settle. ——该句动词 advise 之后的宾语 her 就成了动词不定式 to settle 行为的主语。

The judge permitted the prosecutor to ask questions about prior convictions. ——动词 permitted 之后的宾语 the prosecutor 就成了动词不定式 to ask questions 行为的主语。

最后需要一提的是：当动词之后跟了 too,enough 或 how 等副词,其后的行为只能用不定式而不能用动名词来表达。例如：

The police arrived too late to apprehend the burger.
The defendant is not strong enough to kick the door down.
A 20-year-old woman knows how to protect herself.

六、定冠词与不定冠词的使用规律(a,an,the)[①]

英文中定冠词与不定冠词的用法是 ESL 学生、学者永远的"痛"。很多人学了一辈子英文还是不能准确掌握其用法。不是在英语母语环境中长大和生活,有谁声称自己真正掌握、并且每次都能准确应用(尤其是在口语环境中)定冠词和不定冠词？

这一节的内容是通过复习和梳理冠词和不定冠词的使用规律,来加强包括本人在内的 ESL 学生对法律文本中定冠词和不定冠词用法的认识。如果是众所周知的内容,就不加说明地加以省略。

(一) 不定冠词的语法常识复习

1. 不定冠词 a,an 只用于修饰和限定读者未知其身份或特性的可数名词,如 a contract, an easement, an appellant court。这类词的复数形式在词尾加 s 或 es,如 contracts, easements, appellant courts, glasses。

2. 不可数名词,如 anger, equipment, pollution, wealth 等,顾名思义,是不可数的,所以没有单数或复数形式。

3. 元音开头的名词单数须使用 an,如 an assault, an accident；辅音字母开头但该辅音

[①] 本节的例句,除注明出处的外,均来自 Enne Enquist, Laurel Currie Oates, *Just Writing：Grammar, Punctuation, and Style for the Legal Writer* (2nd Edition),284−295。

不发音的单数名词也同样要使用 an,如 an hour,an honest man;元音字母开头但元音字母不发音的名词,只能用 a 修饰,如 a unique opportunity,a university,a unanimous jury 以及 a one-hour delay。

4. 部分名词可以是可数名词,也可以是不可数名词。其单数和复数形式在词义上往往有较大差异:如 paper 纸(不可数),papers 论文/文件(可数);people 人们(不可数/复数),people 人(单数);peoples 民族(可数)。

5. 不可数名词如果要作为可数名词使用时,不能用 a 或 an,而往往需要用一个量词词组去修饰,如 a piece of paper,an act of violence,two glasses of milk。

(二) 不定冠词 (a,an) 的使用规律

1. 在文本中第一次提到的、对于读者或者作者来说是"身份或性质不明"的某人、某物或某事,用不定冠词 a 或 an 去修饰。例如:

> <u>A truck</u> slowly approached.(首次提到)
> <u>An officer</u> observed a truck slowly approach.(作者不知道 an officer 具体是谁。)

2. 凡已经用了具有专属性质的词(主要为代词)去修饰的名词,不得再使用不定冠词 a 或 an 去限定。如:A <u>this/one</u> officer observed a truck slowly approach.(应去掉 a)。

这类具有专属性质的词包括:Lee's,California's,his,her,its,their,this,that,these,those,every,few,many,more,most,much,either,neither,each,any,all,no,several 以及 some。

3. 极少数名词单数和复数形式无任何变化。例如:I have one sheep. He has two sheep. 我有一只羊,他有三只羊。

对可数名词的数量提问用 how many,如:I can see two pictures on the wall. →How many pictures can you see on the wall? 对不可数名词的数量提问要用 how much,如:There is a lot of pork in the basket. →How much pork is there in the basket? 但对不可数名词之前表示数量名词中的修饰语提问时要用 how many,如:I want three glasses of water. →How many glasses of water do you want?[①]

4. 不可数名词之前不用 a 或 an 量词去限定,所以不可数名词无复数。但究竟哪一些名词或哪一类名词属于不可数类? 主要有:

(1) 饮料食品:如 water,milk,coffee,tea,wine,juice,fruit,fish,chicken,meat

(2) 物料、材料或原料:如 air,coal,dirt,electricity,gasoline,gold,grass,hair,ice,iron,oil,oxygen,paper,plastic,steel,wood

(3) 气候有关词:如 fog,ice,rain,snow

(4) 学科名称:如 architecture,art,chemistry,civics,grammar,music,science,Arabic,Chinese,English

(5) 跟游戏、运动或休闲娱乐有关的名词:如 baseball,basketball,bowling,bridge(桥牌),camping,dancing,golf,hunting,opera,sailing,swimming,tennis,television

(6) 抽象名词:如 advice,anger,beauty,capitalism,communism,confidence,democracy,

---

① news.xinhuanet.com/edu/2008-02/11/content_7587344.htm

education, employment, energy, fun, happiness, health, help, homework, honesty, ignorance, information, intelligence, justice, kindness, knowledge, laughter, liberty, life, love, merchandise, nature, news, pollution, poverty, recreation, research, satisfaction, society, strength, technology, transportation, trouble, truth, violence, virtue, wealth, wisdom, work

（7）跟法律概念有关的名词（大部分属于抽象名词）：如 abandonment, abatement, access, acquiescence, adultery, alimony, arson, authentication, capital, commerce, conduct, depreciation, discretion, duress, evidence, extortion, housing, insolvency, insurance, intent, land, malice, negligence, privacy, real estate, violence

（8）动名词（以 ing 结尾的动词）及动名词短语也属于不可数名词类。如 Drowning was the cause of death, 以及 Most attorney enjoy *making arguments*.

（9）广义类或通称物品：如 ammunition, clothing, equipment, freight, furniture, jewelry, luggage, lumber, machinery, mail, money, propaganda, scenery, stationary, traffic, vegetation

例句如：The detective found a weapon and *ammunition* in the defendant's trunk.（武器可数，弹药不可数）

（三）定冠词（the）使用规律

可数名词（包括单数和复数）和不可数名词均可使用定冠词。在何种情况下需要使用定冠词？情况非常复杂，简单归纳和举例如下：

1. 由于前文已经提及，有关名词的性质或身份已为读者所知：例如：A truck slowly approached. An officer noticed the truck contained several garbage cans. 该段中的第二个 truck 需要加定冠词是因为该 truck 已经在前面句中出现过。

2. 由于有关名词后面跟着修饰语词或限制性定语从句，读者已知该名词的性质或身份。如：The driver of the truck appeared nervous. 即使该句跟上例的句子毫无关系，没有上文，该 driver 之前也必须加定冠词 the，因为该词之后有限制性短语 of the truck，指的是该卡车的司机。又如：What happens if the driver who hit me has no insurance? 该句子中，driver 也必须加定冠词，因为它后面跟了一个限定它的定语从句"who hit..."。（www.mirror.co.uk/）

检验该类词是否需要加定冠词的最佳的办法是确定它是否可以跟在所有格词的后面。例如（就以上例句中的名词而言）：

　　the driver of the truck—the truck's driver
　　the cost of a trial—a trial's cost
　　the length of the skidmark—the skidmark's length

3. 但是，如果有关名词之后跟的是定义性质（define）而非限制性质的短语或定语从句，则该名词之前必须用不定冠词 a 或 an。例如：A contract that has all of its terms in writing is a formal contract. 该句中的 that has all of... 只是给前者 contract 下定义，而非设定限制，所以此处须用 a。

4. 由于读者知道有关名词排行名次或受最高级的形容词修饰，那么这类名词之前须加定冠词。例如：The best example of a public figure is a film star. 以及 The plaintiff was

unable to satisfy the third element. 前者受最高级形容词 best 修饰；后者排行第三位，所以均须用定冠词 the 修饰。值得注意的是，少数形容词没有最高级或比较级的形式，例如 perfect, unique, pregnant, dead, impossible, 以及 infinite 等等。

5. 有关名词的性质或身份你知我知或众所周知。如：The moon provided enough light for the officer to see the defendant open his truck. 以及 Numerous gang-related activities have occurred at the shopping mall. 前者所指的月亮人所共知，后者所指的商场是作者和读者共知的场所。

6. 如何确定需要用定冠词 the 去修饰的特指名词(a specific noun)？最简单的办法是用"哪一个？"(Which one or ones?)对其进行提问。如果是特指的，一定有明确答案。例如（就以上例句中的名词而言）：

  Which driver? 肯定是 The diver of the truck。
  Which example? 肯定是 The best example。
  Which element? 肯定是 The third element。
  Which moon? 肯定是 The moon we all know about。
  Which shopping mall? 肯定是 The shopping mall that we all know or frequently go there shopping。

如果有具体答案的，需要加定冠词 the。如果答案是："任何一个""所有""我不知道究竟是哪一个"或者"不是前面提到的那个"，那么该名词就是不需要加定冠词的非特指或类指名词（a generic *noun*）。

7. 有关名词跟有后饰的修饰词或定语从句的，需要加定冠词。如：The driver of the truck appeared nervous. The jury of the raping case found the defendant innocent. 以及 The defendant who represents himself in court has won the case. (of the truck 与 of the raping case 为后饰的修饰词；who represents himself in court 为 defendant 的定语从句。)

8. 专有名称、政治团体、组织名称、有修饰成分或含有专属词 of 的国名、地理名称（冠名的江、河、湖、海、洋）须加定冠词。例如：the United Nations, the Republic of Korea, the People's Republic of China, the United States of America, the Yellow River, the Mississippi River。

（四）不需要使用定冠词或不定冠词的情形

1. 大多数单数的专有名，如人名、街道名、公园名、城市名、国家名、洲名不需要加定冠词。Smith(人名) went to Africa（洲名）last year. He visited Kenya（国名）and spent several weeks in Tsavo West National Park（公园名）which is about 500 miles away from Nairobi（城市名），the capital city of the Republic of Kenya. 后两个定冠词符合上条特指事物的规定。自然状态的国家名一般不需要加定冠词，如 China, Korean, America；有政治定性的国家名，或者说其后有 of 修饰的国家名、城市名甚或机构名均须加定冠词，如 the Republic of Korea, the city of Los Angeles, the University of California。而人名，如果是复数并有定冠词 the 修饰，则指其一家人，如像 the Johnsons, 指 Johnson 一家人。

2. 指一个类别、群体的名词或泛指的复数名词，不需要加定冠词 the，也不需要不定冠词 a 或 an。例如：

a. <u>Defendants</u> have the right to a lawyer.（该句的"被告人"指的是这个群体。）

b. <u>Information</u> can lead to justice（该句的"资讯"与"公义"均为泛指事物。）

又如：

c. <u>Expert witnesses</u> have become common <u>in court</u>.（该句的以复数形式出现的"专家证人"与"法庭"均非特指具体哪一位或哪方面的专家证人，或哪一个或哪一级的法庭，两者均为泛指的群体名称，所以不需要加定冠词。）

另外，有些集合名词也是可数名词，但不同的是，它们以单数形式出现，表示复数概念，如 people，police，family 等；而有些可数名词本身只以复数形式出现，如 clothes，glasses（眼镜），trousers 等；有的可数名词单、复数形式相同，如 Japanese，sheep，Chinese 等。如：The Chinese people are hardworking and brave.（中国人民勤劳勇敢。）还有某些名词一般情况下无复数形式，但后缀加了-s 或-es 之后，表示该类事物的各种类别，如 steel（钢），复数为 steels（各种钢材。）同类词还有：barley，brass，coffee，copper，corn，fruit，iron，linen，millet，oak，pepper，pine，rye，silk，tea，wheat，wool，基本上都属于原材料的名称。①

---

① 陆谷孙主编：《英汉大字典》(第二版)，上海：上海译文出版社，Plural 词条。

第五章 合同中的 shall 及其他情态动词的使用问题

法律文本中该不该使用 shall 以及如何正确使用 shall，一直是英美法律界长期争论的问题，也是最令法律从业人员困惑的问题。在此简扼提出一些结论性的建议——shall 仍然是表示法律义务的最佳词汇选择。理由如下：

(1) shall 功能上的优越性：法律义务，尤其是合同中规定的义务，蕴含将来需要履行和被要求履行的行为，shall 既含有所需的情态性和人情味（温和强制），又有表示将来的功能（即其原始功能——当与第一人称主语连用时），故 shall 在表述法律义务（尤其是合同中双方商定的义务）时，有"一箭双雕"的功用。

(2) shall 比较上的优越性：虽然它的含义与 must, will, be to do sth, be obligated, be required to, have a duty to, be responsible to 等短语的功用近似，但使用 must 语气太强硬；使用 will 语气太弱，况且 will 与第三人称主语连用主要表示将来时态，此外是表示意愿或同意做某事，如 The tenant will keep the property in good repair——表示租客愿意对房产做适当的维修，并没一定强制租客去维修房产。而在法律文本中，事实上也有纯粹的意愿或将来的状态需要用 will 去表述，所以不应让 will 身兼数职，去"承担"法律文本中繁重的义务表述的功能（这往往是各类合同条款的中心任务）。be to do sth. 尽管有命令的含义，但主要表示将来的安排，专门用以表示法律文本中的义务也有些"越俎代庖"。

而后面的若干短语（be obligated, be required to, have a duty to, be responsible to）又不及 shall 简洁，再且这些短语大部分必须以被动语态的方式才能表示义务，这恰好是上文已经讨论过的、不值得提倡的被动语态的表达方式。

(3) shall 在业界有被滥用的"优势"：数十年来，英、美、加、澳、新的法律界和语言教育界有无数人、无数文章提倡用 must, will 取代 shall 以表示法律义务，但没有取得成功，法律界依然故我、我行我素地使用甚至滥用 shall。语言是一种民主的行为，靠倡议或命令都无法扭转局面，只能因势利导，所以当用 shall 表述法律义务的深厚"群众基础"（律师行）仍然没有改变时，我们唯一能做的就是因势利导：告诉人们如何正确使用 shall，而不是强制用户必须用什么词。

其实，如果法律文本中含有可以用"has a duty to"（有义务，应当）的地方，用 shall 去取代是最合适不过的。而要求更严格、特别需要强调、适合用"be required to"的地方，或违反就会有严重后果的情形，用 must 去表达更合适。

另一个情态动词 may，一般情况下不会错用，它表示"is permitted to"，即允许你做，你可以做，但你未必一定要做，如 Buyer may inspect the property. 购房者可以去察看物业，这是他的权利，但他可以不去做。

在英文所有的情态动词中 shall 是最难用的，也最难翻译成恰当中文，它至少有八种以上的译法。（李克兴，2006）在法律文本中 shall 最常见的被滥用的情形是不问青红皂白、在主句谓语动词之前随意加上一个 shall，尤其常见的滥用是在下定义的句子的谓语动词之前加上一个 shall，如"Driver shall include any person actually driving a motor vehicle at any given time and any person in charge thereof for the purpose of driving whenever the same is stationary on any road；..."；其次是叠床架屋式的滥用：在本身已经能表达法律义务的动词之前加 shall，如"shall have a duty to"，"shall be required to"。

通过分析以下各例句，读者可以更清晰地了解在哪些情形下 shall 用得对还是不对：

The owner of an animal classified as "dangerous" shall keep that animal in wire mesh enclosure as defined in subsection 34(q) and shall not allow that animal outside its enclosure unless it is on a leash capable of restraining it or is being transported in a secure cage.

被列为"危险"类动物的主人须将该动物圈禁在 34(q) 款界定的金属丝网笼内，除了该动物被拴在能够约束得住的绳链上或被关在安全笼子内运输时，否则动物主人不得将该动物放出笼。

在以上语段中两个 shall 用得都是正确的：因为动物属于危险类别的，所以主人有法律责任将动物放在特定规格的笼子内以确保周围其他生命的安全；除非有安全措施，否则禁止主人将该动物放出笼。而在以下的句子情形中，shall 都是被滥用的：

"Vehicle" shall mean....
This option shall expire at noon on March 1, 2014.
The tenant shall have the right to immediate occupancy of the premises.
Buyer shall have the duty to make payment within 10 days of delivery.

总之，在对法律主体(legal subject)或行为者没有强迫、或要求承担义务的法律条款中，使用"shall"都是滥用。以上第一句是下定义，没有强迫任何人或要求谁承担义务；第二句表示一种将来时态，指期权将在何时到期，没有任何强逼到期的意思，如果要更清晰地表示将来时态，倒不妨在动词 expire 之前加一个纯粹表示将来状态的情态动词 will；第三句表达的是法律主体享有的权利而不是义务或法律责任；第四句不用 shall，就已经能够表达义务(have the duty)；如果要用 shall，那么就不需要使用 the duty 这个短语了。Buyer shall make payment within 10 days of delivery 与 Buyer has the duty to make payment within 10 days of delivery 所表达的法律概念是完全相同的。

第六章 合同序言条款的写作和翻译

一、引言

合同序言又叫鉴于条款(Recital/ Preamble /Whereas Clause)。

现代人生活繁忙,反对形式主义,讨厌繁琐的程序,但做任何事仍然又得有一定的程序。写论文有个引言或前言,写合同也不例外,要有一个开场白,但这个开场白一定要开门见山、一语破的。合同里的序言,即开场白,用来陈述事实,说明合同性质,最终引出实质性的实施条款(operative clauses)。

这个最先出现在合同中的序言属于通用条款,有人称之为"序言",有人称之为"鉴于条款",也有人称之为"约因"。这是由于有些合同用 In consideration of 开篇(此处 consideration 解作"约因"),有些用 whereas("鉴于")作引导词,那些较正规、篇幅较长的合同则称之为"序言"(Preamble/Recital)。所以,在英文合同中序言条款叫作 Preamble, Recital, Whereas Clause,均有。但大部分英文合同都用 In consideration of/ Considering that/ Whereas("考虑到/有鉴于")这三个短语引导出序言。

序言条款分为两种,一种为描述事实的陈述部分(narrative recital);另一种为引出事实的陈述部分(introductory recital)。前者用以简单解释实施条款订立的动机,然后马上转入正题,所以篇幅相对较短。后者的作用在于表述合同订立的背景或契据赖以发生的事实的原因以及有关公司成立及存续方面的资料,篇幅一般稍长。以下详介这两种类型的序言。

二、典型合同序言条款的写法

(一) 导言型序言条款

1. This Contract is made by and between the Sellers and the Buyers, whereby the Sellers agree to sell and the Buyers agree to buy the under-mentioned goods on the terms and conditions stated below:

2. Whereas Party A agree to deliver (sell) the goods to Party B within Ten (10) days in accordance with the prices specified herein; Now Therefore, both Parties conclude this agreement as follows:

3. The... (hereinafter referred to as Party A) and the... (hereinafter referred to as Party B) have agreed to complete the following transactions in accordance with the terms and conditions stipulated below:

(二) 陈述型序言条款

1. This Contract, is made and entered into[3] in (place of signature (签约地)) this ____th day of ____ (month), ____ (year), by and between (company name as a party), a corporation duly organized and existing under the laws of (name of country) with its domicile at (address) (hereinafter referred to as Party A), and (name of the other party), a company incorporated and existing under the laws of (name of country) with its domicile at (address) (hereinafter referred to as Party B).

2. In consideration of the mutual promises and undertakings contained in this Agreement, the Parties agree as follows: This XXX Agreement (hereinafter referred to as Agreement) is made and entered into in Hong Kong, China, as the day 10th, 2014 by and between:

ABC Company Limited, established and existing under the law of Hong Kong Special Administrative Region of the PRC, whose registered office is at 12/F Kim Wo Plaza, Causeway Bay, Hong Kong (hereinafter referred to as Party A); and

XYZ Co., established and existing under the law of the PRC, having its headquarter domiciled in Beijing (hereinafter referred to as Party B).

Party A and Party B may be referred to as a Party individually or Parties collectively.

3. Whereas Party A and Party B signed a Memorandum of Understanding dated May 1, 2010 agreeing to start friendly discussion on establishing a joint venture to jointly develop the [Project];

Whereas Party A and Party B reached initial agreement on establishing a joint venture to jointly develop the [Project], and signed the Joint Venture Heads of Agreement on December 1, 2010;

Now, Therefore, in consideration of the above background, Party A and Party B have hereby agreed to establish a joint venture in accordance with the terms and conditions of this joint venture contract to develop the [Project]:

4. This Agreement is made this ____ day of ____ (month), _____ (year), between _____ ("Licensor"), and _____ ("Licensee").

Witnesseth

Whereas Licensor owns certain valuable registered trademarks and service marks, and owns and has merchandising rights to various other Licensor properties as defined in Paragraph 1 of the Rider attached hereto and hereby made a part hereof ("Name"), said Name having been used over the facilities of (certain industries or fields), and in promotional and advertising material in different businesses and being well known and recognized by the general public and associated in the public mind with Licensor; and

Whereas Licensee desires to utilize the Name upon and in connection with the manufacture, sale and distribution of articles hereinafter described;

Now, Therefore, in consideration of the mutual promises herein contained, it is hereby agreed:

5. This Agreement is made this 8th day of August, 2014, by and between Victory Electronic Trading Co., Ltd. (hereinafter called "the Sellers"), a corporation duly organized and existing under the laws of Hong Kong, with its head office (principal place of business) at _____ and Pan American Trading Co, Inc. (hereinafter called "the Buyers"), a corporation duly organized and existing under the laws of California, the United States, with its head office (principal place of business) at _____ , California, the United States.

WHEREAS, the Sellers are desirous of exporting the under-mentioned products to the territory stipulated below;

And

WHEREAS, the Buyers are desirous of importing the said products for sale in the said territory;

NOW, THEREFORE, it is hereby agreed and understood as follows:(薛华业,1989:2—3)

6. ABCD Company (hereinafter referred to as the "Company"), a corporation duly organized and existing under and by virtue of the laws of the People Republic of China with office address at _____, represented by its President and Chief Executive Officer, XXX (name), hereinafter referred to as the "Employer".

and _____, a Chinese citizen of XX years of age with address at _____ , and personal ID♯ (♯ _____) (hereinafter referred to as the "Employee").

Witnesseth that:

Whereas, the Company is in need of a programmer and the Employee possesses the necessary education and professional skills in accordance with the standards and/or qualifications set by the Company;

Whereas, the Employee has applied for the position and fully agreed to the terms and conditions stated herein;

Now, Therefore, for in consideration of the forgoing, the parties freely and voluntarily enter into the Agreement under the following terms and conditions:

三、典型合同序言条款要素

尽管序言写法可以五花八门,具体内容也不尽相同,但归纳而言,较完整的序言一般要包括四大要素:

1. 该合同由谁跟谁签订以及在何时订立:This Contract is made <u>by and between the Sellers and the Buyers</u>;This Agreement is made <u>this 8th day of August,2015,by and between...</u>。

2. 合同方或协议方是谁:ABC Company;各方办公地址在何处;以及各方(如公司)

是根据哪个司法管辖区的法律组建和存续的,以及公司的简称:ABC Company, a corporation duly organized and existing under the laws of (name of country) with its domicile at (address) (hereinafter referred to as Party A), and XYZ Company, a company incorporated and existing under the laws of (name of country) with its domicile at (address) (hereinafter referred to as Party B).

3. 签订合同的原因(约因)或合同的性质——是买卖合同、或是雇佣合同,还是项目合作,等等:the Sellers (or ABC Company) agree(s) to sell and the Buyers (XYZ Company) agree(s) to buy the under-mentioned goods;... agree to deliver (sell) the goods;或 have agreed to complete the following transactions。

4. 引入后续条款的套话:Now Therefore, both Parties conclude this agreement as follows:... 或者 In consideration of the mutual promises and undertakings contained in this Agreement, the Parties agree as follows:... 或者 Now, Therefore, in consideration of the forgoing, the parties enter into the Agreement under the following terms and conditions: 或者 Whereas Party A and Party B reached initial agreement on...; Now, Therefore, in consideration of the above background, Party A and Party B have hereby agreed to do sth. in accordance with the terms and conditions of this contract to develop the [Project].

四、写作序言条款的注意事项

(一) 条款内容繁简的决定因素

如果各方是第一次打交道,自然要谨慎一些,要将对方公司"验明正身",要看一看或查一查、并在合同有关条款中记录下对方的合法身份证明方面的资料,甚至还要验明对方跟你签合同的人是否获得其公司的合法授权(因为并非一切管理层的人员或部门的主管都有权代表公司跟其他公司签约的),这样一来序言条款的内容就比较多,句子也较其他合同通用条款冗长。

但如果是生意上的长期合作伙伴,第一次以后签约再继续做生意,往往无需在序言中写入各方的详细资料以及根据哪一个司法管辖区的法律成立或存续等方面的内容,一般只需要在合同结尾的签字部分写明甲方及乙方是谁或哪家公司即可。这种简洁的序言表达方式如:This Contract is made by and between the Sellers and the Buyers, whereby the Sellers agree to sell and the Buyers agree to buy the under-mentioned goods on the terms and conditions stated below:...

不过,对于并非陌生的合同方,目前更加流行的做法是采用标准合同,省去这种需要由律师起草的套话连篇的序言,在合同题目和合同编号之后采用以下格式,如:

Party A: ABC Company, Ltd.
   Address: 12/F Kim Wo Plaza, Causeway Bay, Hong Kong, PRC
   Tel: (xx) xxxxxxxx; Fax: (xx) xxxxxxxx;
   Company Email: xxxxxx@xxxx.com
Party B: XYZ Company, Inc.

Address:1147 West Vincent Blvd. ,Culver City,CA 91755,USA
Tel:(xx) xxxxxxxx; Fax:(xx) xxxxxxxx;
Company Email:xxxxxxx@xxxx.com

(二) 语法方面的提示

序言条款写作在语法上有一个有目共睹的、违反一般定律的做法。上节已有若干例句,在刚刚提到的例句中(This Contract is made by and between the Sellers and the Buyers, whereby the Sellers agree to sell and the Buyers agree to buy the under-mentioned goods on the terms and conditions stated below):表述过往任何时间发生的行为本来须使用过去时态,但在这一条款的写作中使用一般现在时态几乎是惯例,而且不管句子中发生的行为有无具体日期,都少有例外。例如:This XXX Agreement (hereinafter referred to as Agreement) is made and entered into in Hong Kong, China,as the day 10th,2011 by and between:...; This Contract,is made and entered into in (place of signature 签约地) this ____ th day of _____ (month), _____ (year), by and between (company name as a party), a corporation duly organized and existing under the laws of (name of country) with its domicile at (address) (hereinafter referred to as Party A),and (name of the other party), a company incorporated and existing under...

这些序言条款中都有日期,这表明合同是在过去某一时段签订的,但却一律用现在时态来表述。

(三) 典型条款的语言风格

我们通过实例来分析——This Contract,is made and entered into in (place of signature 签约地) this ____ th day of _____ (month), _____ (year), by and between (company name as a party), a corporation duly organized and existing under the laws of (name of country) with its domicile at (address) (hereinafter referred to as Party A),and (name of the other party), a company incorporated and existing under the laws of (name of country) with its domicile at (address) (hereinafter referred to as Party B).

以上画线部分都属于典型的 legalese 写作风格。is made and entered into... 两者取其一意思已经非常清楚;this ____ th day of _____ (month), _____ (year),属于陈旧和过于正式的表达方式,可以用符合语法规范的普通英文表达方式,即 on 26 January,2014;by and between 属于法律配对词(legal pair)范畴,可以只取其一,如果合同方只有甲乙两方,用 between 也无妨。

duly organized and existing 也是部分重复的表达方式:用何种方式组建公司虽然重要,关键是该公司目前的存续是否合法;有些公司当初合法组建,但如果后来没有缴交需要缴交的公司注册费或营业执照费以及其他的工商或税务费用,其合法地位自然存疑。跟这样的公司打交道,风险太大了,甚至买卖都可能成为非法的。所以,这个短语虽然内容有些重复,大部分律师行还都倾向于将两词合并使用。组建公司最常用的动词无疑是 organize,但在美国经常会用 incorporate。使用前者,公司可能是个体公司(proprietary company),也有可能是合伙人公司(partnership),也有可能是 limited company,当然还有可能是上市公司(listed company);而使用后者,只有一个可能,即有限公司,如简称为 ABC Inc. 即属此类公司,在香港则简称 ABC Ltd.。

最后一个 hereinafter referred to as Party A/B(译为"以下简称'甲/乙方'")是一种啰嗦的表达方式,可以简化为(referred to as "Party A/B")(简称"甲/乙方"),甚至可以更简洁地简化为("Party A/B")——试问,在一个长串公司名称后,加上("甲方"),有谁会误解这不是前文的简称吗?另外还有一种表达方式,即"hereinafter called Party A/B"——虽然比这一段前面提到的短语要短一些,但也同样为旧式的表达方式,在现代合同中越来越少见了。

(四) 特殊古旧词 Witnesseth 的用法、意思与翻译问题

以上第二节的第 7 和第 9 段都用到 Witnesseth。这个词究竟是什么意思?如何使用?法律翻译界众说纷纭。

首先我们要明白,这是一个当前被基本废弃的古旧词,是典型的法律行话,而且几乎所有的英汉普通词典都不收录。即使专业的法律词典或较权威的元照法律词典也没有收录。幸好互联网上还有相关解释:Legal jargon for "to take notice of," used in phrases such as "On this day I do hereby witnesseth the signing of this document."①另一互联网词典也将其界定为"(*LEGALESE*) used in contracts to mean take notice of",用法如:WITNESSETH: WHEREAS, Title 1 of Article 18—A of the General Municipal Law of the State of New York (the "Enabling Act") was duly enacted into law as Chapter 1030 of the Laws of 1969 of the State of New York; and...②

传统上,国内的法律翻译专家都将该词翻译成"证明",其实其意思更接近 shows/records。因此,"见证""标明""记录下"可能更符合原意,因为这个词的根词毕竟是"witness",表示亲临其境见证某事件的发生。所以,我们仍然可以勉强继续将其翻译成"证明""兹证明""现见证"。不过,作为语言工作者,我们必须对这个在法律文本、尤其是序言和结语条款中经常出现的古旧词有较清晰的认识。

首先,这个词的词性是动词,在法律文本中永远与第三人称的主语连用。该词后面加的是 eth,以几百年前古旧英文动词常见的变化形式出现的,相当于当代英语的 es。当代英语中的 You see,如果其主语是第三人称单数,则写成 He sees;而在古旧英文中须写成 He seeth。例如,The righteous shall rejoice when *he seeth* the vengeance.

该词一般在合同中都独占一行,其中的字母往往被全部大写。跟在该词之后的一般是 Whereas;有时也跟 In consideration,如 *WITNESSETH* that in *consideration* of;例句如:NOW THEREFORE THIS AGREEMENT *WITNESSETH* that in *consideration* of the mutual covenants herein contained and other good and valuable...

在合同序言条款的写作中,该词的正确用法如下:

  This AGREEMENT entered into this _____ day of _____,20 ___, by and between the City of Pocatello, a municipal corporation of Idaho, hereinafter referred to as "City," and _____, hereinafter referred to as "Landlord."

  WITNESSETH:

---

① Nolo's *Plain-English Law Dictionary*, http://www.nolo.com/dictionary/witnesseth-term.html
② Legal English Dictionary, http://www.translegal.com/legal-english-dictionary/witnesseth

WHEREAS, the purpose of this Agreement is to provide continuous utility service to the premises specified herein regardless of changes in occupancy.

NOW, THEREFORE, for and in consideration of the mutual promises set forth herein, the parties hereto agree as follows:

该词也用在合同结尾条款,如 in witnesseth whereof, in witnesseth thereof ,这时其作用与 in witness whereof, in witness thereof 相同。

建议:该词用在合同序言和结尾条款中完全是一种过时的写法,仅仅是一种"古色古香"的形式,没有任何实质意义,可以不用去理会,也不需要翻译。

五、标准序言条款的写作及说明

以下扼要介绍各种不同性质的合同序言条款的写法:

(一) 简易买卖合同的序言条款

This Contract is made by and between the Sellers and the Buyers, whereby the Sellers agree to sell and the Buyers agree to buy the under-mentioned goods on the terms and conditions stated below:...

(二) 通用合同的序言条款

This Contract, is made and entered into in (place of signature 签约地) this ____ th day of ____ (month), ____ (year), by and between (company name as a party), a corporation duly organized and existing under the laws of (name of country) with its domicile at (address) (hereinafter referred to as Party A), and (name of the other party), a company incorporated and existing under the laws of (name of country) with its domicile at (address) (hereinafter referred to as Party B).

In consideration of the mutual promises and undertakings contained in this Agreement, the Parties agree as follows:

(三) 材料租借/转让合同的序言条款

(1) This Material Transfer Agreement is made and entered into as of the _____ day of _____ 20 _____ (the "Effective Date") by and between _____ _____ (referred to as "LENDER") having its principle office at _____ _____ and _____ (referred to as "BORROWER") having its principle office at _____ .

(2) In consideration of the mutual covenants contained herein and with the intention of being legally bound under the laws:

(3) BORROWER desires to obtain samples of the MATERIAL (as defined below) and the LENDER is willing to provide the MATERIAL to the BORROWER solely for the permitted uses and on the terms and conditions set forth in this Agreement.

(四) 共同研究合同 (Research Agreement) 的序言条款

THIS AGREEMENT is effective this _____ day of _____, 20 _____ by and between the _____, with an office at _____ (hereinafter "Recipient") and _____ with an office at _____ (hereinafter "Sponsor").

WHEREAS, the parties desire to conduct certain research programs of mutual interest to the parties; and

WHEREAS, such research programs may further the research objectives of Sponsor in a manner consistent with its status as a _____ institution, and may derive benefits for both Recipient and Sponsor through inventions, improvements or discoveries;

NOW, THEREFORE, in consideration of the promises and mutual covenants herein contained, the parties hereto agree to the following: (Frederic Erbisch)

(五) 期权执照 (Option License Agreement) 合同的序言条款

This Agreement is made and entered into between the _____, a research establishment under _____ laws (hereinafter "Grantor") having its principle office at, _____ _____ and _____ a company organized under the laws of _____ (hereinafter "Grantee"), having its principle office at _____.

In consideration of payment of the Option Price by the Grantee to the Grantor, receipt of which the Grantor acknowledges, the Grantor grants the Grantee an exclusive option to obtain a license from the Grantor to the Optioned Rights, in accordance with this Option Agreement.

(六) 复杂的许可证转让合同的序言条款

This agreement is made and entered into between _____, a _____ established under _____ law (hereinafter called Licensor) having its principle office at _____, and _____ a for-profit corporation organized under the laws of _____ (hereinafter called Licensee), having its principle office at _____.

Witnesseth that:

(1) Whereas, Licensor has the right to grant licenses under the licensed patent rights (as hereinafter defined), and wishes to have the inventions covered by the licensed patent rights in the public interest; and

(2) Whereas Licensee wishes to obtain a license under the licensed patent rights upon the terms & conditions hereinafter set forth:

Now, therefore, in consideration of the premises and the faithful performance of the covenants herein contained it is agreed as follows:

(七) 高级人才雇佣合同的序言条款

ABCD Company (hereinafter referred to as "Company"), a corporation duly organized and existing under the laws of the People Republic of China with office address at _____, represented by its President and Chief Executive Officer, XXX (name), (hereinafter referred to as the "Employer").

And _____, a Chinese citizen of years of XX age with address at _____, and personal ID (# _____) (hereinafter referred to as the "Employee").

Witnesseth that:

Whereas, Company is in need of a senior programmer and Employee possesses the necessary education, experience and professional skills in accordance with the standards or qualifications set by Company;

Whereas, Employee has applied for the position and fully agreed to the terms and conditions stated herein;

Now, Therefore, for in consideration of the forgoing, the parties freely and voluntarily enter into the Agreement under the following terms and conditions:

(八) 旧式重大买卖合同的完整序言条款

This Agreement is made this 8th day of August, 1998, by and between Victory Electronic Trading Co., Ltd. (hereinafter called "the Sellers"), a corporation duly organized and existing under the laws of Hong Kong, with its head office (principal place of business) at _____ and Pan American Trading Co., Inc. (hereinafter called "the Buyers"), a corporation duly organized and existing under the laws of California, the United States, with its head office (principal place of business) at _____, California, the United States.

WHEREAS, the Sellers are desirous of exporting the under-mentioned products to the territory stipulated below;

And

WHEREAS, the Buyers are desirous of importing the said products for sale in the said territory;

NOW, THEREFORE, it is hereby agreed and understood as follows:

(九) 推荐条款:通用合同序言条款写作详解

根据序言条款的功能要求和以上所列举的各种序言条款的常用句型和用词特点,我们可以将其汇总荟萃,提供以下更具通用价值和符合时代法律语言特征的序言条款。所以,本节也是有关序言条款写作的精要：

This Contract, is <u>made and entered into</u> in（place of signature 签约地）on 26 January, 2015, <u>by and between</u>（name of a party）, a corporation <u>duly organized and existing</u> under the laws of（name of country）with its registered office at（address）（referred to as "Party A"）, and（name of the other party）, a company incorporated and existing under the laws of（name of country）with its registered office（address）（referred to as "Party B"）.

WHEREAS, the parties desire to do sth...（or Party A is desirous of doing sth...; And WHEREAS, Party B is desirous of doing sth...）,

NOW, THEREFORE, in consideration of the mutual <u>promises and undertakings</u> contained in this Agreement, the Parties agree as follows:

本合同由＿＿＿公司（称为"甲方"），一家依（国家名称）法律正式组建并存续的公司，其注册的营业所在地位于：（公司地址），和＿＿＿公司（称为"乙方"），一家依（国家名称）法律正式组建并存续的公司，其营业所在地位于：（公司地址）于＿＿＿年＿＿＿月＿＿＿日在（签约地点）签署。

鉴于双方欲做某事（或：鉴于甲方欲做某事，而鉴于乙方欲做某事），

考虑到"双方"在本协议中的相互约定和承诺，"双方"协定如下：

就该条款的行为动词而言，我们仍然选用"is made and entered into"及"duly organized and existing"。尽管语法不符合普通英文的规矩（使用一般现在时态）以及表达啰嗦（见上文分析），但毕竟是绝大多数律师行仍在使用的流行写法。根据语言从众的原则，我们继续沿用这一俗套的写法。

就时间的表达而言，我们用普通英文中的较正式的表达方式（"on 26 January, 2015"）而不是诸如"26/01/2014"此类的简便表达方式，同样我们也没有用"This twenty sixth day of 2015"之类的过于老式的写法，目的是为了让合同语言显得庄重、正式，而又不至于过于正式而与时代严重脱节。

就公司地址而言，使用"with its registered office at"比"with its domicile at..."或"having its principle office at..."可以使该推荐条款更具"通用"价值，因为后两者指的是住址和公司总部的地址，而签订合同的公司未必都有总部或分部；即使是分公司、子公司在法理上也仍然有资格签署合同，它们也未必都与公司总部共用一个总部地址，所以选择"with its registered office at..."（"注册办公地址"）去表达，可以使条款更具灵活性，并且在逻辑上也更加合理——任何法人公司都必须有跟政府工商部门登记的或正式注册的办公地址——不过，这个地址一般不应该是民用的住址，但也未必是公司总部的地址。

此外，为了使条款的风格富有时代气息、体现简明法律英文的写作特点，我们把传统的序言条款中常用的古旧词一概省却。以下划线部分是该条款常用的古旧词：<u>hereinafter</u> referred to as Party B; in consideration of the mutual promises <u>herein</u> contained, it is <u>hereby</u> agreed, 或者 it is <u>hereby</u> agreed and understood as follows。由以上条款中的替换写

法可见,古旧词的功能,除了古色古香之外,都是可以省略或用其他表达方式取代。

最后必须说明的是最后一段中的一个短语,即 in consideration of the mutual promises and undertakings contained in this Agreement——这也是一段可以省却而不影响文意和条款功能的文字,但本条款之所以予以保留,是为了使条款的行文更具连贯性,它的意思是"鉴于/考虑到各方在本合同内的相互许诺和保证",由此"前因",可自然过渡到"双方(特此)协定如下"的"后果",即合同的其他核心条款。

六、结语

据从互联网上获得的不完全的资料,在美国以及原为英联邦、以英语为母语或第一工作语言的国家和地区(如新加坡、印度、南非、中国香港等),可供售卖的合同或具有合同性质的法律文书(legal instrument)至少有5 000多种。不同的合同,其序言条款的写法各不相同,但属同类性质的东西,总有共性可言,归而言之,较完整的序言一般要包括四大要素:1. 该合同由谁跟谁签订以及在何时订立;2. 合同方或协议方是谁、各方办公地址在何处、各方是根据哪个司法管辖区的法律组建和存续的、公司的简称;3. 约因,即合同属于何种性质或双方约定进行哪一方面的合作;以及4. 诸如"特协议如下"之类的、以引入后续条款的套话。作者必须接受的一个语法上的悖论是用过去时态来描述过往已经发生的行为,如:This agreement is made and entered this 8th day of August, 2008。传统上,写作该条款会使用许多 hereinafter, herein, hereby, witnesseth, thereof, whereby 以及 whereas 之类的古旧词。但是,俱往矣,除了最后一个,其余古旧词应尽力避免使用。

为方便写作和翻译各种不同类型的序言条款,以下一节将一些常用的双语合同序言条款的写法及其对应的译文汇总,作为附录提供如下:

其他参考条款及对照译文

Recital/ Preamble /Whereas Clause	合同序言(鉴于条款)	用途说明
This Contract is made by and between the Sellers and the Buyers, whereby the Sellers agree to sell and the Buyers agree to buy the under-mentioned goods on the terms and conditions stated below:	兹经买卖双方同意,按下列条件,由卖方出售,买方购进下列货品:	简易买卖合同
Whereas Party A agree to deliver (sell) the goods to Party B within Ten (10) days in accordance with the prices specified herein; Now Therefore, both Parties conclude this agreement as follows:	甲方同意按合同约定的价格在十(10)天内向乙方发货(售货), 特签署本合同如下:	简易买卖/交货合同

续表

Recital/ Preamble /Whereas Clause	合同序言(鉴于条款)	用途说明
The… (hereinafter referred to as Party A) and the… (hereinafter referred to as Party B) have agreed to complete the following transactions in accordance with the terms and conditions stipulated below:	XXX公司(以下简称甲方)于YYY公司(以下简称乙方)同意按照以下条款完成交易:	简易买卖合同
This Contract, is made and entered into in (place of signature 签约地) this ____th day of ____ (month), ____ (year), by and between (company name as a party), a corporation duly organized and existing under the laws of (name of country) with its domicile at (address) (hereinafter referred to as Party A), and (name of the other party), a company incorporated and existing under the laws of (name of country) with its domicile at (address) (hereinafter referred to as Party B). In consideration of the mutual promises and undertakings contained in this Agreement, the Parties agree as follows:	本合同由_____公司(以下称甲方),一家依(国家名称)法律正式组建并存续的公司,其营业所在地位于:(公司地址),和_____公司(以下称乙方),一家依(国家名称)法律正式组建并存续的公司,其营业所在地位于:(公司地址)于____年____月____日在(签约地点)签署。 考虑到"双方"在本协议中的相互约定和承诺,"双方"协定如下:	通用合同
This XXX Agreement (hereinafter referred to as Agreement) is made and entered into in Hong Kong, China, as the day 10th, 2011 by and between: ABC Company Limited, established and existing under the law of Hong Kong Special Administrative Region of the PRC, whose registered office is at 12/F Kim Wo Plaza, Causeway Bay, Hong Kong (hereinafter referred to as Party A); and XYZ Co., established and existing under the law of the PRC, having its headquarter domiciled in Beijing (hereinafter referred to as Party B). Party A and Party B may be referred to as a Party individually or Parties collectively.	本合同由以下双方于2011年5月10日在中国香港签署: ABC有限公司是一家根据中国香港特别行政区法律设立和存续的公司,其注册地址是香港铜锣湾金华广场12层(以下简称甲方);和XYZ公司,一家根据中华人民共和国法律设立和存续的公司,其总部设在中国北京(以下简称乙方); 甲方和乙方以下可单独称为"一方"或合称为"双方"。	万能合同

续表

Recital/ Preamble /Whereas Clause	合同序言(鉴于条款)	用途说明
Whereas Party A and Party B signed a Memorandum of Understanding dated May 1, 2010 agreeing to start friendly discussion on establishing a joint venture to jointly develop the [Project]; Whereas Party A and Party B reached initial agreement on establishing a joint venture to jointly develop the [Project], and signed the Joint Venture Heads of Agreement on December 1, 2010; Now, Therefore, in consideration of the above background, Party A and Party B have hereby agreed to establish a joint venture in accordance with the terms and conditions of this joint venture contract to develop the [Project]:	鉴于甲方和乙方于 2010 年 5 月 1 日签署《谅解备忘录》，同意就设立合资企业共同开发 XX 项目进行友好协商； 鉴于甲方和乙方同意就设立合资企业共同开发 XX 项目初步达成的意向，并于 2010 年 12 月 1 日签署了《设立合资企业原则协议》；(范文祥, 2007:22) 基于上述的前期努力，甲方和乙方兹同意按照本合营合同的条件和条款设立合资企业，共同开发 XX 项目：	适用于经过多轮磋商(需要交代背景)的合资或合营项目合同
This Agreement is made this ____ day of ____ (month), ____ (year), between ____ ("Licensor"), and ____ ("Licensee"). Witnesseth Whereas Licensor owns certain valuable registered trademarks and service marks, and owns and has merchandising rights to various other Licensor properties as defined in Paragraph 1 of the Rider attached hereto and hereby made a part hereof ("Name"), said Name having been used over the facilities of (certain industries or fields), and in promotional and advertising material in different businesses and being well known and recognized by the general public and associated in the public mind with Licensor; and Whereas Licensee desires to utilize the Name upon and in connection with the manufacture, sale and distribution of articles hereinafter described; Now, Therefore, in consideration of the mutual promises herein contained, it is hereby agreed:	本转让协议由 XXX 公司(简称"许可商")与 YYY 公司(被许可商)在____年____月____日签署。 鉴于许可商拥有某些宝贵的注册商标和服务商标，并且拥有本协议附件第一段界定的买卖许可商持有的各种其他财产的权利，并据此协议将该等财产作为本协议之一部分(简称为"财产名称")，而该财产已经在某工业/领域的设施中、在各不同行业的宣传和广告资料中使用，并且得到公众广泛认可、在公众心目中已树立起许可商的形象；以及鉴于被许可商期望在以下描述的物品的制造、售卖和分销中使用该名称； 因此，基于本协议中包含的相互允诺，特协定如下：	适用于商标类转让合同

Recital/ Preamble /Whereas Clause	合同序言(鉴于条款)	用途说明
This Agreement is made this 8th day of August, 2008, by and between Victory Electronic Trading Co., Ltd. (hereinafter called "the Sellers"), a corporation duly organized and existing under the laws of Hong Kong, with its head office (principal place of business) at _____ and Pan American Trading Co, Inc. (hereinafter called "the Buyers"), a corporation duly organized and existing under the laws of California, the United States, with its head office (principal place of business) at _____, California, the United States. WHEREAS, the Sellers are desirous of exporting the under-mentioned products to the territory stipulated below; And WHEREAS, the Buyers are desirous of importing the said products for sale in the said territory; NOW, THEREFORE, it is hereby agreed and understood as follows:(薛华业,1989:2-3)	本协议由香港威科多利电子贸易有限公司(下称"卖方")——一家按香港法律正式组建和存续的公司,总部设在____;与泛美贸易公司——一家按照美加州法律正式组建和存续的公司,总部设在_____,于2008年8月8日签订。 鉴于卖方欲出口下述产品到本合同下文规定的地方; 而买方欲进口所述产品到本合同所述的地方出售; 特协议如下:	适用于国际贸易(进出口)合同
Contact of Employment ABCD Company (hereinafter referred to as the "Company"), a corporation duly organized and existing under and by virtue of the laws of the People Republic of China with office address at _____, represented by its President and Chief Executive Officer, XXX (name), hereinafter referred to as the "Employer". _____ and _____, a Chinese citizen of years of XX age with address at _____, and personal ID # (# ____) (hereinafter referred to as the "Employee"). Witnesseth that: Whereas, the Company is in need of a programmer and the Employee possesses the necessary education and professional skills in accordance with the standards and/or qualifications set by the Company; Whereas, the Employee has applied for the position and fully agreed to the terms and conditions stated herein; Now, Therefore, for in consideration of the forgoing, the parties freely and voluntarily enter into the Agreement under the following terms and conditions:	雇佣合同 ABCD(以下简称"公司"),一家按照中华人民共和国法律组建和存续的公司,其办公地址为_____,公司的法人代表为公司总裁及首席执行官XXX(以下简称"雇主")。 与XXX,中国公民,XX岁,身份证号码(#_____),居住在_____(以下简称"雇员")。 鉴于本公司需要程序员,而雇员拥有所需的教育、专业技能,符合公司规定的水准和/或资格; 鉴于雇员申请了该程序员职位并且完全同意遵守本合同以下条款; 所以,双方根据下列条款自愿订立本合同:	适用于中型公司与个人直接订立的雇佣合同

第七章 定义及解释条款的写作和翻译

一、引言

紧接合同序言的是正文,正文的第一条款往往是合同的定义或解释条款。但定义或解释条款并非每个合同都有,也就是说,简短的合同或合同中专门词语没有歧义的,无需设有定义或解释条款。凡在合同中反复出现的、具有专门的重要意义而又容易产生歧义的词汇,需要在定义或解释条款中加以界定或解释。这样做的目的是为了提高合同行文效率、减少争议以及为争议产生时解释合同提供依据。

不过,某些合同(如大型的合作项目或跨国公司的兼并合同等)篇幅惊人,多达数十页、上百页,甚至近千页。对这类长篇合同而言,为减轻读者或合同有关方的阅读负担,定义或解释条款不但必需,而且往往作为一个单独的附件放在合同正文之后。本节主要阐述放在合同前部的定义或解释条款的常规内容、写作规律以及翻译模式。

二、定义的引言条款以及相关的句型讨论

紧接合同序言的定义条款是对一些反复出现的重要词语进行界定。但在正式进入界定之前,也往往还要先有一个短短的开场白,这就是定义条款的引言。虽然我们在此给出以下若干定义条款的引言句式,但我们还得把"丑话"说在前面:在合同的实际制作中这些定义条款的引言其实没有多少实质意义,只是人云亦云的套话罢了。没有这类引言句子,直接在Definition条款的标题下对有需要的术语进行界定,是更简洁明了的文风。但既然有那么一些受过老式法律写作训练的律师热衷于这套法律"八股",而且在至今依然流行的不少标准合同中常可读到这类套话,我们不妨对其简介如下。如合同作者不怕麻烦,或者希望其制备的合同风格古雅、结构完整、上下文更有呼应,可以酌选以下其中一款:

Introduction to Definition Clause	定义条款的引言
In this Agreement unless the context otherwise requires, the following words or expressions have the meanings assigned to them hereunder:	除本协议上下文另有说明外,下列词语具有如下规定之意义:
The following words and terms used in this AGREEMENT have, unless otherwise specified herein, the following meaning:	除上下文另有明确规定外,在本协议中所用的以下词或术语的意思是:

续表

Introduction to Definition Clause	定义条款的引言
Unless the context requires otherwise, the words and/or expressions have the following meanings:	除上下文另有说明外,以下词语的意思是:
The following words and expressions have the meaning stated in this AGREEMENT, save where the context otherwise requires:	除上下文另有要求外,以下词语在本协议中意思是:
Unless the context requires otherwise, the words appearing in this AGREEMENT in full capitals mean the following:	除上下文另有说明外,本协议中出现的大写字意思是:
In this Agreement the following capitalized terms have the following meaning unless the context clearly requires otherwise:	除上下文另有说明外,本协议中以大写字形式出现的术语意思为:
The definitions set forth in Article 1 of this Contract are equally applicable to the Appendix and have the same meanings ascribed to them in this Contract unless otherwise defined in the Appendix.	本合同第一条中界定的词语定义同样适用于附件;本合同中赋予这些词语的意思,与附件中这些词的含义相同——附件中另有界定者除外;

以上第七条即最后一条定义引言条款是有实质意义的:补充说明合同这一条款中界定的内容也适用于合同的附件,这样可以确保整个合同用词高度统一,避免因附件中的用词而节外生枝地产生争议。

关于定义引言条款的句型:在以上七条定义引言条款中,有一个奇特的、可以构成定义引言条款独特句型的标志性短语,即 unless/ except... otherwise。例如:Unless the context requires otherwise,或 except where the context requires otherwise——这两个短语带出的意思非常明白:如果有关条款对以下定义的词语没有做出其他的特别说明,那这个词才按所定义的意思解释。

有关让步状语的讨论:以上这两个短语实质上是法律写作中常用的、构成让步状语的主要用词。究竟如何看待这类状语从句?有人将之列为以否定形式出现的条件状语从句,有人认为是十种状语从句(时间、地点、原因、结果、目的、方式、比较、程度、让步、条件)以外的第十一种状语从句,即例外状语从句。(李克兴,2011)

其实这两种说法都有道理。将之列为条件状语,那这个条件是以否定形式出现的,如上文的"In this Agreement the following terms have the following meaning unless the context clearly requires otherwise",可以转化为:"In this Agreement the following terms have the following meaning if the context does not clearly requires otherwise"。

如果将这类状语归为单独的一类,即例外状语从句,非常有助于读者或文本使用者对法律语篇做必要的语法和语用分析,因为这类例外状语主要出现在法律文本中,其引导词都与"除非、除外"概念有关,即 unless... otherwise, except(例如:Except as otherwise specifically provided herein),以及古旧词 save(例如:save where the context otherwise requires);有了这个分类,法律文本中这一特殊句型便会有一个名正言顺的"归宿"。其他完整的例句及译文如下：

例 1. In this Ordinance, <u>unless the context otherwise requires</u>, "state" means a territory or group of territories having its own law of nationality. 在本条例中，<u>除文意另有所指外</u>，"国家"指拥有本身国籍法的领域或一组领域。①

"Unless the context otherwise requires"这一句型在条例的释义部分最为常见。在汉语的译文中几乎一律译成"除……另有……外"。根据这一类条例的上下文，OTHERWISE 意思是"不同地"，用来修饰 unless 从句中的动词"requires"。但在被动语态中，OTHERWISE 通常置放在主语与动词之间或置放在被动句的助动词"be"与分词形式的动词之间。汉语中的译法与主动语态相同。以下是若干相关例句：

例 2. <u>Unless in any enactment it is otherwise provided</u>, the period of imprisonment, which may be imposed by a magistrate exercising summary jurisdiction, in respect of the non-payment of any sum of money adjudged to be paid by a conviction, whether it be a fine or in respect of the property the subject of the offence, or in respect of the injury done by the offender, or in respect of the default of a sufficient distress to satisfy any such sum, shall be such period as, in the opinion of the magistrate, will satisfy the justice of the case, but shall not exceed in any case the maximum fixed by the following scale...

<u>除成文法另有规定外</u>，对于因不缴付根据定罪裁定须缴付的款项（不论是罚款或就作为罪行主体的财物而须缴付的款项），或因犯罪者所造成的损害，或因无足够扣押物以抵偿此等款项，则行使简易程式审判权的裁判官，可判处其认为就案情而言是符合公正原则的监禁刑期，但无论如何不得超过下表所定的最长刑期……②

例 3. A notice under subjection (1) shall, <u>unless it otherwise provides</u>, apply to the income from any property specified therein as it applies to the property itself. (Laws of Hong Kong, Cap. 201, Prevention of Bribery Ordinance, Art. 14A [1AA])

根据第(1)款发出的通知书，<u>除其中另有规定外</u>，亦适用于通知书内指明的财产的收入，一如适用于该项财产本身。

例 4. <u>Except as provided</u> in subsections (3) and (4) of this section, "negotiable instrument" means an unconditional promise or order to pay a fixed amount of...③

例 5. <u>Except where the context otherwise requires</u>, the headings of this Chapter apply only to: (a) Separate chemically defined organic compounds, whether or not...④

从以上这些随意选出（从互联网搜索中最先出现的）的例子中可以看出，该例外状语从句主要跟法律文本（法律条文和合同条款）规定中例外状况有密切关系。在法律或合同的实际执行中，发生这种例外状况的概率是极低的。

---

① Laws of Hong Kong, Cap. 30, Wills Ordinance, Art. 2.
② 香港法律第 227 章第 68 条《裁判官條例》www.legislation.gov.hk/.
③ www.lrc.ky.gov/krs/355-03/104.pdf
④ www.customs.gov.ng/Tariff/chapters/Chapter_29.pdf

三、定义条款中的常用动词和句式

给词语下定义最常用的四个动词分别是 mean, refer to, include 以及 have。

被定义的内容一般都使用黑体字或大写词,但也有加引号的。一般不用画线词,例如 Product means the products listed in...。提倡使用的是将被定义词大写(便于辨识)。复杂一点的定义还可以分为若干段,形式如下:

1. Person means

   (1) a natural person and any corporation or other entity which is given, or is recognized as having, legal personality by the law of any country or territory; or

   (2) any unincorporated association or unincorporated body of persons, whether formed in the United Kingdom or elsewhere, concluding a partnership, joint venture or consortium.

2. Expenses include costs, charges and expenses[1] of every description.

在一般情况下,被定义之名词以单数形式出现,故建议使用单数名词。本节基本上穷尽了定义条款引言的各种表达方式。但网上或教科书上出现的这类定义句子,语用上并非一定正确,如 XXXXX shall have the following meanings。又如:Unless the context otherwise requires in this AGREEMENT, the masculine gender shall include the female gender and vice versa and any gender shall include the other genders.

以上两个定义句中的三个 shall 均属滥用。在法律文件中情态动词 shall 与第三人称连用表示一种强制性的法律义务或责任,而在该类语境中,并不涉及法律义务或责任,只不过对某些词汇进行定义而已,故任何情态动词的使用都是滥用和误用。读者需谨慎对待。有关 shall 这个情态动词在法律文本中的使用规律,第五章已有适当论述。

四、合同文本中常被定义的词语及其定义表述

这一部分的内容非常多,因为各类合同都涉及性别、单复数、自然人、法人、法律、税项、工作、关联公司、大小标题、附表/附录与主合同中使用的词语的一致性等一系列的子条款的定义问题。由于绝大部分合同需要定义的内容都不外乎这些,所以这些常被定义的内容,说得好听一点,似乎已约定俗成,成为国际合同惯例的一部分;说得难听一点:是人云亦云、没有多大实质意义的套话,即使全部去之,也不会产生争议。当然这是对律师或合同草拟人员而言;作为译员,他没有选择的余地,只能照本翻译。虽然大部分合同将上述词语归为一类,严格说来,或者按逻辑区分,这类词可以分为两类,一类是真正意义上的被定义或界定的词,另一类则属于被"解释"的常用表达方式。前者可称为"定义"(definition),后者列为"解释"(interpretation)。前者一般是将被定义词放在引号内或将其大写,然后用动词"means"加以界定;后者则无需对有关词语加引号,在解释条款内直接予以解释即可。详见下表:

续表

Common Definition Clauses	常见定义条款	用途说明
"Person" means (1) a natural person and any corporation or other entity which is given, or is recognized as having, legal personality by the law of any country or territory; or (2) any unincorporated association or unincorporated body of persons, whether formed in the United Kingdom or elsewhere, concluding a partnership, joint venture or consortium.	本合同所称"人"为： (1) 自然人、法人公司、或依照任何国家或地区之法律，享有法人资格之实体；或 (2) 在英国或其他地区所组成之非法人组织或非法人团体，包括合伙组织、合资企业或财团。	定义"人"
"He" includes "he" and "she".	本合同所称"他"，包括"他"与"她"。	定义性别
"His" includes "his" and "her".	本合同所称"他的"，包括"他的"与"她的"。	定义所有格的性别
"Him" includes "him" and "her".	本合同所称"他(宾格)"，包括"他(宾格)"与"她(宾格)"。	定义宾格的性别
"Business Day" means a day on which banks and stock exchange houses are open for business in the People's Republic of China, excluding all public holidays.	"营业日"指中华人民共和国的银行及股票交易所营业之日，所有公共假日除外。	定义营业/交易日
"Address" means: 　　in relation to an individual, his usual residential or business address; and 　　in relation to a corporation, its registered or principal office in the People's Republic of China.	"地址"指： 就自然人而言，通常指居所或工作场所。 就公司而言指位于中华人民共和国境内之注册所在地或主营业场所。	定义地址
"Expenses" include costs, charges and expenses of every description.	"费用"包括各种形式的金钱支出。	定义费用
"Property" means property, assets, interests and rights of every description, wherever situated.	"财产"包括不论何地的各种财产、资产及其各种利益或权利。	定义财产
"Work" means all work to be carried out including but not limited to delivery of the Equipment, services of installation, testing and commissioning of the Equipment.	"工作"指进行的所有工作，包括但不限于"设备"的交付，安装、测试及试运行服务。	定义与设备交付使用有关的"工作"

续表

Common Definition Clauses	常见定义条款	用途说明
1. "Intellectual Property Rights" means any and all tangible and intangible: (i) rights associated with works of authorship, including copyrights, moral rights, neighboring rights[4], and derivative works thereof, (ii) trademark and trade name rights, (iii) trade secret rights, (iv) patents, design rights, and other industrial property rights, and, (v) all other intellectual property rights (of every kind and nature however designated) whether arising by operation of law, treaty, contract, license, or otherwise, together with all registrations, initial applications, renewals, extensions, continuations, divisions or reissues thereof.	1."知识产权"指所有有形或无形的权利:(1)与拥有著作权的作品有关的权利,包括版权、精神权利、邻接权以及由此衍生出来的作品权。(2)商标权以及贸易名权,(3)商业秘密权,(4)专利权、设计权和其他工业产权,以及(5)所有其他(无论定为何种性质)知识产权——不管是通过执行法律、条约、合同、许可证或其他方式(包括所有该类文书的注册、始初申请、续期、延期、延续、分拆或重新发行)而产生的。	定义知识产权(定义1为普通意思上的知识产权;定义2对知识产权进行较全面的定义)
2. "Intellectual Property Rights" means any and all tangible and intangible: (i) copyrights and other rights associated with works of authorship throughout the world, including but not limited to copyrights, neighboring rights, moral rights, and mask works[5], and all derivative works thereof; (ii) trademarks and trade name rights and similar rights; (iii) trade secret rights; (iv) patents, designs, algorithms, utility models, and industrial property rights, all improvements thereto; (v) all other intellectual and industrial property rights (of every kind and nature throughout the world and however designated) whether arising by operation of law, contracts, license, or otherwise; and (vi) all registration, applications, renewals, extensions, continuations, divisions, or reissues thereof now or thereafter in force (including any rights in any of the foregoing).	2."知识产权"指所有有形或无形的权利,即(1)与在世界各地的有著作权的作品有关的版权及其他权利,包括但不限于版权、邻接权、精神权利及掩膜作品以及所有由以上述权利衍生而来的权利;(2)商标权以及贸易名权及类似的权利;(3)商业秘密权;(4)专利权、设计权、算法权、实用品模型权及工业产权,及其改进品的权利;(5)所有其他知识及工业产权(包括在世界各地的任何类型和性质的产权——不管以何种形式指定的权利)无论是通过法律、合同、证书或其他方式的运作而产生的;(6)以及所有注册权、应用权、更新权、扩充权、持续权、分割权,或在目前或今后重新签发权(包括对前述任何一项的任何权利)。	

续表

Common Definition Clauses	常见定义条款	用途说明
1. "Affiliate" or "Affiliated Company"[4] means a company which, directly or indirectly through one or more intermediaries, <u>controls or is controlled by</u>[2], or is under common control with a Party or a subcontractor of a Party. For this purpose control means the direct or indirect ownership of in aggregate fifty percent or more of voting capital. （王相国,2008:29） 2. "Affiliate" means any person or company that directly or indirectly controls a Party or is directly or indirectly controlled by a Party, including a Party's parent or subsidiary, or is under direct or indirect common control with such Party. <u>For the purpose of the Agreement</u>[3], "control" shall mean either the ownership of fifty per cent（50%）or more of the ordinary share capital of the company carrying the right to vote at general meetings or the power to nominate a majority of the board of directors of the Company. （孙万彪,2002:62）	1. "关联公司"指直接或通过一个或多个中间体间接控制一方或其承包商的公司；或直接或通过一个或多个中间体间接受该"一方"或其承包商控制的公司；或与一方或其承包商一起共同直接或通过一个或多个中间体间接受别的公司控制的公司。本款中的控制指直接或间接拥有总计百分之五十或以上的具有表决权的资本。 2. "关联公司"指直接或间接控制一方（包括其母公司或子公司）或受一方直接或间接控制的任何人或公司，或与该方共同直接或间接受别的公司控制。在本协议中，"控制"系指拥有在股东大会上有投票权的百分之五十（50%）或以上的公司普通股股本或拥有任命公司董事会中多数董事的权利。	定义关联公司
Unless the context otherwise requires in this AGREEMENT, the masculine gender shall include the female gender and vice versa and any gender shall include the other genders.	除本协议上下文另有说明，男性性别的词应包括女性，反之亦然，任何性别的词应包括其他的性别的词。	定义性别
Unless the context otherwise requires: a word singular and plural in number shall be deemed to include the other.	除上下文另有说明：单复数词均应视为包括单数和复数。	定义单复数
Words importing the singular only shall also include the plural and vice versa where the context so requires.	仅使用单数的词，只要上下文需要，也应包括复数或反之。	定义单复数
Unless the context otherwise requires in this AGREEMENT the singular includes the plural and vice versa.	除非本协议上下文另有说明，单数形式的词包括复数，反之亦然。	定义单复数

续表

Common Definition Clauses	常见定义条款	用途说明
Unless the context otherwise requires, singular nouns and pronouns when used herein shall be deemed to include the plural and vice versa and impersonal pronouns shall be deemed to include the personal pronoun of the appropriate gender.	除上下文另有说明,本合同中使用的表示单数形式的名词或代词应视为包括复数,反之亦然;非人称代词应视为包括适当性别的人称代词。	定义单复数以及人称代词
The words "include" and "including" and words of similar import are not limiting, and shall be construed to be followed by the words "without limitation," whether or not they are in fact followed by such words.	"include","including"(包括)以及类似意思的词并不是限制,应与"without limitation"(不限于)连在一起解读,而不管该词实际是否跟着"without limitation"。	定义"包括"(include)
Unless otherwise specified, the words "hereof," "herein" and "hereunder" and words of similar import refer to this Agreement as a whole and not to any particular provision of this Agreement.	除上下文另有说明,"hereof","herein"和"hereunder"以及类似意思的词指的是本合同的全部,而不是指本合同的某一特定条款。	定义以"here"为词根的古旧词
Unless the context otherwise requires words denoting the singular shall include the plural and vice versa and words denoting any one gender shall include all genders and words denoting persons shall include bodies corporate, unincorporated associations and partnerships.	除上下文另有说明,表示单数形式的词应包括复数,反之亦然;表示一种性别的词应包括所有性别;表示人的词应包括法人、非法人团体以及合伙组织。	定义单复数、性别以及人与公司
Clauses headings and the recitals are inserted for convenience only and shall not be taken into account in construing the provisions of this Agreement. (范文祥、吴怡,2008:31)	条款的标题以及序言仅为方便而加,不得作为本协议之条款内容解释。	定义标题和序言
No heading, index, title, sub-title, or sub-heading of this Agreement shall limit, alter or affect the meaning or operation of this Agreement.	本协议所有标题、索引、题目、副标题、小标题都不应限制、改变或影响本协议的含义和执行。	定义标题、副标题等
The parts, Schedules, Appendices and any other documents referred to in this Agreement shall be <u>taken, read and construed</u>[6] as an essential and integral part of this Agreement. In the event of any inconsistency between the terms of the main body of this Agreement and the Schedules or Appendices to this Agreement the terms of the main body of this Agreement shall prevail (shall take precedence).	本协议中提到的部分、附表、附件以及其他文件均应被视作、解读或解释为本协议之不可或缺的一部分。 万一本协议的主体部分与附表或附件部分的词语有任何不一致之处,以本协议之主体部分的词语为准。	定义附表、附件等

续表

Common Definition Clauses	常见定义条款	用途说明
Technical Meanings. Words not otherwise defined herein that have well known and generally accepted technical meanings are used herein in accordance with such recognized meanings. Unless otherwise agreed to by the Parties, all units of measurement shall be stated in the metric unit (SI) system. (王相国,2008:82)	技术含义。本协议中具有科技或贸易含义的词汇,若非另行界定其含义,均按其为大众认可的通常意义使用。除各方另行协商同意之外,本协议中所有的度量衡单位均使用公制单位。	定义科技词汇(包括度量衡单位)
Headings, Section References. Section headings are for convenience of reference only, do not form part of this Agreement, and shall not be deemed to limit or otherwise affect any of the provisions hereof. References to Articles, Sections, Subsections, Paragraphs, the Preamble or the Recitals, <u>Schedules, Exhibits and Appendices</u>[7], unless otherwise indicated, are references to Articles, Sections, Subsections, Paragraphs, the Preamble or the Recitals, Schedules, Exhibits and Appendices of this Agreement. (王相国,2008:82)	标题,章节引用。本协议中的章节标题仅为引用方便而设,并不构成本协议之一部分,也不应视为是对本协议之规定的限制或对其另有影响。除非另有明示,本协议中所引用之条、节、小节、款、序文或引言、附表、证明及附件,均指本协议本身之条、节、小节、款、序文或引言、附表、证明及附件。	定义标题和章节等
Interpretation. Unless the context otherwise requires: words singular and plural in number shall be deemed to include the other, all references to Applicable Law or to a particular Applicable Law <u>includes a reference</u>[8] to any measures amending, supplementing or repealing any relevant Applicable Law <u>from time to time</u>[9]; all references to any contract or agreement <u>means</u> such contract or agreement and all schedules, appendices, exhibits and attachments <u>thereto</u> as amended, supplemented or otherwise modified <u>and in effect from time to time</u>, and shall include <u>a reference</u> to any document which amends, supplements or replaces it, or <u>is entered into</u>, <u>made or given</u> pursuant to or in accordance with its terms[10]. (王相国,2008:81)	释义。除上下文另有规定外: 单数及复数的单词应视为互相包括; 凡对适用法律或某部特定适用法律之引用应包括对任何相关适用法律不时进行修订、补充或废止的所有措施之引用; 凡对任何合同或协议之引用,皆指对该合同或协议以及其所有有效的不时做出过修订、补充或以其他方式修改的附表、附件、证明及附录之引用;还包括对该合同或协议进行修订、补充或替代,或根据该合同或协议条款而签署的任何文件之引用。	定义单复数、适用法律、合同、合同附表等

续表

Common Definition Clauses	常见定义条款	用途说明
"Force Majeure Events" means any unforeseeable and exceptional events or circumstances affecting the implementation of this Agreement by one or more Parties, which are beyond their control and cannot be overcome despite their reasonable endeavour.	"不可抗力事件"指会影响一方或多于一方执行本协议的任何不可预料或意外的事件或情况,即该有关方做出了合理的努力但仍然无法控制或不能克服的事件或情况。	定义不可以抗力事件

五、对定义文本中的要点和疑难的阐释

以上被定义的内容选自市面上流行的若干本有关合同写作的专著以及有关网站。对其中的语言难点和误区,以作注的方式做如下阐释:

1. & 6. 三联词的翻译:costs,charges and expenses,读了几十年英文,仍然无法区分这三者之间的不同。其实这三个词就是法律英文中常见的、上文述及过的三联词(legal triplet)。法律写手、尤其是大牌律师,会顺手掂来这类词,全部塞进条文。就翻译而言,其处理方法与我们上文讨论的一致:如果能够区别其不同之处的,如果有关近义词的确是反映原作者"良苦用心"的(而不是仅仅为了所谓古雅风格的),区别对待;否则,合三为一。所以,我们将以上三词当作"各种金钱支出"解释,用一个统称名词"费用"来翻译。这一原则也同样适用于注 6:... shall be taken, read and construed as an essential and integral part of this Agreement (……应被视作本协议之不可或缺的一部分。)虽然 be taken, read and construed 可以分别译为"视作、解读或解释",但"视作"的前提是"解读"或"解释";而后者 essential and integral 也属同类性质的配对词(legal pair),可以"或缺"的肯定不是重要的,"不可或缺"的肯定是重要的。

2. 复杂句的理解:语法分析与逻辑推理。以上是两个对"关联公司"的主流定义,从英文文本的表述中可以看出,律师对"关联公司"的定义没有太多的分歧。主要涉及两个基本概念:(1)该公司直接或间接控制别的公司,或直接或间接受别的公司控制,或者该公司与合同中的另一方共同直接或间接受别的公司控制;(2)所谓的控制,必须掌握公司的控制权,该控制权指占有公司股本 50%或以上的股份,在股东会上有 50%以上的选举权,或者掌控公司的董事会。

但是,外国律师的生花妙笔一复杂,我们国内的律师就很难理解条款的确切意思。例如,在"Affiliate" means a company which, directly or indirectly through one or more intermediaries, controls or is controlled by, or is under common control with a Party or a subcontractor of a Party. For this purpose control means the direct or indirect ownership of in aggregate fifty percent or more of voting capital. (范文祥,2007:29)中,译者就被唬弄住了。看一下译文吧:

"关联公司"指与"一方"存在下列关系之一的一家公司:1)该公司直接或通过一个或多个中间体间接控制着该"一方";2)该"一方"直接或通过一个或多个中间体间接控

制着该公司;或该公司与该"一方"直接或通过一个或多个中间体间接受到共同的控制;4)"一方"的分包商。本款中的控制指直接或间接拥有总计百分之五十或以上的具有表决权的资本。

首先,这不是严格意义上的翻译,这叫"诠释"(paraphrase)。用这种方式处理法律文书是不允许的,原作者即律师行根本不允许译者对原文文本的形式做如此之大的改动(如增添编号、随意调动句子顺序和增删内容。

译文的第二句(For this purpose...)勉强可以接受。第一句译文的行文啰嗦,是在解释原文;且还存在一个致命的错误,错在对"'Affiliate' means... with a Party or a subcontractor of a Party"的理解上。译者将该短语翻译成:"'关联公司'指……'一方'的分包商"。这等于说"关联公司"就是"一方"的分包商。这在法理和逻辑都是错误的:分包商的本义指它只分包某承包商的部分业务。但分包商为了生存,往往不得不分包或承包多家、甚至八家、十家的业务,因此分包商不可能家家都是直接的"关联公司",况且,"关联公司就是'一方'的分包商"的表述使关联公司与下文的核心词"控制50%以上的表决权"脱离了关系。如果"关联公司"就是"分包商",那么下文对"控股"的界定就没有意义。出现上述翻译失误,主要是译者对原文未作深入的语法分析和严密的逻辑推理,属于对复杂句理解的常见错误。该段正确的译文应该是这样的:

"Affiliate" means a company which, directly or indirectly through one or more intermediaries, controls or is controlled by, or is under common control with a Party or a subcontractor of a Party. For this purpose control means the direct or indirect ownership of in aggregate fifty percent or more of voting capital.

"关联公司"指直接或通过一个或多个中间体间接控制的一方或其承包商的公司;或直接或通过一个或多个中间体间接受该"一方"或其承包商控制的公司;或直接或通过一个或多个中间体间接受一方或其承包商共同控制的公司。本款中的控制指直接或间接拥有总计百分之五十或以上的具有表决权的资本。(笔者改译)

3. 一个特殊法律句型的翻译:FOR THE PURPOSE(S) OF...

这是法律英文中又一个常用句式。其中的"purpose"可以是复数,也可以是单数。习惯普通英语的人士通常都会认为翻译含有这个短语的句子可以不费任何心思:"为了……目的"便是其对应的译文。而且在国内的中译英法律文献中的确不乏这样的译法。例如:

《中华人民共和国刑法》第二百二十四条:有下列情形之一,以非法占有为目的,在签订、履行合同过程中,骗取对方当事人财物,数额较大的,处三年以下有期徒刑或者拘役,并处或者单处罚金……

Whoever, for the purpose of illegal possession, uses one of the following means during signing or executing a contract to obtain property and goods of the opposite party by fraud, and when the amount of money is relatively large, is to be sentenced to not more than three years of fixed-term imprisonment, criminal detention, and may in addition or exclusively be sentenced to a fine...

在大多数情形下,"目的"一词并非一定要在汉语法律文本中出现。例如:

为保护计算机软件著作权人的利益,调整计算机软件在开发、传播和使用中发生的利益关系,鼓励计算器软件的开发与流通,促进计算器应用事业的发展,依照《中华人民共和国著作权法》的规定,制定本条例。

These Regulations are formulated in accordance with the provisions of the Copyright Law of the People's Republic of China <u>for the purpose of</u> protecting the rights and interests of copyright owner of computer software, of adjusting the interests arising from the development, dissemination and use of computer software, of encouraging the development and circulation of computer software, and of promoting the development of computer application. (*Regulations for the Protection of Computer Software*, Art. 1)

但是,值得注意的是,以上的"for the purpose of"这两种用法都只是典型的中国国内法律译本中的译法。在原文为英文的法律文本中,以表达"为……目的"这层意思而使用"for the purpose of"的句子并不多见,而需要译成"为……目的"的译例则更为罕见。

在法律英文写作中,专家建议用简洁的"for"替代啰嗦的"for the purpose of..."的表达方式,并相信有关法律句子的意义不会有任何改变。(Rylance,1994:82)倘若需要更明确地表达"为了……(目的)"的概念,不定式短语"in order to..."则是更好的、不容易产生歧义的选择。例如:

为了保护发明创造专利权,鼓励发明创造,有利于发明创造的推广应用,促进科学技术的发展,……特制定本法。(Patent Law of the People's Republic of China,Art. 1)

This Law is formulated <u>in order to</u> protect patent rights for invention-creations, encourage invention-creations and facilitate their popularization and application, promote the development of science and technology...

笔者之所以赞同在法律文件中用"for"或"in order to"去表达一个带有真正"目的"的概念、而反对使用"for the purpose of",主要原因是该短语在英文法律文本中的主流用法早已"变味",而且这种"变味"的用法几乎已到了约定俗成、不可逆转的程度。当然其译法更有些匪夷所思。试看若干例句:

(1) <u>For the purpose of</u> these presents any act default or omission of the agents servants workmen or licensees of the Tenant shall be deemed to be the act default or omission of the Tenant.(薛华业,1989:85)

基于这些通知,租户的代理人、佣人、工人或所许可者的任何行为、违约或疏忽,应被认为是租户的行为、违约或疏忽。

(2) <u>For the purpose of</u> the Landlord and the Tenant Ordinance and <u>for the purpose of</u> these presents the rent in respect of the said premises shall be deemed to be in arrear if not paid in advance as stipulated by Clause 1 hereof.(薛华业,1989:85)

基于租务条例并基于这些通知,有关该楼宇的租金,如果未照合约第一条规定的那样提前缴付,就应该被认为是拖欠。

当"purpose"以复数形式,即当"for the purposes of..."出现在法律篇章中、并且与某个具体的法律文本的编号搭配在一起时,该短语的"目的性"更是丧失殆尽。例如:

(3) <u>For the purposes of subsection (1)</u> of this section the attestation of a will by a

person to whom or to whose spouse there is given or made any such disposition as is described in that subsection shall be disregarded if the will is duly executed without his attestation and without that of any other such person. (Laws of Hong Kong, Cap. 30, Wills Ordinance, Art. 10[3])

为第(1)款的施行,获得该款所述的处置的任何人或其配偶,如为遗嘱作见证,而该遗嘱没有其见证或任何这些人的见证亦已属妥为签立,则该人所作的见证须不予理会。

(4) For the purposes of subsection (2), "land" does not include incorporeal hereditament; (Laws of Hong Kong, Chapter 210: THEFT ORDINANCE)

就第(2)款而言——"土地"(land)并不包括无体可继承财产;

(5) For the purposes of subsection (3) permission shall be in writing and—(Laws of Hong Kong, Cap. 201, Prevention of Bribery Ordinance, Art. 4[4])

就第(3)款而言,许可须为书面形式,并且——

以上是"for the purpose(s) of"的主流用法。从上述这一系列有关该短语的用法和译法例句中可以看出,该短语在法律文件中的翻译并非如习惯普通英文句型人士所想象的那么简单。其最恰当的译法是"就……而言"(在以上例(1)、(2)句子中最好译为"就……而言")。

所以,当译员在翻译法律文本、碰到"for the purpose(s) of..."这个句式时,不应急于下笔,而应该首先读完有关段落,准确理解该短语的功用。在大部分情况下,普通辞典里"为……目的"这一解释并不一定适合法律英语中的"for the purpose(s) of..."。正如上文所示:如果紧跟这个短语的是指代某个法律条款的编号(如章、条、款、节或者某个法律文件),首选的译文是"就(有关)章、条、款、节或合同而言",或者干脆作较大的变通,译为"在某有关章节或合同中"。倘若原英文中的"for the purpose(s) of..."与"章、条、款、节等"无关,而该短语又可以用"for"或"in order to"去取代(这种用法在法律英文中属于少数),则可译成"为了"。

所以,在绝大部分情况下法律英文中"for the purpose(s) of..."未必有真正的"目的性"。但有一点是绝对例外的,即当该"purpose"前面有一个修饰它的形容词时,如"for commercial purposes"。此时"purposes"的"目的性"就非常明确,在处理译文时,必须译成"为商业目的"。就本文而言(For the purpose of the Agreement, "control" shall mean either the ownership of fifty per cent (50%) or more of the ordinary share capital of the company...),将画线部分译为"就本协议而言",或者直截了当地译为"在本协议中,'控制'系指拥有在股东大会上有投票权的百分之五十(50%)或以上的公司普通股股本",都未尝不可。

4. & 5. 法律专有概念:copyrights, neighboring rights, moral rights, and mask works.

说到知识产权,大众比较熟悉的就是著作权或版权。但到纽约曼哈顿派克大道的律师楼里,这个概念就变得非常复杂。如果朋友给你一个橙子,普通人会说:"*Here, have an orange.*"但如果一名律师要给另一名律师朋友一个苹果,措辞可能会是这样的:"*I hereby give you all and singular, my estate and interests, right, title, claim, and advantages of and in said orange, together with all of its rind, juice, pulp, pits and all rights and advantages with full power to bite, cut, and otherwise eat the same or give the same away with and without the rind, skin, juice, pulp, or pits, anything herein before or herein after or in any other deed or deeds, instruments of whatever nature or kind whatsoever to the contrary.*" Then a couple of smart Park Avenue lawyers come along and take it away from you. (吴红云,1999:62—63)有了这样完整的书面赠予保证,那个受赠的律师朋友才会无后顾之忧,考虑接受赠品。

虽然这是夸大其辞,但其所包含的信息是不言而喻的:专职律师会把普通人意想不到的各种可能性都考虑进去。就知识产权而言,除了版权之外,还有普通人很少会想得到的许多权利概念,如neighboring rights,moral rights,以及mask works等等。究竟这三者为何物?

neighboring rights(邻接权),也叫"相关权利"(Related rights),它依附于著作权人,没有著作权,邻接权就失去其基础。主要包括图书、报刊出版者的权利,艺术表演者的权利,录音、录像制作人的权利,广播电台、电视台的权利等。

moral rights(道德权)也是由版权/著作权衍生而来,包括发表作品的署名权、匿名权、使用假名权以及保护作品完整性的权利(即不被任意改编的权利)等等。

mask works(掩膜作品),在美国指集成电路布图设计作品,"掩膜作品"的译文是根据美国对该词的定义翻译而成的;在日本,同一概念称作"电路布图"(Circuit Layout),瑞典称为"布图设计"(Layout Design),欧盟许多国家称为拓扑图(Topography)。http://www.netlawcn.com/second/content.asp?no=492

7. schedules,exhibits and appendices 的异同:这几个词均为"附件"的同义或近义词,属于同一概念的还有 rider,addendum,attachment 等等。几乎每个合同都有这类附件。究竟这些词在合同中指的是什么、有何差异、写作中如何恰当地使用?三言两语根本说不清楚。所以,本书专辟一章阐述这类词语的用法和异同,详见最后第二章。

8. 9. & 10. 文本风格和语法问题:在以上有关定义和解释条款的众多引文中,本段的文风,不客气地说,是最恶劣的,其中的谬误也是最多的。将该段的内容再拿出来讨论,有助于读者锻炼自己鉴别法律文本优劣的能力。在当今社会,参考书汗牛充栋,但文本(例句)质量良莠不齐,甚至完全会误人子弟。所以法律文本的作者、译者具备鉴别文本优劣的能力非常重要。试看以下例句:

Interpretation.
Unless the context otherwise requires:
a. words singular and plural in number shall be deemed to include the other;
b. all references to Applicable Law or to a particular Applicable Law includes a reference to any measures amending, supplementing or repealing any relevant Applicable Law from time to time;
c. all references to any contract or agreement means such contract or agreement and all schedules, appendices, exhibits and attachments thereto as amended, supplemented or otherwise modified and in effect from time to time, and shall include a reference to any document which amends, supplements or replaces it, or is entered into, made or given pursuant to or in accordance with its terms;

解释。除依上下文可另作其他理解之外,
a. 单数及复数的单词应被视为彼此互相包含;
b. 所有对于适用法律或某部特定适用法律之引用应包括对任何相关适用法律进行修订,补充或废止的所有措施之引用;
c. 所有对于任何合同或协议之引用都涉指该合同或协议以及其所有表格,附录,证明及附件之本身及所有有效的修订,补充,或以其他方式进行的修改,并应包括任何对于该合同或协议进行修订,补充或替代的文件,或者根据该合同或协议条款之规定而订立,制作或者提供的任何文件之引用;(王相国,2008:79－81)

就以上定义条文而言,无论该段原文是出于中国律师之手还是照搬国外合同相关条文,笔者都为专著中出现这样初级的语法谬误而感到羞愧。在以上摘录的三个句子中,前两个都是中学生一眼就可以看出来的语法错误:(2) all references... <u>includes</u>...;(3) all <u>references... means</u>...;(3) all <u>references... and in effect from time to time, and shall include</u>...。这第三个错误是用了"shall":既然 all references mean,为什么在第二个动词 include 前面非要加一个情态动词 shall? shall 与第三人称主语一起使用表达一种法律义务,而此处仅仅是对词的定义,references 作为非有灵主语根本无法去承担任何法律义务,可见"shall"在此被滥用。

也许读者会问,为什么前述(1)款中所用的 shall (words singular and plural in number <u>shall be deemed</u> to include the other)就不属于这一类滥用或错误呢? 道理很简单:shall be deemed("应被认为")的真实主语是该合同的当事人,只有对有行为能力的人或有灵主语才可以提出需要其执行的义务;shall 与第三人称的主语一起使用,不管是直接的还是间接的,主动的还是被动的,主要都是对该主语提出义务要求,而对无灵主语(如所定义的词汇)提出义务要求,无异于不分对象,滥用"情态"。

不过,该条款的最大问题是使用了我们在论述合同细节的有关章节批评过的滥用同义词和近义词的问题。以上一段的大部分画线部分的内容,均属这一性质。

使用 is entered into, made or given pursuant to or in accordance with its terms 这样的短语,要么说明专著作者对文风好坏没有任何的鉴别能力,拿来就用;要么自己的文风极差。其中 is entered into, made or given 是较为罕见的被滥用的三联词:即使要模仿,也得有个逻辑:任何文件必须先 is made(制作),然后才可以 is entered into(签署),决不可反其道而行之,而 given 则完全是多余的动词,在相关的合同引言条款用语中极为罕见。pursuant to or in accordance with 更是一个不伦不类的仿古短语:在现代的合同文本使用一个古旧词 pursuant to,就已经是在使用不合时宜的法律行话(legalese),更何况还增加一个同义反复的 in accordance with。就 pursuant to 一词而论,我们看一下一位律师出身的法律文体学家对使用该词以及 legalese 的看法吧:

> I despise the phrase "pursuant to." It's not evil or even really bad, but it is used almost exclusively by lawyers. So it's a phrase that says to the reader, "a lawyer wrote this." And I don't want that message to be a part of my writing. Granted that for most of my writing, the reader knows I'm a lawyer. Still, I dislike displaying the fact that way. When I was practicing law, I worked for a lawyer who on occasion put "pursuant to" into a letter I had written. I did the first draft, and he revised it for his own signature, so he had the right to add "pursuant to." But it bothered me, and I developed a strong negative reaction to the phrase. It's not rational with me, I know. I went so far as to banish it from my vocabulary in about 1991. I haven't used it since. And I criticize it in my books and writing whenever I can. It does carry multiple

meanings:"under"and "according to," will often be more precise.①

语言是最民主的。在这一行里,如果大多数人都还在使用或喜欢使用某个词,那么胳膊拧不过大腿,你没有办法扭转局面。但我们至少要知道,使用普通英文中已经被摒弃的 pursuant to 是不良文风,应尽量避免使用。如果你不但继续使用,而且还变本加厉,加上一个与它意思一模一样的 in accordance with,那真有点不可思议了:不得不让人怀疑使用者有无基本的语言鉴赏能力。

最后,all references... means... attachments <u>thereto</u> as amended, supplemented or otherwise modified <u>and in effect from time to time</u>,也是非常不规范的句子,除了上述的语法错误之外,短语 in effect from time to time 用法也非常不妥,其中的 and 是多余的(但可以用 as),其正确的用法应该是这样的:

> Distributor may, subject to Supplier's trademark and branding policies <u>in effect from time to time</u>, use Supplier's name, and the permitted trademarks set forth in Exhibit A for each Product, only to promote and sell Products, as explicitly provided in this Agreement.②;或者 Supplier expressly warrants each Product as provided in Supplier's standard written warranty with respect thereto, <u>as in effect from time to time</u>. (ditto);或者 By using this web site, you agree to be bound by these terms and conditions <u>as in effect from time to time</u>.③画线部分的短语表示的是"在实施中的最新内容"或"时时更新有效的内容"(如政策、保证、条款等)。

就上述 3 段定义文字的翻译而言:凡是有难度的就被 from time to time(不时)地给省略了。在法律翻译中,原文中所有的反映原作者写作意图的实义词(meaningful word),不是那种属于风格型的配对词或三联词,原则上不能省略,原作者用了 from time to time,想表达的是<u>不时</u>做出修订的、也就是最新的文件(在以上译文中该词一概被省略)。

说到底,该段原文文风极差,正确表述类似概念的条文可参考以下写法:References to any document, instrument or agreement (i) shall be deemed to include all appendices, exhibits, schedules and other attachments thereto and all documents, instruments or agreements issued or executed in replacement thereof, and (ii) mean such document, instrument or agreement, or replacement thereto, as amended, modified and supplemented <u>from time to time in accordance with</u> its terms and as the same is <u>in effect</u> at any given time.④

本节(即第 8.9.&10.节)主题讨论的定义条款的译文可修订如下:

解释。除依上下文可另作其他理解之外,
　a. 单数及复数的单词应视为互相包括;
　b. 凡对适用法律或某部特定适用法律之引用应包括对任何相关适用法律不时进行修订、补充或废止的所有议案之引用;

---

① http://www.utexas.edu/law/faculty/wschiess/legalwriting/2005/04/pursuant-to.html
② http://forum.wordreference.com/showthread.php?t=1101934
③ http://www.intellectspace.com/Terms.aspx
④ http://www.fdic.gov/bank/individual/failed/ServicingBusinessAssetPurchaseAgreement.pdf

c. 凡对任何合同或协议之引用,皆指对该合同或协议以及其所有有效的不时做出过修订、补充或以其他方式修改的附表、附件、证明及附录之引用;还包括对该合同或协议进行修订、补充或替代,或根据该合同或协议条款而签署的任何文件之引用;

六、结语:受推荐的定义与解释条款

就合同通用的定义与解释条款而言,以下写法是最具有代表性和包容性的:

Unless the context otherwise requires in this AGREEMENT, word denoting the singular includes the plural and vice versa, and word denoting any one gender includes all genders, and word denoting person includes a natural person, body corporate, unincorporated association and partnership.

原因很简单:1.任何合同都会涉及名词的单数和复数问题,根据此处定义或解释:复数就是单数,单数就是复数;2.任何合同都会涉及男女两个性别的问题,根据此处的定义或解释:一个性别应包括所有性别(言外之意还包括变性人或双性人);任何合同中表示人的词应包括自然人、法人团体、非法人团体以及合伙组织。

至于给具体的词下定义,尽管有四个常用动词——mean, refer to, include 以及 have,但笔者只建议使用 mean。例如:Property *means* property, assets, interests and rights of every description, wherever situated.

第八章
合同语言与文本条款写作和翻译

一般而言,本书各章大同小异的结构包括:1.引言(定义,有关通用条款的作用和写作原理);2.主要句型结构;3.关键词及词义辨识;4.典型条款及点评;5.改善或推荐条款及原理;6.特殊条款介绍;7.可供借鉴的条款及参考译文;8.参考文献。但本着"有话则长,无话则短"的写作原则,这一章我们要适当简化程序、缩短篇幅。首先,我们开门见山,省去各章应有的序言部分,因为合同的语言和文本条款的内容,无论从法理还是从语言表达上讲,都是通用条款中最简单的一条。

其实,在以英语为母语的法律管辖区,合同的这一部分内容几乎都被省却,因为合同各方通常都认为用英语写合同是天经地义的。只有在国力日益强盛而国家官方语言在国际商务活动中还未获得认可或与其国力相称的地位时,这一条款往往是必要的。直接地说,在用非母语签订的合同中或在中国与外国用英语签订的合同中,几乎都有这么短短的一条。以下是我们时常会在中外合同中见到的有关条款的内容:

一、典型条款及例句

This Contract and all appendices hereto shall be written in Chinese and English in duplicate. Each Party shall hold three (3) original copies of each version. Both versions are equally authentic.

This Agreement shall be written in both English and Chinese. If there is any conflict between the English and Chinese versions, the English version shall prevail.

The parties hereby covenant and agree that this Agreement is executed and delivered in both English and Chinese, and that in the event of any discrepancy between the two versions, the English version shall prevail.

This Agreement may be executed in any number of counterparts and they shall have the same effect as if the signatures on the counterparts were on a single copy of the Agreement. (范文祥、吴怡,2008:232)

This Agreement may be executed in any number of counterparts, each of which will be deemed an original of this Agreement, and which together will constitute one and the same instrument. Neither Party will be bound to this Agreement unless and until both Parties have executed a counterpart. (范文祥、吴怡,2008:232)

This Agreement is executed in English only, and the executed English language Agreement shall prevail in all cases. This Agreement may be executed in one or more counterparts, each of which shall constitute one and the same agreement, and by facsimile or electronic signature.

This Agreement is signed in _____ originals, with each of equally binding force, and the Parties shall each keep _____ originals. This Agreement is made in both Chinese and English. In case of any dispute as to the interpretation, the English version shall prevail.

This contract is made out in duplicate in Chinese and in English language, one Chinese original copy and one English original copy for each Party, both texts being equally authentic. This contract shall come into force from the date it is signed by the authorized representatives of both parties. The annexes as listed in Article 10 shall form an integral part to this Contract. Any amendment and/or supplement to this contract will be valid only after the authorized representatives of both parties have signed written documents, forming integral parts of the Contract.（王相国，2008：93）

All notices, demands, requests, statements or other communications to be made or given by the Borrower hereunder shall be in the English language. Any documents other than financial statements required to be delivered pursuant to this Agreement which are not in the English language must be accompanied by a certified English translation thereof and in the event of any conflict between the original of the document and the English language translation thereof, the English language translation shall for all purposes be deemed to be the correct and controlling version. （王辉，2008：96）

二、关键词解说

"签订合同"——合同语言与文本条款的核心是合同用何种语言拟就及签订，其关键词无疑是"写"和"签"。其实，这两个貌似不同的词在该条款中属于同一概念，至少在英文合同中是这样的，即"签订"。合同用中文撰写，用英文签订，或反之，几乎是不可能的，尽管签名者可能只签中文名或英文名，甚至法文名。所以，尽管在英文中"签订"有很多不同的表达方式，翻译成中文时——虽然也有"拟就""签署""签订"等词语，但实质上都只有一个概念：使合同生效。为此，除了经授权人士在合同上签名外，往往还需盖上公司印章，并把已签名的文本提交给对方。这个过程可能涉及返签，即乙方（合同的起草方）先在若干份合同上签字、盖章后，全部寄给甲方；甲方签字、盖章后，除留下给甲方自己的合同正本外，将约定份数的合同通过挂号邮件寄送或亲自提交给乙方。在以上典型例句中，表达该概念的句式有：

This Contract and all appendices hereto shall be written in Chinese and English;
This Agreement is executed and delivered in both English and Chinese;
This Agreement is executed in English only;
This Agreement may be executed in one or more counterparts;
This Agreement is signed in _____ originals; and
This Agreement is made in both Chinese and English.

上述例句中特别要引起对法律概念比较陌生的读者注意的是 execute 一词，它不但指签署,还指盖印并将文本递交给对方负责人以使合同正式生效。虽然有时合同作者会额外使用一个 be delivered 的词,但其实真正懂英文法律概念的人都知道 be executed 已经包含这层意思,多用一个 be delivered 虽然不怎么画蛇添足(就普通英文而言,似乎还挺有逻辑、自然),但在一般情况下可以推断出作者对法律英文中 execute 这个词的含义缺乏足够的认识。

随着科技进步,签立合同的方式也与时俱进:(1)传统的方式当然是双方代表亲力亲为,举行签字仪式,交换文本,握手言欢;(2)后来是返签、挂号信寄回;(3)再后来是使用传真方式将签名后的合同文本传回给对方,(4)而目前开始流行以电子方式签署合同。但事实上,以上四种签立合同的方法都在使用。重大合同,尤其是国与国之间的合作项目或大额交易,常采用第一种最传统的方式,有时甚至由外访的国家领导人亲自签署。当然,这类合同的签订,除了经济上的实质意义外,更主要是政治上和外交上的象征性意义。以上第四种方法在合同条款中是这样写的:

> This Agreement <u>may be executed</u> in one or more counterparts, each of which shall constitute one and the same agreement, and <u>by facsimile or electronic signature</u>.

由上述例句还可以看出,合同的有效文本可以有多个(in one or more counterparts)。又如:

> This Agreement <u>may be executed in any number of counterparts</u> and they <u>shall have the same effect</u> as if the signatures on the counterparts were on a single copy of the Agreement.

这个例句强调的是合同可以有多个副本,而且各个副本都跟正本同样有效,但条件是这个副本上的签字必须与正本上的签字一致(signatures on the counterparts were on a single copy of the Agreement)。

除了上述签署合同的概念之外,写作这一条款还牵涉的其他概念有:

合同何时生效:come into force from the date...(自……之日起生效);

合同效力:be equally authentic 同等效力 / have equally binding force。同等法律效力——读者所熟悉的 validity 一词倒不在此处使用。

三、条款内容解析

"语言与文本"这部分内容相对其他通用条款而言,形式较为单一,内容相对简单、固定。从第1部分10段例句中可以看出,该条款一般包括如下三个主要方面的内容:

首先,指出该合同或协议(及其附件)以何种语言拟就或订立,一式几份。一般表达方式包括:This Contract/Agreement shall be written/executed and delivered/made out in (language) in (duplicate/...);

例1. This Agreement <u>is executed</u> in English only, and the executed English language Agreement shall prevail in all cases.

例2. This Agreement <u>is made</u> in both Chinese and English.

例3. This Contract and all appendices hereto <u>shall be written</u> in Chinese and English in duplicate.

例4. This Agreement shall be written in both English and Chinese. 或 This Agreement is executed and delivered in both English and Chinese.

例5. This contract is made out in duplicate in Chinese and in English language, one Chinese original copy and one English original copy for each Party, both texts being equally authentic.

除例1之外,以上各条均阐明合同用双语拟就或签订。就条款的语言表述而言,例3、4均在滥用法律英语中的情态动词shall。如果这样的表述出现在相关法律条文中,如民法或合同法,那是可以接受的,因为法律规定合同应当用何种语言拟订;但此处在陈述本合同的一种状态或已经发生的状态:该合同是用何种语言拟订的,所以用一般现在式表达比较妥当。当然,除本合同和附件外,还有其他一些后续文件,如通知、财务报表之类的,该用何种语言制订则可用以下句式来表达:

例6. All notices, demands, requests, statements or other communications to be made or given by the Borrower hereunder shall be in the English language.

例7. Any documents other than financial statements required to be delivered pursuant to this Agreement which are not in the English language must be accompanied by a certified English translation thereof.

毫无疑问,以上表述就语言而言已有些过时。可以更简明地写成:

All communications, including notices, demands, requests, statements, etc. to be made or given by the parties shall be in the English language. 以及 Any documents other than financial statements required to be delivered under this Agreement which are not in the English language must be accompanied by a certified English translation.

其次,为述明文本的效力,一般会在条款中指出两个版本具有同等法律效力,表达方式包括:both versions/each version are/is equally authentic /have the same effect;

例8. Both versions are equally authentic.

例9. This Agreement may be executed in any number of counterparts and they shall have the same effect as if the signatures on the counterparts were on a single copy of the Agreement.

再次,如果要规定在两个或多个文本或版本出现内容不一致或冲突的情形下应以哪个版本为准,标准的表达方式为:If there is any conflict between English and Chinese versions/ in the event of any discrepancy between two versions/ in case of any dispute, the English version shall prevail/ shall be deemed to be the correct and controlling version. 其实,例8的写法貌似公正,两个版本同具法律效力,实际上在发生内容不一致的情形下,该条款是相当令其中一方头痛的,有时甚至是劳民伤财的,因为"公说公有理,婆说婆有理",各执己见是不能解决问题的,最后可能为此而闹到"公堂对簿"。依笔者之见,应该以起草合同时的主要用语为准,这样在发生分歧时就会有据可依,因为翻译必然有词不达意的时候,也不可能保证百分百正确。

例 10.　If there is any conflict between the English and Chinese versions, the English version shall prevail.

例 11.　In the event of any discrepancy between the two versions, the English version shall prevail.

例 13.　In case of any dispute as to the interpretation, the English version shall prevail.

例 14.　In the event of any conflict between the original of the document and the English language translation thereof, the English language translation shall for all purposes be deemed to be the correct and controlling version.

以哪个文本或版本为准条款的表述一般都采用典型的法律条件句句型：条件部分的引导词为 if, in the event that（of）或者 in case（of）。笔者更倾向使用例 10 的句式，但 conflict 和 dispute 在此语境中并非是最合适的，更恰当的应当用 discrepancy（分歧）。两个版本有分歧，才会产生争端（dispute），或引起冲突或矛盾（conflict）。再说，in the event that（of）是个长词，可以用一个短短的 if 解决，没有必要用一个冗长的词组，表达一个极为普通、通常都会发生的概念；况且，后者一般都用来引导发生"大事件"或特别不幸的事件（李克兴，2013）。

所以，表达这个概念更合理的句式应该这样：If there is any discrepancy between the English and Chinese versions, the English version shall prevail. 当然，in case of discrepancy 的表达方式也可以接受，一则可以丰富表达形式，另则也符合条件句引导词 in case that（of）的用法特点：主要表达不常发生的状况；同一合同的不同语言的文本产生分歧，当然是偶发状况（李克兴，2008）。

还值得注意的是，以上表述是在 20 世纪末中国对外改革开放、希望多多益善地吸引外资和使产品打进国际市场的特殊历史时期、带点"委曲求全"的条款用语，因此，即使合同签署地是在中国，也不得不把非母语文本作为具有更高地位的"统治文本"（controlling version）；以后，随着中国国力的逐渐增强，中国产品在国际市场上地位的提高，这一条的说法有所改变，这就是两种版本同时有效的写法：This contract is made out in duplicate in Chinese and in English language, one Chinese original copy and one English original copy for each Party, both texts being equally authentic. 近年，也曾出现 "If there is any discrepancy between the Chinese and English versions, the Chinese version shall prevail" 的写法。对于这类写法，笔者持有异议，详见下文"推荐条款"中的解析。

四、其他附加内容及特殊条款

保险公司、医疗服务业、律师行、投资公司等等，在客户向其购买产品或服务时，根据有关监管条例或法律必须向客户提供翻译服务——至少他们有义务不能让客户对其出售的产品完全地莫名其妙。他们撰写的产品介绍或销售条款其实构成其与客户之间合同的一部分。因此向他们提供翻译服务是避免日后被诉讼的必要的预防措施（"已把丑话说在前"），所以这一部分是某些公司合同中的语言与文本条款的内容之一，只是写法上与上文介绍的普通合同中的语言与文本条款有所不同而已。试看以下保险公司保单中的有关条款：

INSURER is required to provide oral translation services of information to any Enrollee who speaks any non-English language regardless of whether an Enrollee speaks a language that meets the threshold of a prevalent non-English language. INSURER is required to notify Enrollees of the availability of oral interpretation services and to inform them of how to access such services. There shall be no charge to Enrollee for translation services. INSURER shall make all written materials available in English, Chinese, and all other appropriate foreign languages.

Each Party shall hold three (3) original copies of each version.

保险公司要为非以英语为母语的客户(不管其英语是否达到相应的水准)提供有关保险业务的口译服务。保险公司要告知投保人有此口译服务以及如何获得服务。服务是免费的。除此之外,保险公司提供给这类客户的书面资料必须是双语的。

五、推荐条款

This Agreement and all its appendices (if any) is executed in English, and the Chinese version is a translation. In case of any discrepancy between the English and Chinese versions, the English version shall prevail. All communications, including notices, demands, requests, statements, etc. to be made or given by the parties in performing the Agreement shall also be in the English language. If they are not originally in English, a certified English translation shall be accompanied.

This Agreement may be executed in any number of counterparts and they shall have the same effect as if the signatures on the counterparts were on a single copy of the Agreement.

这么明白的"白话"英文,其实已经不需要任何英文译文了。当然,感性上,笔者非常赞成合同以中文文本为准、或者两种文本具有同等效力的较平等的措辞;但理性上,如果合同是用英文撰写的,仍然应以英文文本为准(也许此"媚说"二十年之后不再成立),因为经济领域或生意辞令跟政治领域或外交辞令(那是在传递"国家的立场")毕竟有别,况且要让老外真正读懂中文合同谈何容易。在经贸领域,为了不弄巧成拙,方便交流以使合同顺利执行,对强势的英文语言还应表示应有的尊重。做成生意,在经济领域的得益其实就是最大的政治。

六、其他双语参考条款

Languages and Counterparts	语言与文本
This Contract and all appendices hereto <u>shall be written in Chinese and English in duplicate</u>. Each Party shall hold three (3) original copies of each version. Both versions are <u>equally authentic</u>.	本合同及其所有附件应以中文和英文拟就,一式两份。合同双方各持有三(3)份中、英文原件。中英文两个版本具有同等效力。

续表

Languages and Counterparts	语言与文本
This Agreement shall be written in both English and Chinese. <u>If there is any conflict between</u> the English and Chinese versions, <u>the English version shall prevail.</u>	本协议以英文和中文两种语言拟就。如英文版本和中文版本有任何抵触,则以英文版本为准。
The parties hereby covenant and agree that this Agreement is <u>executed and delivered</u> in both English and Chinese, and that <u>in the event of any discrepancy between</u> the two versions, the English version shall prevail.	协议方特此同意以英文和中文两种语言签订该协议,并同意:一旦两个版本出现任何不一致的地方,以英文版本为准。
This Agreement is executed in English only, and the executed English language Agreement shall prevail in all cases. This Agreement may be executed in one or more counterparts, each of which shall constitute one and the same agreement, and by facsimile or electronic signature.	本协议仅以英文签订,且在一切情形下均以英文文本的协议为准。本协议可以一个或多个副本签订,各个副本构成同一协议,可通过传真或电子签名签署。
This Agreement is signed in ____ originals, with each of <u>equally binding force</u>, and the Parties shall each keep _____ originals. This Agreement is made in both Chinese and English. <u>In case of any dispute</u> as to the interpretation, the English version shall prevail.	本协议以一式____份签署,各个正本具有同等法律效力,协议方各执____份。本协议以中英文两种语言拟就。如果两种语言解释出现争议,则以英文为准。
This contract <u>is made out in duplicate in Chinese and in English language</u>, one Chinese original copy and one English original copy for each Party, both texts being equally authentic. This contract shall <u>come into force from the date</u> it is signed by the authorized representatives of both parties. The annexes as listed in Article 10 shall form an integral part to this Contract. Any amendment and/or supplement to this contract will be valid only after the authorized representatives of both parties have signed written documents, <u>forming integral parts of the Contract</u>.(王相国,2008:93)	本合同用中文和英文书就,一式两份,双方各执一份中文正本和一份英文正本。两种文本具有同等效力。本合同自双方授权代表签字之日起生效,第十条中列出的附件为本合同不可分割的组成部分。对本合同的任何修改和/或补充,只有在双方授权代表在书面签字后方为有效,并成为本合同不可分割的组成部分。
INSURER is required to provide oral translation services of information to any Enrollee who speaks any non-English language regardless of whether an Enrollee speaks a language that meets the threshold of a prevalent non-English language. INSURER is required to notify Enrollees of the availability of oral interpretation services and to inform them of how to access such services. There shall be no charge to Enrollee for translation services. INSURER shall make all written materials available in English, Chinese, and all other appropriate foreign languages.	保险公司要求向任何操非英语语言的投保者提供信息的口头翻译服务,不论该投保者所操语言是否符合非英语类的流行语种的范畴。保险公司要求通知投保者公司提供口头翻译服务,并通知他们如何获取该服务。该翻译服务不收取任何费用。保险公司应以英文、中文和所有其他适当的外国语言准备所有书面材料。

Languages and Counterparts	语言与文本
All notices, demands, requests, statements or other communications to be made or given by the Borrower hereunder shall be in the English language. Any documents other than financial statements required to be delivered pursuant to this Agreement which are not in the English language must be accompanied by a certified English translation thereof and <u>in the event of any conflict between</u> the original of the document and the English language translation thereof, the English language translation shall for all purposes <u>be deemed to be the correct and controlling version.</u>（王辉,2008:96）	本协议项下所有借款人发出或接收的通知、要求、请求、声明或其他通信均应以英语书就。除财务报表外任何根据本协议需要提交的文件如果不是以英语书就,则必须附有该文件的经认可的英文译文。一旦文本原件和英文译文不一致,则以英文译文为准。
This Agreement may be executed in any number of counterparts and they shall have the same effect as if the signatures on the counterparts were on a single copy of the Agreement.（范文祥、吴怡,2008:232）	本协议签订的份数不限,具有同等效力,所有协议副本上的签字就如同在协议正本上签字一样。
This Agreement may be executed in any number of counterparts, each of which will be deemed an original of this Agreement, and which together will <u>constitute one and the same instrument</u>. Neither Party will be bound to this Agreement unless and until both Parties have executed a counterpart.（范文祥、吴怡,2008:232）	本协议签订的份数不限,每一份都应被视作本协议的原件,而加在一起也仅构成一份相同的协议。本协议只有各协议方签署后才对双方具约束力。

第九章 不可抗力条款的写作、翻译和研究

一、引言：不可抗力事件的定义

几乎每一个合同中都有不可抗力这一通用条款。但几乎每一个合同中提到的不可抗力事件都不尽相同。一个识多见广或具有国际视野的合同起草人在脑子里对可能发生的不可抗力事件都有一个自己的"排行榜"：他们会根据自己对合同方所在国家的政治、经济、法律、地理和季节条件等因素做出恰当的判断，在合同中写入某几项最可能发生的不可抗力事件。例如，对一个历史悠久、政权民选、政治稳定的国家，一般不会在这一条提到外敌行为、叛乱、军事政变、革命等；而对海岛国家一定会提到海啸、台风、飓风等。为了对不可抗力事件有一个全面了解，笔者根据权威词典的定义以及各类常用合同中提到的内容，将该法律术语所包含的内容列举如下：

不可抗力来自一个合成的法文词(Force Majeure)，本意为"主要力量"(仍然保留法语词序，修饰词放在被修饰的名词之后)。在法律上，该词包括本义和广义两层含义：1. 其本义是超出合同双方或其中一方合理控制范围的类似事件(superior or irresistible force, an event or effect that cannot be reasonably anticipated or controlled)；2. 广义上指天灾(act of God)、自然力(force of nature)(an extraordinary interruption by a natural cause of the usual course of events that experience, prescience, or care cannot reasonably foresee or prevent)。

前者包括：战争/war；敌对行动/hostilities；入侵/invasion；外敌行为/act of foreign enemies；叛乱/rebellion；骚乱/riots；暴动/insurrection；恐怖主义事件/acts of terrorism；革命/revolution；军事政变或篡夺政权/military or usurped power；内战/civil war；内乱/civil unrest, commotion；爆炸/explosion；破坏/sabotage, destruction；罢工/strikes；其他集体性的工业行动/other concerted acts of workers or industrial actions；劳资纠纷/labor disturbance；闭厂/lockout；交通或通讯系统全面瘫痪/general failure of transportation or telecommunication systems；原材料供应不足或无法供应/lack or failure of supply of raw materials；禁运/embargoes；法庭判令/judgment or decree of a court of competent jurisdiction；政府行为/acts of governments (restrictions)；法律或准据法的改变/changes in law。

后者主要包括：火灾/fire；洪灾/flood；地震/earthquake；海啸/tsunami (seaquake)；台风 typhoons/；风暴/storm；飓风/hurricane；火山活动/volcanic activity；山体滑坡/landslide；雪崩/avalanche；龙卷风/tornado。

不可抗力还包括其他一些特殊的灾难性事件，如战争军火、爆炸材料、电离辐射或放射性(核辐射)污染引起的事件——当然从事这一行业业务的一方往往是不被免责的。

二、不可抗力条款的内容、句型及语用特征分析

不可抗力条款一般包括四方面的内容:第一,各方都无需为不可抗力事件负责;第二,就本合同而言,可能会使合同各方受到影响的不可抗力事件有哪几项;第三,万一发生不可抗力事件,发生地一方(一般为卖方)有哪些责任或需要采取哪些善后措施;第四,间接受事件影响的另一方(如买方)拥有哪方面的权利,或往往会采取哪些行动以及在何种条件下可以采取这些行动(如事件持续 60 天以上)。

(一) 无须对不可抗力事件负责的表述方式

笔者审察了数以百计的包括不可抗力条款的合同,开门见山的基本句型可归纳如下:

(1) Neither Party A nor Party B shall be held responsible for...;

(2) Neither party shall be liable to the other for...;

(3) No party shall be liable to the other party for...;

(4) The Seller shall not be held liable for...;以及

(5) ...such failure or delay(caused by a force majeure) shall not be deemed as a breach of contract.

以上 1)到 3)的句式是免除双方对不可抗力事件的责任;(4)到(5)适用于免除单方的责任。但所有句式一概采用否定的形式。核心谓语动词是 be(be held /hold sb.) responsible for 和 be(be held /hold sb.) liable for。

至于 be responsible for 与 be liable for 之间有何不同? 笔者倾向于使用后者,而且从频率上讲,选择使用后者的合同起草者占绝对多数。前者一般用来表示对某项工作和任务需要肩负的执行之责,往往不涉及金钱利益的责任;后者所意含的负责是一种法律上的民事责任,主要涉及金钱方面的赔偿,它的名词复数形式(liabilities)在英汉法律词典里的意思就是"负债"或"债务"。对于违约,只要违约方负责赔偿,其他都不是问题。所以,此处"shall be liable (to the other) for"是更加合适的用词选择。就语气而言,"hold sb. liable for"(或其被动语态,都有"强制贵方负责"的含义)比前者更加强硬,但在此没有必要如此强硬,因为因发生不可抗力事件的违约都是迫不得已,不是任何一方自己能力所能控制的。另外还有一个类似的、在不可抗力条款中常用的、表示"负责"的短语是 be under the obligation to,但使用频率较低。例如:The Seller, however, is still under the obligation to take all necessary measures to hasten the delivery of the goods.

如果该通用条款的首句不是开门见山的"谁无须为不可抗力事件负责",而是先用一个条件句,陈述发生了什么,或违约的原因是什么(例如:If the performance by either party of any of its obligations is prevented by a force majeure event,或者 If an event of Force Majeure occurs),则一般须采用肯定的复合句式去表达,而最常用的谓语动词是 be excused from。例如:

1. ...such party shall be excused from the performance of that obligation for the duration of the event.

2. contractual obligations affected by such an event shall be suspended during the

period of delay caused by the Force Majeure and shall be automatically extended, without penalty or liability, for a period equal to such suspension.

以下是有关无须对不可抗力事件负责的一些完整的表述方式：

1. <u>Neither the Seller nor the Buyer shall be held responsible for</u> late delivery or non-delivery owing to generally recognized "Force Majeure" causes.

2. Neither the SELLER nor the BUYER <u>shall be liable for</u> any failure to fulfil any terms or conditions of the PURCHASE ORDER if fulfillment has been delayed, interfered with or prevented by FORCE MAJEURE.

3. <u>Neither party shall be liable to the other for</u> any failure to perform or delay in performance of the terms of this agreement, ... caused by any circumstances beyond its reasonable control.

4. <u>No party shall be liable to the other party for</u> any delay in or failure of performance under this Agreement due to a Force Majeure.

5. <u>No party shall be liable for</u> the failure to perform its obligations under this Agreement if such failure is occasioned by a contingency beyond such party's reasonable control, including, but not limited to,...

6. The Seller <u>shall not be held liable</u> for the delay in shipment or non-delivery of the goods under the Contract in consequence of Force Majeure, which might occur during the process of manufacturing or in the course of loading or transit.

7. ... such <u>failure or delay shall not be deemed as a breach</u> of contract.

8. If the performance by either party of any of its obligations under this Agreement is prevented by circumstances beyond its reasonable control, then <u>such party shall be excused from</u> the performance of that obligation for the duration of the event.

9. <u>Each party shall be excused from liability for</u> the failure or delay in performance of any obligation under this Agreement by reason of any event beyond such parties reasonable control including but not limited to...

10. If an event of Force Majeure occurs, a Party's <u>contractual obligations affected by such an event under this Contract shall be suspended during the period of delay caused by the Force Majeure and shall be automatically extended, without penalty or liability, for a period equal to such suspension.</u>

11. Any such delay or failure shall <u>extend the period of performance to such extent as is reasonably necessary to enable complete performance</u> by a party if reasonable diligence is exercised after the causes or delay or failure have been removed.

(二) 不可抗力事件的范畴

按照该条款写作的逻辑流程，阐述完各方对不可抗力事件的责任后，应当对什么是不可抗力事件加以界定。为了不与前面的内容重复，本节只罗列部分与某个合同有关的事件以及相关的语言表达方式。

1. A Force Majeure <u>is</u> fire, explosion, earthquake, storm, flood, strike, labor difficulties, war, insurrection, riot, act of God or the public enemy, or any law, act, order, export or import control regulations, proclamation, decree, regulation, ordinance, or instructions of local, state, federal or foreign governmental or other public authorities, or judgment or decree of a court of competent jurisdiction (but excluding a court injunction against a Party's performance).

2. ... <u>including but not limited to</u> defaults of suppliers or subcontractors and all types of industrial disputes, lockouts and strikes.

3. Each party <u>shall be excused from</u> any breach or default with respect to this Agreement to the extent that the party was prevented from performance by reason of <u>anything beyond the party's control and not reasonably avoidable</u> such as a <u>strike or other labor disturbance, act of any governmental authority or agency, fire, flood, terrorism, wind storm, or any act of God, or the act or omission of any person or entity not controlled by that party</u> ("FORCE MAJEURE").

4. ... which <u>are</u> unforeseen, unavoidable or insurmountable, and which prevent total or partial performance by either of the Parties.

5. ... the happening and consequences of which <u>are</u> unpreventable and unavoidable.

6. Such events <u>shall include without limitation</u> earthquakes, typhoons, flood, fire, war, strikes, riots, acts of governments, changes in law or the application thereof or any other instances which cannot be foreseen, prevented or controlled, including instances which are accepted as Force Majeure in general international commercial practice.

以上各句的表述都十分简单,只用到两个最常用的动词或短语:be 和 include but not limited to/ include without limitation。上述的例(3)表述最为经济:不但对不可抗力事件做了较为全面的定义,还同时把各方对不可抗力事件的责任也包括在内。笔者建议在简短、没有特殊要求的合同中使用。接着要阐述的是直接受不可抗力事件影响一方的责任和权利。

(三) 不可抗力直接受害方的责任和权利的表述

发生不可抗力事件后,通常受影响的都是提供产品或服务的一方(卖方)。虽然合同的这一条规定可免除或减轻直接受害方因不可抗力而违约的责任,但该方仍然应当采取必要的应对措施。按照常识,该方应马上将事件通告对方,并在规定的时间内向对方提供发生该事件的官方证明文件;与此同时,还应采取积极的补救措施,将损失减至最少。所以,有关这一部分的写法不外乎:

1. ... the Party so affected shall <u>give prompt written notice to the other Party</u>, stating the period of time the occurrence is expected to continue and shall <u>use diligent efforts to end the failure or delay</u> and ensure that the effects of such Force Majeure are

minimized.

2. ... the Seller shall immediately advise by cable or telex the Buyer of the accident and airmail to the Buyer within 15 days after the accident, a certificate of the accident issued by the competent government authority... which is located at the place where the accident occurred as evidence thereof.

3. The party claiming Force Majeure shall promptly inform the other parties in writing and shall furnish within fifteen (15) days thereafter sufficient proof of the occurrence and duration of such Force Majeure.

4. ... then such party shall be excused from the performance of that obligation for the duration of the event.

5. The Party claiming Force Majeure shall also use all reasonable endeavors to terminate the Force Majeure.

以上的其中一些提法已经过时。例如，随着通讯技术的进步，如今已经没有人会去使用电报、电传之类的通讯工具，所以 advise by cable or telex 是 20 世纪的流行说法，再将此写入合同太不合时宜。但是，即便国际长途电话是平日联系业务的常用通讯工具，使用该方法将不可抗力事件通知对方仍然不妥，因为"口说无凭"。根据目前的商业惯例，一般还是先用电邮以及传真将事件告知对方，然后在半个月内通过航空邮寄的方式将当地有关政府部门出具的或经过公证的事件证明书寄送对方。而 use diligent efforts to end the failure or delay 以及 ensure that the effects of such Force Majeure are minimized 是没有实质意义的套话、客气话，凡是想继续合作、继续做生意的公司，都会做出努力、恢复生产、减少损失。至于直接受天灾人祸影响的一方，英文中说法众多，有称之为 the Party so affected, the party suffering such occurrence, 也有 the Party claiming Force Majeure 或 the non-performing party。但最适当的应称之为 the affected Party，因为言简意赅而又毫无歧义。以下是相关例句：

1. In the event of the occurrence of such an event, the Party so affected shall give prompt written notice to the other Party, stating the period of time the occurrence is expected to continue and shall use diligent efforts to end the failure or delay and ensure that the effects of such Force Majeure are minimized.

2. The Seller shall immediately advise by cable or telex the Buyer of the accident and airmail to the Buyer within 15 days after the accident, a certificate of the accident issued by the competent government authority... which is located at the place where the accident occurred as evidence thereof.

3. The party claiming Force Majeure shall promptly inform the other Parties in writing and shall furnish within fifteen (15) days thereafter sufficient proof of the occurrence and duration of such Force Majeure.

4. The affected Party shall notify the other Party by cable without delay and, within fourteen (14) days thereafter, provide information regarding the event of force majeure and valid certificate thereof, explaining the reason for its inability to perform all or part of this Contract or the delay in performance hereof.

5. Notice of a party's failure or delay in performance due to force majeure must be given to the other party within ten (10) days after its occurrence.

6. The party suffering such occurrence shall immediately notify the other party and any time for performance hereunder shall be extended by the actual time of prevention, delay, or interruption caused by the occurrence.

7. Such certificate as proof of the existence of force majeure shall be issued by the notary public office at the locality where the event of force majeure occurred.

8. The affected party shall promptly notify the other party in writing should such circumstances arise, give an indication of the likely extent and duration thereof, and shall use commercially reasonable efforts to resume performance of its obligations as soon as practicable.

9. The party suffering such occurrence shall immediately notify the other party and any time for performance hereunder shall be extended by the actual time of prevention, delay, or interruption caused by the occurrence.

10. The Seller, however, is still under the obligation to take all necessary measures to hasten the delivery of the goods.

(四) 不可抗力间接受害方的责任和权利的表述

发生不可抗力事件后,间接受影响的都是购买产品或服务的一方(买方)。天灾人祸发生在对方身上,间接受害方除了深表同情之外,能做的事情不多。最严重、最严厉的措施就是取消合同的全部或尚未履行部分的合同,最宽容的就是允许适当延期。采取前一措施的,几乎无需商量,但允许延期的就需要跟对方协商。所以,有关这一内容,只有两种表述方式。就前者而言:

1. Buyer shall have the right to cancel the Contract if the force majeure event lasts more than sixty (60) days.

2. The Buyer shall have the right to cancel the whole or the undelivered part of the order for the goods as stipulated in Contract.

3. The other party may then terminate this Agreement by written notice to the non-performing party, with the consequences of such termination as set forth in Sections xx.

4. The Parties shall, through consultation, decide whether to terminate this Contract, or release part of the affected Party's responsibilities to perform this Contract, or delay the performance hereof.

就后者而言,因为牵涉双方的合作,所以:

1. The Parties shall immediately consult with each other in order to find an equitable solution and shall use all reasonable endeavors to minimize the consequences of such Force Majeure.

2. Any such delay or failure shall extend the period of performance to such extent as is reasonably necessary to enable complete performance by a party if reasonable

diligence is exercised after the causes or delay or failure have been removed.

相关例句还有:

3. The Party claiming Force Majeure shall also use all reasonable endeavors to terminate the Force Majeure. In the event of Force Majeure, <u>the Parties shall immediately consult with each other in order to find an equitable solution</u> and shall use all reasonable endeavors to minimize the consequences of such Force Majeure.

4. Any <u>such delay or failure shall extend the period of performance to such extent as is reasonably necessary to enable complete performance by a party</u> if reasonable diligence is exercised after the causes or delay or failure have been removed.

5. The Parties shall, through consultation, <u>decide whether to terminate this Contract, or release part of the affected Party's responsibilities to perform this Contract, or delay the performance hereof</u>.

6. If the said "Force Majeure" cause lasts over 60 days, <u>the Buyer shall have the right to cancel the whole or the undelivered part of the order for the goods</u> as stipulated in Contract.

三、标准不可抗力条款的写法及原理说明

以上句子是根据不可抗力条款的不同内容而分解的例句。以下提供一条(段)完整的(包括以上分析的四方面内容)、比较有通用价值的不可抗力条款,并且对其写作原理进行综合分析和点评:

1. Neither party shall be liable to the other for any failure to perform or delay in performance of the terms of this Contract, if such a failure or delay is caused by a Force Majeure event.

2. Force Majeure includes earthquakes, typhoons, flood, fire, war, strikes, riots, acts of governments, changes in law during the contracting period or any other instances which cannot be foreseen, prevented or controlled and are accepted as Force Majeure in general international commercial practice.

3. In the event of the occurrence of such an incident, the Party so affected shall immediately notify (via both email and fax) the other Party, stating the period of time the occurrence is expected to continue and shall use diligent efforts to end the failure or delay and ensure that the effects of such Force Majeure be minimized.

The affected Party shall also, within 15 days after the incident, send to the other party a certificate of the incident issued by the competent government authority which is located at the place where the accident occurred as its evidence.

4. The Parties shall, through consultation, decide whether to terminate this Contract, or release part of the affected Party's responsibilities to perform this Contract, or delay its performance. In case the Force Majeure lasts more than 60 days, the other party shall have the right to cancel the whole or the unperformed part

of the Contract by giving a written notice to the non-performing party.

第一节陈述双方在不可抗力事件中的责任:双方均无须负责。第二节讲不可抗力事件主要包括哪些内容。第三节讲直接受不可抗力事件影响的一方须做的两件事:马上通过电邮和传真将事件通知对方,并在事发后的15天内寄送一份由官方签发的事件证明书。第四节讲述合同双方须共同采取的补救措施,以及陈述非违约方应有的权利。

这样的写法,几乎"面面俱到""无懈可击",同时又"放之四海而皆准",放到任何合同中几乎都合适,真正具有了通用条款的"通用性"。

在以上写作中,重复最多的是"事件"这个词,指的都是不可抗力事件。在不同合同译本里,不少称之为"事故"。但准确说来,只能称之为"事件",理由可以不言而喻:战争、敌对行动、入侵、叛乱、骚乱、暴动、革命、军事政变、罢工等等,都包括在不可抗力范畴之内,把这些事件都称为或归为"事故",说法也太不"专业"。在英文中,表达这一概念的词有 occurrence, happening, cause, event, incident, accident, contingency, 等等。虽然有些词意思基本相同,如前五者,是同义词,在普通英文中可以互相取代。但在法律英文中,应当尽可能少用这类近义或同义词。因为法律英文的最高追求是表述的精确性,而达到精确表述的途径之一是用词的一致性和同一性。在论述法律翻译的基本原则时,就法律文本用词的一致性和同一性问题作者曾经有过较详细的论述:

在文学作品、新闻报告及日常信函的写作和翻译中,用同义词和近义词来表达相同的概念或思想,被认为是写作和翻译的一种积极风格。在这方面通常只有那些对语言文字有较深造诣的作者及译者,才能驾轻就熟:得心应手地调词遣句、使用各种同义词、近义词或寓意词;而读者往往因此会感到作品的句子错落有致、词汇丰富、可读性强。如果用词重复、句式单调,读之会让人味同嚼蜡。若用"信、达、雅"的标准来衡量一部文学译作,如果作品中重复词汇用之过多,句型"千篇一律",不管译文如何"准确""通顺",恐怕很难被认为是一部"雅"作。

但是,在日常法律文本的写作和翻译中,即便是从同义词词典中拣取意义完全相同的词汇来表达同一法律概念,也是不可取的。在法律文本的写作和翻译中坚持在整个文件中用同一词汇表示同一概念、甚至使之与其管辖的法律体系中的有关概念保持一致,都是非常值得推崇的作业规矩,有时即便会使译文读起来味同嚼蜡也在所不惜。这是因为法律文件最高的翻译准则,是准确性和精确性,任何同义词、等义词或近义词的使用都不得以这个准则为代价。而重复使用同一词汇表达同一概念也是法律文本写作和翻译的一种值得提倡的风格。反之,为了避免词汇的重复而绞尽脑汁,用五花八门的同义词取而代之,其效果将适得其反。《法律文体》一书的作者 Henry Weihofen 强调说:

". . . exactness often demands repeating the same term to express the same idea. Where that is true, never be afraid of using the same word over and over again. Many more sentences are spoiled by trying to avoid repetition than by repetition." (Chen, 1992:164—165)

更明确地说,此处提出的法律翻译的同一性标准指的是用同一词汇表达同一法律概念或思想;而所谓的一致性标准指的是在整个法律文本中自始至终要保持具有特定法律概念的词汇用词的一致性,并要求与有关管辖法律中对该词的释义(如果有的话)保持一致。只有在法律写作和翻译中保持这种同一性和一致性,才有可能使法律文本中的概念或思想保持前后一致、上下一致以及与有关的官方释义一致,从而使寻求司法公正的人士有据可查、有法可依、使善于咬文嚼字或钻牛角尖的诉讼师或试图曲解文意以至别有用心的当事人都无文字空子可钻。……很显然,法律文本中用词缺乏一致性和同一性无疑会使法律概念混淆,使读者不必要地去揣测不同词语的含义差别,从而影响所要表达的法律概念的精确度。

四、不可抗力参考条款及译文

以下供对比的双语条款选自目前中国书刊市场上若干本与合同或法律写作或翻译相关的书籍以及包含本条款的网站。但原文以及原译文中都存在各种瑕疵。故笔者对以下附文中的原文和译文都做了适当的订正和修改。如未注明出处者,译文由笔者提供。

Force Majeure	不可抗力
Neither the Seller nor the Buyer shall be held responsible for late delivery or non-delivery owing to generally recognized "Force Majeure" causes. However in such a case, the Seller shall immediately advise by cable or telex the Buyer of the accident and airmail to the Buyer within 15 days after the accident, a certificate of the accident issued by the competent government authority or the chamber of commerce which is located at the place where the accident occurred as evidence thereof. If the said "Force Majeure" cause lasts over 60 days, the Buyer shall have the right to cancel the whole or the undelivered part of the order for the goods as stipulated in Contract. (王辉,2007:95)	因公认的不可抗力事件致使迟延交付或交付不能,无论买方还是卖方均无须负责。然而,在这种情况下,卖方应立即以电报或电传的方式通知买方该不可抗力事件,并在该事发15天内以航空邮件方式寄送由该事件发生的当地主管政府部门或商会出具的该事件的证明书以资证明。如果上述不可抗力事件持续超过60天,则买方应有权取消整个合同或本合同规定货物订单未交付部分。
Neither party shall be liable to the other for any failure to perform or delay in performance of the terms of this agreement, other than an obligation to pay monies, caused by any circumstances beyond its reasonable control, including but not limited to defaults of suppliers or subcontractors and all types of industrial disputes, lockouts and strikes. (乔焕然,2008:118)	除付款义务外,任何一方当事人均无须为因超出其可合理控制的因素造成的未能履行或迟延履行本协议条款而负责。这些因素包括但不限于供应商或分包商违约、各种类型的行业纠纷、闭厂和罢工。
If the performance by either party of any of its obligations under this Agreement (except the obligation to pay money) shall be prevented by circumstances beyond its reasonable control which could not have been avoided by the exercise of reasonable diligence, then such party shall be excused from the performance of that obligation for the duration of the event. The affected party shall promptly notify the other party in writing should such circumstances arise, give an indication of the likely extent and duration thereof, and shall use commercially reasonable efforts to resume performance of its obligations as soon as practicable.	如协议一方在履行本协议规定的义务时(除付款义务)遭受超出其合理控制能力的事件,该事件即使通过合理努力也无法避免,则该协议方在事件发生期间无须履行该义务。如发生该类事件,受影响的一方应立即书面通知另一方,告知该类事件可能的影响范围和持续时间,并应做出商业上合理的努力尽早重新履行其义务。

续表

Force Majeure	不可抗力
Each party shall be excused from any breach or default with respect to this Agreement to the extent that the party was prevented from performance by reason of anything beyond the party's control and not reasonably avoidable such as a strike or other labor disturbance, act of any governmental authority or agency, fire, flood, terrorism, wind storm, or any act of God, or the act or omission of any person or entity not controlled by that party ("FORCE MAJEURE"). No party shall be liable to the other party for any delay in or failure of performance under this Agreement due to a Force Majeure. Any such delay or failure shall extend the period of performance to such extent as is reasonably necessary to enable complete performance by a party if reasonable diligence is exercised after the causes or delay or failure have been removed.	如果协议方违反或不履行本协议是由于超出其控制能力且无法合理避免,比如罢工或其他劳资纠纷,任何政府机构或代理机构的行为、火灾、洪水、恐怖袭击、风暴、或任何天灾、或是不受该协议方控制的任何人或实体的行为或忽略行为("不可抗力"),那么该协议方的违反或不履行本协议的责任应予免除。如由于不可抗力导致任何延误或不履行本协议,则协议一方无须向另一方负法律责任。如果这类事件的原因、延误或不履约因素被排除后而该方做出了合理的努力,那么因该延误或不履行而耽误的履行协议的时间应予适当延长,直至该协议方有能力完成履行协议。
"Force Majeure" shall mean all events which are beyond the control of the Parties to this Contract, and which are unforeseen, unavoidable or insurmountable, and which prevent total or partial performance by either of the Parties. Such events shall include without limitation earthquakes, typhoons, flood, fire, war, strikes, riots, acts of governments, changes in law or the application thereof or any other instances which cannot be foreseen, prevented or controlled, including instances which are accepted as Force Majeure in general international commercial practice. If an event of Force Majeure occurs, a Party's contractual obligations affected by such an event under this Contract shall be suspended during the period of delay caused by the Force Majeure and shall be automatically extended, without penalty or liability, for a period equal to such suspension. The party claiming Force Majeure shall promptly inform the other Parties in writing and shall furnish within fifteen (15) days thereafter sufficient proof of the occurrence and duration of such Force Majeure. The Party claiming Force Majeure shall also use all reasonable endeavors to terminate the Force Majeure. In the event of Force Majeure, the Parties shall immediately consult with each other in order to find an equitable solution and shall use all reasonable endeavors to minimize the consequences of such Force Majeure. (乔焕然,2008:120)	"不可抗力"指超出本合同双方控制范围、无法预见、无法避免或无法克服、使得本合同一方部分或者全部不能履行的事件。这类事件包括但不限于地震、台风、洪水、火灾、战争、罢工、骚乱、政府行为、法律或准据法的变化,或者其他任何无法预见、无法避免或者无法控制的情况,包括在国际商务惯例中通常被认定为不可抗力的事件。如果发生不可抗力事件,一方在本合同项下受不可抗力影响的义务在不可抗力造成的延误期间内自动中止,并且其履行期限自动延长,延长期间相当于延误的期间,该方无须为此遭受惩罚或承担法律责任。提出受不可抗力影响的一方应及时书面通知另一方,并且在随后的十五(15)日内向另一方提供不可抗力发生以及持续期间的充分证据。提出受不可抗力影响的一方还应尽一切合理的努力以终止不可抗力事件。发生不可抗力时,双方应立即进行磋商,寻求一项公正的解决方案,并且要尽一切合理的努力将不可抗力的影响降至最小。

续表

Force Majeure	不可抗力
No party shall be liable for the failure to perform its obligations under this Agreement if such failure is occasioned by a contingency beyond such party's reasonable control, including, but not limited to, acts of terrorism, strikes or other labor disturbances, lockouts, riots, wars, fires, floods or storms. A party claiming a right to excuse performance under this paragraph 26 shall immediately notify the other party in writing of the extent of its inability to perform, which notice shall specify the occurrence beyond its reasonable control that prevents such performance and an estimate of the time that the inability to perform is anticipated to last.	如协议方由于受该协议方不能合理控制的偶发事件影响而未能履行本协议规定的义务(偶发事件包括但不限于恐怖袭击、罢工或其他劳资纠纷、闭厂、骚乱、战争、火灾、水灾或暴风雨),则该协议方无须负责。根据本协议第26款而享有索赔免责权利的协议方应立即书面通知另一方其无法履行协议的程度,该通知应注明发生了超出其合理控制能力而阻止其履行协议的偶发事件以及无法履行协议的大致持续时间。
Any prevention, delay or interruption of performance by any party under this Agreement shall not be considered a breach of this Agreement if and to the extent caused by occurrences beyond the reasonable control of the party affected, including but not limited to acts of God, embargoes, governmental restrictions, strikes or other concerted acts of workers, fire, flood, earthquake, explosion, riots, wars, civil disorder, rebellion or sabotage. The party suffering such occurrence shall immediately notify the other party and any time for performance hereunder shall be extended by the actual time of prevention, delay, or interruption caused by the occurrence.	如果偶发事件是由于超出受影响一方的合理控制范围以外的,本协议任何一方阻止、延误或中断根据本协议履行协议的行为不应视为违反协议规定,该偶发事件包括但不限于天灾、禁运、政府管制、罢工或其他工人的集体行动、火灾、水灾、地震、爆炸、骚乱、战争、内乱、暴乱或破坏。受该偶发事件影响的一方应立即通知另一方,且本协议规定的协议履行时间应根据偶发事件阻止、延误或中断协议履行的实际时间而延长。
Except for either Party's obligation to make payments to the other Party hereunder, neither Party shall be liable for any failure or delay in performance under this Agreement to the extent such failure or delay arises from Force Majeure. A Force Majeure is fire, explosion, earthquake, storm, flood, strike, labor difficulties, war, insurrection, riot, act of God or the public enemy, or any law, act, order, export or import control regulations, proclamation, decree, regulation, ordinance, or instructions of local, state, federal or foreign governmental or other public authorities, or judgment or decree of a court of competent jurisdiction (but excluding a court injunction against a Party's performance). In the event of the occurrence of such an event, the Party so affected shall give prompt written notice to the other Party, stating the period of time the occurrence is expected to continue and shall use diligent efforts to end the failure or delay and ensure that the effects of such Force Majeure are minimized.	除本协议一方有义务向另一方付款之外,任何一方对由于不可抗力引发的未能或延迟履行本协议行为均不负责。不可抗力指火灾、爆炸、地震、暴风雨、洪灾、罢工、劳资问题、战争、暴动、骚乱、天灾、公敌,或当地的、州的、联邦的或外国政府的或其他公众机构的任何法律、法案、命令、进口或出口管制规则、公告、法令、规则、条例、指令,或拥有司法权的法院判词或法令(但不包括针对协议方行为的法院禁令)。万一发生上述事件,受影响的一方应立即书面通知另一方,述明该事件将持续多长时间,并应努力结束未能履行或延迟履行协议的行为,以确保将不可抗力的影响降至最低。

Force Majeure	不可抗力
Except for the obligation to make payment when due (which shall be fairly adjusted as a result of the effect of the applicable Force Majeure), each party shall be excused from liability for the failure or delay in performance of any obligation under this Agreement by reason of any event beyond such parties reasonable control including but not limited to Acts of God, fire, flood, explosion, earthquake, or other natural forces, war, civil unrest, accident, destruction or other casualty, any lack or failure of transportation facilities, any lack or failure of supply of raw materials, any strike or labor disturbance, or any other event similar to those enumerated above. Notice of a party's failure or delay in performance due to force majeure must be given to the other party within ten (10) days after its occurrence. All delivery dates under this Agreement that have been affected by force majeure shall be tolled for the duration of such force majeure. In no event shall any party be required to prevent or settle any labor disturbance or dispute. Notwithstanding the foregoing, should the event(s) of force majeure suffered by a party extend beyond a three (3) month period, the other party may then terminate this Agreement by written notice to the non-performing party, with the consequences of such termination as set forth in Sections 11.	除到期需要付款(由于不可抗力事件可适当做出调整),如有关的由于发生超出协议方合理控制能力之外的任何事件,包括但不限于天灾、火灾、水灾、爆炸、地震、或其他自然力、战争、内乱、突发事件、破坏或其他事故、交通设施缺乏或不运作、原材料供应不足或无法供应、任何罢工或劳资纠纷、或任何其他与上述列举相似的事件,则协议方应免除不履行或延误履行本协议规定的任何义务。协议一方由于不可抗力不履行或延误履行的通知必须在该事件发生的十(10)日内通知另一方。受不可抗力影响的本协议规定的一切发货日期应在该不可抗力发生期间征税。任何一方绝不能要求另一方阻止或解决任何劳资纠纷。尽管有上述规定,如受不可抗力影响的一方超过三(3)个月,则另一方可书面通知不履行协议的一方终止该协议,该终止的后果参见第11款规定。
If an event of force majeure occurs, <u>neither</u> Party <u>shall be responsible for</u> any damage or loss which the other Party may sustain by reason of its failure to perform or delay in performing this Contract, and such failure or delay shall not <u>be deemed</u> as a breach of contract.	如发生不可抗力事件,合同双方无须就另一方未能履行或迟延履行本合同可能遭受的任何损坏或损失而负责,且该未能履行或迟延履行不应视为违约。
The Seller shall not <u>be held liable</u> for the delay in shipment or non-delivery of the goods under the Contract in consequence of Force Majeure, which might occur during the process of manufacturing or in the course of loading or transit. The Seller shall inform the Buyer promptly of the occurrence mentioned above and within fourteen (14) days thereafter, send by airmail to the Buyer for his acceptance a certificate of the <u>incident</u> issued by the Competent Government Authorities where the incident occurred as evidence <u>thereof</u>. In such circumstances, the Seller, however, <u>is still under the obligation</u> to take all necessary measures to hasten the delivery of the goods. In case the incident lasts for more than ten(10) weeks, the Buyer <u>shall have the right to cancel</u> the Contract.	本合同中所述的货品如在制造、装货或运输过程中因可能发生的不可抗力事件而延迟装运或未能交货,卖方概不负责。卖方应立即通知买方上述事件,并在该事件发生十四(14)日内向买方以航空邮件方式寄送由主管政府机构出具的该事件的证明书,以资证明。然而,在该情况下,卖方仍有责任采取一切必要措施尽快交货。万一该事件持续超过十(10)周,则买方有权取消本合同。

续表

Force Majeure	不可抗力
Should a Party be directly prevented from performing this Contract or be delayed in performing this Contract by an event of Force Majeure, such as earthquake, typhoon, flood, fire and war and other unforeseen events, the happening and consequences of which are unpreventable and unavoidable, the affected Party shall notify the other Party by cable without delay and, within fourteen (14) days thereafter, provide information regarding the event of force majeure and valid certificate thereof, explaining the reason for its inability to perform all or part of this Contract or the delay in performance hereof. Such certificate as proof of the existence of force majeure shall be issued by the notary public office at the locality where the event of force majeure occurred. The Parties shall, through consultation, decide whether to terminate this Contract, or release part of the affected Party's responsibilities to perform this Contract, or delay the performance hereof.	如合同一方由于不可抗力事件（如地震、台风、洪灾、火灾和战争以及其他不可预见的事件，该事件的发生和后果无法阻止、无法避免）的发生而无法履行本合同或迟延履行本合同，则受影响的一方应立即以电报通知另一方，并在事发后的十四（14）日内提供不可抗力事件的信息和有效证明，解释其无法履行全部或部分合同或迟延履行本合同的原因。作为不可抗力事件发生的证明应由该事件发生地公证处出具。合同方应通过磋商决定是否终止合同，或减轻受影响一方履行本合同的责任，或迟延履行本合同。
Neither the SELLER nor the BUYER shall be liable for any failure to fulfil any terms or conditions of the PURCHASE ORDER if fulfillment has been delayed, interfered with or prevented by FORCE MAJEURE, provided that the respective PARTY is not already in default of those obligations under the PUCHASE ORDER whose performance is being delayed, interfered with or prevented. FORCE MAJEURE for this purpose shall refer to Acts of God or force of nature or similar events beyond the reasonable control of the PARTIES or either of them, which may include: war, hostilities (whether war be declared or not), invasion, act of foreign enemies, rebellion, terrorism, revolution, insurrection, military or usurped power, or civil war, riot, commotion, disorder, strike or lockout by persons other than the Contractor's Personnel and other employees of the Contractor and Subcontractors, munitions of war, explosive materials, ionizing radiation or contamination by radio-activity, except as may be attributable to the Contractor's use of such munitions, explosives, radiation or radio-activity, and Natural catastrophes such as earthquake, hurricane, typhoon or volcanic activity.	如由于不可抗力事件而迟延、中断或阻止完成订单，则买卖双方无须为未能完成订单的任何条款或条件负责，但前提是各方在履行本订单义务时并未事前已经违约，即未迟延、中断或阻止履行本订单。本条所指不可抗力指天灾、自然力或超出买卖双方合理控制范围的类似事件，包括： 战争、敌对行动（无论宣战与否）、入侵、外敌行为； 叛乱、恐怖主义、革命、暴动、军事政变或篡夺政权或内战； 承包商人员以及承包商和分包商的其他雇员范围以外的人员的骚乱、动乱、混乱、罢工或闭厂； 战争军火、爆炸物资、电离辐射或放射性污染，但可能因承包商使用此类军火、炸药、辐射或放射性引起的除外； 自然灾害，如地震、飓风、台风或火山活动。

本章附录：

对一段不可抗力条款译作的批改

引言：以下汉译英文本选自一名修习翻译专业硕士生的作业。原文内容来自几段买卖合约的条文。总体上讲，该篇译文表达清晰，句子通顺，语法无大错，能达到基本的传意（communicative）目的。但从合同翻译、法律条文翻译的专业要求来讲，译文还存在不少瑕疵；从文体上讲，译文的问题更加严重。一个真正合格的专业法律文本译者，应该可以看出并能纠正译文中存在的至少20个问题。读者可以此检验自己的合同翻译和写作水平。笔者以逐条注释的方式，对其中近30个问题进行详细讲解。最后提供一段参考译文。

原文：本合同内所述的全部货品，在制造和装运过程，如因不可抗力原因，拖延装运或不能交货，则卖方概不负责。卖方必须将上述事故立刻通知买方，且在其后的14天内航空邮寄一份由出事地点政府主管部门签发的事故证明书给买方作为证据。但是，卖方仍应负责采取必要的措施尽快交货。万一事故持续超过10个星期，则买方有权取消合同。

在收货或货物抵达目的港之后的45天内，假如发现货品的品质、规格或数量与合约规定不符，买方凭当地商品检验局颁发的检验证书，有权提出更换品质合格的新货品或要求赔偿。

译文：The Sellers shall not be responsible for(1) the late-shipment or none-delivery(2) of all the contracted goods owing to(3) force majeure which occurs(4) in the process of manufacturing or shipping. The Sellers should intimate(5) the Buyers at once(6) of the accident(7) within 14 days after such an event taking place(8), and the Sellers shall(9) send by airmail to the Buyers for their acceptance a certificate of the incident issued by a competent local government authority(10) where the event occurs(11) as evidence of such an event(12). However, the Seller shall still be responsible to(13) take all essential(14) measures to accelerate the delivery of the commodities(15). If(16) an accident(17) lasts more than 10 weeks, the Buyer(18) shall be entitled to(19) end(20) the contract.

Within 45 days after the delivery of the goods(21) or the arrival of the goods at the destination port, in case(22) the quality, specification(23), or quantity are found not checking with(24) those stipulated in the contract, the Buyers shall, based on(25) an inspection certificate(26) issued by the competent organization for commodity inspection of the local government, have the right to(27) claim for replacement with the new qualified goods(28) or for compensation.

翻译讲评：

1. "……拖延装运或不能交货，则卖方概不负责"——此处的"负责"或"责任"显然跟不能按时交货造成买方经济损失的赔偿有关，根据我们在第六章有关"负责"四种基本表述，be responsible for 只表示对某项工作和任务需要肩负的执行之责，往往不涉及金钱利益的责任，所以此处使用 be responsible for 显然不够到位；而选用 shall not be liable for 或其被动语态的 shall not be held liable for 是更为适当的选择，因为这个"负责"背后是赔偿经济损失;不过就语气而言,后者(hold sb. liable for 或其被动语态)比前者更加强硬,故在此没有必要使用,不必把话说得太绝,买卖不成交情在。

2. 其实此处包含两个技术层面的瑕疵:the late-shipment or none-delivery;定冠词 the 是没有必要的,"迟交货"并非是个专有名词,也没有特指哪一次迟交货。而 none-delivery 是个小小的失误,none 永远不能作为某一个名词的前缀以构成新词,正确的构词是 non-delivery。

3. owing to 用在此处,语法上没有错,但"人力不可抗拒事件"是大型的天灾人祸(force majeure),是非常负面的消息,将该词用在此处太 positive;due to, as a consequence of 或者 because of 都比 owing to 更加得体。

4. 此处的 occurs 语法上并没有错;force majeure 不是必然会发生的,更不是经常发生的。但从逻辑上讲,在"不可抗力事件"发生这个动词之前,加一个情态动词 might,语气上、逻辑上都更加得体。

5. 根据法律翻译的规范,"卖方必须……通知"以译成"the Buyers must… advise/notify"更加规范;inform 语域较低,似乎更似口语用词;intimate 在当今生意人中间越来越陌生,年轻一代只把该词当作形容词使用,解作"亲密的",作动词使用的 intimate 虽然数十年前在商务英语丛书中频繁出现,的确解作"通知",但太书面语了,如今该词已不常使用,在该语境作为"通知"的对应词似乎已有些过时。should 通常不作法律文本中表示"强制"的情态动词使用,而 shall 似乎语气不够强烈,因此,must 是最合适的。

6. 法律翻译的选词一定要注重语域适切。此处的 at once 主要为英文中的口语用词,用在非常正式的法律文本中似乎语域太低,immediately, without delay, promptly, forth with, 都表达相同的概念,但最后者,即 forth with 已经被法律语言的专家们列入了 legalese 或古旧词的行列,在现代法律写作中尽可能不用;相比较而言,immediately 和 promptly 较为中性,语域更适切。

7. 天灾之类的事件可以称之为 incident, event, occurrence,就是不能称其为 accident (事故),事故与事件性质是有差异的,用 incident 指代 force majeure 是最合适不过的。

8. 事实上,该句的翻译是错误的。为了验证法律译文的对错,可以用"回译"(back-translation)程序来检验(李克兴,2013:39)。倘若将该半句"The Sellers should intimate the Buyers at once of the accident within 14 days after such an event taking place"回译成英文,其译文应该是"在事件发生的 14 天内,卖方应该立即将事件通知买方",这句话的逻辑本身就有问题:"14 天"跟"立即"是互相矛盾的,任何人对"立即"的理解都比"14 天"要短得多。

9. "……且在其后的 14 天内航空邮寄一份由出事地点主管政府当局签发的事故证明书作为证据给买方"这半句应该跟前半句分享一个情态动词"必须",所以,该句可以省略 shall。

10. a competent local government authority:英文中冠词的使用历来是以汉语为母语而学习英语人士的一大困惑,在该短语前究竟用定冠词还是不定冠词?逻辑告诉我们该用定冠词 the,因为这类"主管政府当局"不是随便找一个就可以出具有效证明的。

11. where the event occurs as evidence of such an event,画线部分的 occurs 不是太恰当,因为这类 event 是指前述已经发生的事件,故将 occurs 改为过去式 occurred,才符合语言表达的时间逻辑。

12. 此句中的 event 应该与前文的 incident 用词保持一致。为了追求译文的精确性,法律的写作和翻译不怕用词重复,故没有必要选择一个同义词或近义词去表达"事件"这个相同的概念。

13. 将该句子中"负责"翻译成 be responsible to 其实是正确的选词,如果用了 be liable to 反倒不妥,因为该语境中的"负责"并不直接涉及金钱或索赔的问题,这里只是规定卖方的义务,应该在该种情形下负责采取何种措施。

14&15. 原文是"必要措施",但 essential 的基本词义是"重要的",就法律翻译的严格要求而言,这算是小小的偏差。而另一个用词 accelerate,则太"scientific",太"机械化"了,因为这个语境中的"加快"是一个模糊或不确切的用词,用 hasten 或 expedite 就可以了。

16&17. "万一事故持续超过 10 个星期",这里的"事故"是"不可抗力事件",本身就是大事件,而且"持续超过 10 个星期":这个假设事件发生的可能性是微乎其微的,所以根据法律条件句引导词的用词规律,对这样既是大事件、又是不幸事件、而且发生的概率特别低,选用 in the event that 更加到位。此外,如前所述,法律翻译非常强调用词的同一性,前面用 incident 来翻译"事件",此处就不可以再选用其他词,再说,如上文所述,accident 还是不恰当的选择。再次,不定冠词 an 也是错用,前文已经提及 incident,此处是复指,自然只能用定冠词 the。

18. 法律文本写作还讲求用词的对应性或配对性,如果是一份租约,称甲方为 tenant,则乙方为 landlord;如果称甲方为 leasee,则乙方为 leasor;如果付款人是 payer,那么收款人一定是 payee。在该文本中,虽然 Seller 与 Buyer 是配对词,但单复数并不对称:在前文,Sellers 是以复数形式出现的,那么此处的 Buyer 必须是对应的复数;同样,如果前面的 Sellers 之前没有定冠词 the,那么此处的 Buyers 也不能加定冠词,反之亦然。

19&20. 正确表述英文中的"有权"并不容易。"有权"可以是 have the right to,也可以是 have the power to,be entitled to,reserve the right to 或者是 have the authority to,在此用三言两语说不清楚(李克兴,2013:130－145)。简而言之,be entitled to 通常用来表述具有"特权"性质的权利(而不是权力)。在该语境中我们并未发现可以使买方获得特权的条件,天灾人祸,而且持续 10 个星期,对卖方来说已经是很不幸的事件,如果因此而让买方获得特权,于情于理都说不过去,但也不能让买方遥遥无期地等待,所以,用比较中性的 have the right to 去表达该语境中的"有权"是更适当的选词。此外,如果一份合同不是在规定的到期日终止,而是"半途而废",则 terminate 是更准确的用词。有关该词在合同中与 end 的区别,可以参阅本书关于"合同期限及终止条款的写作、翻译和研究"一章。

21. Within 45 days after the delivery of the goods 该短语的本身没有错,也与"在收货……之后的 45 天内"的原文吻合,但如果读者非常懂国际贸易,会发现该译文是经不起推敲的,因为 delivery 并不一定是"收货","交货"也同样用这个词,如果交易双方在同一个城市或两地距离是在合理的路程之内的,那么"交货"之日就是"收货"之日;但此文是有关国际贸易的合同,从前文的 shipment 以及本句的"抵达目的港"等词语,我们都可以断定这是需要经过长途海运的国际买卖,为避免双方发生可能的争议或节外生枝,把该短语翻译成"after taking the delivery of the goods"或者"after receipt of the goods"会更加保险些。

22. 23&24. "... in case the quality, specification, or quantity are found not checking with those stipulated in the contract",该条件句并无大错,但存在若干可以改正的地方:倘若不改变条件句的引导词,则动词 are found 应该改为 is found,因为该动词短语之前罗列的

几个并列的主语词是用 or 连接在一起的,而最后一个 quantity 又是单数;若连接词是 and,则我们可以以一加一等于二的逻辑认为主语是复数,那么 are found 在语法上是正确的。其次,该短语中的 specification 应该是复数才符合逻辑,因为任何规格都不可能只有一个参数。再次,该条件句属于假设性质,在法律文本中假设性质的条件句的引导词以 should 引导或用虚拟语态的方式表达更为恰当,在买卖合约中更是如此。所以,该条件句改为 should the quality, quantity or specifications be found not in conformity with those stipulated in the contract, 是更规范的表述,原文的 not checking with 用词,在法律文本中非常少见,用词不够正式,如同口语词,表达这类性质的符合或合格与否,以 in conformity with 最为合适,也最为通用。

25&26. ... based on an inspection certificate issued by the competent organization for commodity inspection——表达"根据"的英文词多得不胜枚举:based on, on the basis of, because of, on account of, on the ground of, by reason of, in light of, by virtue of, in view of, on the strength of, in accordance with, according to 等等。在这一系列表达"根据"的词汇中,"根据"之基础最牢靠的应该是 on the strength of。在本语境中,该短语也是最到位的。inspection certificate 之前应该有定冠词 the;为了得到索赔,不是随便取得一份商检证书就可以作为证据的,而且商检局也不可能为同一批受损商品出具多份检验证书。

27. 此处的 have the right to 应该由 be entitled to 取而代之,因为买方此时已得到政府部门颁发的商检证书,这是索赔的凭证,算得上是一把"尚方宝剑"吧,因此,买方凭此得到了一种对方所没有的"特权",故此,be entitled to 是最恰当的表达此处"有权"的词语。

28. 译文中这最后一个短语 claim for replacement with the new qualified goods,其中的定冠词 the 是多余的,因为究竟用哪一批新产品去取代商检证书中认定有缺陷或瑕疵的产品,是不能确定的,故该将定冠词去除。

至此,我们可以将以上经过修改的译文缀篇如下:

The Seller shall not be liable for late-shipment or non-delivery of all the contracted goods due to force majeure which might occur in the process of manufacturing or shipping. The Seller must advise the Buyer promptly of the incident, and within 14 days after its occurrence (thereafter), send by airmail to the Buyer for its acceptance a certificate of the incident issued by the competent local government authority where the incident occurred evidencing the incident (as evidence thereof). However, the Seller shall still be under obligation to take all necessary measures to hasten the delivery of the goods. In the event that the incident lasts more than 10 weeks, the Buyer shall have the right to terminate the contract.

Within 45 days after taking delivery of the goods or the arrival of the goods at the destination port, should the quality, quantity or specifications be found not in conformity with those stipulated in the contract, the Buyer shall, on the strength of the inspection certificate issued by the Commodity Inspection Bureau of the local government, be entitled to claim for replacement with new qualified goods or for compensation.

第十章
保证条款的写作、翻译和研究

一、引言：保证条款的定义及基本内涵

根据 Black's *Law Dictionary* 的解释，法律英文里保证条款中的关键词 "representations（陈述）" 的含义是 "a representation of fact—either by words or by conducts, made to induce someone to act, esp., to enter into a contract（通过言辞或行为呈现某种事实，以促使相对方做出相应行为，比如订立合同）"。合同保证条款中的 "representations" 大多用来说明当事人的主体资格或权利能力、行为能力等问题。而另一个关键词 "warranties（保证）" 则指 "an express or implied promise that something in furtherance of the contract is guaranteed by one of the contracting parties; esp., the seller's promise that the thing being sold is represented or promised.［合同一方提供的明示或默示的保证条款，尤其是在买卖合同中乙方（卖方/销售方）向甲方（买方）做出的质量保证］。

但是基于两者都是当事人针对过去曾经发生或现在存在，并可能影响合同效力的事实，所以现时的英文合同常将两者连用，构成一组配对词（represent and warrant 或 representations and warranties，陈述与保证）。

合同中属于通用条款的陈述与保证分为两大类。

第一类是对产品或服务的保证。当今世间的绝大部分合同都会涉及产品或服务的问题。就产品保证而言，既有明示的保证，如达到一定的标准和使用期限（express warranties），又有暗含或默示的保证（implied warranties: merchantability, fitness），如适于作某种用途，以及对所售产品的所有权或法律上的保证（statutory warranties）。如顾客买空调，产品能够进行一般意义上的制冷是暗含保证；噪音水平、用电量、压缩机能运转几年是明示保证；卖方合法获得所出售的空调是法律上的保证（如果是窃取物或赃物厂家就不提供法律上的保证）。本书的写作重心是条款的语言表述，讨论的重点仍然放在这类条款的写作和翻译的本身。

第二类纯粹是法律层面的保证。如：(1)对公司是否有权签署本协议所做的陈述与保证，包括公司组建设立情况以及公司是否授予签约人适当的权力去签署这份合同的保证；(2)依据合同性质和合同标的要求合同另一方做出特别保证的内容，比如公司是否存在或正在进行的诉讼（打官司）等。对于这些信息，合同一方很难从其他渠道获取，因此要求另一方通过这个条款对其合同中提供的相关信息做出保证，确保其真实有效。如果另一方违反这个保证，则合同一方可以采取包括终止合同在内的救济措施，从而最大限度保护恪守合同承诺的一方。（范文祥、吴怡，2008:32）

二、保证条款的基本句型和关键用词/语

（一）保证方式

- Party A and Party B hereby undertake that...
- Party A represents and warrants that...
- breaches the representation and warranty...
- makes no warranties(不保证……)
- disclaim...(不保证……)
- express and implied warranties
- The Buyer has waived/given up the (implied) warranties of merchantability and of fitness for ... purpose.
- The seller does not warrant the condition of the goods and they are sold "as is" or "in present condition."

（二）保证内容

- new and not refurbished or reconditioned
- shall be of good quality and free from defects in materials and workmanship
- shall not infringe any patent, copyright, mask work, trademark, trade secret or other intellectual property
- shall be fit and serviceable
- shall have good and marketable title to all goods
- all material, work product, and merchandise supplied under the Order (a) shall strictly conform to all specifications, drawings, samples, or other descriptions
- in conformity with all applicable contractual commitments
- in a professional and workmanlike manner
- all services shall be provided in a professional and workmanlike manner, with a degree of skill and care consistent with current, good and sound professional procedures
- free of all liens and encumbrances
- no licenses are required for Buyer to use such goods
- replacement of the product/repair or replace
- indemnify and hold harmless
- a refund of the purchase price of the product

（三）保证条件

- under normal use
- at Seller's option

- in its sole discretion
- sold "as is" or "in present condition"

有一定经验的作者或译者，利用这些"零部件"就可以"组装"出各种保证条款；但他们往往很难确定哪些写法是流行的、哪些是过时的、哪些在语言风格上是得体、哪些已经迂腐。以下我们来看一些完整的保证条款语段，以便在再下一节分析各种写法的风格和特点。

三、传统保证条款的主要表达方式

（一）产品保证条款

任何一个商品，小至纳米芯片，大至高楼大厦，只要是售卖的产品，特别是新货品，都有品质保证，都要有保修、保养、调换的期限和规则，除非是 sell "as is" 的旧货或次品。保证条款写法同样是五花八门的。主要写法有如下几种：

1. In the event of breach of this warranty, Buyer may rescind this Agreement and any consideration paid by it to Sellers will be returned.

2. The Party A will promptly repair or replace any Goods that malfunction, fail to operate, or are otherwise defective and that area covered under the warranty, regardless of whether the Party B or the Party B's customer own the goods at the time.

3. If any of the above representations and warranties of a Party are not accurate in all material respects on the date hereof or the Effective Date, then such Party shall be in material breach of this Contract.

4. ... all Products sold hereunder shall be new and not refurbished or reconditioned, and free from defects in materials and workmanship under normal use for a period of twelve (12) months from the date of original retail purchase (from the date of Buyer's receipt) ("Warranty"). Your exclusive remedy under this Section shall be, at Seller's option, a refund of the purchase price of the product or replacement of the product which is returned to Seller or a Seller's authorized representative with a copy of the receipt.

这是我们日常生活中购买消费耐用品的典型保证条款。但就保修或调换品质有问题的产品而言，在同一城市有保修点的厂家或卖方可以这样做：客户或买方自己带货上门维修或调换；而在大多数国际贸易中，货品保修期内出现问题都是按下列方式处理的：

5. In the event of a breach of this Warranty, Seller shall, at Seller's option, either (i) repair the applicable product at the original F.O.B. point of delivery, (ii) refund an equitable portion of the contract price, or (iii) furnish replacement equipment or parts, as necessary to the original F.O.B. point of delivery.

一旦违反本保证，卖方由自己选择：(i) 在原先 FOB 交货地点修复瑕疵产品；或 (ii) 返还合同价的对等金额；或 (iii) 在原先 FOB 交货地点提供替换产品或部件。

国际贸易中最常用的两个报价时使用的专业术语是 F.O.B.（离岸价）和 C.I.F.（到岸

价)(都必须包括交货城市或港口名称)。对于卖方来说后者是最贵的价格,需支付的包括货品成本(Cost)、保险费(Premium)以及运费(Freight);前者对卖方而言付出相对较少,卖方只需要将货品交给货(船)运公司(Free on board,即货品越过货轮的船舷,放上甲板),就算履行完合同规定的交货义务,至于到达目的港的运费、保险费均由买方自己负担。该 F.O.B. 用在此处旨在厘定买方只负责有关问题产品的维修、或提供替换的零部件,至于所需的运费概由买方自己承担。在保证条款中加上以下这一句,就是为了避免双方在执行货品质量保证时在此问题上产生争执:

6. Except as specifically set forth in the preceding sentences, Seller makes no warranties either express or implied with respect to the products sold hereunder.

这样一来,合同世界中最常见的保证条款,也就完成。

(二) 服务保证条款

但合同标的或买卖的内容可以有无数种类。以下略举仅次于货品买卖的服务类合同的保证条款的写作范例:

1. Seller warrants that all services shall be provided in a professional and workmanlike manner, with a degree of skill and care consistent with current, good and sound professional procedures.

卖方保证根据现行适用的行业标准程序,提供技术合格、态度专业的服务。

以上是最基本的服务保证。较详细一点、对所提供的服务所产生的后果不予承担或只承担部分后果的条款可以这样写。

2. Each service performed or otherwise delivered or provided, as the case may be, by Seller in the operation of the Business, has been in conformity with all applicable contractual commitments and all express and implied warranties, and Seller does not have any liability for any damages in connection therewith. No service provided by Seller in the operation of the Business is subject to any guaranty, warranty or other indemnity beyond the terms and conditions of service contained in the customer Contracts. The maximum potential liability of Seller under any guaranty, warranty or other indemnity set forth in the Contracts is limited to the cost of reprocessing the products (if required) and the manufacturing costs of the customer's product being processed.

在经营生意中卖方履行或提供的每项服务(视具体情况)与所有适合的合同承担和所有明示和暗示的保证相符;卖方对与服务相关的任何赔偿不承担任何法律责任。在经营生意中,卖方提供的服务不受客户合同包含的服务条款和条件以外的任何保证、担保或其他补偿的限制。卖方根据本合约中订明的保证、担保或其他补偿条款中所需承担最大责任,仅限于产品再处理(如要求)的成本和正在处理的客户产品的制造成本。

四、标准保证条款写作及说明

由于保证涉及的范围广泛,故该通用条款的标准写法也极其多样。以下分门别类予以简述。

(一) 产品保证条款写作原理

Seller warrants that all Products sold hereunder shall be new and not refurbished or reconditioned, and free from defects in materials and workmanship under normal use for a period of twelve (12) months from the date of original retail purchase. Should a breach of the warranty occur, Buyer's exclusive remedy under this Section shall be, at Seller's option, a full refund of the purchase price of the product, or replacement of the product which is returned to Seller or a Seller's authorized representative with a copy of the receipt. In the case of replacement, the parties shall respectively pay the shipping cost.

卖方保证根据本合同所售的所有产品为全新产品,无翻新或修复品,其用料和做工在正常使用情况下自原零售购买日期起十二(12)个月内均无瑕疵。一旦违反本保证,买方的唯一补偿是根据卖方选择,得到产品购买价的全额退款,或将产品(附上收据)退还给卖方或其授权的代理商后获得替换品。就后者而言,各方自行负责退货或发货的运费。

1. 如前所述,保证条款的主句有四种基本表达方式:

  Seller <u>warrants that</u> ...,
  Party A <u>represents and warrants</u> that...,
  Party A <u>represents and warrants</u> to Party B that...,
  Party A and Party B hereby <u>undertake that (or to indemnify and keep indemnified</u> the other Parties for...,

以上四种不同的保证写法,最值得推荐的是开门见山、简明扼要的第一种;虽然目前最流行的仍然是第二种,其中的 represents and warrants 是法律英语中典型的配对词(legal pair)的表达形式,其实 represents 是没有实质意义的:已经做出了保证,无需多此一举再表述或陈述(represent)一番,难道合同中的保证还可以不用表述?但我们只需认识到这一点就已足够,因为广大的职业写手在写作保证条款时仍然会继续使用这一对只有一个意思的配对词,就像 terms and conditions 一样,在一个合同中,究竟哪条是条款(term),哪条是细则,哪条是条件,往往无人分得清,也不需要分清;这一组词仍然是目前法律界职业写手(律师)用起来得心应手、读起来朗朗上口的配对词。只是我们需要知道,现代英语语言是越简洁越好,只要把意思表达清楚了,不应该多用一个多余的字。

2. 就产品的保证而言,"所有产品为全新产品,无翻新或修复品"是理所当然的,如果是旧货或次货,卖方通常都不提供任何保证,其写法也比较固定,如果售卖的是一辆旧车,无保证的条款一般这样写:The Buyer understands that he/she is purchasing this vehicle (the goods) "as is" and agrees not to hold the Seller responsible for any problems that may arise with the vehicle (the goods) after the purchase, whether or not those issues were known by either party at the time of purchase. 其中的关键词是"as is",即"就是当时那个状况",卖方不对产品出现的任何问题承担责任。不过,有时也可用"in present condition"来表达"就是当时那个状况"的概念,但从语言简洁要求来讲,"as is"更值得推荐。

3. 保证内容最先提到的 free from defects in materials and workmanship under normal use for a period of twelve (12) months from the date of original retail purchase. (其用料和做工在正常使用情况下、自原零售购买日期起十二(12)个月内均无瑕疵。)其中四个条件都

是合情合理的:a."用料和做工无瑕疵";b.但必须"在正常使用情况下"——滥用、误用、非正常操作造成的损害让卖方负担肯定是不合理的;c."自原零售购买日期起十二(12)个月内"这个时间条件适用于耐用消费品,否则,保证期可能会缩短至 3 个月;d. 但保证期从哪一天开始计算? 当然不是分销商从厂家购得产品的那一天开始计算,而是按零售给用户的(end user)那一天算起。

4. Should a breach of the warranty occur, Buyer's exclusive remedy under this Section shall be, at Seller's option, a full refund of the purchase price of the product, or replacement of the product which is returned to Seller or a Seller's authorized representative with a copy of the receipt. (一旦违反本保证,买方的唯一补偿是根据卖方选择,得到产品购买价的全额退款,或将产品(附上收据)退还给卖方或其授权的代理商后获得替换品。)一般来说,卖方给予的保证条件都是基于对自己产品品质的信心,否则卖方给予这样的保证是在自找麻烦。但也不排除有万一的状况,所以该句的条件部分用 Should 开头,表示一种假设;不过,也可以这样写:In case a breach of the warranty occur,或者 In case of a breach of the warranty。用 In case 这个短语引导一个条件,表示一种不是经常发生的"万一"状况。按照卖方的意志,解决问题的办法有两种:买方退货,卖方全额退款;或者换成合格的产品。但货退到何处? 要么直接退给卖方,要么退给卖方授权的代理商。当然,为了证明货品的确是通过适当途径购买的,并且仍在保修期内,买方须附上收据凭证。

5. In the case of replacement, the parties shall respectively pay the shipping cost. (如更换货品,各方须自行负责退货或发货的运费。)这是为了消除退货时所涉及的运费争拗:将有问题货品寄还给卖方的费用由买方支付,但卖方将替换品寄返买方的运费则由卖方支付。这样安排也算公平,双方均有所付出,不会因产品的一些小瑕疵而轻易退货。当然,如果卖方对自己的货品信心十足,或者买方是强势一方、是众多卖方争相竞夺的"财神爷",那么有时该换货或退货条款还可以这样写:

If a breach of warranty occurs, Buyer may, in its sole discretion, and without waiving any other rights, return for credit or require prompt correction or replacement of the nonconforming goods or services.

如果违反本保证,买方可在不放弃任何其他权利的情况下单方面决定退货并要求将货款计入买方的贷方账户,或要求立即更正或更换不合格之产品或服务。

(二) 复杂保证条款的写作

不过,在笔者见到的保证条款中,内容最面面俱到、保证最周全的条款恐怕就数下面这一条:既包括产品的保证,也包括服务的保证,还包括知识产权、商标使用权以及留置权等方方面面的保证。但一般的商品买卖合同未必需要这么周全的保证条款,正所谓"杀鸡焉用牛刀"。不妨将该复杂条款立此存照,以备不测之需。

Warranties: Seller warrants that <u>all material, work product, and merchandise supplied under the Order (a) shall strictly conform to all specifications, drawings, samples, or other descriptions</u> furnished to and approved by Buyer, (b) <u>shall be fit and serviceable for the purpose intended</u>, as agreed to by Buyer and Seller, (c) <u>shall be of good quality and free from defects in materials and workmanship</u>, (d) shall be new and not refurbished or reconditioned, unless expressly agreed in writing by Buyer, and (e) shall not infringe any patent, copyright, mask work, trademark, trade secret or other intellectual property, proprietary or contractual right of any third party. In addition, Seller warrants that Buyer shall have good and marketable title to all goods (including all components thereof) purchased by Buyer pursuant to the Order, free of all liens and encumbrances and that no licenses are required for Buyer to use such goods. With respect to services, Seller warrants that all services shall be provided in a professional and workmanlike manner, with a degree of skill and care consistent with current, good and sound professional procedures. Neither receipt of material, work product or merchandise nor payment therefor shall constitute a waiver of this provision. If a breach of warranty occurs, Buyer may, in its sole discretion, and without waiving any other rights, return for credit or require prompt correction or replacement of the nonconforming goods or services.

保证:卖方保证本订单下供应的所有原料、制成品和商品(a)须严格符合买方提供和认可的产品规格、图纸、样品或其他说明,(b)均为双方约定的合格产品并符合预期的用途,(c)品质优良,无原料和工艺缺陷,(d)除有买方明确的书面同意者外,为全新产品,无翻新或修复品,(e)无侵犯任何第三方的任何专利权、著作权、掩膜作品权、商标权、商业秘密或者其他的知识产权、专有权或合同权。此外,卖方保证买方拥有根据订单所购全部货物(包括货物的全部零部件)的合法交易权,无任何留置权或抵押权,且买方在使用上述货物时无须任何许可证。就服务而言,卖方保证根据现行适用的行业标准程序,提供技术合格、态度专业的服务。买方接受原料、制成品和商品或者支付其货款并不代表放弃该保证条款。如果违反本保证,买方可在不放弃任何其他权利的情况下单方面决定退货并要求将货款计入贷方账户,或要求立即更正或更换不合格之产品或服务。

(三) 服务保证条款写作原理

Seller warrants that all services provided by Seller in the operation of the Business shall be in a professional and workmanlike manner, with a degree of skill and care consistent with current, good and sound professional procedures, and in conformity with all applicable contractual commitments. No service provided by Seller is subject to any guaranty, warranty or other indemnity beyond the terms and conditions of service contained in the contract, and the maximum potential liability of Seller under any guaranty, warranty or other indemnity set forth herein is limited to the cost of reprocessing the products (if required) and the manufacturing costs of the Buyer's product being processed.

卖方保证在经营的业务中根据现行适用的行业标准程序,提供技术合格、态度专业的服务,并与所有适合的本合同所承担的保证相符。卖方提供的服务不受本合同包含的服务条款和条件以外的任何保证、担保或其他补偿的限制;卖方根据本合同订明的保证、担保或其他补偿条款所需承担的最大责任仅限于产品再处理(如要求)的成本和正在处理的客户产品的制造成本。

1. all services... shall be provided in a professional and workmanlike manner, with a degree of skill and care consistent with current, good and sound professional procedures,/ and in conformity with all applicable contractual commitments.

这是标准的服务保证。前半句是人云亦云的客套话：服务提供者肯定要根据当下适用的行业标准提供服务，并且要技术合格、态度专业；后半句（提供的服务与所有适合的本合同所承担的保证相符）是根据具体需要或合同附件或其他条款中详细说明的内容［服务项目、服务人员的资格、服务水准（如随叫随到或在多少工作日内解决问题）等］提供特别的服务。值得注意的是，合同的其他条款或附件必须有相关内容提及较详细、较具体的服务内容，否则这半句就是多余，可以免除。

2. 本段第二句讲的是卖方不提供超出合同规定范围的服务（No service... is subject to any guaranty... beyond...）；卖方在提供服务时万一有失，最高的赔偿是什么……：根据本款，卖方最大责任是承担问题产品的所有维修或重新制造的成本而已（is limited to the cost of reprocessing the products... and the manufacturing costs of... the Buyer's product being processed）。这也算公平了，产品出了问题难道要让卖方赔得"家破人亡"、关门大吉？

（四）不提供保证条款的写法

除了以上的 No service... shall be beyond...，以及 liability of Seller... is limited to 这两种之外，还有另外三种常用的表达方式：

a. Party A <u>makes no warranties</u>, express or implied, and <u>hereby disclaim</u>...

b. Seller <u>makes no warranties about</u> the condition of the goods. The goods are sold "AS IS."

c. Seller <u>shall not be liable for</u> any direct, consequential, or other damages suffered by Buyer or any third parties resulting from the use, production, manufacture, sale, lease, consumption, or advertisement of the product.

（五）保证期限条款的写法

写作保证条款时，有时还会涉及保证期限问题，基本写法是：The foregoing representations and warranties shall terminate as of the third (3rd) anniversary of the Effective Date of this agreement.

但这类表述一般只适用于对纯粹的服务项目的保证，因为对产品的保证一般都已经在保证条款中明确提及，如 <u>free from defects in materials and workmanship under normal use for a period of twelve (12) months</u>。

（六）对土地买卖的保证条款

商品性质不同，保证条款的内容和条件可以完全不同。以下是土地买卖的保证条款：

<u>Party A represents and warrants that</u> there are <u>no conditions at</u>, on, under, or <u>related to</u>, <u>the real property</u> constituting all or any portion of the land which presently or potentially pose a hazard to human health or the environment, whether or not in compliance with law, and there has been no manufacture, use, treatment, storage, transportation, or disposal of any hazardous or toxic substance, pollutant, or contaminant on the Land nor any release of any hazardous or toxic substance, pollutant, or contaminant into or upon or over the land.

(七) 对公司和合同合法性的保证

除了对产品保证之外,还有不少保证条款是用来保证公司存在的合法性,合同的合法性和签署合同人员身份的合法性的。例如:

The XXX Company is duly organized and registered and in good standing in the United States, has power and authority to enter into and perform this Agreement and any other agreements and documents executed or delivered by it in connection herewith.

Party A is validly created and existing under the laws of Delaware, the USA, has full power, authority, and approval to execute this Agreement and has all the necessary power, authority, and approval for the performance of its obligations under this Agreement.

Party A has taken all necessary corporate actions to authorize the execution of this Agreement. In signing this Agreement, Party A's representatives have full authority to execute and bind Party A to the Agreement by virtue of a valid power of attorney.

This Agreement shall constitute the legal, valid, and binding obligations of Party A, enforceable in accordance with the provisions of this Agreement.

The execution of this Agreement and the performance by Party A of its obligations hereunder will not violate any applicable laws, regulations, ordinances, permits or approvals of any governmental bodies or institutions or Party A's articles of association; nor will it lead to or constitute a breach or non-performance of such laws, regulations, ordinances, permits, approvals, articles of association.

Each Party represents and warrants that: Its execution, delivery and performance of the Documents have been duly authorized by all necessary action.

If Disclosing Party breaches the representation and warranty in Clause 2.1, this Agreement will immediately terminate without any further action of any Party, and Disclosing Party will indemnify and hold harmless Receiving Party and its Affiliates from any losses, costs, damages or claims of any kind as a result of that breach.

(八) 对产品用途合法性的保证

第三种保证是保证产品用途的合法性。跟美国人做生意、尤其是跟高科技产品有关的生意,特别麻烦(就像跟一个穷极无赖的人纠缠不休一样),因为美国政府要求买方保证不让产品作军事用途或转售给美国认为是敌对的任何国家,尤其是落入恐怖分子的手中(否则,哪怕是亲兄弟也会被它搞得家破人亡)。这类保证通常这样写:

Buyer represents and warrants that it: (a) understands that the Equipment is subject to export controls under the U.S. Commerce Department's Export Administration Regulations ("EAR"); (b) is not located in a prohibited destination country under the EAR or U.S. sanctions regulations (currently Cuba, Iran, Iraq, Libya, North Korea, Sudan and Syria); (c) will not export, re-export, or transfer the Equipment to any prohibited destination, entity, or individual without the necessary export licenses or authorizations from the U.S. Government; (d) will not use or transfer the Equipment for use in any sensitive nuclear, chemical or biological weapons, or missile technology end-uses unless authorized by the U. S. Government by regulation or specific license; (e) <u>understands and agrees</u> that if it is in the United States and exports or transfers the Equipment to eligible end users, it will, as required by EAR Section 741. 17 (e), submit semi-annual reports to the Commerce Department's Bureau of Industry & Security (BIS), which include the name and address (including country) of each transferee; and (f) understands that countries other than the United States may restrict the import, use, or export of encryption products and that it <u>shall be solely responsible for compliance with</u> any such import, use, or export restrictions.

五、参考条款及译文

合同的内容可以有千差万别，所以保证条款可以因合同标的不同而有所差异。以下提供各类不同合同保证条款的写法以及译法（笔者对其中一些注明出处的译文做了订正）：

Representations and Warranties	陈述及保证
对普通商品的保证：	
The Seller <u>warrants that</u> all commodities will conform to the description set out in Clause 1. Save as aforesaid all representations, conditions and warranties of whatsoever nature are hereby excluded and extinguished. （王辉，2007：81）	卖方保证所有商品符合第 1 条规定的规格说明。除了前述本协议在此排除和废止所有任何性质的声明、条件或保证。
Limited Warranty on Media. Apple warrants the media on which the Apple Software is recorded and delivered by Apple to <u>be free from defects in materials and workmanship</u> <u>under normal use</u> <u>for a period of ninety (90) days from the date of original retail purchase</u>. Your <u>exclusive remedy</u> under this Section shall be, <u>at Apple's option</u>, <u>a refund of the purchase price of the product</u> containing the Apple Software <u>or replacement of</u> the Apple Software which is returned to Apple or an Apple authorized representative with a copy of the receipt. This limited warranty and any implied warranties on the media including, but not limited to, the implied <u>warranties of merchantability, of satisfactory quality, and of fitness for a particular purpose</u>, are limited in duration to ninety (90) days from the date of original retail purchase.	最新近的大品牌保证条款：给予媒体工具的有限保证。苹果公司保证：由苹果公司用以录制和提供苹果软件的媒体工具无任何材料和工艺上的缺陷，给予正常情况使用的九十(90)天保证（从原零售购买之日起）。根据本条，给予贵方的唯一补偿是凭退货收据副本退还包含苹果软件产品的购买款、或者更换退还给苹果公司或苹果公司授权代理商的苹果软件产品（由苹果公司决定）。给予媒体工具的有限保证及默示保证包括但不限于产品适销性保证、质量满意度保证以及适合特定用途保证，保证期为从原零售购买之日起的九十(90)天。

续表

Representations and Warranties	陈述及保证
Some jurisdictions do not allow limitations on how long an implied warranty lasts, so the above limitation may not apply to you. The limited warranty set forth herein is the only warranty made to you and is provided in lieu of any other warranties (if any) created by any documentation or packaging. This limited warranty gives you specific legal rights, and you may also have other rights which vary by jurisdiction.	某些司法管辖区不允许对隐含保证期长短加以限制,因此上述限制可能并不适用于你。本保证条款规定的有限保证是对你做出的唯一保证,取代任何产品文件或包装材料上的任何其他保证(如有)。本有限保证书赋予你特定的法律权利,你可能还拥有因司法管辖区而异的其他权利。
Seller warrants that all Products sold hereunder shall be free from defects in materials and workmanship for a period of six (6) months from the date of Buyer's receipt ("Warranty"). In the event of a breach of this Warranty, Seller shall, at Seller's option, either (i) repair the applicable product at the original F.O.B. point of delivery, (ii) refund an equitable portion of the contract price, or (iii) furnish replacement equipment or parts, as necessary to the original F.O.B. point of delivery. Except as specifically set forth in the preceding sentences, Seller makes no warranties either express or implied with respect to the products sold hereunder.	卖方保证根据本合同所售的所有产品的用料和做工自买方获取收据("保证书")之日起六(6)个月内均无瑕疵。一旦违反本保证,卖方应由自己选择,可(i)在原先 FOB 交货地点修复瑕疵产品;或(ii)返还合同价的对等金额;或(iii)在原先 FOB 交货地点提供替换产品或部件。除上句具体规定外,卖方对根据本合同售出的产品不做任何其他明示或暗示的保证。
The Party A will give the Party B the same limited warranty for each of the Goods sold as the Party A provides for its own customers. The Party B must furnish the Party A's warranty to every person that purchases any Goods from it. The Party B is prohibited from altering any terms of the Party A's warranty. The Party A will promptly repair or replace any Goods that malfunction, fail to operate, or are otherwise defective and that area covered under the warranty, regardless of whether the Party B or the Party B's customer own the goods at the time. (乔焕然,2008:103)	甲方应为每件货品给予乙方如甲方提供给自己的客户的同样的有限保证。乙方必须将甲方的保证提供给每一个购买其货品的人。乙方不得对甲方的担保条款做出任何变更。甲方应及时修理或替换任何出现故障、无法操作、有其他缺陷或本保证书担保的其他问题货品,无论乙方或乙方的顾客在此时是否拥有该货品。

续表

Representations and Warranties	陈述及保证
Seller warrants that all material, work product, and merchandise supplied under the Order (a) shall strictly conform to all specifications, drawings, samples, or other descriptions furnished to and approved by Buyer, (b) shall be fit and serviceable for the purpose intended, as agreed to by Buyer and Seller, (c) shall be of good quality and free from defects in materials and workmanship, (d) shall be new and not refurbished or reconditioned, unless expressly agreed in writing by Buyer, and (e) shall not infringe any patent, copyright, mask work, trademark, trade secret or other intellectual property, proprietary or contractual right of any third party. In addition, Seller warrants that Buyer shall have good and marketable title to all goods (including all components thereof) purchased by Buyer pursuant to the Order, free of all liens and encumbrances and that no licenses are required for Buyer to use such goods.	卖方保证本订单下供应的所有原料、制成品和商品(a)须严格符合买方提供和认可的产品规格、图纸、样品或其他说明,(b)均为双方约定的合格产品并符合预期的用途,(c)品质优良,无原料和工艺缺陷,(d)除有买方明确的书面同意者外,为全新产品,无翻新或修复品,(e)无侵犯任何第三方的任何专利权、著作权、掩膜作品权、商标权、商业秘密或者其他的知识产权、专有权或合同权。此外,卖方保证买方拥有根据订单所购全部货物(包括货物的全部零部件)的合法交易权,无任何留置权或抵押权,且买方在使用上述货物时无须任何许可证。
对提供的服务的保证:	
Seller warrants that all services shall be provided <u>in a professional and workmanlike manner</u>, with a degree of skill and care consistent with current, good and sound professional procedures. Neither receipt of material, work product or merchandise nor payment therefor shall constitute a waiver of this provision. If a breach of warranty occurs, Buyer may, <u>in its sole discretion</u>, and without waiving any other rights, return for credit or require prompt correction or replacement of the nonconforming goods or services.	卖方保证根据现行适用的行业标准程序,提供技术合格、态度专业的服务。买方接受原料、制成品和商品或者支付其货款并不代表放弃该保证条款。如果违反本保证,买方可在不放弃任何其他权利的情况下单方面决定退货并要求将货款计入贷方账户,或要求立即更正或更换不合格之产品或服务。
<u>Each service</u> performed or otherwise delivered or provided, as the case may be, by the Seller in the operation of the Business, <u>has been in conformity with all applicable contractual commitments and all express and implied warranties</u>, and <u>the Seller does not have any liability</u> (and, to the knowledge of the Seller, there is no basis for any action, suit, proceeding, hearing, investigation, charge, complaint, claim or demand against the Seller) <u>for any damages in connection therewith</u>, subject only to the reserve for warranty claims set forth in the Financial Statements. <u>No service provided by the Seller in the operation of the</u>	在经营生意中卖方履行或提供的每项服务(视具体情况)与所有适合的合同承担和所有明示和暗示的保证相符,卖方对与服务相关的任何损害不承担任何法律责任(据卖方所知,没有针对卖方的任何法律行动、诉讼、程序、听证、调查、控告、投诉、索赔或要求),

续表

Representations and Warranties	陈述及保证
Business is subject to any guaranty, warranty or other indemnity beyond the terms and conditions of service contained in the customer Contracts, and except as set forth on Schedule 3.1(0), the maximum potential liability of the Seller under any guaranty, warranty or other indemnity set forth in the Contracts with the 25 largest customers of the Business (as such Contracts are referenced in Section 3.1(l)(ii)) is limited to the cost of reprocessing the products (if required) and the manufacturing costs of the customers product being processed.	但仅受财务报表中列明的担保索赔的管制。在经营生意中,卖方提供的服务不受客户合同包含的服务条款和条件以外的任何保证、担保或其他补偿的限制;除附表 3.1(0)规定之外,卖方与 25 名最大客户在合同(该等合同详见于第 3.1(l)(ii)条)订明的保证、担保或其他补偿条款中所需承担的最大责任,仅限于产品再处理(如要求)的成本和正在处理的客户产品的制造成本。
卖方的保证条款:	
4.1 The Sellers warrant to the Buyer in the terms of the Warranties. 4.2 Any information supplied by or on behalf of the Company or on behalf of the Sellers in connection with the Warranties, the Disclosure Letter or otherwise in relation to the business and affairs of the Company shall not constitute a representation or warranty or guarantee as to the accuracy thereof by the Company and the Sellers undertake to the Buyer and the Company (and its respective directors, officers, employees, agents and advisers) that they will not bring any claims which any of them might otherwise have against the Company or any of its respective directors, officers, employees, agents or advisers in respect thereof. 4.3 Each of the Warranties shall be construed as a separate warranty, and (unless expressly provided to the contrary) shall not be limited by the terms of any of the other Warranties or by any other term of this agreement. 4.4 The liability of the Sellers under the Warranties and the Tax Warranties shall be limited in the manner set out in Schedule 4. 4.5 The Sellers shall give to the Buyer all such information and documentation relating to the Company as the Buyer shall require to enable it to satisfy itself as to whether there has been any breach of the Warranties.	4.1 卖方向买方保证遵守本保证书的条款。 4.2 由公司或代表公司或代表卖方提供的与本保证书有关的任何资料、披露信或与公司生意及事务有关的其他方面的任何资料不构成公司对这些资料准确性的陈述、保证或担保,卖方向买方和公司(及其相关的董事、高级职员、雇员、代理及顾问)承诺:卖方不会就上述资料的准确性对公司或其任何相关的董事、高级职员、雇员、代理或顾问提起索赔诉讼。 4.3 每个保证书应解释为单独保证书,除明文有相反规定,各保证书不受任何其他担保条款或本协议中任何其他条款的限制。 4.4 本保证书及税务保证书项下的卖方责任受附表 4 规定的限制。 4.5 卖方应向买方提供有关公司的所有的这一类资料和文件,因为买方需要充分了解卖方是否存在任何违反本保证书的情况。

续表

Representations and Warranties	陈述及保证
不提供额外保证的条款：	
No product or service manufactured, sold, leased, licensed or delivered by the Company <u>is subject to any guaranty, warranty, right of return, right of credit or other indemnity</u> other than (i) the applicable standard terms and conditions of sale or lease of the Company, which are set forth in Section 2.2 of the Disclosure Schedule; and (ii) manufacturers warranties for which the Company does not have any liability. Section 2.2 of the Disclosure Schedule <u>sets forth the aggregate expenses incurred by the Company in fulfilling its obligations under its guaranty, warranty, right of return and indemnity provisions</u> during each of the fiscal years and the interim period covered by the Financial Statements; and the Company does not know of any reason why such expenses should significantly increase as a percentage of sales in the future.	公司制造、出售、租赁、特许或交付的任何产品或服务不接受任何担保、保证、退货权、债权或其他赔偿，但下列情况则属例外：(i)第2.2款披露附表述明的适用于公司租售的标准条款和条件；以及(ii)制造商保证公司不负任何责任。第2.2款披露附表述明公司在每个财政年度和资产负债表涵盖的过渡期内为履行其担保、保证、退货权和赔偿义务而产生的总费用；公司不知晓为何该费用会在将来销售比重中大幅增加。
对土地买卖的保证：	
Party A <u>represents and warrants</u> that <u>there are no conditions at, on, under, or related to, the real property constituting all or any portion of the land which presently or potentially pose a hazard to human health or the environment</u>, whether or not in compliance with law, and there has been <u>no manufacture, use, treatment, storage, transportation, or disposal of any hazardous or toxic substance, pollutant, or contaminant on the Land nor any release of any hazardous or toxic substance, pollutant, or contaminant into or upon or over the land</u>. Party A further represents and warrants that the Land <u>is free and clear of any and all claims, charges, easement, encumbrances, lease, covenants, security interest, liens, option, pledge, rights of others, or restrictions</u>, whether imposed by agreement, understanding, law, equity or otherwise.（乔焕然，2008：102）	甲方陈述和保证，构成土地全部或任何部分的房地产，其内部、上面、下面或其相关的部位现在不存在，也不可能存在危害人体健康或环境的状况（无论是否符合法律规定），且土地上从未生产、使用、处理、储存、运输或处置过任何危险的或有毒的物质、污染物、或致污物。 甲方进一步陈述和保证，土地不存在（无论是以协议、谅解、普通法、衡平法还是其他方法设定的）任何权利主张、抵押、地役权、产权负担、租约、契约、担保权益、留置权、购买权、质押、他人权利或限制。

续表

Representations and Warranties	陈述及保证
对出售的业务（生意）的保证条款：	
Sellers hereby represent and warrant that there is no pending administrative, civil, or criminal litigation involving the business sold, nor any demands or claims that would materially and adversely affect the same or Seller's financial condition. In the event of breach of this warranty, Buyer may rescind this Agreement and any consideration paid by it to Sellers will be returned.（王辉，2007:77）	卖方兹陈述并保证所出售之业务没有涉及任何未决之行政、民事或刑事方面的诉讼，也不存在可能会对该业务或卖方的财务状况产生重大不利影响的任何要求或权利请求。 一旦违背本保证，买方可解除本协议，已支付给卖方的任何对价应退还买方。
知识（信息）产权保证条款：	
2.1 Disclosing Party represents and warrants to Receiving Party that it has the right and authority to disclose the Confidential Information to Receiving Party under this Confidentiality Agreement. 2.2 If Disclosing Party breaches the representation and warranty in Clause 2.1, this Agreement will immediately terminate without any further action of any Party, and Disclosing Party will indemnify and hold harmless Receiving Party and its Affiliates from any losses, costs, damages or claims of any kind as a result of that breach.（范文祥，2008: 106）	2.1 披露方向接受方陈述及保证，他有权向接受方披露本协议项下的保密信息。 2.2 如披露方违反第2.1款的陈述及保证，任何一方无须采取任何行动即可立刻终止本协议，而披露方应对接受方及其关联公司做出补偿，使接受方及其关联公司不会因披露方违反该保证和陈述而遭受任何种类的损失、费用、损害或索赔。
Licensors make no warranties, express or implied, and hereby disclaim all such warranties, as to the merchantability, or fitness for a particular purpose of the invention or product; or that the use of the licensed product will not infringe any patent, copyrights, trademarks, or other rights. Licensors shall not be liable for any direct, consequential, or other damages suffered by any licensee or any third parties resulting from the use, production, manufacture, sale, lease, consumption, or advertisement of the product. Notwithstanding the foregoing, Licensors represent and warrant to Licensee that they have no actual knowledge of invalidity of any of the Intellectual Property Rights licensed to Licensee under this Agreement. Licensors further represent and warrant that they have the full power and authority, without any conflict with the rights of others, to grant the licenses to Licensee contained in this Agreement. Licensors will promptly bring to the attention of the Licensee any Licensed Intellectual Property Rights or Additional Licensed Intellectual Property Rights not theretofore disclosed to Licensee.	许可方不做明示或暗示的保证，因此否认以下的所有保证：具有某种发明或产品特定用途的适销性或适用性；或使用许可产品不侵犯任何专利、版权、商标权或其他权利。由于产品的使用、生产、制造、销售、租赁、消费或广告宣传而给任何被许可方或第三方带来的任何直接、间接或其他损害，许可方不负任何法律责任。尽管有上述规定，许可方仍向被许可方陈述及保证：许可方并不知晓根据本协议规定向被许可方提供的任何知识产权是否无效。许可方做进一步陈述及保证：许可方有完全权利（与其他权利并不相冲突）向被许可方授予本协议包含的执照。许可方将即时提请

续表

Representations and Warranties	陈述及保证
	被许可方注意任何尚未披露给被许可方的被许可的知识产权或额外被许可的知识产权。
对公司合法性的保证条款：	
Party A hereby represents and warrants to the other Parties that: Party A is validly created and existing under the laws of Delaware, the USA, has full power, authority, and approval to execute this Agreement and has all the necessary power, authority, and approval for the performance of its obligations under this Agreement; Party A has taken all necessary corporate actions to authorize the execution of this Agreement. In signing this Agreement, Party A's representatives have full authority to execute and bind Party A to the Agreement by virtue of a valid power of attorney; This Agreement shall constitute the legal, valid, and binding obligations of Party A, enforceable in accordance with the provisions of this Agreement; The execution of this Agreement and the performance by Party A of its obligations hereunder will not violate any applicable laws, regulations, ordinances, permits or approvals of any governmental bodies or institutions or Party A's articles of association; nor will it lead to or constitute a breach or non-performance of such laws, regulations, ordinances, permits, approvals, articles of association. Party A and the Guarantor hereby undertakes to indemnify and keep indemnified the other Parties for any costs, expenses, liabilities, and losses which arise as a result of any breach by Party A or the Guarantor of its representations and warranties hereunder. （范文祥、吴怡，2008：100）	甲方向合同其他方保证： 甲方是一家根据美国特拉华州法律组建并存续的公司，完全有权力并已获得批准签署本协议，而且有必要的权力并获得必要的批准执行本协议项下的义务； 甲方已获得所有必要的公司决议授权签署本协议。甲方代表在签署本协议时通过有效的授权书完全有权签署本协议并对甲方具有约束力。 本协议对甲方构成合法、有效并有约束力的义务，根据本协议条件能够得以执行。 甲方签订本协议并履行协议项下的义务并不违反任何法律、法规、法令、政府部门或机构的许可或批准，或甲方的公司章程，也不会导致或构成违反或不遵守这些法律、法规、法令、政府部门或机构的许可或批准，或甲方的公司章程。 甲方及其担保人在此承诺，赔偿合同其他方因甲方或其担保人违反其陈述及保证而产生的所有费用、开支、负债或损失。
Each Party represents and warrants that: (a) It is duly organized and registered and in good standing in the United States, has power and authority to enter into and perform this Agreement and any other agreements and documents executed or delivered by it in connection herewith (collectively, with this Agreement, "the Documents").	各方陈述并保证： (a)它是在美国国内合法成立和注册的公司，符合各项规定，它有权力签订并履行本协议及由其签署并递交的、与之有关的任何其他协议和文件（本协议内统称为"文件"）。

续表

Representations and Warranties	陈述及保证
(b)Its execution, delivery and performance of the Documents have been <u>duly authorized</u> by all necessary action. (范文祥、吴怡,2008:33)	(b)文件的签署、递交和履行已经通过一切必要行动做了正式授权。
Each Party represents and warrants to the other Party that on the date hereof and as of the effective Date: (a)it is an independent legal person duly organized, validly existing in good standing under the laws of the place of its establishment or incorporation; (b)it has full authority to enter into this Contract and to perform its obligations hereunder; (c)it has authorized its representative to sign this Contract and from and after the Effective Date the provisions of this Contract shall be legally binding upon it; (d)its execution of this Contract and its performance of its obligations hereunder: (i) will not violate any provision of its business license, articles of incorporation, articles of association or similar organizational documents; (ii) will not violate any Applicable Laws or any governmental authorization or approval; and (iii) will not violate or result in a default under any contract to which it is a party or to which it is subject; (e)no lawsuit, arbitration or other legal or governmental proceeding is pending or, to its knowledge, threatened against it that would affect its ability to perform its obligations under this Contract; (f)and it has disclosed to the other Party all documents issued by any governmental department that may have a material adverse effect on its ability to fully perform its obligations under this Contract, and the documents previously provided by it to the other Party do not contain any misstatements or omissions of material facts. If any of the above representations and warranties of a Party are not accurate in all material respects on the date hereof or the Effective Date, then such Party shall be in material breach of this Contract. (乔焕然,2008:103)	双方互为陈述并保证,于本合同签订日以及生效日: (a)根据其组建或成立地的法律,该方为独立法人、依法定程序设立、有效存续,且相关手续完备; (b)该方有全权订立本合同以及履行本合同项下义务; (c)该方已授权其代表签署本合同,从生效日开始,本合同的条款对其具有法律约束力。 (d)该方签署本合同并履行本合同项下义务:(i)不违反其营业执照、成立章程、经营章程或类似组织文件的任何规定;(ii)不违反任何相关法律或任何政府授权或批准;并且(iii)不违反其作为当事人一方(或受之约束)的其他任何合同,也不会导致其在该合同项下违约; (e)不存在将影响该方履行本合同项下义务的能力的、待决的诉讼、仲裁或其他司法或行政程序,而且根据其所知也无人威胁将采取上述行动;并且 (f)该方已经向另一方披露任何政府机构颁发的可能对其全面履行其在本合同项下义务的能力造成重大不利影响的所有文件,并且该方此前提供给另一方的文件中没有对任何重要事实的不实陈述或遗漏。 如果在本合同签订日或生效日,一方上述的任何陈述或担保在所有重要方面不准确,则构成该方重大违约。

续表

Representations and Warranties	陈述及保证
对签署合同的内容和执行合同的合法性的保证：	
Micron represents and warrants to Intel that, to the best of Micron's knowledge, as of the Effective Date: (a) Micron has full title to, and ownership of, the free and clear of all liens and has the right to transfer such ownership to Intel; (b) [* * *]; (c) Micron has the right to transfer the Tangible Design Package to Intel; (d) Micron has the right to grant the licenses to the Supported Materials granted hereunder; (e) Micron has not granted any rights in or to the Pre-existing Product Designs or Supporting Materials that conflict with the rights granted to Intel under this Agreement; (f) there are no unresolved claims, demands or pending litigation relating to the Pre-existing Product Designs or Supporting Materials; and (g) the Pre-existing Product Designs and Supporting Materials do not contain any Publicly Available Software. The foregoing representations and warranties shall terminate as of the tenth (10th) anniversary of the Effective Date, except for Section 5.1 (f), which shall terminate as of the second (2nd) anniversary of the Effective Date. Any claim by Intel that any representation or warranty was untrue must be made before expiration of the applicable foregoing time period, otherwise Micron shall have no liability whatsoever with respect to any such representations and warranties.	据Micron知晓，自生效日期起Micron向Intel陈述及保证：(a)Micron完全有权和所有权免除所有留置权，并有权将该所有权转让给Intel；(b)[* * *]；(c)Micron有权将有形设计包转让给Intel；(d)Micron有权准许根据本协议准许的支持材料的执照；(e)Micron不准许与本协议规定准许Intel权利相冲突的既有产品设计或支持材料的任何权利；(f)没有与既有产品设计或支持材料相关的未解决的索赔、要求或未决诉讼；以及(g)既有的产品设计和支持材料不包含任何公共获取的软件。上述陈述和保证应于生效日期的第十(10)个周年之时终止，除5.1(f)条规定应于生效日期第二(2)个周年之时终止。Intel提出的任何索赔(即任何陈述或保证不准确)必须在上述期间到期之前，否则Micron对任何该等陈述和保证不承担责任。
OMP represents and warrants to Triax that: (a) OMP has full authority to execute and perform this Agreement; (b) this Agreement has been duly executed and delivered by OMP and constitutes the legal, enforceable and binding obligation of OMP; (c) OMP's execution and performance of this Agreement will not conflict with the terms or conditions of any other agreement or contract to which OMP is a party or is otherwise bound; (d) no approval, action or authorization by any governmental authority or agency is required for OMP's execution and performance hereof which has not already been obtained; and (e) OMP will notify Triax within twenty-four (24) hours of receiving any notice or upon discovery of any adverse event arising from the sale or use of the Products.	OMP向Triax陈述和保证：(a)OMP完全有权签署和履行本协议；(b)本协议由OMP合法签署和递交，并构成OMP合法、可强制执行和具有约束力的义务；(c)OMP签署和履行本协议与其他OMP为协议方或受约束的任何协议的条款或条件不冲突；(d)OMP签署和履行尚未获取的本协议不要求任何政府部门或代理机构的批准、作为或授权；以及(e)OMP将于接到任何通知

续表

Representations and Warranties	陈述及保证
	或发现由产品销售或产品使用带来的任何不利事件的二十四(24)小时内通知 Triax。
Lessor represents and warrants that Lessor has good clear and marketable title to the System and the Equipment, free from any and all liens and encumbrances, and shall defend the title to the System and Equipment against any adverse claims. Lessor represents and warrants that no person holds a claim or interest in the System and Equipment that arise from an act or omission of an act by Lessor that will interfere with Lessee's use of the Equipment during the Term. Lessor represents and warrants that the equipment and software complies with federal and state gaming laws and regulations. Lessor agrees to hold harmless and indemnify Lessee for any damages, losses, claims, causes of action, expenses (including attorney's fees) for any injury to person or damage to property caused by or related to the System, equipment, or parts supplied to Lessee by Lessor. Lessor will not indemnify Lessee or End User for loss of profits, reimbursement for prizes, use of coupons, or other promotional items.	出租人陈述和保证出租人对系统和设备享有良好的销售权,不受一切留置权及其他权利的负担影响,并应针对任何不利诉求维护其对系统和设备的所有权。出租人陈述和保证任何人不得由于出租人行为或忽略行为导致承租人在合同期间中断使用设备而对系统和设备提出权利或利益诉求。出租人陈述和保证设备和软件遵守联邦和州的诉因和费用(包括律师费)法律和法规。出租人同意不伤害且同意赔偿承租人因出租人提供给承租人的系统、设备、部件而造成人身和财产损害或与之有关的任何损坏、损失、索赔、诉讼。出租人将不赔偿承租人或终端用户利润损失、奖品偿还、优惠券使用或其他促销商品。
遵守进出口条例的保证条款:	
2.1 Buyer represents and warrants that it: (a) understands that the Equipment is subject to export controls under the U. S. Commerce Department's Export Administration Regulations ("EAR"); (b) is not located in a prohibited destination country under the EAR or U. S. sanctions regulations (currently Cuba, Iran, Iraq, Libya, North Korea, Sudan and Syria); (c) will not export, re-export, or transfer the Equipment to any prohibited destination, entity, or individual without the necessary export licenses or authorizations from the U. S. Government; (d) will not use or transfer the Equipment for use in any sensitive nuclear, chemical or biological weapons, or missile technology end-uses unless authorized by the U. S. Government by regulation or specific license; (e) understands and agrees that if it is in the United States and exports or transfers the Equipment to eligible end users, it will, as required by EAR Section 741.17(e), submit semi-annual reports	2.1 买方陈述及保证:(a)买方理解,该设备受美国商务部《出口管理条例》的出口管制;(b)买方不在上述《出口管理条例》或美国制裁措施所涉及的任何被禁目的国(目前指古巴、伊朗、伊拉克、利比亚、朝鲜、苏丹及叙利亚)境内;(c)未经美国政府许可或授权,买方不会向任何被禁地区、实体或个人出口、转口销售或转让该设备;(d)除非由美国政府合法授权或经特别许可,买方不会将该设备用于任何敏感的核

续表

Representations and Warranties	陈述及保证
to the Commerce Department's Bureau of Industry & Security (BIS), which include the name and address (including country) of each transferee; and (f) understands that countries other than the United States may restrict the import, use, or export of encryption products and that it <u>shall be solely responsible for compliance with</u> any such import, use, or export restrictions. 2.2 If Buyer is in breach of this <u>presentation and warrants</u> in Clause 2.1 herein, Seller shall have the right to terminate this Purchase Agreement by a mere notice of termination and claim any loss and/or damage thus incurred. (范文祥、吴怡,2008:105)	能、化学或生物武器或导弹技术的最终应用目的,也不会将之转让给他人用于此类目的;(e)买方理解并同意,如其在美国境内向合格的终端用户出口或转让设备,则买方将按上述《出口管理条例》第741.17(e)条的规定,每半年向美国商务部的行业安全局提交一份报告,说明各受让人的姓名、地址(包括所属国)等情况;且(f)买方理解,美国以外的其他国家可能会限制密码产品的进口、使用或出口,买方应对遵守这些进口、使用或出口限制负完全责任。 2.2 如由于买方违反本协议第2.1条的陈述或保证,卖方有权通过终止通知即可终止本协议,并有权要求买方承担由此造成的任何损失和/或损害。

第十一章 责任及义务条款的写作和翻译

一、引言

在探索合同的责任和义务条款的写作规律中,笔者经过查阅数以百计的含有此条款的合同后发现:绝大多数这类条款都与高级职员的雇佣有关。其实,绝大部分合同的责任条款都要落实到具体的人事任命上,笼统地让一家公司或抽象的法人承担义务和责任的文字非常有限。而雇佣合适的人才,要有适当的任命,赋予相应的职责和权力。所以,我们也就容易明白为何责任条款都与公司或机构的重要人员雇佣有关。

此外,各种合同条款中出现频率颇高的几组法律概念词往往离不开"权利"与"义务"[①]。这两个概念也总是相辅相成的:某个个体或法人要享有合同规定的某种"权利",就必须承担起相应的"义务"或责任。"义务"和"职责"有各种表达方式。在汉语中表述这类概念的词非常有限,主要是"负责"以及"承担责任或义务";在法律英文中表示这类概念的词汇就非常丰富。因此,在将汉语中的"负责"概念翻译成确切的英文时,难度非常大。所以,从本章的第五部分开始,将重点讨论法律英文中有关"负责"和"义务"概念的其他各种表述。

[①] 对"义务""职责""责任",本文不做任何严格界定或区分,可以翻译成 duty, obligation, responsibility 等等。《中华人民共和国宪法》的官方英译本,将"职责"和"义务"等同,在绝大部分情况下翻译成 duty,但有时也译成 obligation 和 responsibility。例如:第五十五条 保卫祖国、抵抗侵略是中华人民共和国每一个公民的神圣职责。依照法律服兵役和参加民兵组织是中华人民共和国公民的光荣义务。(It is the sacred duty of every citizen of the People's Republic of China to defend the motherland and resist aggression. It is the honorable duty of citizens of the People's Republic of China to perform military service and join the militia in accordance with the law.)而另一个版本则将其翻译成:It is the sacred obligation of every citizen of the People's Republic of China to defend the motherland and resist aggression. It is the honorable duty of citizens of the People's Republic of China to perform military service and join the militia in accordance with the law. 不过,也有把"职责"翻译成 responsibility 的译法,例如:第八十九条 国务院行使下列职权:……(三)规定各部和各委员会的任务和职责,统一领导各部和各委员会的工作,并且领导不属于各部和各委员会的全国性的行政工作;(Article 89... (3) to formulate the tasks and responsibilities of the ministries and commissions of the State Council, to exercise unified leadership over the work of the ministries and commissions and to direct all other administrative work of a national character that does not fall within the jurisdiction of the ministries and commissions;) 总之,这三个词可视为同义词,其定义就如同普通人所理解的,在法律文本中均指一种义不容辞的责任。

二、责任及义务条款的样本及译文

Duties/Responsibilities and Obligations	责任及义务	使用说明
During the Term, Employee shall[1] <u>devote his full time and efforts to</u> the service of THE COMPANY, shall[1] <u>perform his duties</u> honestly, diligently, competently, in good faith and <u>in the best interests of</u> THE COMPANY and shall <u>use his best efforts to</u> promote the interests of THE COMPANY. Employee shall <u>perform the duties consistent with his role as</u> President and Chief Executive Officer, <u>subject to</u> direction from THE COMPANY's Board of Directors.	在雇佣期限内,雇员应当全职和全力为公司服务,应当诚实勤勉、尽其能力为公司的最佳利益而履行职责,应当竭尽所能为增进公司的利益服务。雇员应当履行与其作为公司总裁和首席执行官的角色相符的职责,但仍然必须遵循公司董事会的指示。	笼统规定公司总裁或首席执行官的职责
The Company hereby <u>engages Executive as a</u> full-time executive employee and Executive accepts such employment, on the terms and <u>subject to</u>[2] the conditions set forth in this Agreement. During the Term, Executive shall <u>devote all of his business time and best efforts to</u>, and shall <u>perform</u> faithfully, loyally and efficiently, his duties as President of the Company and shall <u>exercise such powers</u> and <u>fulfill such responsibilities</u> as may be duly <u>assigned to or vested</u> in him by the Operating Agreement or by the Managers of the Company (the "Managers") consistent with the responsibilities of the President. During the Term, Executive will not <u>engage</u> in other employment or consulting work or any trade or business for his own account or on behalf of any other Person. <u>Notwithstanding the foregoing</u>, Executive may (i) <u>serve</u> on such corporate, civic, industry or charitable boards or committees as are approved by the Managers and (ii) manage his own and his immediate family's personal investments, provided that the activities permitted by clauses (i) and (ii) above shall not, individually or in the aggregate, interfere in any <u>material</u> respect with the performance of Executive's responsibilities hereunder.	本公司兹雇佣"执行官"作为本公司的全职主管级雇员,"执行官"按照本协议订明的条件接受此雇佣。在雇佣期间,"执行官"应当尽忠职守、全心全意、高效努力地以公司总裁身份履行职责,将其上班时间全部奉献给公司,还应当按照经营协议或公司管理层("管理层")可能正式赋予的与公司总裁职责一致的权力和责任去行使这些权力和履行这些职责。在任职期间,"执行官"不得接受其他雇佣或顾问工作或为自己或代表他人经营生意。尽管有前述规定,"执行官"如得到管理层的批准可以(i)在公司、民间、行业或慈善之类机构任职;(ii)管理自己及其家庭的个人投资,但上述第(i)和第(ii)款允许的活动,无论一项或数项活动,都不得在实质上干扰本协议以下规定的"执行官"职责的履行。	适合雇佣全职首席执行官的责任条款

续表

Duties/Responsibilities and Obligations	责任及义务	使用说明
Employee shall <u>serve as</u> the Chief Financial Officer of Employer <u>on a full-time basis</u> and shall <u>report to</u> the Chief Executive Officer of Employer. Employee shall <u>perform such duties and responsibilities assigned to</u> her from time to time by the Chief Executive Officer and by the Board of Directors of the Employer that are consistent with the titles held by Employee. If requested by the Board of Directors, Employee shall <u>serve</u> on any committee established by the Board of Directors without additional compensation. Employee agrees to <u>use her best efforts to perform</u> any and all <u>duties, responsibilities</u> and other services necessary or appropriate to <u>perform the functions of her position</u>, as modified, expanded or assigned, from time to time, by the Chief Executive Officer and/or the Board of Directors of Employer. During the term of this Agreement, Employee shall <u>devote</u> substantially all of her business <u>time and efforts to</u> the performance of her duties and responsibilities to the Employer. Employee agrees not to work for any other <u>business or enterprise</u> during the course of her employment with Employer, whether as an employee, agent, independent contractor or in any other capacity whatsoever, except passive ownership of real estate interests.	"雇员"将作为雇主公司全职的首席财务官受雇,"雇员"向雇主公司的首席执行官报告。"雇员"应当履行首席执行官及雇主公司董事会不时分派给她的与其职务相称的各项义务和职责。如果应董事会要求,"雇员"须担任董事会设立的各类委员会的职位而无额外报酬。"雇员"同意尽其所能履行其职务要求其行使或与其职务相称的所有职责及提供其他服务,而该职责和服务可由雇主公司的首席执行官和/或董事会不时予以修改、扩充或分配。在本协议期限内,"雇员"应当把她的上班时间和精力主要用于履行其对雇主公司的职责上。"雇员"同意在其受雇期间不为其他公司或企业工作,无论是以雇员、代理、独立承包人或以任何其他身份,但被动拥有地产利益则属例外。	首席财务官的职责,适合任何中型以上公司
The Consultant shall <u>perform</u> such <u>consulting and advisory</u> services <u>pertaining to</u> the Company's business as the Board of Directors and Chief Executive Officer of the Company shall from time to time request, which shall include, without limitation, <u>assisting</u> with the integration of the Company's and ABC's business <u>pursuant to</u> the Merger, and <u>assisting in</u> the growth of the Company. The Consultant further agrees to <u>perform</u> his duties <u>honestly, diligently, competently, in good faith</u> and <u>in the best interests of</u> the Company and shall give his best	"顾问"应当根据公司董事会及首席执行官不时提出的要求,履行与公司业务相关的顾问或咨询服务,其中包括但不限于就合并事宜协助公司与ABC业务的融合,协助公司的业务发展。"顾问"还同意在履行职责时尽职尽力、诚实勤勉、事事以公司利益为重。"顾问"还同意,在提供顾问服务期间应当代表本公司为服务工作奉献适当的时间,并遵守本公司所有的适用于"顾问"的政策和程序。本公司	适用于雇佣非全职的公司顾问(尤其适合与公司合并事宜相关的业务)

续表

Duties/Responsibilities and Obligations	责任及义务	使用说明
efforts in performing these duties for the Company. The Consultant further agrees that during the Consulting Period the Consultant shall <u>devote proper time to</u> the <u>rendering of services</u> on behalf of the Company and shall <u>follow</u> all policies and procedures of the Company applicable to the Consultant. The Company understands and acknowledges that the Consultant will not be providing full time services to the Company but only as requested and on a part time basis as requested by the Company in accordance with the scope of duties as provided in this Section 3.	理解并确认,"顾问"并非为本公司提供全职的服务,而是根据本公司请求、根据本协议的第3款在其职责范围内提供兼职服务。	
You agree to <u>perform the duties</u> of your positions, which shall be consistent with those customarily <u>assigned to</u> individuals serving in such positions, and such other duties consistent with your positions as may reasonably be <u>assigned to</u> you by the Board from time to time. You also agree that, while employed by the Company, you will <u>devote your full business time and your best efforts</u>, <u>business judgment, skill and knowledge exclusively to</u> the advancement of the business and interests of the Company in a manner consistent with your duties and to the <u>discharge of your duties and responsibilities</u> for the Company, except for vacation time, absence for sickness or disability, and reasonable time spent <u>performing services for</u> any charitable, religious or community organizations, so long as such services do not violate the Company's Confidentiality Agreement or the Company's Fair Competition Agreement (as defined in Section 3 hereof), or otherwise materially interfere with the performance of your duties hereunder.	你同意按你的职务履行职责以及执行其他任务。该职责应当与根据惯例分派给担任此职位的个人的职责相称;该其他任务也应当与公司董事会可能合理地不时分派给你、与你的职务任务相称。你还同意,在你受本公司雇佣期间,你会竭尽全力将你的全部上班时间、业务判断、技能知识完全用来发展公司的业务和增进公司的利益,尽本分为公司行使你的职责,履行你的义务;但在你的假期、因病或身体伤残而缺席期间则属例外,同时,你可以花适当的时间为慈善机构、宗教组织或社区团体提供服务——只要这些服务不违背本公司的保密协定或公平竞争协定(定义见本合约的第3款),或以其他方式严重干扰你履行本合同规定的职责。	适合任何全职雇员的通用责任条款

Duties/Responsibilities and Obligations	责任及义务	使用说明
You shall <u>provide advice to</u> the Company <u>with respect to</u>, <u>identify and evaluate</u> potential acquisitions, dispositions and/or business combinations in order to strengthen the Company's business prospects and to <u>increase</u> the Company's shareholder <u>value</u>, and <u>provide advice with respect to</u> such other matters as the Company's Board of Directors may request <u>from time to time</u> (the "Services"), all on a non-exclusive basis. You shall[1] <u>devote</u> the appropriate portion of your <u>time to</u> perform diligently the Services; however, nothing herein shall prevent you from <u>fulfilling</u> any of your obligations as a director of the Company or <u>engaging in</u> other businesses and activities that are not in violation of your obligations hereunder. You shall <u>inform</u> the Company promptly of any conditions or limitations which will or might affect your performance of the Services contemplated hereunder, including legal, ethical and personal conflicts; however, your failure to <u>comply with</u>[2] these provisions shall not <u>relieve you of</u> any of your <u>duties</u>, <u>liabilities or obligations</u> hereunder.	你应当为本公司鉴别、评估潜在的兼并、物业处置和/及业务合作机会，并提供咨询，以增进本公司的业务前景和股东利益，并就公司董事会可能不时提出要求的其他有关事项（"服务"）提供咨询，但所有该类咨询均属非独家性质。你应当勤勉地提供服务，奉献适量的时间；但是，本协议的规定并不阻碍你履行作为公司董事的任何义务、参与其他业务和活动，只要这些业务或活动不违背本协议中对你规定的义务。如有任何状况或限制会或可能会影响你履行本协议预定你须提供的"服务"——无论是法律上的、道德上的还是个人冲突方面的，你都应当及时通知公司；但是，如果你未能遵守这些规定，你根据本合同应尽之职责、责任或义务则不获免除。	雇佣非全职的公司顾问

三、责任条款的写作规律

在审阅与人事任命有关的责任和义务条款中，我们发现适用的表达方式相当多样，相关的关键词也非常丰富。例如：

（一）关键词

- perform faithfully, loyally and efficiently, and in the best interests of...
- engages sb. as
- devote one's full business time and one's best efforts, business judgment, skill and knowledge exclusively to
- use one's best efforts to perform any and all duties, responsibilities
- perform his duties and responsibilities assigned to him honestly, diligently, competently, and in good faith

- exercise such powers and fulfill such responsibilities
- give his best efforts
- performing these duties for
- engaging in other businesses and activities
- provide services
- rendering of services
- assisting in
- report to
- observe and comply with Company's material policies, rules and regulations

(二) 写作逻辑

在写作责任条款时,最常用的动词依次是 engages (somebody) as, accept, perform, report to, assist in, fulfill (responsibilities), devote to, exercise powers, provide/render services, observe and comply with。

其写作逻辑是这样的:

1. 先要雇某人担任某职位,而某人也要乐意受雇,如:Employer hereby engages Employee as the full-time Chief Financial Officer of Employer and Employee accepts such employment。这两个动词之前都不能加 shall,否则这项雇佣就成为强制性的。因此,凡发现该两动词之前加情态动词的,不管是 shall 还是 may,或其他,皆属滥用情态动词,而且这种状况并不少见。

2. Employee shall report to the Chief Executive Officer of Employer. Employee shall perform such duties and responsibilities assigned to him from time to time by the Chief Executive Officer and by the Board of Directors of Employer that are consistent with the titles held by Employee. report 这个词厘清了他与公司首席执行官的关系;明确与上司关系之后,他就要履行一定的职责;而这些职责当然是由他的上司不时(from time to time)分配给他的,并且应该是与他的职务相称的(consistent with the titles held by Employee),也就是说不能让他去打杂或"越俎代庖",要他做他"分内"的事。

3. 如果是一份全职的工作,雇主就会要求雇员奉献上班时的全部时间和精力(devote all of his business time and best efforts to)去履行相应的职责(perform faithfully, loyally and efficiently, his duties)和行使相应的权力(exercise such powers and fulfill such responsibilities)。

4. 如果除了本职工作之外,还要求受雇者担任一些"分外"的、没有额外报酬的职务,则这一条中还需加上一句:If requested by the Board of Directors, Employee shall serve on any committee established by the Board of Directors without additional compensation.

5. 当然,如果还有些公司的政策或程序是受雇者必须遵守的,则该职责条文还须订明:Employee shall observe and comply with the Employer's material policies, rules and regulations regarding the performance of his duties.

以上第 2 至第 5 条的主要动词之前都必须加上情态动词 shall,因为这是雇员的义务,shall 最适合用来表达这种温和强制的条规;就其翻译而言,"应当"是最正式的汉语对应词,"须"和"应"也都是适当的选择。很多研究法律文本情态动词的专家认为,shall 与 must 在法律文本中的功能是一样的,因此建议一律用 must 取代 shall,以摆脱这个困惑法律文本作者几百年的问题。其实,在不少情形下,shall 与 must 的功能未必一样,至少两者在 tone 与 register 上是不一样的。在以上一系列描述职责、行为动词前用了 shall 之处,如果用 must 取而代之,那么各个句子的语调完全变了:仿佛是在强制"下人"做事似的。

其他写作注意事项:

此外,在写作责任条款时,我们还注意到:最通用的修饰词是 honestly, diligently, competently, in good faith, with best efforts;或者另外一组较简单的副词是 faithfully, loyally and efficiently。这就是说受雇者履行职责或提供服务要诚实(honestly)/(faithfully)、有诚信(in good faith)、要勤勤恳恳(diligently)、能胜任工作(competently),并且要尽其所能(with best efforts or use his/her best efforts to)。这些副词或作副词用的介词短语所修饰的动词或动作往往是 perform(his duties and responsibilities)。

如果是全职的职位,雇主还会要求受雇者 devote all of his business time and best efforts to (his duties as...)(将其全部的上班时间和最大的努力投入其所担当的角色之中);如果是兼职的职位,雇主往往只要求受雇者 devote proper time to (the rendering of services)/devote the appropriate portion of your time to perform diligently the Services(为提供的服务投入适当的或合理的时间)。

如果受雇者的角色是全盘负责,一般会用以下词语:serve as, engages as(担任什么职位);如果受雇者是个副手,或非主要角色,一般会用以下词语:report to[向(主管)报告], assist sb. in doing sth.(辅助某人做某事)——语域较低的 help 一般不在法律文本的语境中使用。

但是,无论是全职还是兼职受雇者,都必须遵守雇佣公司相关的规定或政策。表达这一概念的词汇主要有 follow, observe and comply with, subject to(all policies and procedures/rules and regulations of);其中的 observe and comply with 是一个法律配对词,只用其中更常用的 comply with,即可完全表达所要表达的概念,如"comply with these provisions"。而最后一个词组,虽然被动意味强烈,但事实上是要求最严格、当事人一定要服从的,否则往往就会有严重后果的表述方式。例如:Employee shall perform the duties consistent with his role as President and Chief Executive Officer, <u>subject to</u> direction from THE COMPANY's Board of Directors.(雇员必须遵循公司董事会的指示,履行与其作为公司总裁和首席执行官的角色相符的职责。)该词往往译成"必须"。有关遵循、遵照、按照、依照、根据等词,在法律文本中使用频率非常高,汉语中都当作同义词使用,但英文中却有不同的表达方式。较详细的论述见作者另一本专著《高级法律翻译与写作》(李克兴,2013)。

四、责任和义务条款示范语段

如果将上述关于雇用全职的首席财务官的责任条款句焊接起来,一段逻辑连贯、表达清晰、行文规范、内容全面的责任条款便呼之欲出:

Employer hereby engages Employee as the full-time Chief Financial Officer of Employer and Employee accepts such employment. Employee shall report to the Chief Executive Officer of Employer and shall perform such duties and responsibilities assigned to him from time to time by the Chief Executive Officer and by the Board of

Directors of Employer that are consistent with the titles held by Employee. Employee shall devote all of his business time and best efforts to, and shall perform faithfully, loyally and efficiently, his duties as the Chief Financial Officer of Employer and shall exercise such powers and fulfill such responsibilities as may be duly assigned to or vested in him by the Chief Executive Officer and by the Board of Directors of Employer consistent with the responsibilities of the Chief Financial Officer. If requested by the Board of Directors, Employee shall serve on any committee established by the Board of Directors without additional compensation. Employee shall observe and comply with the Employer's material policies, rules and regulations regarding the performance of his duties. However, Employer's failure to comply therewith shall not relieve him of any of his duties, liabilities or obligations hereunder. ("雇主"据此协议雇佣"雇员"为本公司的全职财务总管。"雇员"接受该职位的雇佣。"雇员"应当向"雇主"公司的总执行官报告,并执行总执行官及公司董事会不时下达给他的与其职位相称的职责。"雇员"应尽其所能,将其全部的上班时间和最大的努力投入其所担任的公司财务总监职务工作中,"雇员"应忠于职守、勤勉高效地工作,行使公司总执行官及董事会授予其行使的、与其财务总监职位相称的权力和职责。如应董事会要求,"雇员"应加入董事会设立的各种委员会,但不获额外报酬。"雇员"应当遵守"雇主"公司有关其职责行使的各项重要政策及规章制度。但"雇员"未能遵守有关政策或规章制度,并不免除其根据本合同应尽之职责、责任或义务。)

五、"责任"和"义务"在其他法律文本中的各种表述

在法律英文中表示"责任"和"义务"概念的词汇非常丰富。例如:

be responsible for/to (bear the responsibility of, be borne by), be liable to/for (liability/liabilities), be accountable to (accountability), be in charge of (take charge of), have the duty to, be under the obligation of/be obliged to/be obligatory/compulsory/mandatory 等等。

它们都是同义词吗?可以互相替换吗?如果不可以,那么它们之间究竟有哪些差异?在合同的写作和翻译中如何正确使用这些词汇?

当然,在将上述有关"负责"的英文表述翻译成中文时,译文可能都一样,即"负责(做某事)"或者"承担……责任",译者也较少会犯错。但反之,译者面临的就远远不只是"两难"的选择。据笔者了解,绝大部分的翻译系研究生无法搞清上述英文中这一系列"负责"概念之间的差别,因此翻译中时常出错。本章的目的就是要阐明英文合同中这些表示类似概念的词汇之间的异同,用一些权威双语法律文本中的例证,来演示其正确的使用方法,以便为从事合同以及法律文本写作的人员提供一个实务指引。

(一) be in charge of 与 be responsible for 的用法比较

我们首先来看一下在法律文本中用得相对较少的 in charge of 的用法。下例选自权威法律文本《中华人民共和国宪法》及其英译本:

1. 第九十条 国务院各部部长、各委员会主任<u>负责</u>本部门的工作；召集和主持部务会议或者委员会会议、委务会议，讨论决定本部门工作的重大问题。

Article 90 Ministers <u>in charge of</u> the ministries or commissions of the State Council <u>are responsible for the work</u> of their respective departments and they convene and preside over ministerial meetings or general and executive meetings of the commissions to discuss and decide on major issues in the work of their respective departments.《中华人民共和国宪法》

从以上的英文译文中我们可以观察到：跟随 in charge of 之后的是与其所界定或修饰之职位名称相称的工作，即职能范围的、比较笼统的工作，或人们通常认为的该职位的"分内"之事：Ministers <u>in charge of</u> the ministries; government officials or other personnel <u>in charge of</u> government affairs——由部长负责其部门的事务、由政府官员负责其部门的事务是理所当然的。而 responsible for 虽然在语法上其用法（后置修饰词）可以跟 in charge of 一样（如 government officials or other personnel <u>responsible for</u> government affairs），但两者是有实质性差异的：responsible for 所"负责"可以是任何性质的事务——工作、任务、职责、违约责任，等等，可以是"分内"的，也可以是"分外"的，但在跟第三人称搭配使用时，一般都指强制性地"负责"某项具体事务，而不是笼统地担负某项职责或是描述性的负责。上例就有一个非常鲜明的对比（见画线部分），两者不可调换使用，不可以写成："Ministers <u>responsible for</u> the ministries or commissions of the State Council <u>are in charge of the work</u> of their respective departments"，因为部长负责自己的部门是天经地义的，无需另作规定强制他去负责。凡 responsible for 之后所跟随的都是较具体的任务或事务，并且都是强制行为者承担的责任。又如：

2. 第十四条 中央人民政府<u>负责</u>管理香港特别行政区的防务。香港特别行政区政府<u>负责</u>维持香港特别行政区的社会治安。

Article 14 The Central People's Government shall <u>be responsible for the defence of</u> the Hong Kong Special Administrative Region. The Government of the Hong Kong Special Administrative Region shall <u>be responsible for the maintenance of public order</u> in the Region.（《基本法》）

3. In the event of non-compliance with or contravention of any of the requirements of this section, a director or other person <u>responsible for the prospectus</u> shall not incur any liability by reason of the non-compliance or contravention.

如本条任何规定不获遵从或被违反，董事或其他<u>对招股章程负责</u>的人在下列情况下，不会因有关规定不获遵从或被违反而招致任何法律责任。（《公司条例》）

4. The company shall be <u>responsible for any loss</u> incurred by any person by reason of the company entering in the register the name of a bearer of a share warrant in respect of the shares therein specified without the warrant being surrendered and cancelled.

如公司在有关认股权证没有交出及注销的情况下，就认股权证所指明的股份，将认股权证持有人的姓名或名称记入登记册，以致任何人招致任何损失，则公司须<u>对该等损失负责</u>。（同上）

只要读者对以上句子与前面包含 in charge of 的例句用心比较或细心体会,就会发现 be responsible for 所表达的"负责"项目与前者非常不同:例3中负责的是十分明确的、强制性的"防务"和"治安"(与情态动词 shall 的搭配使用更增强了这种强制性),其余两例中所要负责的更是非常繁杂具体的工作,如"招股章程""损失"等。比较而言,in charge of 几乎纯粹是"描述"或"界定"性质的,其所意含的责任都是伴随职务而来而并非义务性质的。

(二) be liable to/for 的寓意与用法

就法律文本中,be liable to/for 比前两个短语用得更加频繁。与 be liable to/for 配合使用的宾格往往都是跟金钱或债务有关的,其真正寓意是行为者将被逼负上金钱方面的责任,在英译汉法律文本中该词往往都被翻译成"负上法律责任"①,而且这几乎是香港数以千部计的法律译本中的标准译法。例如:

1. No person shall be liable under subsection (1) if he proves—(a) that, having consented to become a director of the company, he withdrew his consent before the issue of the prospectus, and that it was issued without his authority or consent;

任何人如能证明下述各项,则无须根据第(1)款负上法律责任——(a) 该人虽曾同意成为该公司董事,但在招股章程发出前已撤回同意,且该招股章程是未经其批准或同意而发出的;(《公司条例》)

2. In the event of the winding up of a company re-registered in pursuance of this section, the following provisions shall have effect—(a) notwithstanding section 170(1)(a), a past member of the company who was a member thereof at the time of re-registration shall, if the winding up commences within the period of 3 years beginning with the day on which the company is re-registered, be liable to contribute to the assets of the company in respect of debts and liabilities of its contracted before that time;

如依据本条重新注册的公司清盘,以下条文即具效力——(a) 即使第170(1)(a)条另有规定,如清盘在该公司重新注册之日起计3年内开始,一名过去的成员,在重新注册时若是该公司的成员,则有法律责任就公司在该时间之前所订约承担的债项及债务,分担提供公司的资产;(同上)

从以上两个例子中,我们还可以观察到 liable 之名词性质的 liability 与 liabilities 之间的不同:单数形式的 liability 仍然解作并译为"法律责任",复数形式的 liabilities 与 debts 配对使用(形成同义反复的 legal pair),显然只有"债务"的意思——香港法律条文的译者在翻译过程中将该词的单复数形式做出如此区分,既合情合理,也符合法理和语境。这一点很值得法律文本的译者和作者的重视,可以作为借鉴。在以下例子中,我们还可以进一步观察到 be responsible for 与 be liable to 之间的另一层差异:

3. Where a person is personally responsible under this section for the relevant debts of a company, he is jointly and severally liable in respect of those debts with the

---

① 国内的大部分英译汉文本很少将该词(be liable to/for)翻译成"(负有)法律责任",但可喜的是国内编写的两部主要法律词典均给了合理的翻译。《法律词典》译为"有(法律)责任的""应受罚的""有义务责任的";《元照法律词典》译为"有(法律)责任的""有义务的"。

company and any other person who, whether under this section or otherwise, is so liable.

凡任何人根据本条对某家公司的有关债项承担个人责任,该人须与该公司及任何其他不论是否须根据本条就该等债项承担个人法律责任的人,就该等债项承担共同及个别的法律责任。(同上)

由上例可见,其中 be responsible for 所要负责的纯粹是一种义务,而 be liable 所要负责的是跟金钱有关(在本案中指的是"债项")的"法律责任"。但一个需要对"债项"负上"法律责任"的人具体如何去承担责任? 当然,有钱人履行"法律责任"可以通过支付金钱(包括罚款)。无钱人又如何承担? 法律界人士均知:在某些案例中,法理上允许"以罚代刑"或"以刑代罚",即可让付不起钱的当事人承担起刑事责任,而 liable 这个词在法律文本中还可以用来表述这一层意思。例如:

4. Where a statement in lieu of prospectus delivered to the Registrar under subsection (1) includes any untrue statement, any person who authorized the delivery of the statement, in lieu of prospectus for registration shall be liable to imprisonment and a fine, unless he proves either that the untrue statement was immaterial or that he had reasonable ground to believe and did up to the time of the delivery for registration of the statement in lieu of prospectus believe that the untrue statement was true.

凡根据第(1)款向处长交付的代替招股章程陈述书内,载有任何不真实陈述,则任何授权将该份代替招股章程陈述书交付注册的人,除非能证明该项不真实陈述不具关键性,或能证明有合理理由相信,以及直至该份代替招股章程陈述书被交付注册时,仍相信该项不真实陈述乃属真实,否则可处监禁及罚款。(同上)

据笔者初步审察,在香港的 1100 多部法律中译本中,除了"承担法律责任"外,"处……惩罚"(监禁或罚款等)便是 be liable to 最基本的对译了。虽然是否有更佳的翻译,尚需进一步推敲,但至少在语言逻辑上该译法与"承担法律责任"是一致的,因为"处……惩罚"也是"承担法律责任"的一种形式。至此,我们已经完成本文三个"负责"词汇的讨论,最后要讨论的另一个表示"负责"概念为"be accountable to"。

(三) be accountable to 的用法、译法以及与 be responsible to 的异同

本章这一部的讨论已经超出合同条款的范畴,但法律条文与合同条款在词语的使用和翻译上本质上是一脉相承的,前者永远管辖后者,相同的概念无论在法律文本中还是在合同条文理应一致。不过,这一节讨论的 be accountable to,在合同条款中甚少出现。该词同样表达"负责的"概念,但用法比较特殊:

1. Article 43 The Chief Executive of the Hong Kong Special Administrative Region shall be accountable to the Central People's Government and the Hong Kong Special Administrative Region in accordance with the provisions of this law.

香港特别行政区行政长官依照本法的规定对中央人民政府和香港特别行政区负责。(*Basic Law*)

2. Article 57 A Commission Against Corruption shall be established in the Hong Kong Special Administrative Region. It shall function independently and be

accountable to the Chief Executive.

香港特别行政区设立廉政公署,独立工作,对行政长官负责。(同上)

《基本法》是一个起草过程透明度非常高的双语法律文本,几乎每一条文、每一个用词都经过中国香港地区、中国内地、英国法律专家、语言专家的反复商榷、一再推敲[①]。除个别词句外,其语言可视为双语法律的一个楷模。基于以上两条《基本法》中表述"责任"的用词以及前文的讨论,我们不难发现这样一个规律:上级对下级的"负责"都用 responsible for 来表述;而下级对上级的"负责"(问责)更地道的表述应该是 accountable to。该短语所表述的"负责"的对象一定是权力或职位高于施动者(句子中的主格)的上级的"人"或"法人"(广义上包括机构/部门),也就是说,这个上级的"人"或"法人"是可以向其做出交代或汇报的"有灵"(animate)宾格或由其主理的机构;而 responsible for 所"负责"的对象一定是下级,所跟随的宾格可以是任何事物,如"违约"等。在某些情形下,accountable to 所"负责"的对象在职务上可能没有施动者那么有权有势,但在理念上他一定是施动者的上级。例如,在一个民主制度中,某个统治者个人可以权倾朝野,但他必须对其人民负责("accountable to his people"),这就是说,作为一个集合概念的人民依然是他的上级,即我们传统概念中的所谓"衣食父母"。

在国内法律文本的英译实践中,用 be accountable to 表述下级对上级"负责"这一专业用法往往被完全疏忽或没有被译者意识到。在《中华人民共和国宪法》中表述这种关系的"负责"概念共有 15 处,无一处是译成 be accountable to 的,其表达方式是非常容易混淆的 be responsible to。例如:

3. 第三条……全国人民代表大会和地方各级人民代表大会都由民主选举产生,<u>对人民负责</u>,受人民监督。

Article 3 The National People's Congress and the local people's congresses at various levels are constituted through democratic elections. They <u>are responsible to the people</u> and subject to their supervision. (《中华人民共和国宪法》)

4. 第九十四条 中央军事委员会主席对全国人民代表大会和全国人民代表大会常务委员会<u>负责</u>。

Article 94 The Chairman of the Central Military Commission <u>is responsible to</u> the National People's Congress and its Standing Committee. (同上)

值得欣慰的是,在英文惯用法上这些 be responsible to 用得并无任何不妥,但如改用 be accountable to,则译文中所涉及的当事人的"上下级"关系会更加清晰,表达的意思会更加准确,从而译文也会更加地道、专业。不过,既然本文是系统讨论法律文本中表述"负责"概念的文章,在此还须提醒读者注意 be responsible for 与 be responsible to 语义上的重大差别:前者是自上而下、必须有承担的负责;而后者是自下而上、对上级有报告义务的负责。

---

① 由于《基本法》起草委员会的成员绝大多数是香港本地的各界名流以及内地的法律专家,该法的最初版本是以中文形式形成的。起草委员会每商定部分条文后,即由政府语文组的高级译员翻译成英文以征询香港社会各界(尤其是不谙汉语但当时仍在统治香港的英籍高官)的意见。每一条文的定稿,无论是内容、形式还是个别措辞都经过广泛咨询、反复商榷及几经修改。因此,可以说这是一个经过"千锤百炼"(但并不等于无懈可击)的双语法律文件。

六、结语

本文在责任表述方面有以下几点发现：

就"义务"和"责任"而言，汉语中主要的动词表达形式是"负责"和"承担责任/义务"，法律英文中最主要的表达词语有 be in charge of, be accountable to, be responsible for/to 以及 be liable to/for。但 in charge of 所表达的是"职务"（并非是"义务"）性质的"负责"，是一个表示"负责"的"描述性"而并非"强制性"的用词；be accountable to 专门表达下级对上级的"负责"；上级对下级的负责以及除对金钱（包括债务）之外一切工作和杂务的负责，均以 be responsible for 去表达更加稳妥；与 be liable to/for 这个短语配合使用的宾格往往都跟金钱或债务有关，将该词翻译成"（负）法律责任"是香港中文法律文本中最标准的译法，也是值得推荐的合理译法。

第十二章 知识产权条款的写作和翻译

一、引言

知识产权的条款和保密条款实质上是保证条款的延续。也就是说,合同各方拥有专有权的知识和商业机密,各方保证予以保护。这类条款在"知识就是力量"的时代越来越受重视。虽然并非每一类合同都涉及或需要这两类条款(如普通货物买卖,租赁合约或地产买卖),但合资企业、技术转让、各种网站使用条件等等,都涉及保密和保护知识产权的议题。由于这两个条款的通用度不及其他条款,故本章只做简短讨论。

保密条款与知识产权条款有两点重大的不同:(1)知识产权直接受法律保护,因为商标和专利等都有注册的所有权。受到侵犯时可直接通过法庭进行民事诉讼;而保密协议被违反了,往往只有间接的后果,很难直接对泄露方提起诉讼。此外,(2)保密条款通常在协议终止后的很长时间内(一般是两到三年)仍然有效;而知识产权的保护不受合同期限的限制,只要知识产权的有效期仍然生效,该知识就一直受保护,如商标或专利只要向政府规管部门缴纳规定的维持费,便一直受法律保护。

不过,作为知识产权主要项目的专利的保护是有一定限制的。如在美国、日本,新药专利保护期限是 20 年。今年,辉瑞药厂的"伟哥"(威而钢)专利保护期到期,"伟哥"价格就大降。所以知识产权得到保护,产权所有人的利益就有法律上的保障。合同中订立知识产权条款主要目的是加强合同双方的知识产权意识,同时为一些没有注册或明确受到法律保护的项目提供保护。就已获注册的知识产权而言,即使合同中没有该条款,当一方的该权利受到侵害时,任何时候都可以依法对侵害方(无论其是否合同的签署方)追究法律责任。

二、知识产权条款样本和译文

Intellectual property	知识产权
The Party A understands that the Party B <u>owns the exclusive rights</u> in the designs, patents, trademarks, trade names, and company names (the "Intellectual Property") used in connection with the Party B's Goods. The Party A <u>is given no rights</u> in any of the Party B's Intellectual Property. The party A <u>will not use the Party B's Intellectual Property</u> as if were the Party A's own property, nor will the Party A <u>register the Party B's Intellectual Property in any country</u> as if it were the Party A's own. The Party A acknowledges that its unauthorized use or registration of the Party B's Intellectual Property, or of any intellectual property that is confusingly or deceptively similar to the Party B's Intellectual Property, will be <u>deemed an infringement</u> of the Party B's exclusive rights. (乔焕然,2008:122)	甲方知晓乙方对其所售商品的设计、专利、商标、商号及公司名称("知识财产")拥有专有权利。甲方无权拥有乙方的任何知识产权。甲方不得如使用自己的财产那样使用乙方的知识产权,亦不得如属于自己的知识财产那样对乙方知识产权在任何国家进行注册。甲方承认其擅自使用或注册乙方知识产权,或者与乙方知识产权相混淆的知识产权将构成侵害乙方的专有权。

续表

Intellectual property	知识产权
Party A warrants that any design or instruction furnished or given by Party A to Party B shall not be such as will cause Party B to infringe any patent, copyright, registered design or trade mark or any other intellectual property rights in the execution of Party A's order. These Terms and Conditions and/or the Contract and/or the giving of technical assistance or other information by Party B shall not grant to, convey or confer upon Party A or Party A's customer or upon anyone claiming under Party A a license, express or implied, under any patent rights, copyrights, trade marks, registered designs or other intellectual property rights of Party B covering or relating to any combination, machine or process in which the Goods might be or are used or for any product of which the Goods might form part. (乔焕然, 2008:166)	甲方保证其向乙方提供或给出的任何设计或说明,都不会使乙方在执行甲方命令之时侵犯任何专利权、版权、注册设计或商标或任何其他知识产权。 本条款和条件和/或合同/或乙方提供的技术支持或其他信息,都不明示或暗示地构成对甲方或甲方顾客或任何以甲方名义提出请求的人,就任何专利权、版权、商标、注册设计或乙方的其他知识产权之许可的授权、转让、授予,该知识产权包括货物可能被用来制造产品或成为产品之一部分的合成物、机器或工艺,或与该合成物、机器或工艺有关。
ViroPharma shall be the sole and exclusive owner of any and all writings, documents, works made for hire, inventions, discoveries, know-how, processes, chemical entities, compounds, plans, memoranda, tests, research, designs, specifications, models and data that Consultant makes, conceives, discovers or develops, either solely or jointly with any other person in performance of the Services (collectively, "Work Product"). Consultant shall promptly disclose to ViroPharma all information relating to Work Product. Consultant acknowledges that all of the Work Product that is copyrightable shall be considered a work made for hire under United States Copyright Law. To the extent that any copyrightable Work Product may not be considered a work made for hire under Copyright Law or to the extent that, notwithstanding the foregoing provisions, Consultant may retain an interest in any Work Product that is not copyrightable, Consultant hereby irrevocably assigns and transfers to ViroPharma, and to the extent that an executory assignment is not enforceable, Consultant hereby agrees to assign and transfer to ViroPharma, in writing, from time to time, upon request, any and all right, title, or interest that Consultant has or may obtain in any Work Product without the necessity of further consideration. ViroPharma shall be entitled to obtain and hold in its own name all copyrights, patents, trade secrets and trademarks with respect thereto. At ViroPharma's request and expense, Consultant shall assist ViroPharma in acquiring and maintaining its right in and title to, any Work Product. Such assistance may include, but will not be limited to, signing applications and other documents, cooperating in legal proceedings, and taking any other steps considered necessary or desirable by ViroPharma.	由顾问在提供服务的过程中单独或与他人合作制作、构想、发现或开发的所有作品、文件、受雇作品、发明、发现、技术、工艺、化学实体、化合物、计划、备忘录、测试、研究设计、说明书、模型及数据(统称为"工作成果"),为ViroPharma公司所专有。顾问应即时向ViroPharma透露有关工作成果的一切信息。顾问承认享有版权的一切工作成果应根据美国版权法规定视为受雇佣制作的作品。任何享有版权的工作成果不得视为根据版权法规定为雇佣而做的作品,或尽管上述规定,顾问对于没有版权的任何工作成果可维持利益,因此顾问不可撤销地分派并转让给VirPharma,尚未履行的任务无须实施,顾问在此书面同意无须经过进一步考虑按要求将任何一切顾问从任何工作成果已经获取或可获取的权利、所有权或利益分派和转让给ViroPharma。ViroPharma有权获取并以自身名义持有该等工作成果之所有版权、专利、商业秘密和商标。应ViroPharma要求并由其支付费用,顾问应协助ViroPharma获取并维持其对任何工作成果的权利和所有权。该等协助包括但不限于签署申请书和其他文件,在法律程序中合作,并采取ViroPharma认为必要或想要的任何其他措施。

续表

Intellectual property	知识产权
Section 1. Notification of Infringement. Each Party shall immediately notify the other Party and provide to the other Party all relevant background facts upon becoming aware of (i) any registrations of or applications for registration of, marks that do or may conflict with any Licensed Trademark in the Core Merchandise Field or the New Merchandise Field, and (ii) any infringement, misappropriation, imitation, dilution, illegal use or misuse of the Licensed Trademarks, Licensed Patents, and Other Licensed Intellectual Property in the Core Merchandise Field or the New Merchandise Field. Section 2. Action Against Infringer. ABC shall have the first right, but not the obligation, to take action against others in the courts, administrative agencies or otherwise, at XYZ's cost and expense, to prevent or terminate infringement, misappropriation, imitation, illegal use or misuse of the Licensed Trademarks, Licensed Patents, and Other Licensed Intellectual Property in the Core Merchandise Field or the New Merchandise Field, and to oppose or cancel applications or registrations of trademarks, service marks, trade dress, characters and designs that do or may conflict with any of the Licensed Trademarks in the Core Merchandise Field or the New Merchandise Field. XYZ agrees to cooperate with ABC in any litigation or other enforcement action that ABC may undertake to enforce or protect the licensed Trademarks, Licensed Patents, and Other Licensed Intellectual Property in the Core Merchandise Field or the New Merchandise Field and, upon ABC's request, to execute, file and deliver all documents and proof necessary for such purpose, including being names as a party to such litigation as required by law. All reasonable out-of-pocket expenses incurred by XYZ in connection therewith shall be reimbursed by ABC. XYZ shall have the right to participate and be represented in any such action, suit or proceeding by its own counsel at its own expense. XYZ shall have no claim of any kind against ABC based on or arising out of ABC's handling of or decisions concerning any such action, suit, proceeding, settlement, or compromise, and XYZ hereby irrevocably releases ABC from any such claim, provided, however, that ABC shall not enter into any settlement or compromise of such action, suit or proceeding that affects or concerns the validity, enforceability, or ownership of any Licensed Trademarks, Licensed Patents, or the Other Licensed Intellectual Property in the Core Merchandise Field or the New Merchandise Field Confidential Treatment requested for redacted portion without the prior written consent of XYZ, which consent shall not be unreasonably withheld. (乔焕然,2008:237)	第1条 侵权通知。各方在知晓(i)任何可能与核心商业领域或新兴商业领域中任何被许可的商标相冲突的标志注册或注册申请,以及(ii)在核心商业领域或新兴商业领域中任何对被许可的商标、专利权和其他知识产权的侵权、盗用、模仿、淡化侵权、非法使用或滥用之时,该方应立即通知另一方,并向另一方提供所有的相关背景事实。 第2条 反侵权诉讼。ABC有第一位的权利(但无义务),以向法院、行政机构或其他方式对其他人提出控告,去阻止或终止在核心商业领域或新兴商业领域中对被许可的商标、专利权和其他知识产权的侵权、盗用、模仿、淡化侵权、非法使用或滥用,以及对在核心商业领域或新兴商业领域中任何与被许可的商标肯定相冲突或可能相冲突的商标、服务标志、商品外观、特征和设计之注册或注册申请提出反对或使之被撤销,而诉讼费用则由XYZ承担。XYZ同意在ABC为强制执行或保护核心商业领域或新兴商业领域中的被许可商标、专利权和其他知识产权而可能采取的任何诉讼或其他强制行动中,与ABC合作,并且在ABC提出请求之时,签署、提交和交付为上述目的而必要的所有文件和证据,包括按照法律要求在上述诉讼中成为一方当事人的名称。XYZ所产生的,与此相关的所有合理的现金支出应由ABC进行补偿。XYZ有权自行承担费用,聘请律师代表其参加任何诉讼或法律行动或程序。XYZ不得基于ABC对任何此类诉讼、法律行动、程序、解决或妥协的处理或决定而对ABC提出任何性质的权利主张,XYZ兹不可撤销地放弃对ABC的此类权利主张,但ABC不得对任何影响或关乎其核心商业领域或新兴商业领域中被许可的商标、专利权和其他被许可的知识产权之诉讼、法律行动或程序做出任何解决或妥协处理,除非经XYZ事先书面同意(该同意无正当理由不得拒绝)。

续表

Intellectual property	知识产权
The Company <u>owns or possesses</u> or is currently seeking to develop adequate <u>rights or licenses to use all trademarks, trade names, service marks, service mark registrations, service names, patents, patent rights, copyrights, inventions, licenses, approvals, governmental authorizations, trade secrets</u> and rights necessary to conduct their respective businesses as now conducted. The Company does not have any knowledge of any infringement by the Company trademark, trade name rights, patents, patent rights, copyrights, inventions, licenses, service names, service marks, service mark registrations, trade secret or other similar rights of others, and, to the knowledge of the Company there is no claim, action or proceeding being made or brought against, or to the Company's knowledge, being threatened against, the Company regarding trademark, trade name, patents, patent rights, invention, copyright, license, service names, service marks, service mark registrations, trade secret or other infringement; and the Company is unaware of any facts or circumstances which might give rise to any of the foregoing.	公司拥有或享有或目前正在寻求发展充分的权利或许可去使用,以满足经营目前各自经营的业务所需而使用的所有商标、商号、专利、专利权、版权、发明、许可证、核准书、政府授权书、商业秘密和商业权利。公司不知晓公司商标、商号权利、专利、专利权、版权、发明、许可证、服务名称、服务标记、服务标记注册、商业秘密或其他类似权利是否受到任何侵犯,且据公司所知没有针对公司的任何权利主张、法律行动或诉讼,或据公司所知也没有针对公司及其商标、商号、专利、专利权、发明、版权、许可证、服务名称、服务标记、服务标记注册、商业秘密或其他侵权而拟将提出的权利主张、法律行动或诉讼;公司对可产生上述的任何事实或情况也并不知情。
Health West agrees that any and all intellectual property and intellectual property rights that Health West conceived, reduced to practice or developed during the course of its performance of services as a director, officer, employee or consultant for PST, together with any and all intellectual property and intellectual property rights that Health West conceives, reduces to practice or develops during the course of its performance of the Services pursuant to this Agreement, in each case whether alone or in conjunction with others (all of the foregoing being collectively referred to herein as the "Inventions"), <u>shall be the sole and exclusive property</u> of PST. Accordingly, Health West hereby: (i) <u>assigns and agrees to assign to PST its entire right, title and interest in and to all Inventions</u>; and (ii) <u>designates PST as its agent for</u>, and grants to the officers of PST a power of attorney (which power of attorney shall be deemed coupled with an interest) <u>with full power</u> of <u>substitution solely</u> for the purpose of, effecting the foregoing assignments from Health West to PST. Health West further agrees to cooperate with and <u>provide reasonable assistance to PST to obtain and from time to time enforce any and all current or future intellectual property rights</u> covering or relating to the Inventions in any and all jurisdictions.	Health West 同意不论是单独还是与他人协作的,在其作为 PST 主管、高级职员、雇员或顾问的过程中任何和所有由 Health West 构想、然后实施或开发的知识产权和知识财产权利以及根据本协议在履行服务的过程中由任何和所有 Health West 构想、然后实施或开发的知识产权和知识财产权利(上述的一切于本协议中共称为"发明")应为 PST 独有财产。因此,Health West 特此:(i)转让或同意将其与所有发明相关的所有权利、权力和利益转让给 PST;以及 (ii) 指定 PST 作为其代理人,给予 PST 高级职员授权书(授权书应视为与利益相结合),由 PST 单独全权代理以实现 Health West 向 PST 转让上述权利的事宜。Health West 进一步同意与 PST 合作,向其提供合理协助,以帮助在任何及一切管辖范围内不时获取并执行与发明相关的任何及一切现有或将来会带来的知识财产权利。

续表

Intellectual property	知识产权
(a) The Intellectual Property <u>consists</u> on the date hereof <u>of the Trade Mark</u>, the NDA and the "cortrosyn. com" and "cortrosyn. us" domain names and <u>is sufficient to carry on the business of the production</u>, <u>manufacture</u>, <u>marketing</u>, <u>distribution and sale of</u> Cortrosyn. To the best of Amphastar's knowledge and belief, the Trade Mark ownership has been validly transferred from Organon Inc. to Organon on June 19, 2003 by recordation of a change of name document within the records of the United States Patent and Trade Mark Office. <u>The Trade Mark ownership has been validly assigned by</u> Organon to Amphastar on June 26, 2003 and <u>such assignment has been duly recorded by</u> the United States Patent and Trade Mark Office. Amphastar <u>is the registered owner of the Trade Mark free and clear of all Encumbrances.</u> Amphastar has not, and to its knowledge, Organon has not allowed or acquiesced in the use of the Trade Mark by any other Person in the Territory. To the best of Amphastar's knowledge and belief, <u>the Trade Mark is distinctive and is not confusing with any other trade mark or trade name</u>. The United States trade mark registration of the Trade Mark in the name of Amphastar as the owner thereof is valid in good standing and is not the subject of any expungement or cancellation proceedings. To the best of Amphastar's knowledge, <u>use of the Trade Mark does not constitute infringement of any Person's common law or statutory trade mark rights</u> within the Territory. Amphastar is not aware of any infringement or passing off relating to the Trade Mark within the Territory. (b) The NDA <u>is in full force and effect</u> and, <u>to Amphastar's knowledge</u>, <u>has been duly and validly issued</u>. To Amphastar's knowledge, there <u>is no proceeding by</u> any Governmental Agency pending, nor is any Governmental Agency threatening with respect to Cortrosyn a <u>product recall or market withdrawal</u>, <u>or the revocation or suspension of</u> the NDA. To Amphastar's knowledge all required notices, supplemental applications and annual or other reports, including adverse experience reports, with respect to the NDA which are required to maintain the NDA in good standing have been filed with the FDA and true and correct copies of such documents have been provided to DRC prior to the Closing Date. (c) To Amphastar's knowledge, as of the Closing Date, the	(a) 自本协议签订之日起,知识产权包括商标、保密协议(NDA)以及"cortrosyn. com"和"cortrosyn. us"的域名,该产权足以支持 Cortrosyn 的生产、制造、营销、分销和销售。Amphastar 相信,商标所有权已于 2003 年 6 月 19 日通过于美国专利及商标局记录更改名称的文件从 Organon 公司合法转让至 Organon。商标所有权已于 2003 年 6 月 26 日由 Organon 合法转让给 Amphastar,且该转让已在美国专利及商标局正式存档。Amphastar 为该无留置权的商标的注册拥有者。据 Amphastar 所知,Organon 不允许或不默许美国境内的其他任何人使用该商标。就 Amphastar 所知所信,该商标与众不同,不会与其他任何商标或商号混淆。该商标以 Amphastar 为商标,所有权人在美国专利及商标局注册是有效的,并非是任何撤销不当注册商标之法律程序的对象。据 Amphastar 所知,在美国境内使用该商标不构成对任何法人的普通法或成文法商标权的侵权行为。Amphastar 对美国境内与该商标相关的任何侵权或冒充行为并不知情。 (b) 据 Amphastar 所知,NDA 完全有效,是经合理合法签发的。据 Amphastar 所知,没有任何政府代理机构就 Cortrosyn 产品召回或从市场撤回或撤销或暂停 NDA 提出或拟将提出的诉讼。据 Amphastar 所知,所有与 NDA 相关要求 NDA 维持良好信誉的通知、补充申请和年报或其他报表,包括不良事件报表,都已于食品和药物管理局(FDA)存档,且该等文件的真确版本于截止期之前提交给 DRC。 (c) 据 Amphastar 所知,自截止期起,美国境内 Cortrosyn 的生产、制造、营销、分销和销售不会侵犯任何第三方的知识产权,Amphastar 和 Organon 没有收到与任何其他人的任何专利、商标或其他专利相关的任何通知、投诉、威胁或权利主张。

续表

Intellectual property	知识产权
production, manufacture, marketing, distribution and sale of Cortrosyn in the Territory <u>does not infringe any third party's intellectual property rights</u>, and neither Amphastar nor Organon has received any notice, complaint, threat or claim concerning alleging infringement of any patent, trademark or other intellectual property right of any other Person.	
The parties agree as follows: The Party A <u>owns valuable property rights in all of the marks, names, designs, patents, and trade secrets (the "Intellectual Property") connected with the Goods. None of these rights are being granted to the Party B.</u> The Party B must not represent that he or she owns any rights in the Party A's Intellectual Property, nor is the Party B permitted to use the Party A's name as any part of its own name. <u>The rights to Intellectual Property remain vested in the Party A.</u> The Party B <u>is granted a right to use the Intellectual Property of the Party A in connection with operating the distributorship and reselling, leasing, and renting the Goods.</u> The Party B <u>has no right to use the Intellectual Property for any other purpose.</u> <u>All advertisements</u>, promotional materials, quotations, invoices, labels, containers, and <u>other materials used in conjunction with Goods must include a notice stating that the Party A owns the Intellectual Property</u> associated with the Goods. Such material must also state that the Party B is an authorized dealer or distributor of the Goods. The Party B <u>is prohibited from altering in any way the Party A's Intellectual Property</u> used in connection with the Goods. All details, colors, and designs must be exactly as provided by the Party A. The Party B may resell, lease, or rent Goods only if the Party A's Intellectual Property is used in connection with Goods. The Party B is prohibited from using the Party A's Intellectual Property in connection with any products that are not furnished by the Party A. The Party B <u>will not duplicate or attempt to duplicate any of the Goods</u>, will not make the Goods available to another person for purposes of duplication, and will not make or sell	双方同意： 甲方拥有与产品相关的所有商标、名称、设计、专利和商业秘密的有价值财产的权利（"知识产权"）。该等权利未授予乙方。乙方不得声称自己拥有甲方的知识产权，亦不得使用甲方的名义作为自己的名义。知识产权均保留于甲方。 乙方在进行经销、转销、租赁货物时，被授权使用甲方的知识产权。非为此目的，乙方不得使用甲方的知识产权。 所有与货物相关的广告、促销材料、报价单、发票、标签、包装箱以及其他材料必须包含声明甲方拥有该等知识产权的通知。并且这些材料亦必须声明乙方是被授权的销售者或经销商。 乙方不得在使用与货物相关的知识产权过程中对其进行任何改变。所有的细节、色彩和设计必须与甲方规定的完全一致。只有甲方的知识产权用于与货物相关的目的，乙方才可以转售、租赁货物。乙方不得在销售任何非由甲方提供的产品中使用甲方的知识产权。 乙方不得仿冒或试图仿冒任何货物，不得向意图仿冒的其他人提供货物，或生产或销售与货物相混淆，或会产生欺骗性后果的产品。

续表

Intellectual property	知识产权
any products that are confusingly or deceptively similar to the Goods. The Party B undertakes not to do any act that would or might invalidate or the Party A's registrations of, or title to, the Intellectual Property. The Party B will not attempt to vary or cancel any registrations of the Intellectual Property. The Party B will not assist any other person in any of these actions. Violation of this entire Paragraph will result in immediate termination of this Agreement. Further, both parties agree that violation of this Paragraph will result in the dilution or destruction of the Party A's valuable rights in its reputation, goodwill, and intellectual property, resulting in substantial damages. These damages will be impractical or impossible to measure because of the difficulty in measuring intangible rights. Therefore, the parties agree that if the Party B violates this Paragraph, the Party A has right to assess liquidated damaged against the Party B in an amount equal to [number] percent of the price listed on the Party A's Current Product List for each of the Good that is subject of the violation. (乔焕然,2008:190)	乙方不得为导致或可能导致甲方知识产权登记无效的任何行为。乙方不得试图改变或取消知识产权的任何登记。乙方不得协助他人从事此等行为。 违反本条款将立即导致本协议的终止。而且,双方同意违反本条款将导致对甲方声誉、商誉、知识财产价值的减损或毁坏,从而会导致实质的损害。此等损害将是无法估量的,因为无形财产的减损是难以计算的。因此,双方同意如果乙方违反本条款,则甲方有权就每种违约货物向乙方索取预定的违约金,金额以甲方当前产品目录上所列明价格的 X% 为基础进行计算。
Intellectual Property Rights. Except as stated herein, you acknowledge that SendThisFile owns all right, title, and interest in and to the Site and Service, including, without limitation, all content and intellectual property rights therein, which are protected by U. S. and international intellectual property laws. SendThisFile is a service mark and SendThisFile and the Yellow File Folder Logo are federally registered service marks of SendThisFile, Inc.. Other product and company names mentioned herein may be the trademarks or service marks of their respective owners. You agree that you will not in any way, directly or indirectly copy, reproduce, produce, distribute, transmit, alter, modify, or create derivative works of the Site, the Service, or any content therein. Any rights not expressly granted herein are reserved.	网站常用的知识产权条款

三、知识产权条款的核心内容以及基本句型

从法律概念上讲,知识产权的主题可能是合同条款中最复杂的一项。它本身包含的内容实在太多,涉及的范围或机构太广。

在定义条款写作的一章,我们对知识产权已有界定,不妨再摘录于此,以便加深我们对这一复杂议题的理解:

"Intellectual Property Rights" means any and all tangible and intangible: (i) rights associated with works of authorship, including copyrights, <u>moral rights</u>, <u>neighboring rights</u>, and derivative works thereof, (ii) trademark and trade name rights, (iii) trade secret rights, (iv) patents, design rights, and other industrial property rights, and, (v) all other intellectual property rights (of every kind and nature however designated) whether arising by operation of law, treaty, contract, license, or otherwise, together with all registrations, initial applications, renewals, extensions, continuations, divisions or reissues thereof.

"Intellectual Property Rights" means any and all tangible and intangible: (i) copyrights and other rights associated with works of authorship throughout the world, including but not limited to <u>copyrights</u>, <u>neighboring rights</u>, <u>moral rights</u>, and <u>mask works</u>, and all derivative works thereof; (ii) trademarks and trade name rights and similar rights; (iii) trade secret rights; (iv) patents, designs, algorithms, utility models, and industrial property rights, all improvements thereto; (v) all other intellectual and industrial property rights (of every kind and nature throughout the world and however designated) whether arising by operation of law, contracts, license, or otherwise; and (vi) all registration, applications, renewals, extensions, continuations, divisions, or reissues thereof now or thereafter in force (including any rights in any of the foregoing).

"知识产权"指所有有形或无形的权利:(1)与拥有著作权的作品有关的权利,包括版权、精神权利、邻接权以及由此衍生出来的作品权。所有由以上述权利衍生而来的权利;(2)商标权以及贸易名权,(3)商业秘密权,(4)专利权、设计权和其他工业产权,以及(5)所有其他(无论定为何种性质)知识产权——不管是通过执行法律、条约、合同、许可证或其他方式(包括所有该类文书的注册、始初申请、续期、延期、延续、分拆或重新发行)而产生的。

"知识产权"指所有有形或无形的权利,即(1)与在世界各地的有著作权的作品有关的版权及其他权利,包括但不限于版权、邻接权、精神权利及掩膜作品①以及所有由以上述权利衍生而来的权利;(2)商标权以及贸易名权及类似的权利;(3)商业秘密权;(4)专利权、设计权、算法权、实用品模型权及工业产权,及其改进产品的权利;(5)所有其他知识及工业产权(包括在世界各地的任何类型和性质的产权——不管以何种形式指定的

---

① 说到知识产权,大众比较熟悉的就是著作权或版权。专职律师会把普通人意想不到的各种可能性都考虑进去。就知识产权而言,除了版权之外,还有普通人很少会想得到的许多权利概念,如 neighboring rights, moral rights, mask works 等等。究竟这三者为何物? Neighboring rights(邻接权),也叫"相关权利"(Related rights),它依附于著作权人,没有著作权,邻接权就失去其基础。主要包括图书、报刊出版者的权利,艺术表演者的权利,录音、录像制作人的权利,广播电台、电视台的权利等。Moral rights(道德权)也是由版权/著作权衍生而来,包括发表作品的署名权、匿名权、使用假名权以及保护作品完整性的权利(即不被任意改编的权利)等等。Mask works(掩膜作品),在美国指集成电路布图设计作品,"掩膜作品"的译文是根据美国对该词的定义翻译而成的;在日本,同一概念称作"电路布图"(Circuit Layout),瑞典称为"布图设计"(Layout Design),欧盟许多国家称为拓扑图(Topography)。http://www.netlawcn.com/second/content.asp?no=492

权利)无论是通过法律、合同、证书或其他方式的运作而产生的;(6)以及所有注册权、应用权、更新权、扩充权、持续权、分割权,或在目前或今后重新签发权(包括对前述任何一项的任何权利)。

综上所述,我们可以将该条款的写作归为四个方面:

(一) 如何定义与本合同有关的知识产权?谁拥有知识产权以及该产权有没有法律上的问题?

1. The Intellectual Property <u>consists</u> on the date hereof <u>of the trade mark, trade names, service marks, service mark registrations, service names, patents, patent rights, copyrights, inventions, licenses, approvals, governmental authorizations, trade secrets</u> and rights necessary to conduct their respective businesses as now conducted …

2. The Company <u>owns or possesses</u> <u>all trademarks</u>…

3. … shall be <u>the sole and exclusive owner of any and all writings, documents, works made for hire, inventions, discoveries, know-how, processes, chemical entities, compounds, plans, memoranda, tests, research, designs, specifications, models and data</u> that Consultant <u>makes, conceives, discovers or develops</u>, either solely or jointly with any other person in performance of the Services (collectively, "Work Product").

4. Party B <u>owns the exclusive rights in the designs, patents, trademarks, trade names, and company names</u> (the "Intellectual Property") used in connection with the Party B's Goods.

5. … owns all right, title, and interest in and to the Site and Service, including, without limitation, all content and intellectual property rights therein, which are protected by U.S. and international intellectual property laws.

6. The Company does not have any knowledge of any infringement by the Company trademark, patents, copyrights, inventions, trade secret, and, to the knowledge of the Company there is no claim, action or proceeding being made or brought against the Company regarding their intellectual property; and the Company is unaware of any facts or circumstances which might give rise to any of the foregoing.

(二) 如何使用该知识产权?哪些使用是允许的、适当的?哪些使用属于违约?

1. The Party B may resell, lease, or rent Goods only if the Party A's Intellectual Property is used in connection with Goods.

2. The Party B is prohibited from using the Party A's Intellectual Property in connection with any products that are not furnished by the Party A.

(三) 如何保护(协助保护)有关的知识产权?有关方就保护知识产权做出的保证

1. You agree that you will not in any way, directly or indirectly copy, reproduce, produce, distribute, transmit, alter, modify, or create derivative works of the Site, the Service, or any content

therein.

2. XYZ agrees to cooperate with ABC in any litigation or other enforcement action that ABC may undertake to enforce or protect the licensed Trademarks...

3. Party A warrants that any design or instruction furnished or given by Party A to Party B shall not be such as will cause Party B to infringe any patent...

4. The party A will not use the Party B's Intellectual Property as if were the Party A's own property, nor will the Party A register the Party B's Intellectual Property in any country as if it were the Party A's own.

5. ...has no rights in or to the use of, any trademark, trade name, logo, service mark or other mark, identification or name of SUPPLIER or any Intellectual Property Right of SUPPLIER.

6. ...shall promptly notify SUPPLIER of any known infringement or improper use of SUPPLIER's Intellectual Property Rights.

7. Registrant agrees to reasonably cooperate with SUPPLIER in any action taken by SUPPLIER against such third parties, provided that all expenses of such action shall be borne by SUPPLIER and all damages which may be awarded or agreed upon in settlement of such action shall accrue to SUPPLIER.

8. The Party B will not duplicate or attempt to duplicate any of the Goods, will not make the Goods available to another person for purposes of duplication, and will not make or sell any products that are confusingly or deceptively similar to the Goods.

9. Each Party shall immediately notify the other Party and provide to the other Party all relevant background facts upon becoming aware of (i) any registrations of...

(四) 什么样状况构成违约以及发生违约使用时的处置方法

1. ...its unauthorized use or registration of the Party B's Intellectual Property, or of any intellectual property that is confusingly or deceptively similar to the Party B's Intellectual Property, will be deemed an infringement of the Party B's exclusive rights;

2. ...the parties agree that if the Party B violates this Paragraph, the Party A has right to assess liquidated damaged against the Party B in an amount equal to [number] percent of the price listed on the Party A's Current Product List for each of the Good that is subject of the violation.

四、知识产权标准条款的写作

我们假设甲方与乙方签约,甲方获得特许销售或生产乙方拥有知识产权的若干产品。那么该保护知识产权的条款该如何撰写?根据对以上条款样本、内容、句型和关键用词的分析,我们可以推出以下四段标准条款:

Party B owns or possesses the Intellectual Property which consists its trade marks, trade names, service names, service marks, service mark registrations, patents, patent rights, copyrights, inventions, licenses, approvals, governmental authorizations, trade secrets and rights necessary to conduct its businesses as now conducted. To the knowledge of Party B, there is no claim, action or proceeding being made or brought against Party B regarding any of the foregoing Intellectual Property items.

乙方拥有或享有以满足经营目前业务所需而使用的知识产权,包括其商标、商号、服务名称、服务标记、服务标记注册专利、专利、专利权、版权、发明、许可证、核准书、政府授权书、商业秘密和商业权利。据乙方所知,没有任何一方就上述知识产权项目对乙方提出权利主张或提起诉讼。

Party A may resell, lease, rent or manufacture the Goods only if Party B's Intellectual Property is used in connection with the Goods. Party A is prohibited from using the Party B's Intellectual Property in connection with any Goods that are not furnished or approved by Party B.

只有乙方的知识产权用于与货品相关的目的,甲方才可以转售、租赁或制造货品。甲方不得在销售任何非由乙方提供或批准的货品中使用乙方的知识产权。

Party A's unauthorized use or registration of the Party B's Intellectual Property, or of any intellectual property that is confusingly or deceptively similar to the Party B's Intellectual Property, shall also be deemed an infringement of the Party B's exclusive rights. In such case, Party B may terminate this Agreement upon the giving of thirty (30) days' prior written notice and Party A shall still be liable to Party B for any such infringement under the applicable laws.

甲方如擅自使用或注册乙方知识产权或者与乙方知识产权相混淆的知识产权将构成侵害乙方的专有权。在该种情况下,乙方可提前给予甲方三十天的书面通知而终止本协议。但甲方仍须按照相关法律对其侵害行为负法律责任。

Party A shall promptly notify Party B of any known infringement or improper use of Party B's Intellectual Property Right in its region or territory. Party A will reasonably cooperate with Party B in any action taken by Party B against such third parties, provided that all expenses of such action shall be borne by Party B and all damages which may be awarded or agreed upon in settlement of such action shall accrue to Party B.

甲方如发现在其区域或地区内有人侵害或不当使用乙方的知识产权,甲方应及时通知乙方,并在乙方对有关的第三方展开法律行动时给予合理的配合;但所有的诉讼花费应由乙方自行负责,而诉讼中所获的赔偿或解决获益亦归乙方所有。

第十三章 保密条款的写作和翻译

一、引言

保密条款和知识产权条款一样,实质上保证条款的延续。也就是说,合同各方的商业机密与拥有专有权的知识都必须予以保护,各方必须在合同中做出承诺。虽然并非每一类合同都涉及或需要这两类条款(如租赁合约或地产买卖,普通货物买卖等),但合资企业、技术转让、高科技产品代理或销售等等,都涉及需要保密和特殊保护的内容。由于这两个条款的通用度不及其他条款,故本章只做比较简短的讨论,主要提供写作和翻译样本,所以篇幅仍然相等可观。但必须指出的是,如果合同内容敏感(materials of a highly sensitive nature),各方甚至可能单独签署一份保密协议。

保密条款的功能至少包括以下三项:(1)在英美国家,它能为普通法或商业秘密法令保护范围未能涵盖的救济的信息提供保护,在中国,它同样也能对该等尚未取得知识产权保护的信息提供契约上的保护;(2)可以为一方设定保守其从另一方所获信息之秘密的义务;(3)有助于公开信息的一方证明,为保护其专有信息它已经尽到了合理努力。(王相国,2008:137)

保密条款与上一章讨论的知识产权条款有两点重大的不同:(1)知识产权直接受法律保护,因为商标和专利等都有注册的所有权。受到侵犯时可直接通过法庭进行民事诉讼,而保密协议被违反了,往往只有间接的后果,而且举证相当困难,所以很难直接向泄露方提起诉讼。[①]此外,(2)保密条款往往在协议终止后的很长时间内(一般是两到三年)仍然有效;而知识产权的保护不受合同期限的限制,只要知识产权的有效期仍然生效,该知识就一直受保护,如商标或专利只要向政府规管部门缴纳规定的维持费,便可保持生效。不过,专利有一定期限。如在美国、日本,新药专利保护期限是 20 年。所以知识产权是否受到保护,与产权所有人的利益有重大关系。

---

① 一旦提起刑事诉讼,可按《中华人民共和国刑法》第二百一十九条有关侵犯商业秘密罪,对个人或法人行为人处三年以下有期徒刑或者拘役,并处或者单处罚金;造成特别严重后果的,处三年以上七年以下有期徒刑,并处罚金。

二、保密条款样本和译文

Confidentiality	保密条款
All information provided by the Disclosing Party which the Disclosing Party wishes to remain confidential shall be clearly marked as being confidential. Confidential Information includes：	信息披露方提供的所有信息，如果披露方希望予以保密，应明确标示为机密。 保密信息包括：
Party B agrees that it will not at any time after the signature of this Agreement disclose any information in relation to the Company's method of manufacture or design or Party B's method of distribution in relation to the Products.（乔焕然，2008：108）	乙方同意其在签订本合同后的任何时间内，都不得泄露任何与公司制造或设计方法或乙方经销本产品的方法相关的信息。
The Parties shall not disclose to any third parties the Data with regard to this Contract during the Contract terms and two years after the termination of the Contract.	在本合同生效期限内以及终止后的两年内合同双方不得将与本合同有关的任何资料披露给第三方。
The Receiving Party shall not disclose the Confidential Information to anyone other than its own employees without a prior written consent from the Disclosing Party provided that such a prior written consent shall not be unreasonably withheld. The Receiving Party undertakes to disclose the Confidential Information furnished to it only to its employees who have a legitimate and absolute need to know the Confidential Information in order to perform their duties relating to the purpose set out herein.（范文祥、吴怡，2008：63）	除非事先获得信息披露方书面允许，否则，信息接受方不得将该信息披露给除其雇员以外的任何人，但信息披露方不得无故拒绝。信息接受方承诺，提供给的保密信息只披露给那些为履行与本协议所规定的目的有关的义务而合法且绝对有必要知晓该保密信息的员工。
The Disclosing Party hereby represents and warrants that it has the right and authority to disclose the Confidential Information to the Receiving Party in accordance with terms and conditions herein. Neither Party shall be liable in an action initiated by one against the other for special, indirect or consequential damages resulting from or arising out of this Agreement, including without limitation, loss of profit or business interruptions, however the same may be caused.	信息披露方兹保证：披露方有权根据本协议条款向信息接受方披露该保密信息。 在一方对另一方提起的诉讼中，双方均不对对方的由于本协议而引起或产生的特殊的、间接的或后果性的赔偿（包括但不限于不管由何种原因引起的盈利损失或业务中断）负责。

续表

Confidentiality	保密条款
The Recipient <u>may disclose Confidential Information to</u> only those of its Representatives who (a) require the Confidential Information for the Permitted Use (but to the extent practicable, only the part that is required); (b) are informed in writing by the Recipient of the confidential nature of the Confidential Information; and (c) <u>agree in writing to be bound by the obligations of this Article.</u>(乔焕然,2008:228)	接受方只能将保密信息向其满足下列条件的代表做出披露：(a)需要将保密信息用作"被许可的用途"（但应在可行的限度内,且限于所需部分）；(b)已接到接受方关于这些保密信息之保密性质的书面通知；以及（c）书面同意受本条义务约束。
During and after the term of this Agreement, the Recipient <u>shall take all commercially reasonable measures necessary to keep the Confidential Information confidential</u>, including, without limitation, all measures it takes to protect its confidential information of a similar nature. Without limiting the effect of the preceding sentence, the Recipient shall take commercially reasonable actions, legal or otherwise, necessary to cause its Representatives to comply with the provisions of this Agreement and to prevent any disclosure of the Confidential Information by any of them. The Recipient <u>shall give prompt written notice to the Company of any unauthorized use or disclosure of the Confidential Information</u> and shall assist the Company in remedying each unauthorized use or disclosure. Giving assistance does not waive any breach of his Article by the Recipient, nor does acceptance of the assistance constitute a waiver of any breach of this Article.（乔焕然,2008:228）	在本协议生效期间及其后,信息接受方应采取所有必要的商业上合理的手段（包括但不限于其用来保护自己的性质类似的保密信息的所有手段）,以保持保密信息的保密性。除此之外,信息接受方还应采取商业上合理的合法的或其他必要的行动以促使其代表遵守本协议之规定并且阻止任何代表对保密信息做出任何披露。 信息接受方应及时将任何对保密信息的无权使用或披露情况以书面形式通知公司,且应协助公司对该种无权使用或披露情况做出救济。提供协助并不代表放弃对接受方违反本条规定的追究,接受协助也不代表对违反该条行为不予追究。
Upon the end of the confidential obligation herein, the Receiving Party shall promptly: (a) <u>return or, at the option of the Disclosing Party, destroy all Confidential Information that is in tangible form</u> (including, without limitation, Confidential Information contained on computer disks or other electronic media) furnished to the Receiving Party; and (b) <u>destroy all analyses, compilations, studies or other documents based upon Confidential Information</u>, except to the extent such Confidential Information is incorporated into corporate documents or reports which the Receiving Party is required to retain by law or its internal procedures, in which case the Receiving Party <u>shall take appropriate measures to preserve its continuing confidentiality.</u>	本合同规定的保密义务结束后,信息接受方应立即： (a)返还或根据信息披露方选择,销毁以有形形式提供给信息接受方的保密信息（包括但不限于计算机硬盘中或其他带电子媒介中储存的保密信息）；以及 (b)销毁任何基于该保密信息所作出的分析、编纂、研究或其他文件,但根据法律或信息接受方内部程序该保密信息已经并入公司文件或报告的内容除外,但信息接受方仍应采取适当措施,继续对这些信息予以保密。

Confidentiality	保密条款
Party A acknowledges and agrees that the Technology it will receive from Party B during the term of this Contract <u>shall be kept secret and confidential</u>. Party A agrees that it and all of its employees and personnel <u>shall use the Technology only for the purposes specified in this Contract</u> and <u>shall not disclose in anyway whatsoever any of the Technology to any third Party or Parties without the prior written consent of Party B. Such confidentiality shall be maintained during the terms of this Contract and for a period of two (2) years after the termination of this Contract</u>. (王辉,2007:100)	甲方承认并同意在本合同期间内对将从乙方收到的技术应予保密。甲方同意其与所有员工和人员仅为本合同规定之用途使用该技术,未经乙方事先书面同意,不会以任何方式向任何第三方披露该技术的任何信息。该保密义务在本合同期间以及本合同终止后两(2)年内继续有效。
In the course of performing consulting services, the parties recognize that Consultant may come in contact with or become familiar with information which the Company or its subsidiaries or Affiliated Companies may consider confidential. This information may include, but is not limited to, information pertaining to the Company, such as financial, statistical, technical, strategic, product, customer, and personnel data, which information, is not generally available to the public, and may be of value to a competitor. Consultant agrees to keep all such information confidential and not to discuss or divulge it to anyone other than appropriate Company personnel or their designees. The provisions of this paragraph are in addition to, and not in lieu of, any other obligations of confidentiality entered into by Consultant and Company and/or any Affiliated Companies.	在提供咨询服务的过程中,合同方承认顾问可接触或熟悉公司或其附属公司或其关联公司视为机密的信息。该信息包括但不限于与公司相关的信息,即公众一般无法获取但对竞争者可能有价值的信息,比如金融、统计、技术、战略、产品、客户和个人资料。顾问同意对所有上述信息保密,不与除适当公司员工或其指定人员以外的任何人讨论或向其泄露。本条款是对顾问与公司和/或任何附属公司签订的任何其他保密义务的补充,而并非代替。
Unless he obtains the prior written consent of the Employer, the Executive shall at all times, both during and following the Retention Period, keep confidential and shall refrain from using for the benefit of himself, or any person or entity other than the Employer or its subsidiaries or affiliates, any material document or information obtained from the Employer or its subsidiaries, affiliates or predecessors, in the course of his employment with any of them concerning their properties, operations or business (unless such document or information is readily ascertainable from public or published information or trade sources or has otherwise been made available to the public through no fault of his own) until the same ceases to be material (or becomes so ascertainable or available); provided, however, that nothing in this Section 7(a) shall prevent the Executive, with or without the	除获得雇主的事先书面同意,执行官应在保管期间和之后的任何时候对信息保密,且不得在雇佣期间在其财产、运作或业务方面为自身或除雇主或其下属机构或附属机构的任何人或实体的利益使用从雇主或其下属机构、附属机构或前任雇主获取的任何实质文件或信息(除非该文件或信息确定可从公众或已公布信息或贸易资源获取或是通过非自身过失已经公之于众的资料),直至同样信息不再是实质信息(或可如此确定或获取);但第7(a)条的规定不得阻止执行官(不管有或没有雇主同意)参与或泄露与任何

续表

Confidentiality	保密条款
Employers consent, from participating in or disclosing documents or information in connection with any judicial or administrative investigation, inquiry or proceeding or the Company's public reporting requirements to the extent that such participation or disclosure is required under applicable law.	司法或行政调查、询问或诉讼或公司公众报告要求的相关文件或信息——只要该等参与或泄露是准据法所要求的。
From and after the date of execution of this Settlement Agreement, this Settlement Agreement shall be kept and maintained confidentially among the Parties. No Party shall disclose any part or term of this Settlement Agreement to any other person or entity, without the prior written consent of all other parties, except, (i) AGU shall be entitled to disclose such facts concerning this Settlement Agreement as may be required under applicable laws, rules and regulations governing the conduct of business by public corporations, including, among other laws, the United States Securities Laws; (ii) any Party shall be entitled to disclose any or all of the terms of this Settlement Agreement, if compelled to do so by an order of a court of competent jurisdiction, or a subpoena issued in connection with a judicial proceeding, only after a protective order is issued by a court preventing further disclosure of the terms of this Settlement Agreement by any of the parties to any such litigation; and (iii) any Party shall be entitled to disclose any or all of the terms of this Settlement Agreement in any judicial or arbitral proceeding commenced in order to enforce the terms of this Settlement Agreement.	自调解书订立之日起,各方应对本调解书的一切内容保密。任何一方未经所有其他方事先书面通知不得向任何其他人或实体泄露本调解书的任一部分或条款,但下列情况则属例外,(i)根据管辖公营公司商业行为的适用法律、法则和法规的要求(包括《美国证券法》及其他法律),AGU 有权泄露有关本调解书的事实;(ii)如拥有司法管辖权的法院禁制令,或与法律诉讼相关的传票(仅在法院签发保护令阻止其向任何诉讼机构进一步泄露本调解书之后),任何一方有权泄露本调解书的任何或全部条款;和(iii)任何一方有权在任何已开始的司法或仲裁程序中泄露本调解书的任何或全部条款,以实施本调解书的条款。
Party A has supplied and during the period of this Agreement will continue to supply to Party B certain technical and commercial information relating to the Licensed Software and Party A Services in order to assist Party B to carry out its duties hereunder. Such information may include that found in specifications and drawings related to the design and manufacture of the Licensed Software and Party A Services, of which Party A has been and remains the sole proprietor. Party B undertakes: (a) to use such information only for that purpose; (b) to keep confidential and not to reproduce, distribute or disclose any or all such information as is not freely available to the public (including without limiting the generality thereof such information as Party A may from time to time specifically designate as confidential); (c) to return to Party A on termination of this Agreement all material embodying information	甲方已经提供并且在本协议有效期间内继续向乙方提供与被许可软件以及甲方服务相关的技术、商业信息以帮助乙方履行其在本协议项下的义务。上述信息包括包含在与被许可软件、甲方服务设计、制作相关说明书及图纸中的信息。甲方对这些信息享有所有的专有权。乙方保证:(a)仅为该等目的使用该等信息;(b)由于这些信息不为公众所知,乙方为信息保密,并且不复制、散布、披露任何上述信息(包括但不限于一般性的具有上述性质的信息,甲方可以随时特别指定某信息具有保密性质);(c)本协议终止

续表

Confidentiality	保密条款
designated by Party A as confidential and all copies thereof; and (d) to ensure that its staff concerned with the Licensed Software is aware of and observe the provisions of this paragraph. (乔焕然,2008:107)	后,应向甲方公司返还所有包含由甲方公司所指定为机密的资料及其副本;并且(d)确保与本许可软件相关之人员知悉并遵守本条款。
All information furnished by Company A to Company B or by Company B to Company A in connection with this Agreement and the transactions contemplated hereby, as well as the terms, conditions and provisions of this Agreement, shall be kept confidential by Company B and Company A and shall be used by Company B and Company A only in connection with this Agreement and the transactions contemplated hereby, except in connection with the enforcement of rights or exercise of remedies under this Agreement and the Security Agreement and except to the extent that such information (i) is already known by the party to whom the information is disclosed or in the public domain at the time the information is disclosed; (ii) thereafter becomes lawfully obtainable from other sources; (iii) is required to be disclosed in any document to be filed with any federal, state, provincial, municipal or other governmental department, commission, board, bureau, agency or instrumentality, domestic or foreign; or (iv) is required to be disclosed under securities laws or regulations applicable to Company A or its affiliates, or by court order. Notwithstanding the foregoing, either Party may disclose such information to its Affiliates, directors, officers, investors, bankers, advisors, trustees and representatives, provided that such Persons shall be informed of the confidential nature of such information and shall be obligated to keep such information confidential pursuant to the terms of this Section 7.17.	对于公司A向公司B或公司B向公司A提供的与本协议相关的一切信息和本协议打算进行的交易的一切信息以及本协议的条件、条款和规定,公司A和公司B应予以保密,并仅用于双方与本协议相关和本协议打算进行的交易,但与本协议和安全协议的权利实施或补救相关的信息除外,且不包括下列信息(i)披露信息的一方已经知悉该信息或在信息披露时公众已经知悉;(ii)披露之后从其他来源合法获取的信息;(iii)要求在任何提交给下述机构的文件中披露的信息,即任一联邦、州、省、市或其他政府部门、委员会、董事会、办事处、代理处或其他国内外媒介;或(iv)适用于公司A或其附属机构的证券法律或法规或法院命令要求披露的信息。尽管有上述规定,任何一方可向其附属机构、主管、高级职员、投资商、开户银行、顾问、信托公司和代表披露该等信息,但有关方应告知该人这些信息的保密性质,且该人有义务根据第7.17条规定对该等信息予以保密。
7.1 The Parties each undertake to keep confidential and not to disclose to any third party, or to use themselves other than for the purposes of the Projects or as permitted under or in accordance with this Agreement (including for the purpose of enjoying the benefit of the rights and licenses granted under Clause 5), any confidential or secret information in any form directly belonging or relating to the other, its Affiliates, its or their business or affairs, disclosed by the one and received by the other pursuant to or in the course of this Agreement, including without limitation any Technology and the existence and terms of this Agreement (Confidential Information)	7.1 合同各方皆承诺,对于根据本协议执行过程中一方披露、另一方接受的以各种形式直接或间接属于或关系到对方、对方的关联公司、对方或关联公司的业务或事务的各种机密信息或秘密信息,包括但不限于对方的任何技术及本协议的存在及其条件("保密信息")予以保密,并不会将该保密信息向任何第三方做出披露或用于除项目目的或本协议允许的目的(包括为享有根据第5条授予的权利和许可的

续表

Confidentiality	保密条款
7.2 Each Party undertakes to only disclose the Confidential Information of the other to those of its officers, employees, agents and contractors to whom, and to the extent to which, such disclosure is necessary for the purposes contemplated under this Agreement. Each Party shall ensure that all such personnel enter into and observe the terms of an individual confidentiality undertaking in the form set out in Schedule 3. 7.3 The obligations contained in this Clause 7 shall survive the expiry or termination of this Agreement for any reason, but shall not apply to any Confidential Information which: (a) is publicly known at the time of disclosure to the receiving party; or (b) becomes publicly known otherwise than through a breach of this agreement by the receiving Party, its officers, employees, agents or contractors; or (c) can be proved by the receiving party to have reached it otherwise than by being communicated by the receiving party to have reached it otherwise than by being communicated by the other Party including: (i) being known to it prior to disclosure; or (ii) having been developed by or for it wholly independently of the other party; or (iii) having been obtained from a third party without any restriction on disclosure on such third party of which the recipient is aware, having made due enquiry; or (d) is required by law, regulation or order of a competent authority (including any regulatory or governmental body or securities exchange) to be disclosed by the Receiving party provided that, where practicable, the disclosing Party is given reasonable advance notice of the intended disclosure. (范文祥、吴怡,2008:128)	目的)以外的任何目的。 7.2各方皆承诺,仅将对方的保密信息披露给其管理人员、雇员、代理或承包商,所披露的人员和内容范围以执行本协议计划之目的而应予披露的范围为限。各方保证,所有这些人员都应签署一份单独的附表3形式的保密承诺书并予以遵守。 7.3不管出于何种原因,第7条规定的义务在本协议到期或终止后仍然有效,但并不适用于下列机密信息: (a)向接受方披露之时已为公众知晓的信息; (b)非由于本协议保密信息接收方、其管理人员、雇员、代理或承包商违反本协议规定而为公众知晓的信息。 (c)接受方能够证明其获得的信息并非协议对方交流传递给接收方的,包括: (i) 在披露之前接受方已知晓的信息; (ii) 完全由接受方独立开发出来的信息; (iii) 接受方知道第三方不受任何披露限制并经过恰当的询问后从该第三方处获得的信息;或 (d) 法律、法规或主管当局(包括规管或政府机构或证券交易所)的命令要求信息接收方披露的信息,但如果可能,接受方应合理提前将该打算之披露通知信息披露方。
The Receiving Party may disclose the Confidential Information without the Disclosing Party's prior written consent to an Affiliate (as hereinafter defined) company in the performance of the Agreement, provided that the Receiving Party guarantees the adherence of such Affiliate company to the terms of this Clause X. "Affiliate" means a company which, directly or indirectly through one or more intermediaries, controls or is controlled by, or is under common control with a Party, or a subcontractor of a Party. For this purpose control means the direct or indirect ownership of in aggregate fifty percent or more of voting capital. The Receiving Party shall be entitled to disclose the Confidential	信息接受方可以不经披露方事先书面同意将保密信息披露给执行本协议的一家关联公司(如下文定义),但接受方保证该关联公司遵守第X条的保密规定。"关联公司"指直接或通过一个或多个中间体间接控制"一方"的公司;或直接或通过一个或多个中间体间接受该"一方"控制的公司;或直接或通过一个或多个中间体间接与该"一方"共同控制的公司;或是该"一方"的分包商。本款中的控制指直接

续表

Confidentiality	保密条款
Information without the Disclosing Party's prior written consent to such of the following persons to the extent that they have a clear need to know in order to carry out the Agreement: (i) Employees, officers, and directors of the Receiving Party; or (ii) Employees, officers, and directors of the said Affiliate company of the Receiving Party. The Receiving Party <u>shall ensure that all the persons</u> to whom the Confidential Information is disclosed under this Agreement <u>keep such Confidential Information confidential and do not disclose or divulge the Confidential Information on to</u> any unauthorized person.① Prior to making any disclosures to the persons permitted under the above-mentioned, the Receiving Party shall obtain an undertaking of confidentiality from the recipients, enforceable by both the Disclosing Party and the Receiving Party, substantially in the same form and content as this Agreement.	或间接拥有总计百分之五十或以上的具有表决权的资本。 信息接受方有权不经披露方事先书面同意向下列人员披露保密信息,但应限于这些人为执行合同而明确需要知道的范围: (i) 接受方的雇员、高级职员和董事;或 (ii) 上述接受方之关联公司的雇员、高级职员和董事。 信息接受方保证所有根据本协议接受保密信息的有关人员应对这些保密信息保密,不得向任何未授权人员披露或泄露保密信息。 在向上述条款中允许的有关人员披露信息之前,信息接受方应从这些信息接受者那里获得本协议信息披露方与接受方均有权执行的保密承诺,其内容和形式应基本与本协议相同。②
1.1 Confidentiality. "Confidential Information" <u>means</u> any and all tangible and intangible information (whether written or otherwise recorded or oral) of Party B that: (a) <u>derives independent economic value, actual or potential, from not being generally known to, and not being readily ascertainable by proper means by</u>, other persons who can obtain economic value from its disclosure or use and is the subject of efforts that are reasonable under the circumstances to maintain its secrecy; (b) <u>Party B designates as confidential</u> or, given the nature of the information or the circumstances surrounding its disclosure, <u>reasonably should be considered as confidential</u>. Confidential Information <u>includes</u>, without limitation: (i) <u>nonpublic information relating to Party B's technology, customers, business plans, promotional and marketing activities, finances and other business affairs</u>; (ii) <u>the terms and conditions of this agreement</u>; and (iii) <u>any nonpublic information relating to any activities conducted hereunder</u>. Notwithstanding the above, the term "Confidential	1.1 保密条款。"保密资料"指乙方之所有有形或无形的资料(不论是书面的、口头的或以其他方式录制的):(a) 该资料由于一般不为他人所知,他人使用常规方法无法轻易获得,其披露、使用可使该他人从中获得经济价值,因而具有独立的经济价值(实际的或潜在的),并且是要做出合理努力以维持其保密状态的主体;(b) 乙方指定其为保密的资料,或根据该资料的性质或围绕其披露状况而应合理地认为是保密的资料,其中包括(但不限于)(i) 与乙方的技术、客户、营商计划、促销和营销活动、财务及其他业务有关的非公开的资料;(ii) 本合同的条款;以及(iii) 与根据本合同开展的活动有关的任何非公开的资料。尽管有以上规

---

① Divulge: To give sb. information that is supposed to be secret (泄露/透露); Disclose: 比较中性, to make sth. known publicly, 透露的含义占主导。

② 译文参阅范文祥:65－66;但做了若干订正,其中原文中的"关联公司"与原作者在该书第29页下过定义的"关联公司"拼法和措辞都不一致,本译文将其更正为与其前文界定词一致的"Affiliate",而不是"Affiliated Company"。

Confidentiality	保密条款
Information" does not include any information that is readily discernible from publicly-available products or literature. 1.2 Use of Confidential Information. Party A shall only use Confidential Information solely in furtherance of the activities contemplated by this agreement, and it shall not disclose Confidential Information to third parties without Party B's prior written consent. 1.3 Required Disclosures. Party A may disclose Confidential Information as required to comply with binding orders of governmental entities that have jurisdiction over it or as otherwise required by law, provided that Party A (i) gives Party B reasonable written notice to allow it to seek a protective order or other appropriate remedy (except to the extent compliance with the foregoing would cause Distributor to violate a court order or other legal requirement), (ii) discloses only such information as is required by the governmental entity or otherwise required by law, and (iii) and uses its best efforts to obtain confidential treatment for any Confidential Information so disclosed. 1.4 Survival. The parties hereto covenant and agree that this Section 1 shall survive the expiration, termination, or cancellation of this agreement for a period of three (3) years, except for Confidential Information described in Section 1(a), which shall survive the expiration, termination, or cancellation of this agreement for so long as such Confidential Information remains a trade secret as defined by relevant laws.	定,"保密资料"一词并不包括从已经可以公开得到的产品或文献中获得的任何资料。 1.2 保密资料的使用。甲方应将保密资料只用于促进本合同打算执行的各项活动;没有乙方的书面许可,甲方不得将保密资料披露给第三方。 1.3 必需的披露。甲方可以根据对机密资料有管辖权的政府部门必须服从的命令或其他法律要求披露机密资料;但甲方(i)要以合理的书面形式通知乙方,以允许乙方寻求保护令或寻求其他适当的补救措施(但如果因此会造成甲方违反法庭命令或其他法律要求则属例外),(ii)只披露政府部门或其他法律要求而需要披露的资料,以及(iii)尽一切努力对以上方式披露的资料采取保密措施。 1.4 存续条款。本合同双方兹同意:本合同上述1条(Section 1)的保密资料在本合同到期、终止或取消之后的三年内存续有效,但上述1(a)条的保密资料只要仍属于有关法律界定的商业机密、即使在本合同到期、终止或取消之后仍然存续有效。

Confidentiality. The parties agree to maintain discussions and proprietary information revealed pursuant to this agreement in confidence, to disclose them only to persons within their respective organizations having a need to know, and to furnish assurances to the other party that such persons understand this duty on confidentiality.

Effective upon, and only upon, the Closing Date, the Confidentiality Agreement shall terminate with respect to Confidential Information relating solely to the Business or otherwise in connection with the Purchased Assets; provided, however, that Purchaser acknowledges that any and all other Confidential Information provided to it by any Seller or its representatives concerning any Seller and its Subsidiaries (other than as it relates to the Business and/or the Purchased Assets) shall remain subject to the terms and conditions of the Confidentiality Agreement after the Closing Date. This provision shall survive the Closing or termination of this Agreement.[1]

---

[1] https://www.sendthisfile.com/policy/terms-of-use.jsp

续表

Confidentiality	保密条款
Confidentiality. <u>During the process of fulfilling this Agreement</u>, <u>all information</u> obtained by a Party (the "Receiving Party") from the other Party (the "Disclosing Party") <u>in connection with its business activities, products, services, intellectual property rights, technical details and performance and structure of company's management</u> shall be deemed to be confidential and shall not be disclosed to any third party, unless mandated by law, and shall not be used by the Receiving Party except in the performance of this Agreement. Confidentiality. (a) Purchaser acknowledges and agrees that all Confidential Information provided to it in connection with this Agreement, including under <u>Section 8.1</u>, <u>shall be maintained in confidence by</u> Purchaser, and <u>returned to Sellers</u>, at Purchaser's cost, promptly if this Agreement is terminated for any reason. In addition, Purchaser <u>shall deliver to</u> Sellers <u>all other due diligence information</u>, material and reports obtained independently by Purchaser if Purchaser terminates this Agreement. For purposes of this <u>Section 8.5</u> "<u>Confidential Information</u>" <u>shall mean</u> any confidential information with respect to, without limitation, methods of operation, customers, customer lists, Products, prices, fees, costs, Technology, inventions, trade secrets, know-how, software, marketing methods, plans, personnel, suppliers, competitors, markets or other specialized information or proprietary matters. (b) Sellers have had access to and contributed to information and materials of a highly sensitive nature (including Confidential Information) regarding the Purchased Assets and the Business. Each Seller agrees that unless it first secures the written consent of an authorized representative of Purchaser, <u>it shall not use for itself or anyone else</u>, and shall not disclose to others, any Confidential Information except to the extent such use or disclosure is required by Law or is required in connection with the Chapter 11 Cases (in which event it shall inform Purchaser in advance of any such required disclosure, shall cooperate with Purchaser in all reasonable ways in obtaining a protective order or other protection in respect of such required disclosure, and shall limit such disclosure to the extent reasonably possible while still complying with such requirements). Each Seller shall use reasonable care to safeguard Confidential Information and to protect it against disclosure, misuse, espionage, loss and theft.①	

三、保密条款的要素、句型和关键词

有学者总结:一个完整的保密条款包括保密主体、保密客体、保密方式和保密时间。保密主体是签约方;保密客体是与项目相关的数据资料;保密方式是不向第三方披露;保密时间是整个合同有效期及合同终止后两年内。(范文祥、吴怡,2008:60)其实,主体客体之类的界定没有任何意义。任何一个合同条款都涉及签约方,任何条款都有客体,即主题或针对的问题。就保密条款而言,内容可以说得更具体一些,要素有五个:

(一)哪些资料需要保密或对保密资料如何定义?

1. "Confidential Information" (shall) <u>mean</u> any confidential information with

---

① http://contracts.onecle.com/sco/unxis-sale-2009-06-15.shtml

respect to, without limitation, methods of operation, customers, customer lists, products, prices, fees, costs, technology, inventions, trade secrets, know-how, software, marketing methods, plans, personnel, suppliers, competitors, markets or other specialized information or proprietary matters.

2. ... all information obtained by a Party (the "Receiving Party") from the other Party (the "Disclosing Party") in connection with its business activities, products, services, intellectual property rights, technical details and performance and structure of company's management shall be deemed to be confidential.

3. ... all Confidential Information provided to it in connection with this Agreement, including...

4. Confidential Information includes:

5. Notwithstanding the above, the term "Confidential Information" does not include any information that is readily discernible from publicly-available products or literature.

这最后一条写法非常经济,"保密资料不包括任何显然已为公众所知的产品或文献"。那些啰唆的写法可以让读者看得失去耐心,例如:(a) is publicly known at the time of disclosure to the receiving party(接受方获得保密资料之前已为公众所知); or (b) becomes publicly known otherwise than through a breach of this agreement by the receiving Party, its officers, employees, agents or contractors (并非由于接受方违约泄密而为公众所知的资料); or (c) can be proved by the receiving party to have reached it otherwise than by being communicated by the receiving party to have reached it otherwise than by being communicated by the other Party including...(接受方能够证实并非由提供方提供而已经获得的资料,包括……); (i) being known to it prior to disclosure(在泄露前接受方已经获悉); or (ii) having been developed by or for it wholly independently of the other party(由其他方独立开发或为其开发的资料); or (iii) having been obtained from a third party without any restriction on disclosure on such third party of which the recipient is aware, having made due enquiry(不受任何披露条件限制从接受方认识的或向其适当征询过的第三方获得的资料); or (d) is required by law, regulation or order of a competent authority (including any regulatory or governmental body or securities exchange) to be disclosed by the Receiving party provided that, where practicable, the disclosing Party is given reasonable advance notice of the intended disclosure(最后包括法律、法规、政府行政机关、规管机构、证券交易所要求接受方披露的资料)。

(二) 保密资料使用的尺度

1. ... to the extent such use or disclosure is required by Law.

2. ... it shall inform Purchaser in advance of any such required disclosure.

3. ... shall cooperate with Purchaser in all reasonable ways in obtaining a protective order or other protection in respect of such required disclosure.

4. ... shall limit such disclosure to the extent reasonably possible while still complying with such requirements.

5. Party A agrees that it and all of its employees and personnel shall use the Technology <u>only for the purposes specified in this Contract</u> and <u>shall not disclose</u> in anyway whatsoever any of the Technology to any third Party or Parties <u>without the prior written consent</u> of Party B.

6. ... <u>shall only use</u> Confidential Information solely in furtherance of the activities contemplated by this agreement.

(三) 如何保密?

1. ... <u>shall not be disclosed to</u> any third party.

2. ... <u>shall be clearly marked as being confidential</u>.

3. ... <u>shall be maintained in confidence</u> by Purchaser.

4. ... it shall not use for itself or anyone else, and shall not disclose to others, any Confidential Information.

5. Each Seller <u>shall use reasonable care</u> to safeguard Confidential Information and <u>to protect it against disclosure, misuse, espionage, loss and theft</u>.

6. The Technology <u>shall be kept secret and confidential</u>.

7. <u>No Party shall disclose</u> any part or term of this Settlement Agreement to any other person or entity, <u>without the prior written consent</u> of all other parties, except...

8. Party A <u>shall not disclose</u> Confidential Information <u>to third parties</u> without Party B's prior written consent.

9. The Receiving Party <u>shall ensure that all the persons</u> to whom the Confidential Information is disclosed under this Agreement <u>keep such Confidential Information confidential and do not disclose or divulge the Confidential Information on to</u>.

(四) 合同终止后如何处置保密资料?

1. ... <u>shall remain subject to the terms and conditions of</u> the Confidentiality Agreement after the Closing Date.

2. This provision <u>shall survive</u> the Closing or termination of this Agreement.

3. ... <u>shall be returned to</u> Sellers, at Purchaser's cost, promptly if this Agreement is terminated for any reason.

4. ... <u>shall deliver to</u> the Seller all other due diligence information, material and reports obtained independently by...

5. Such <u>confidentiality shall be maintained</u> during the terms of this Contract and for a period of two (2) years after the termination of this Contract.

6. ... <u>shall not disclose to any third parties the Data with regard to</u> this Contract during the Contract terms and two years after the termination of the Contract.

7. ... <u>return or, at the option of the Disclosing Party, destroy all Confidential Information that is in tangible form</u>.

（五）违反保密协定如何处理？

1. Without limiting the effect of the preceding sentence, the Recipient shall take commercially reasonable actions, legal or otherwise, necessary to cause its Representatives to comply with the provisions of this Agreement and to prevent any disclosure of the Confidential Information by any of them.

2. The Recipient shall give prompt written notice to the Company of any unauthorized use or disclosure of the Confidential Information and shall assist the Company in remedying each unauthorized use or disclosure. Giving assistance does not waive any breach of his Article by the Recipient, nor does acceptance of the assistance constitute a waiver of any breach of this Article.

3. Neither Party shall be liable in an action initiated by one against the other for special, indirect or consequential damages resulting from or arising out of this Agreement, including without limitation, loss of profit or business interruptions, however the same may be caused.

泄露机密情况造成的后果一般是间接性的，造成的损失也较难做出实际估值而且举证相当困难，所以除终止合同或辞退泄密员工外，一般都不对泄密行为进行追究，故上述的补救措施都是轻描淡写的，很少有对合同当事人或泄密方提起民事诉讼或追究刑事责任的（当然斯诺登①和阿桑奇②事件是例外）。所以，我们在标准保密合同写作中，不对这最后一部分的内容做任何明确的提述。合同是实用性文本，也不应让其充斥无用或很少用得到的形式主义的东西。

以务实的态度，我们推荐以下三款不同风格、可用于不同类型合同的保密条款。第一款适用于对资料保密有极高要求的合同，第二款用于中型合同，第三款用于对保密只有适度要求的简易合同。

四、标准保密条款的写作

第一款：

1.1 Confidentiality. "Confidential Information" means any and all tangible and intangible information (whether written or otherwise recorded or oral) of Party B that：(a) derives independent economic value, actual or potential, from not being generally known to, and not being readily ascertainable by proper means by, other persons who can obtain economic value from its disclosure or use and is the subject of efforts that are reasonable under the circumstances to maintain its secrecy; (b) Party B designates as confidential or, given the nature of the information or the circumstances surrounding its disclosure, reasonably should be considered as confidential. Confidential Information includes, without

---

① Edward Joseph Snowden，前美国中央情报局职员，美国国家安全局外判技术员。因于2013年6月在香港将美国国家安全局关于棱镜计划监听项目的秘密文档披露给了英国《卫报》和美国《华盛顿邮报》，遭到美国和英国的通缉。

② Julian Paul Assange，澳大利亚记者，"维基解密"董事与发言人。

limitation: (i) nonpublic information relating to Party B's technology, customers, business plans, promotional and marketing activities, finances and other business affairs; (ii) the terms and conditions of this agreement; and (iii) any nonpublic information relating to any activities conducted hereunder. Notwithstanding the above, the term "Confidential Information" does not include any information that is readily discernible from publicly-available products or literature.

1.1 保密条款。"保密资料"指乙方之所有有形或无形的资料(不论是书面的、口头的或以其他方式录制的):(a)该资料由于一般不为他人所知,他人使用常规方法无法轻易获得,其披露、使用可使该他人从中获得经济价值,因而具有独立的经济价值(实际或潜在的),并且是要做出合理努力以维持其保密状态的主体;(b)乙方指定其为保密的资料,或根据该资料的性质或围绕其披露状况而应合理地认为是保密的资料,其中包括(但不限于)(i)与乙方的技术、客户、营商计划、促销和营销活动、财务及其他业务有关的非公开的资料;(ii)本合同的条款;以及(iii)与根据本合同开展的活动有关的任何非公开的资料。尽管有以上规定,"保密资料"一词并不包括从已经可以公开得到的产品或文献中获得的任何资料。

1.2 Use of Confidential Information. Party A shall only use Confidential Information solely in furtherance of the activities contemplated by this agreement, and it shall not disclose Confidential Information to third parties without Party B's prior written consent.

1.2 保密资料的使用。甲方应将保密资料只用于促进本合同打算执行的各项活动;没有乙方的书面许可,甲方不得将保密资料披露给第三方。

1.3 Required Disclosures. Party A may disclose Confidential Information as required to comply with binding orders of governmental entities that have jurisdiction over it or as otherwise required by law, provided that Party A (i) gives Party B reasonable written notice to allow it to seek a protective order or other appropriate remedy (except to the extent compliance with the foregoing would cause Distributor to violate a court order or other legal requirement), (ii) discloses only such information as is required by the governmental entity or otherwise required by law, and (iii) and uses its best efforts to obtain confidential treatment for any Confidential Information so disclosed.

1.3 必需的披露。甲方可以根据对机密资料有管辖权的政府部门必须服从的命令或其他法律要求披露机密资料;但甲方(i)要以合理的书面形式通知乙方,以允许乙方寻求保护令或寻求其他适当的补救措施(但如果因此会造成甲方违反法庭命令或其他法律要求则属例外),(ii)只披露政府部门或其他法律要求而需要披露的资料,以及(iii)尽一切努力对以上方式披露的资料采取保密措施。

1.4 Survival. The parties hereto covenant and agree that this Section 1 shall survive the expiration, termination, or cancellation of this agreement for a period of three (3) years, except for Confidential Information described in Section 1.1(a), which shall survive the expiration, termination, or cancellation of this agreement for so long as such Confidential Information remains a trade secret as defined by relevant laws.

1.4 存续条款。本合同双方兹同意:本合同上述 1 条(Section 1)的保密资料在本合同到期、终止或取消之后的三年内存续有效,但上述 1.1(a)条的保密资料只要仍属于有关法律界定的商业机密、即使在本合同到期、终止或取消之后仍然存续有效。

第二款：

Confidentiality. "Confidential Information" means all information obtained by a Party (the "Receiving Party") from the other Party (the "Disclosing Party") in connection with its business activities, products, services, intellectual property rights, technical details and performance and structure of company's management. It shall be deemed to be confidential. But the term does not include any information that is readily discernible from publicly-available products or literature.

保密。"保密资料"指一方（"接受方"）从另一方（"披露方"）获得的与披露方生意活动、产品、服务、知识产权、详细技术资料和技术性能以及与其公司管理架构有关的所有资料。该资料应视为保密性质。但该词并不包括从已经可以公开得到的产品或文献中获得的任何资料。

The Receiving Party agrees that it and all of its employees and personnel shall use the Confidential Information only for the purposes specified in this Contract and shall not disclose in anyway whatsoever any of the Confidential Information to any third Party without the prior written consent of the Disclosing Party.

接受方同意其与所有员工和人员仅为本合同规定之用途使用该保密资料，未获披露方事先书面同意，不会以任何方式向任何第三方披露该保密资料。

The Receiving Party also agrees that the Confidential Information shall survive the expiration, termination, or cancellation of this agreement for a period of two (2) years. It shall either be returned to the Disclosing Party, at the Receiving Party's cost, promptly if this Agreement is terminated for any reason, or be destroyed if it is in tangible form.

接受方还同意该保密资料条款在本协议到期、终止或取消之后的两（2）年内存续有效。不管本协议因何种原因而终止，接受方应以自费方式将该保密资料及时还返给披露方，或将以有形形式提供给接受方的保密资料予以销毁。

第三款：

Party A acknowledges and agrees that the Technology it will receive from Party B during the term of this Contract shall be kept secret and confidential. Party A agrees that it and all of its employees and personnel shall use the Technology only for the purposes specified in this Contract and shall not disclose in anyway whatsoever any of the Technology to any third Party or Parties without the prior written consent of Party B. Such confidentiality shall be maintained during the terms of this Contract and for a period of two (2) years after the termination of this Contract.（王辉，2007：100）

甲方承认并同意在本合同期间内对将从乙方收到的技术予以保密。甲方同意其与所有员工和人员仅为本合同规定之用途使用该技术，未经乙方事先书面同意，不会以任何方式向任何第三方披露该技术的任何信息。该保密义务在本合同期间以及本合同终止后两（2）年内继续有效。

第十四章 合同期限及终止条款的写作、翻译和研究

合同终止条款在多数情况下不作为一条单独冠名的通用条款,它一般会跟合同期限(Term/Duration)条款合并在一起,置放在其后。这样安排是比较合理的:先有期限,然后才可以在期限前或后终止它。

一、关于合同期限的写作

有关合同期限部分的写作比较简单,不管合同属何性质,其内容一般都包括两方面(后两者二选一):

1. 本合同几时开始生效:This Agreement shall <u>come into effect on the Commencement Date</u> and shall <u>continue in force until</u> the 5th Anniversary of the Commencement Date. 或者 This Agreement shall <u>commence as of the date hereof</u> and remain in full force and effect for an initial term of 5 years (the "Initial Term"). 无论采用何种写法,合同的其他部分(一般是序言部分)必须订明合同正式生效的日期。

2. 几时自动失效:On such date (the 5th Anniversary of the Commencement Date) this Agreement shall <u>terminate</u> automatically by expiry. 或者 This Agreement shall <u>end</u> on the last day of such term if written notice is provided by either party at least 120 days before the end of the then-current term.

3. 可否延长以及可延长多少时间:This Agreement may <u>be extended by</u> written agreement between the Parties hereto. 或者 Thereafter (after the 5th Anniversary of the Commencement Date), this Agreement shall <u>be renewed</u> automatically for a successive 5 year term.

关键词解析:此处有两个用词需要特别注意:

Term(s) of Contract——单数的 term 是期限,尤其指任期、有效期;复数的 terms 指合同条款、条件或细则,并且一般跟 conditions 连用,构成一组法律配对词(legal pair),可翻译成条款,或条款与细则,例如:... in the event of any such termination, the <u>terms and conditions</u> of this agreement shall continue to be binding upon the parties in connection with all Products shipped by Seller to Buyer. 即使 term 不跟 condition 连用,只要是复数,跟本章标题中的 term 就不属同一概念,例如:... OMP pays a reasonable price not to exceed the price that would have applied if Triax had delivered such Products according to the <u>terms</u> of the applicable Purchase Orders. 此处 terms 指的是"条款",即有关订单上的条款。

另一词是 expiry——该词与 expiration 同义,用法相同。但为何有些合同用 expiry,有

些则用 expiration？学了一辈子英文或做了一辈子翻译的非母语人士往往是搞不清的，其实美国和英国都用这两个词，只是 expiry 在英国和前英联邦国家比较流行而已；而在美国律师界，虽然两者都用，但主要使用 expiration[①]。

另外，以上引文中的用词还涉及典型法律英文的写作风格问题。在第 1 段中，有两个司空见惯的用词：as of the date hereof 和 remain in full force and effect。其实这一段的原文是这样的：

> This Agreement shall commence as of the date <u>hereof</u> and remain <u>in full force and effect</u> for an initial term of 5 years (the "Initial Term"). <u>Thereafter</u>, this Agreement shall be renewed automatically for a successive 5 year term, unless written notice is provided by either party at least 120 days before the end of the then-current term, in which event this Agreement shall end on the last day of such term. The Initial Term and any renewals shall <u>be constitute</u> the "Term."[②]

该段中前三个画线词均反映典型的"师爷风格"：陈腐的古旧词和累赘的配对词——属于第二章论述的"吸血鬼"性质的用词。在现代法律英文写作中对其如何处置，第二章中有详细的对策。简言之，古旧词一般可以删除而文意不受影响，必要时重复前文的有关用词（使用以 here，there，where 为词根的古旧词主要为避免用词重复）；对付配对词和累赘词一般是只保留其中一个最为读者熟悉的用词，例如，在 remain in full force and effect，去掉 effect，留下 force；remain in full force 完全可以表达相同的意思。上段最后一句中的 be，应该是多余的误用词。

二、关于合同终止条款的写作

分析完合同期限条款之后必然要讲合同期的终止条款，因为 Friends must part——天下无不散之宴席。任何合同都有一个终止期：可能是"寿终正寝"（前面已经做过介绍），也可能以前的合作半途而废或买卖双方不欢而散。不管发生何种情况，合同的起草者都得防患于未来，或把丑话说在前，或把"善后事宜"（如继续保持商业秘密或支付余款）安排妥帖。合同终止条款就是为此目的而设的。由于"善后事宜"总是繁杂的，因此简短明了的合同终止条款几乎是不存在的，除非碰到严重的"不可抗力"事件（这样一来整个合同就可一笔勾销）。

合同终止条款通常包括两个方面内容：

（一）合同终止的条件

非常复杂，因为当初订立合同之时谁都不愿看到这种"夭折"局面。凡合同走到用 terminate 这一步，一般都不是"善终"。当然合同终止首先可以想到的原因或条件有：

---

① 互联网上对两词的使用也有较多的讨论，基本观点跟本文一致：I found an interesting trend："Expiry" is a UK style and "Expiration" is an American style. https://answers.yahoo.com/question/index?qid=20100325011222AAAJuDT
② http://agreements.realdealdocs.com/supply-contract-clauses/71-term-17999933/#ixzz39sxWrSd5

1. 其中一方(严重)违约

- any breach or default by the other party;
- either Party may terminate this Agreement... in the event that the other Party breaches or fails to fulfill any of its material obligations under this Agreement;
- the other Party has materially breached this Agreement... and, in case of a remediable breach other than a persistent breach, has failed to remedy that breach within thirty days of the date of service of a written notice from the other Party specifying the breach and requiring that it be remedied;

2. 双方自愿终止

- by any other contract or arrangement between the parties;

3. 对方将公司转让给或准备转让给债权人,或为了债权人利益而重组

- in the event of any assignment for the benefit of creditors;
- if the other party makes an assignment for the benefit of creditors, or
- upon the appointment of a receiver for the other Party or the reorganization of the other Party for the benefit of creditors;

4. 对方公司进入破产程序

- the commencement of any proceedings under any bankruptcy laws by or against the other Party;
- becomes the subject of any proceeding under state or federal law for the relief of debtors or otherwise becomes insolvent, bankrupt;

5. 对方公司已宣告或被颁令清盘或破产

- the insolvency of the other Party;
- becomes insolvent, bankrupt;
- the other Party is declared bankrupt;
- an order is made or a resolution passed for the winding up of that other Party or for the appointment of an administrator, receiver, liquidator or manager of that other Party;

6. 对方公司不再营业、常规业务被中断或被清盘或无力按时偿还债务

- the other Party ceases to carry on its business;
- the suspension or liquidation of the other Party's (Buyer's) usual business;
- is unable to pay its debts when they fall due;

7. 对方公司主要资产或财产被转让

- any transfer (either voluntary or involuntary) of a substantial part of Buyer's property or assets other than in the ordinary course of business;

（二）无过失一方的权利

合同可以提前终止，但无过失一方在此条件下须受到一定的保护。否则，这样的条款会纵容违约方或欠债方在遇到业务困难时采取不负责任或毁约行为。因此，即使发生上述的合同终止状况，与违约公司关联的各方仍然受本合同条款限制(the terms and conditions of this shall continue to be binding upon the parties in connection with... the other Party)。直白一点说，你买了一家有债务的公司，你也买了它的债务，新的老板也受原先公司签订的合同条款的约束，以及该终止不影响无过失一方在合同终止时期向对方索赔或要求履行合同义务的权利：

(1) Termination of this Agreement by either Party shall not prejudice the right of it or the other Party to recover any monies or require performance of any obligations due at the time of such termination.

(2) Without prejudice to any other right or remedy, either Party may terminate this Agreement at any time by notice in writing to the other Party, if...

(3) The expiry or termination of this Agreement does not affect any rights or obligations of either Party which have arisen or accrued up to and including the date of expiry or termination including the right to payment under this Agreement.

在条款的写作中，有关无过失方的权利的表达可以置放在合同终止条件的陈述之前或之后。上例(1)的 Termination of this Agreement by either Party shall not prejudice... 和例(3)的 The expiry or termination of this Agreement does not affect...，均置放在合同终止条款之后。例(1)还在该条款有关内容之前冠以名为 Rights After Termination 的小标题。而例(2)的相关内容(Without prejudice to any other right or remedy...)则置放在合同终止条件之前。

关键词解析：(1)本条款最常用、也是最重要的动词莫过于 terminate 与 end。一般来说，两词都可译为"终止"。如果文本是由训练有素的写手而为，读者可辨别出。自然结束或"寿终正寝"他会用 end；而半途夭折或非正常结束他会用 terminate。例如：(1) This Agreement shall end on the last day of the end of the current term. 以及 (2)The Licensee may terminate this Agreement at any time on 60 days' notice in writing to CE. 或 (3) Termination by either Party：Without prejudice to any other right or remedy, either Party may terminate this Agreement at any time by notice in writing to the other Party, if the other Party has materially breached this Agreement. 任何善于体会文意的读者都会从例(2)和(3)的句子中读出这两种状况的结束并非是"寿终正寝"的自然结束。

在以上陈述合同终止原因的文字中，有一系列非常近似的概念，这就是 becomes insolvent, bankrupt, or makes an assignment for the benefit of creditors,... arrangement, or the reorganization of the other Party for the benefit of creditors; for the winding up of that other Party; the suspension or liquidation of Buyer's usual business... 在这些画线词中，除了 makes an assignment 与 suspension 比较容易理解之外，其余的概念，尤其是这些概念之间细微差别，即便是法律专业户也未必说得清。依靠逻辑推理和权威字典的帮助，特简

述如下:

Arrangement:"安排"是普通人最熟悉不过的概念,但是在法律上它指的是和解或和解协议,是一个法律程序,指在破产程序中调整财务(即重新安排财务)使失去支付能力的债务人实现复兴,所以此处的 arrangement 是一个和解协议。

Reorganization:虽然也可以指公司的结构调整,译作重组或改组,但在以上语境中指的是公司破产过程中的重组,包括公司的合并或收购、公司的分立、公司资本结构的重大调整。[1]总之,这是破产程序的一环,重组成功,该公司可以逃过一劫或浴火重生;重组不成功,依然走向破产。

Insolvency:指无力偿还债务或资不抵债的财务状况;这是破产(bankruptcy)或清盘(liquidation/winding up)的前奏。如果是个人,无力偿还债务的结果大抵是走向破产;如果是公司资不抵债,其结局大抵是被清盘。破产或清盘程序通常是由债权人向法庭提出(file a bankruptcy petition),法庭会任命 insolvency practitioner,这个人可称作 administrator,administrative receiver(财产管理人/接管人)或 liquidator(清算人/清盘人),由其来处理资不抵债公司的财务,变卖其资产和偿付给其债权人。

Winding up:指公司停业/结业清理,通过清算账目、清理资产、将资产分给股东或者合伙人的程序,该程序可以在公司解散时发生,也可以在破产时发生。公司结业一般是公司自愿的行为(voluntary)。

Liquidation:清算,停业清理,清盘,在终止公司业务的情况下,变卖公司资产、清抵债务,将其资产分配给债权人、合伙人、股东或继承人。清盘一般是强制行为(involuntary/compulsory),即公司被迫结业,变卖资产,以偿还债务。

Bankrupt:这是英文中一个少有的全能词,意为"破产"或"破产者"(名词),或作形容词"破产的",作动词为"破产"。个人破产不可用 wind up 或 liquidate(均为动词),只能用 bankrupt。但 bankrupt 也可以指合伙人、公司或市政法人等无力偿还到期债务的状况。虽然破产令只能由法庭发出,但申请破产可以自愿提出,也可以被他人申请破产。破产程序开始后,法庭可以组织对债务人的剩余资产进行清算并分配给债权人,从而彻底免除债务人的债务;或者对债务人进行重整,允许其继续从事经营活动,以经营所得来偿还债务,从而避免破产。[2]

尽管有以上解析,这些概念仍然会令法律专业人士困惑,因为其意思非常相近,有些甚至同义。要想绝对厘清几乎是不可能的。但这些相关概念的逻辑关系大致是这样的:

首先公司发生资不抵债或欠债不还(insolvency)的状况,然后被债权人向法庭申请清盘(file a bankruptcy/ liquidation petition)。法庭会根据具体情况做出命令,可能会先对该公司实行债务和解安排(arrangement)或重组(reorganization),如被收购。不能实现债务和解或通过重组解决债务问题的,由法庭将公司关门(winding up),停止其业务(suspension of its business),然后任命财产管理人/接管人或清算人/清盘人(insolvency practitioner/liquidator)来处理该公司的财务,变卖其资产(liquidation),或将公司的业务、资产转让给有兴趣的买家(make an assignment)以达致变现,然后将所得偿付给债权人,如果还有剩余,则分配给合伙人、优先股股东或继承人。最后,该公司被宣布破产(bankrupt)。当然,以上是一个强制性(involuntary/compulsory)的清盘程序。

---

[1] 《元照法律字典》。
[2] 薛波:《元照英美法词典》,北京:法律出版社,2003 年,见 bankruptcy proceedings 词条。

三、模式条款及译文

以下是笔者通过分析各种文本写法的利弊，归纳并重写的"合同期限及终止"条款，可以作为标准模式来推介：

Duration. This Agreement shall come into effect on the Commencement Date and shall continue in force until the 5th Anniversary of the Commencement Date. On such date this Agreement shall terminate automatically by expiry, but it may be extended by written agreement between the Parties.

期限。本协议自协议开始日起生效，到第五个周年日一直有效，自该日起自动失效，但双方可通过书面协议使本协议展期。

Early Termination. If the other Party has materially breached this Agreement such as ... and, in case of a remediable breach other than a persistent breach, has failed to remedy that breach within thirty days of the date of service of a written notice from the other Party specifying the breach and requiring that it be remedied; or the other Party ceases to carry on business; or is unable to pay its debts when they fall due, or is to be assigned for the benefit of creditors; or is declared bankrupt, or a court order is made or a resolution of board of directors passed for the winding up of that other Party; or is in a situation of similar nature, the non-default party may immediately terminate this agreement by giving written notice to the other party.

提前终止。如果另一方严重违约，诸如……；如该等违约并非持续行为而是可以补救的、但另一方在对方指出其违约行为并要求其采取补救措施的书面通知送达后的30天内仍未采取补救措施；或另一方停止其业务；或债务到期而无法偿还；或打算以转让其公司的方式向债权人还债；或被宣布破产、或法庭颁令或公司董事会通过决议决定公司结业；或处于类似性质的状态，未违约一方可书面通知另一方立即终止本协议。

Rights After Termination. The expiry or termination of this Agreement does not affect any rights or obligations of either Party which have arisen or accrued up to and including the date of expiry or termination including the right to payment under this Agreement. In the event of any such expiry or termination, the terms and conditions of this agreement shall continue to be binding upon the parties in connection with the obligations and payment on the part of the default party under this Agreement.

协议终止后的权利。本协议到期或终止并不影响各方直至协议到期或终止日（包括该日）而产生或累积的权利和义务，其中包括获得根据本协议付款的权利。如本协议到期或终止，本协议的条款继续对与本协议违约方根据本协议须履行的义务或支付的款项有关联的各方具有约束力。

推荐理由是写作脉络清晰、逻辑严谨，内容面面俱到，且要点突出，但该含糊处又有充分的发挥余地，适用的合同性质范围非常广，语言也是明白如话，一读就懂。

四、特定终止条款的解析及译文

以上分析的条款属于通用性质。在不同性质合同的具体领域，该条款的写法稍有不同。

以下三个终止条款的内容与前文分析的差异最大的是第一个,即《雇佣协议的终止条款》,而内容最近似的(同时也是最有用的)则是第后一个,即《购销协议的终止条款》。因此,我们对这两个完整的终止条款做重点分析。

Nature of the Clause	条款名称	条款名称及用途说明
Termination of Employment Agreement	雇佣协议的终止	
Unless the Employees' employment (shall) sooner terminate for any reason pursuant to paragraph 5 of this Agreement, the "Employment Period" shall <u>commence on</u> the Effective Date and shall initially <u>terminate on</u> the third anniversary of the Effective Date, except that beginning on the third anniversary of the Effective Date, the <u>Employment Period will automatically extend for one year</u> unless either the Employee or the Company gives at least <u>90 days advance written notice of non-extension.</u> In the event that the Employees employment is terminated during the Employment Period (i) by the Employee for Good Reason (as defined in Appendix A) or (ii) by the Company without Cause (as defined in Appendix A), other than as a result of the Employees death or disability (within the meaning of the Company's long-term disability program then in effect), <u>subject to</u> the Employees <u>execution and delivery</u> of a <u>valid and effective release and waiver</u> in a form satisfactory to the Company, the Company shall <u>pay the Employee a lump sum cash amount</u> equal to one (1) times Employees Base Salary, within thirty (30) days following the effective date of such release and waiver.	雇员的雇佣期除非根据本协议第5段的任何理由提前终止,否则本协议的雇佣期首次将在本协议生效之日起的三周年日终止,但从生效日三周年日开始,雇佣期自动延长一年,除非雇员或雇主至少提前90天书面通知对方不做延长。万一雇员的雇佣在雇佣期内(i)由雇员凭合理的因由(见附录A的界定)或(ii)公司无故(见附录A的界定),但并非是由于雇员的死亡或病残(根据当时实施的公司长期病残计划中的定义)所致的结果而予以终止,公司须向雇员支付相当于雇员一个月基本工资的一次性现金补偿,但雇员必须签署一份有效的、使公司满意的索赔弃权书,公司应当在雇员签署的该弃权书生效日期起的三十(30)天内做出支付。	高级雇员雇佣协议终止条款
Notwithstanding anything herein to the contrary, upon the termination of the Employees employment for any reason, the rights of the Employee with respect to any shares of restricted stock or options to purchase Common Stock held by the Employee which, as of the Termination Date, have not been <u>forfeited</u> shall be <u>subject to</u> the applicable rules of the plan or agreement under which such restricted stock or options were granted as they exist from time to time. In addition, upon the termination of the Employees employment for any reason, the Company shall <u>pay to the Employee his Base Salary through the Termination</u>	尽管本协议有任何相反的规定,在雇员的雇佣因任何因由终止时,就雇员原本拥有的购买限制性股票或购买普通股期权的权利而言,如在雇佣终止日尚未被收回,必须受准许购买该限制性股票或期权的计划或协议不时订定的有关规定的规管。此外,在雇员的雇佣因任何因由而终止时,公司应当在雇佣终止之日向雇员支付相当于其一个月基本工资的补偿金,再加上直至雇佣终止日所累积的假期。雇	高级雇员雇佣协议终止条款

续表

Nature of the Clause	条款名称	条款名称及用途说明
Date, plus any unused vacation time accrued through the Termination Date. Any vested benefits and other amounts that the Employee is otherwise entitled to receive under any employee benefit plan, policy, practice or program of the Company or any of its affiliates shall be payable in accordance with such employee benefit plan, policy, practice or program as the case may be, provided that the Employee shall not be entitled to receive any other payments or benefits in the nature of severance or termination pay. In the event that the Agreement expires pursuant to paragraph 5(a) or the Employee resigns without Good Reason, is terminated for Cause, or dies or becomes disabled (within the meaning of the Companies long-term disability program then in effect) during the Employment Period, no benefits shall be payable to the Employee under paragraph 5(b) of this Agreement, but the terms and conditions of paragraph 5(c) shall remain in effect.	员根据公司或其附属公司的任何雇员福利计划、政策、惯例或安排原本有权得到的既得利益或其他款额应当按各有关个案的这类雇员福利计划、政策、惯例或安排予以支付,但雇员无权享有任何属于遣散费或雇佣终止金性质的其他付款或福利。万一本协议根据第5(a)段到期,或雇员无正当理由辞职,或因故协议被终止,或雇员在雇佣期间内死亡、病残(根据当时实施的公司长期病残计划中的定义),雇员不得享有本协议第5(b)段中规定的福利,但第5(c)段中的条款和条件仍然继续有效。	
Termination of Stock Purchase Agreement	股票购买协议的终止	
The M Company shall have the option to terminate this Agreement and the transactions contemplated herein at or prior to Closing if any of the S Company's or S Company Partner's warranties, representations or covenants contained in this Agreement are breached. S Company shall have the option to terminate this Agreement and the transactions contemplated herein at or prior to Closing if any of the following (shall) occur: (a) if for any reason whatsoever there is no closing of the 2015 Stock Purchase; or (b) if any of the M Company's warranties, representations or covenants contained in this Agreement are breached. In the	如果S公司或其合作伙伴违反其在本协议中所做的保证、陈述或允诺,M公司可选择在合同到期或之前终止协议,以及取消本协议中仍在筹划的交易。如果发生以下情形,S公司亦可选择在合同到期或之前终止本协议以及取消本协议中仍在筹划的交易:(a)无论因何原因2015年股票没有成交;或(b)M公司违反其在本协议中所做的保证、陈述或允诺。万一S公司因本款未提及的任何其他原因而选择终止本协议,S公司须将其公司的决定以书面形式通知M	适合股票买卖协议的终止

续表

Nature of the Clause	条款名称	条款名称及用途说明
event S Company <u>elects to terminate</u> this Agreement for any reason other than those provided in this Section, S Company shall <u>notify</u> the M Company <u>of</u> S Company's decision in writing and S Company shall <u>pay</u> the M Company <u>a termination fee of</u> One Hundred Thousand Dollars ($100,000.00) within ten (10) days S Company of demand therefor (the "Termination Fee").	公司,S 公司须在提出其终止本协议要求的十(10)日内向 M 公司支付十万(100 000)整美元的终止费("终止费")。	
Termination of Sales Agreement	购销协议的终止条款	
This Agreement and the covenants, representations, warranties, and agreements contained herein shall <u>terminate</u> upon the earlier of the mutual agreement of the parties or the Expiration Date. Upon any termination of this Agreement, this Agreement shall thereupon <u>become void and of no further force and effect</u>, and there shall be <u>no liability</u> in respect of this Agreement <u>on the part of any party hereto</u> or any of its directors, officers, partners, stockholders, employees, agents, advisors, representatives or Affiliates; provided, however, that <u>nothing</u> contained herein shall <u>relieve any party from any liability</u> for such party's willful breach of this Agreement <u>prior to termination</u>. Any termination of this Agreement pursuant to this Section 11(k) shall be effected by written notice from the Company to the Buyer, or the Buyer to the Company, as the case may be, setting forth the basis for the termination hereof. The representations and warranties of the Company and the Buyer contained in Sections 2 and 3 hereof, the indemnification provisions set forth in Section 8 hereof and the agreements and covenants set forth in Section 11, shall <u>survive the Commencement and any termination</u> of this Agreement. No termination of this Agreement shall affect the Company's or the Buyer's rights otherwise available under applicable law or the	本协议及其包含的契约、陈述、保证以及协定可经双方同意提前或在协议期满之日终止。本协议终止之时,本协议便告失效,协议各方或各方董事、高级职员、合伙人、股东、雇员、代理人、顾问、代表或附属公司均不对本协议负责;但本协议的任何内容均不得解除本协议终止之前各方蓄意违反本协议而需要承担的责任。根据第 11(K)款终止本协议须按不同个案酌情处理:由公司以书面形式通知买方,或由买方以书面形式通知公司。该通知须说明本协议终止的基础。本协议第 2 款或第 3 款包括的本公司及买方的陈述及保证,第 8 款订定的补偿规定以及第 11 款订定的协定和契诺在本协议开始生效和终止之后仍然有效。本协议的终止并不影响公司或买方根据有关法律享有的其他权利或本协议有关未完成之买卖的义务;公司与买方应当完成本协议项下任何未完成买卖之各自义务。	购销协议的终止条款

续表

Nature of the Clause	条款名称	条款名称及用途说明
obligations under this Agreement with respect to pending purchases and the Company and the Buyer shall complete their respective obligations with respect to any pending purchases under this Agreement.		

（一）雇佣合同终止条款的关键词和基本内容

首先，我们就大公司高级职员雇佣合同终止条款的基本元素和写作要点来做些分析。其中的关键词有：

- commence on the Effective Date
- employment shall be terminated on the third anniversary of the Effective Date
- extend for one year
- gives at least 90 days advance written notice of non-extension
- in the event that employment is terminated during the Employment Period by the Employee for Good Reason/by the Company without Cause
- subject to
- execution and delivery of a valid and effective release and waiver
- a lump sum cash amount
- the rights of the Employee with respect to any shares of restricted stock
- be forfeited
- be subject to the applicable rules
- pay to the Employee his Base Salary through the Termination Date
- unused vacation time accrued through the Termination Date
- vested benefits
- provided that
- severance or termination pay

大公司，尤其是上市公司高级职员的合约终止条款，一般应包括四个方面的内容：

1. 雇佣合同一般为"三年死（期）、一年活（期）"。这类高级职员，如果合约期只有一年或两年，合资格的能人，一般不会辞去现有的职位，去应聘一个充满风险的新职位，而且，如果干满三年，没有延续合同的可能，会使该职位失去吸引力，此外，如果任期太短，也会给用人公司招聘人才造成诸多不便和开销（尤其是猎头公司的费用）：须不断组织面试班子和频繁刊登招聘广告，还会给下层员工一个坏印象：领导层像走马灯一样。当然，如果雇员和雇主磨合不佳，也会彼此容忍到合同的最后一天；但在去意已决的情况下，彼此都要给三个月的提前通知，以便双方都可为各自的未来做出安排。要表达这几层意思，英文的条款可以这样写：The Employment Period shall commence on the Effective Date of Employees reporting to duty and shall initially terminate on the third anniversary of the Effective Date. The Employment Period will automatically extend for one year unless either the

Employee or the Company gives at least 90 days advance written notice of non-extension.

2. 雇佣可能提前终止，原因不外乎三者：a. 雇员与公司领导层无法成功磨合；b. 雇员能力受到怀疑或业绩很不理想；c. 雇员犯错或严重违规；d. 雇员另有高就或其他合理的原因，当然另有高就不是提前离职的"good reason"。但在前两种情形下雇员被提前解雇，公司一般会采取常规的补偿措施：给一笔相当于一个月基本工资的一次性补偿金，同时让雇员休完以前累积下来的假期或以薪代假，不过雇员需签署一份不再为提前解雇而日后与公司纠缠不休的弃权书。这些概念可以这样表述：In the event that the Employees employment is terminated during the Employment Period (i) by the Employee for Good Reason (as defined either in Appendix or a clause hereunder) or (ii) by the Company without Cause (as defined either in Appendix or in a clause hereunder), subject to the Employees execution and delivery of a valid and effective release and waiver in a form satisfactory to the Company, the Company shall pay the Employee a lump sum cash payment equal to one (1) time Employees Base Salary, within thirty (30) days following the effective date of such release and waiver, plus any unused vacation time accrued through the Termination Date.

3. 上市公司通常会给高层雇员在任职至一定期限后按优惠价购买或免费获得自己公司股票的权利，但为了使雇员安心工作、与公司同命运，不让他们思忖上任才几天就想着卖股走人，认购这类股份的权利通常都有特殊的规定或安排，往往要等到雇员在公司有一定年资或有一定业绩后才可以行使，而这类股票通常称为"限制性股票"。有关这一类安排，表述通常是这样的：Upon the termination of the Employees employment for any reason, the rights of the Employee with respect to any shares of restricted stock or options to purchase Common Stock held by the Employee which, as of the Termination Date, have not been forfeited shall be subject to the applicable rules of the plan or agreement under which such restricted stock or options were granted as they exist from time to time.

4. 有些公司业绩辉煌、员工福利制度健全，除各种福利计划外，还有退职金或遣散费之类的安排，但福利计划与后者往往只能择其一，故此，雇佣合同终止条款还可能包括这样的规定：In addition, any vested benefits and other amounts that the Employee is otherwise entitled to receive under any employee benefit plan, policy, practice or program of the Company or any of its affiliates shall be payable in accordance with such employee benefit plan, policy, practice or program as the case may be, provided that the Employee shall not be entitled to receive any other payments or benefits in the nature of severance or termination pay.

雇佣合同终止条款实例及译文：

1. "The Employment Period shall commence on the Effective Date of Employees reporting to duty and shall initially terminate on the third anniversary of the Effective Date. The Employment Period will automatically extend for one year unless either the Employee or the Company gives at least 90 days advance written notice of non-extension.

雇佣期从雇佣合同生效、即雇员述职之日起开始，首个雇佣期至合同生效日的三周年日终止，并会自动延长一年，除非雇员或雇主至少提前90天书面通知对方不作延长。

2. In the event that the Employees employment is terminated during the Employment Period (i) by the Employee for Good Reason (as defined either in Appendix or a clause hereunder) or (ii) by the Company without Cause (as defined

either in Appendix or in a clause hereunder), subject to the Employees execution and delivery of a valid and effective release and waiver in a form satisfactory to the Company, the Company shall pay the Employee a lump sum cash payment equal to one (1) time Employees Base Salary, within thirty (30) days following the effective date of such release and waiver, plus any cash payment of the unused vacation time accrued through the Termination Date on the basis of the daily rate of employees Base Salary.

万一雇员的雇佣在雇佣期内(i)由雇员凭合理的因由(见附录或本合同下文的界定)或(ii)公司无故(见附录或本合同下文的界定)予以终止,公司须向雇员支付相当于雇员一个月基本工资的一次性现金补偿,但雇员必须签署一份有效的、令公司满意的索赔弃权书,公司应当在雇员签署的该弃权书生效日期起的三十(30)天内做出支付,再加上直至雇佣终止日所累积的假期薪金(按照基本工资的日薪计算)。

3. Upon the termination of the Employees employment for any reason, if the rights of the Employee with respect to any shares of restricted stock of the Company, as of the Termination Date, have not been forfeited, they shall be subject to the applicable rules of the plan or agreement under which such shares of the restricted stock were granted as they exist from time to time.

不管雇员的雇佣因何因终止,在雇佣终止时,就雇员原本拥有的购买本公司限制性股票的权利而言,如在雇佣终止日尚未被收回,必须受准许购买该限制性股票的计划或协议不时订定的有关规定的规管。

4. In addition, upon the termination of the Employees employment for any reason, any vested benefits and other amounts that the Employee is otherwise entitled to receive under any employee benefit plan, policy, practice or program of the Company or any of its affiliates shall be payable in accordance with such employee benefit plan, policy, practice or program as the case may be, provided that the Employee shall not be entitled to receive any other payments or benefits in the nature of severance or termination pay.

此外,在雇员的雇佣因任何因由而终止时,雇员根据公司或其附属公司的任何雇员福利计划、政策、惯例或安排原本有权得到的既得利益或其他款额应按各有关个案的这类雇员福利计划、政策、惯例或安排予以支付,但雇员无权再享有任何属于遣散费或雇佣终止金性质的其他付款或福利。

(二) 销售合同终止条款的关键词及基本内容

世间各类合同的数量,除了雇佣合同外,恐怕就数买卖或购销合同。做买卖,要讲诚信。购销合同被提前终止往往与合同内的虚假陈述或保证相关。谁需要为这些不实之词负责?如何进行补救?在发现这类不实之词或虚假陈述之时,生意往往已经在进行,合同被提前终止,对未完成的买卖应如何处理?买卖合同的终止条款主要就是为了处理这类问题的。其关键词如下:

- terminate upon the earlier of the mutual agreement
- become void and of no further force and effect
- shall be no liability...on the part of any party hereto

- provided, however, that
- nothing contained herein shall relieve any party from any liability
- willful breach
- shall be effected
- setting forth the basis for the termination
- representations and warranties
- the indemnification provisions
- shall survive the Commencement and any termination
- pending purchases
- complete their respective obligations

销售合同基本条款:没有节外生枝、顺利做了买卖,但因为各种原因(如赚不到钱)双方都觉得应该按时或提前结束关系的,其销售合同的终止条款通常这样写:This Agreement, and the covenants, representations, warranties, and agreements contained herein if any, shall terminate upon the earlier of the mutual agreement of the parties or the Expiration Date. Upon any termination of this Agreement, this Agreement shall thereupon become void and of no further force and effect, and there shall be no liability in respect of this Agreement on the part of any party hereto or any of its directors, officers, partners, stockholders, employees, agents, advisors, representatives or Affiliates; provided, however, that nothing contained herein shall relieve any party from any liability for such party's willful breach of this Agreement prior to termination. 这一段的最后部分(用 provided...that 引导的条件句)属于法律文本中典型的"但书"(proviso),用以提出补充或例外状况。当然在买卖合同终止条款中加上这个补充性质的例外条件也是合情合理和必需的:尽管本协议根据双方意愿(upon the earlier of the mutual agreement of the parties)提前终结或在到期日(upon... the Expiration Date)圆满终结,但买卖双方仍然需要为其在协议终止之前(prior to termination)的蓄意违约行为(willful breach)承担责任。

在技术层面,上段所述的买卖合同如何终止呢?自然是由买方或卖方以书面形式通知对方: Any termination of this Agreement shall be effected by written notice from the Seller to the Buyer, or the Buyer to the Seller, as the case may be, setting forth the basis for the termination hereof. 合同的终止并不等于可以既往不咎,除了前面所提及的合同期内的违约赔偿或寻求其他法律救济外,买卖双方还要对尚未完成的买卖履行各自的义务: No termination of this Agreement shall affect the Sellers or the Buyers rights otherwise available under applicable law or the obligations under this Agreement with respect to pending purchases and the Seller and the Buyer shall complete their respective obligations with respect to any pending purchases under this Agreement.

以上内容可以逻辑地组合在一起,便构成一则可供参考的买卖终止条款实例:

This Agreement, and the covenants, representations, warranties, and agreements contained herein if any, shall terminate upon an earlier date mutually agreed by both parties or the Expiration Date. Upon any termination of this Agreement, this Agreement shall thereupon become void and of no further effect, and there shall be no liability in respect of this Agreement on the part of any party hereto or any of its directors, officers, partners, stockholders, employees, agents, advisors, representatives or Affiliates; provided, however, that nothing contained herein shall relieve any party from any liability for such party's willful breach of this Agreement prior to termination.

本协议及其包含的契约、陈述、保证以及约定可经双方同意提前或在协议期满之日终止。本协议终止之后,本协议便告失效,协议各方或各方董事、高级职员、合伙人、股东、雇员、代理人、顾问、代表或附属公司均无需对本协议负责;但本协议的任何内容均不得解除本协议终止之前各方蓄意违反本协议行为而需要承担的责任。

Any termination of this Agreement shall only be effected by written notice from the Seller to the Buyer, or the Buyer to the Seller, as the case may be, setting forth the basis for the termination hereof. No termination of this Agreement shall affect the Sellers or the Buyers rights otherwise available under applicable law or the obligations under this Agreement with respect to pending purchases, and the Seller and the Buyer shall complete their respective obligations with respect to the pending purchases.

终止本协议须按不同个案由卖方以书面形式通知买方,或由买方以书面形式通知卖方的形式执行,该通知须说明本协议终止的基础。本协议的终止并不影响卖方或买方就本协议未完成之买卖,根据有关法律所享有的合同权利或需要履行的义务;卖方与买方仍须完成未完成之买卖的各自义务。

从实例到范例,至此,一个内容完整而已排除许多繁文缛节的通用销售合同终止条款便告完成。但英文条款本身的语言并不简明易懂。倘若用简明英文加以"润色",以上条款可进一步改善如下:

This Agreement, including all its attachments if any, shall terminate on an earlier date mutually agreed by both parties or on its Expiration Date. Upon such termination, this Agreement will become void, and both parties and all their employees and other personnel shall have no liability regarding this Agreement, except that they shall still be liable for any willful breach of this Agreement prior to the termination.

Each party may terminate this Agreement by written notice in which the basis for the termination should be set forth. No termination of this Agreement shall affect the parties' rights available under applicable law and their obligations for pending purchases under this Agreement. Both parties shall complete their respective obligations for the pending purchases.

五、结语

以上是用简明英文重写的合同终止条款,其内容与前面用法律英文传统风格写成的条款是基本一致的,功能上完全一样。前者多用了63词(共184词)去表达与后者(121词)相同的意思,字数上足足多出50%。就读者理解而言,后者可以一目了然,无需读第二遍;而前者即便是专家也要琢磨再三。由此可见,在法律英文领域,提倡使用简明英文写作大有可为,可以收到事半功倍的效果。这一点,也是作者写作本书的初衷之一。希望有读者在这方面的共鸣,更希望有读者的共同参与,使法律英文不再是与时代脱节的精英语言。

本章附录：

其他终止参考条款

1. 简易协议终止条款

   TERMINATION

   This agreement shall immediately terminate without notice by or to, or other action by, either party in the event of any assignment for the benefit of creditors or offer to make an extension to creditors by Buyer; the insolvency (as such term is defined to the Uniform Commercial Code) of Buyer; the commencement of any proceedings under any bankruptcy laws by or against Buyer; the suspension or liquidation of Buyer's usual business; or any transfer (either voluntary or involuntary) of a substantial part of Buyer's property or assets other than in the ordinary course of business; provided, however that in the event of any such termination, the terms and conditions of this agreement shall continue to be binding upon the parties in connection with all Products shipped by Seller to Buyer.

2. 常用协议终止条款

   TERM AND TERMINATION

   Term. This Agreement shall commence as of the date hereof and remain in full force and effect for an initial term of 5 years (the "Initial Term"). Thereafter, this Agreement shall be renewed automatically for a successive 5 year term, unless written notice is provided by either party at least 120 days before the end of the then-current term, in which event this Agreement shall end on the last day of such term. The Initial Term and any renewals shall be constitute the "Term."

   Termination For Breach. Either Party may terminate this Agreement upon 30 days' prior written notice to the other Party in the event that the other Party breaches or fails to fulfill any of its material obligations under this Agreement (including, without limitation, making deliveries of Products within the deadlines specified on any Purchase Order, or providing Products that do not meet the Specifications). However, if during such 30 day notice period the other Party shall have remedied such failure, this Agreement shall continue in full force and effect as if such failure had not occurred.

   Termination For Other Reasons. This Agreement shall terminate forthwith, at the option of either Party by written notice to the other Party, if the other Party ceases to carry on its business or becomes the subject of any proceeding under state or federal law for the relief of debtors or otherwise becomes insolvent, bankrupt or makes an assignment for the benefit of creditors, or upon the appointment of a receiver for the other Party or the reorganization of the other Party for the benefit of creditors.

   Rights After Termination. Termination of this Agreement by either Party shall not prejudice the right of it or the other Party to recover any monies or require performance of any obligations due at the time of such termination. ①

3. 许可证使用协议期限及终止条款

Duration and Termination

Commencement and termination by expiry

This Agreement, and the licences granted hereunder, shall come into effect on the Commencement Date and, unless terminated earlier in accordance with this clause 7, shall continue in force until the 5th Anniversary of the Commencement Date and on such date this Agreement and the licences granted hereunder shall terminate automatically by expiry. This Agreement may be extended by written agreement between the Parties hereto.

Early termination by the Licensee

The Licensee may terminate this Agreement at any time on 60 days' notice in writing to CE.

Early termination by either Party

Without prejudice to any other right or remedy, either Party may terminate this Agreement at any time by notice in writing to the other Party, if the other Party has materially breached this Agreement (and for the avoidance of doubt non-payment by the Licensee under clause 5 shall be deemed a material breach) and, in case of a remediable breach other than a persistent breach, has failed to remedy that breach within thirty days of the date of service of a written notice from the other Party specifying the breach and requiring that it be remedied; or the other Party ceases to carry on business, is unable to pay its debts when they fall due, is declared bankrupt, or an order is made or a resolution passed for the winding up of that other Party or for the appointment of an administrator, receiver, liquidator or manager of that other Party.

Consequences of termination

Upon termination of this Agreement for any reason:

The Licensee and its Affiliates shall destroy the Cell Line and Licensed Products in its possession or control; and each Party shall return to the other (or destroy at the other's request) all Confidential Information disclosed to it by the other and all materials containing any Confidential Information in its possession or control including, in the case of the Licensee, in the possession or control of its Affiliates.

The expiry or termination of this Agreement does not affect any rights or obligations of either Party which have arisen or accrued up to and including the date of expiry or termination including the right to payment under this Agreement.

Clauses 2.3, 2.4, 3.5 (in respect of payments due on or before termination), 6, 7.4, 8 and 9 survive expiry or termination (for whatever reason).

---

① http://agreements.realdealdocs.com/supply-contract-clauses/71-term-17999933/#ixzz39sxWrSd5

4. 最详尽的服务协议期限及终止条款

Term/Termination

a. The initial term of this Agreement shall be as set forth in the Order Form (the "Initial Term"). The Initial Term shall begin upon commencement of the Services to Customer. After the Initial Term, this Agreement shall automatically renew. ADDITIONALLY AFTER THE INITIAL TERM,YOU ACKNOWLEDGE,AGREE AND AUTHORIZE Multacom Corporation TO AUTOMATICALLY BILL AND/OR CHARGE ON YOUR CREDIT CARD FOR SUCCESSIVE TERMS OF EQUAL LENGTH AS THE INITIAL TERM, UNLESS TERMINATED OR CANCELLED BY EITHER PARTY AS PROVIDED IN THIS SECTION. The Initial Term and all successive renewal periods shall be referred to,collectively,as the "Term."

b. This Agreement may be terminated

i. by either party by giving the other party thirty (30) days prior written notice (subject to an early cancellation fee payable by Customer as provided below),

ii. by Multacom in the event of nonpayment by Customer,

iii. by Multacom,at any time,without notice,if,in Multacom's sole and absolute discretion and/or judgment,Customer is in violation of any term or condition of the this Agreement and related agreements, AUP, or Customer's use of the Services disrupts or, in Multacom's sole and absolute discretion and/or judgment, could disrupt,Multacom's business operations and/or

c. If you cancel this Agreement prior to the end of the Initial Term or any Term thereafter,

i. you shall be obligated to pay all fees and charges accrued prior to the effectiveness of such cancellation,

ii. Multacom shall refund to you all pre-paid fees for basic hosting services (shared,dedicated and/or managed) for the full months remaining after effectiveness of cancellation (i. e.,no partial month fees shall be refunded),less any setup fees and any discount applied for prepayment,

iii. you shall be obligated to pay 100% of all charges for all Services for each month remaining in the Term (other than basic hosting fees as provided in (ii) above) and (iii) you shall pay an early cancellation fee of $50. Any cancellation request shall be effective thirty (30) days after receipt by Multacom,unless a later date is specified in such request.

d. Multacom Corporation may terminate this Agreement

i. if the Services are prohibited by applicable law, or become impractical or unfeasible for any technical,legal or regulatory reason,by giving Customer as much prior notice as reasonably practicable or

ii. immediately by giving written notice to Customer,if Multacom determines in good faith that Customer's use of the Customer Website or the Customer Content violates any term or condition. If Multacom cancels this Agreement prior to the end of the Term for your breach of this Agreement and related agreements, the Customer's use of the Services disrupts, Multacom shall not refund to you any fees paid in advance of such cancellation and you shall be obligated to pay all fees and charges accrued prior to the effectiveness of such cancellation; further, you shall be obligated to pay 100% of all charges for all Services for each month remaining in the Term and Multacom shall have the right to charge you an administrative fee of $50.00.

e. Upon termination of this Agreement for any cause or reason whatsoever, customer shall not have any further rights or obligations under this Agreement, except as expressly set forth herein. Termination of this Agreement and retention of pre-paid fees and charges shall be in addition to, and not be in lieu of, any other legal or equitable rights or remedies to which Multacom Corporation may be entitled.

f. Additional Resource Charges. You will be charged additional nonrefundable fees in the event that you used excessive resources including, without limitation, additional bandwidth, file transfer or disk space in excess of the amount included with your account. You agree to pay for any and all charges that may coincide with the usage of Multacom's services at the then current prices.

g. Late payment. If your payment is received late, you may be responsible for paying a late charge fee of $10 per month for shared hosting and $25 for dedicated server or colocation services. Services and your account may remain suspended until payment is received by Multacom. If your account is left unpaid for 30 days for shared hosting and 15 days for dedicated servers, your account and your files and data will be deleted. A termination under this condition, or any other, will not relieve you from paying any past due fees plus interest that have accrued prior to the termination. In the event of collection enforcement, you will be liable for any costs, including, without limitation, attorneys' fees, court costs, and collection agency fees. (http://www.multacom.com/terms.html, accessed on August 11, 2014)

第十五章 违约条款的写作和翻译

一、引言

"违约条款"与"责任条款""保证条款""弃权条款""仲裁条款"以及"适用法条款"和"诉讼地选择条款"等都有紧密关联,甚至互为因果。一般来说,合同方履行自己的职责,没有违反合同中的保证,就不构成违约;构成违约了,但未违约一方不予追究,就产生了"弃权条款";但如果违约严重,未违约一方决定对违约方的行为加以追究,那么诉讼之外的廉价解决办法是仲裁;仲裁可能解决不了问题的,势必要诉诸法律。要诉诸法律,必然要以"适用或管辖法律"为依据(准居法),并且要按照"诉讼地选择"条款选择诉讼的司法管辖区或法庭。

但如果违约并不严重,可能双方未必要走"仲裁"或"诉讼"这两步。双方可能按照"违约条款"的有关安排或规定,自行解决因违约而引起的纠纷。所以,从逻辑上讲,违约条款应该安排在"保证条款"之后,但一定先于上述的其他四个通用条款。根据"违约条款"就可以解决的违约行为,一般都并不十分严重。通常都是签订合同前做了一些虚假的陈述或在签订合同后未能依约履行义务。解决办法不外乎让违约方"亡羊补牢",做出适当的补救;或终止合同;更严重一点的则要求赔偿,甚至在合同终止后仍然要违约方继续做出赔偿。所以违约条款基本上都是按照这个思路写作的。由于"责任条款"主要出现在雇用合约中,一般是针对个人签约方,故本章甚少收集与"责任条款"相关的违约条款样本(只有下文的第 11 段),以下第 1 到第 10 段都是针对公司类违约行为的。

二、违约责任条款及译文

Breach of Contract	违约责任	使用说明
1. Neither the execution and delivery of this Agreement by Buyer, nor the consummation by Buyer of the transactions contemplated hereby, nor <u>compliance</u> by Buyer with any of the provisions hereof, will <u>violate or cause a default</u> under any statute (domestic or foreign), judgment, order, writ, decree, rule or regulation of any Governmental Authority applicable to Buyer or any of its material properties; <u>breach or conflict with any of the terms, provisions or conditions</u>	根据适用于买方或买方之任何重要物业所在地的任何政府主管部门颁发的法律(国内的或国外的)、判决、命令、令状、法令、规章,买方签署本协议,或根据本协议的安排完成了交易,或买方遵守了本协议的所有条款,则买方便没有违约;	适用于购买房地产的合同,但英文原文风极差,无用的近义词连篇累牍

续表

Breach of Contract	违约责任	使用说明
of the organization documents of Buyer[1]; or violate, conflict with or breach any agreement, contract, mortgage, instrument, indenture or license to which Buyer is party or by which Buyer is or may be bound, or constitute a default thereunder, or result in the creation or imposition of any Encumbrance[2] upon, or give to any other party or parties, any claim, interest or right, including rights of termination or cancellation in, or with respect to any of Buyer's properties.	也不违反买方之机构文件的任何条款或条件;也不违反买方是签约方或受其或可能受其约束的任何协议、合同、按揭、契据或许可证书,也不构成对该类文件项下条款的违约;也不会对买方任何物业产生或施加任何留置权;也未给予任何其他方对买方物业提出权利或利益主张的权利(包括终止或取消买方的物业协议的权利)。	
2. The sole remedy of this agreement in respect of any material breach of this Agreement by Consultant shall be to terminate this Agreement upon the giving of thirty (30) days' prior written notice, but no such termination shall affect the fees payable pursuant to Paragraphs 3 hereof.	就顾问严重违反本协议而言,本协议之唯一补救是提前三十(30)天给予书面通知,终止本协议。本协议提前终止并不影响根据本协议第 3 段需要支付的各种费用。	顾问违约条款
3. If a Party fails to perform any of its material obligations under this Contract, or if a representation or warranty made by a Party is untrue or materially inconsistent with the fact, such Party is deemed to have breached this Contract.	如果一方未能履行本合同的重要义务,或者一方做出的陈述或保证不真实或与事实有重大出入,则视该方已违反本合同。	一般性违约条款,适合合资企业合同
4. Any violation of any provision hereof, any incomplete or mistaken performance of any obligation provided hereunder, any misrepresentation made hereunder, any material nondisclosure or omission of any material fact, or any failure to perform any covenants provided hereunder by any Party shall constitute a breach of this Agreement. The breaching Party shall be liable for any such breach pursuant to the applicable laws.	任何一方违反本协议的任何条款,或未完全或错误地履行本协议的任何义务,在本协议中做出虚假陈述,或对重要事实未做重要披露或疏忽,或未履行本协议规定的条款,即构成违约。违约方须依有关法律为违约行为负责。	一般性违约条款

续表

Breach of Contract	违约责任	使用说明
5. During the Contract Period, any <u>failure to perform the obligations</u> required herein, in whole or in part, or any <u>violation of any provisions</u> herein by either Party B or Party A <u>constitutes breach</u> of contract and the breaching Party shall <u>compensate</u> the non-breaching Party <u>for the loss incurred</u> as a result of this breach.	在合约期内,无论甲方或乙方未按本协议规定全部或部分履行义务,或违反本协议任何条款都构成违约,违约方须就该违约给未违约一方造成的损失做出赔偿。	简单通用型违约条款
6. The Purchaser <u>is not assuming nor shall they be responsible for</u> any Liabilities of the Sellers for any <u>breach or failure to perform</u> any of the Sellers <u>covenants and agreements</u> contained in, or made <u>pursuant to</u>, this Agreement, or, <u>prior to</u> the Closing, any other contract or agreement, whether or not assumed hereunder, including breach arising from assignment of contracts hereunder without consent of third parties.	买方既不承担也无须负责因卖方违约或未能履行本合同所包括的任何卖方的契约或协定而产生的任何卖方的债务,该契约或协定包括卖方根据本协议或其他合同或协议在本协议终止之前(不管是否根据本协议而承担的——包括在没有取得第三方同意情况下转让合同而产生的违约行为)而签署的契约或协议。	购销合同违约(行文啰唆,表达不够清晰)
7. <u>Notwithstanding</u> anything to the contrary in this Article XX, either Member <u>purporting</u>³ to Transfer its Membership Interest, or any part thereof; in violation of this Article XX shall <u>be liable to</u> the Company and the other Member <u>for all liabilities</u>, obligations, damages, losses, costs and expenses (including reasonable attorneys fees and court costs) <u>arising as a direct or consequential result of</u> such non-complying transfer, attempted transfer or <u>purported</u>³ transfer, including specifically, any additional cost or taxes created by non-compliance with any of the requirements and conditions <u>provided for</u> in Section 10.1.	尽管第 XX 条有任何相反的规定,打算转让会员利益或会员利益之一部分的会员,凡违反第 XX 条者应对公司及其他会员的就其未遵守合同规定转让、企图转让或打算转让之直接或间接后果所产生的全部债务、义务、损害、损失以及费用(包括合理的律师费以及诉讼费)负责;以上费用还特别包括未遵守第 10.1 款规定的要求或条件而产生的额外费用或税款。	会员转让违约条款
8. If either party <u>terminates</u> this Agreement under Section 18.1, the breaching party shall, in addition to reimbursing the non-breaching party for all amounts due for equipment and supplies procured and services rendered hereunder, <u>reimburse</u> the non-breaching party <u>for</u> its direct costs of termination, which shall <u>include</u> (without any double counting) all reasonable <u>costs and expenses</u> of Operator moving out or being removed from the Facility.	任何一方根据第18.1款终止本协议,违约方除了须向非违约方偿还根据本协议所购的所有设备、器材及服务费用外,还须向非违约方支付因违约而产生的直接开支,其中包括(不得重复计算)将操作员撤离工厂的所有合理花费。	适合工程项目协议

续表

Breach of Contract	违约责任	使用说明
9. In the event of a default by Party B, Party A shall not be required to return any part of the security deposit. Party A may <u>retain all or any part of the security deposit as liquidated damages</u> or apply all or any part of the security deposit against actual damages sustained by reason of Party B's default. The retention of the security deposit shall not be the only remedy to which, Party A shall <u>have all recourse against</u> Party B provided by this Lease and by law. Party B agrees to pay Party A's reasonable attorneys' <u>fees and expenses incurred in</u> enforcing any of the terms of this Lease, in collecting past due rent, and in recovering possession from Party B.	乙方违反本合同的,甲方无需返还任何押金。甲方可以保留全部或部分押金作为约定违约金,亦可以押金之一部分或全部用于抵偿甲方违约所造成之实际损害。甲方不因押金之没收而丧失依照本合同或依照法律对乙方行使的其他请求。乙方同意补偿甲方为执行本合同、收取所欠租金及收回租赁物所支付之合理律师费用。(乔焕然,2008:129)	违反租约
10. If a Party <u>materially fails to perform</u> any of its obligations under this Contract or if a Party's <u>representation or warranty</u> under this Contract is <u>materially untrue or inaccurate</u>, the Party shall be <u>deemed to have breached the Contract</u>. The Party in breach shall have thirty (30) days from receipt of a notice from the other Party specifying the breach to correct such breach if it is remediable. The Party in breach shall in any case <u>be liable to</u> the other Party for all damages caused by the breach. <u>Liabilities</u> for such damages <u>shall not be waivered</u> in the event the non-breaching Party terminates this Contract under XX. All remedies provided for herein and under the law shall <u>be cumulative</u>.	如果一方实质上未履行其在本合同项下的任何义务,或一方在本合同项下的陈述或保证是不真实的或不准确的,该方应被视为违反了本合同。违约方应在收到另一方指明其违约行为的通知后三十(30)日内,纠正其违约行为(若该违约行为是可以纠正的)。无论如何,违约方有责任赔偿另一方因该等违约而造成的一切损害。如果守约方根据XX条款终止本合同,违约方仍应给予损害赔偿。本合同规定的及法律规定的一切救济应是累积的。(同上)	适合各种性质的违约行为
11. The Executive hereby <u>represents</u> to the Corporation that: (i) the <u>execution and delivery</u> of this Agreement by the Executive and the Corporation and the performance by the Executive of the Executives duties hereunder <u>shall not constitute a breach of</u>, or otherwise <u>contravene</u>, the terms of any other agreement to which the Executive is a party or otherwise bound; and (ii) that in the performance of his duties hereunder the Executive <u>shall not use any</u> information (including, without limitation, confidential information and trade secrets) which the	总经理兹向公司保证:(1)总经理与公司签署本协议以及总经理行使本协议规定之总经理职责,并不构成对总经理是其中签约方(或以其他方式受制于该协议)的任何其他协议之条款的违约或在其他方面违反该协议条款;(2)在行使其本协议的职责时,总经理不得使用并非由其合法所得或合约上允许泄露给公司的任何资料(包括但不限于机密资料或商业秘密)。总经	总经理的违约责任:是相当于disclaimer(免责条款)之类的防范措施——要求受雇者保证其所作所为均为合法行为,万一雇主受到指控,该雇员要负起个人责任。

续表

Breach of Contract	违约责任	使用说明
Executive is not legally and contractually free to disclose to the Corporation. The Executive <u>represents</u> that any confidentiality, trade secret or similar agreement to which he is a party or otherwise bound <u>will not interfere with</u> the effective performance by the Executive of his duties hereunder.	理保证：涉及总经理是签约方或以其他方式受制约的任何机密资料、商业秘密或类似协议，都不会妨碍总经理对本协议职责之有效行使。	

三、关键词解说

在以上 11 段有关违约的不同条款中，我们给很大一批数量的词画了引人注目的"底线"。其实在本书的其他章节，我们都曾经对这类词以某种方式做过注释或讲解。如果读者能领会作者将这些词画线的意图，那作者就会感到十分欣慰：因为这些词基本上都是写作有关合同条款的核心用词，是这些词及其特殊的用法，构成了英文法律文本的一大语篇特征。限于篇幅，作者无法在此对其一一进行讲解。但读者可细心揣摩，省悟其用法，然后便可融会贯通于合同文本的写作和翻译之中。但有些词或概念，太专业或冷僻，仍然有必要在此提出讨论：

1. The organization documents of Buyer：即使非常忠实地将该短语翻译成"买方的组织文件"也没有人能明白"个中奥秘"。翻译的确需要百科全书的知识，但是有时百科全书未必会给你提供相关的答案。这时我们就需要善用互联网的搜索引擎。当然仅仅搜索 The organization documents of Buyer 是不会有结果的，因为范围太宽。通过观察上下文，其中 mortgage，Encumbrance，the Buyer's properties 都跟物业或地产相关，因此在搜索该短语时，加上一个 property 或 mortgage，就会出现以下相关资料：When the seller or buyer is not a natural born person, the settlement agent and title insurer must verify that the entity was properly formed and that the person(s) signing the documents are duly authorized and have the power to sell and/or loan money, or to buy and/or borrow money. If the closing documents are not signed by a duly authorized representative of the corporation, trust, company, partnership, etc., the transaction may be voidable.[①]于是，我们将其翻译成"买方之机构文件"，也明白这是非个人买家，如公司或社团，在购买物业时，该买家或经手人是否身份合法、得到适当的授权等资料。

2. Encumbrance：这是一个典型的行话式的法律术语，即圈外人士很难明白其复杂的内涵，越解释越令人糊涂。它指按揭、地役权、留置权、押记等等。那么，什么是留置权、地役权、押记？总之，一个物业上有了这些东西，在出售或向银行作抵押贷款时，就会有麻烦。例如，某个物业有违章建筑，政府有关部门下令清拆，但业主置之不理，政府有关部门会视情况而定，如果暂时不妨碍公众安全的，可能不会强制对其进行拆除，但往往会在政府的产权管

---

① https://www.fntic.com/commercialescrow.asp, 资料提取日期为 2013 年 5 月 30 日。

理部门对该物业施加一个"押记";当业主今后要出售该物业时,买家就会认为该物业产权"不干净",从而会影响物业的交易。这时,业主就要主动采取必要清拆行动,或将物业恢复原状,在通过有关工程部门的检查之后,再申请撤销该"押记"。由于 encumbrance 一词包括内容太多,故该词一般就笼统地翻译成"产权负担"。

3. Purporting,purported:法律英语中的"purport"问题,在以往任何论述法律语言特点和翻译方法的文章中很少受到重视。因为该词使用的频率远没有古旧副词那么普遍。但在翻译过程中处理该词的难度,远比任何其他典型的法律专用词更加困难。之所以把它选出来讨论是因为它的确是读者、译者的共同讨厌词(nuisance),理解和翻译都非常困难,另一个原因是本段恰好又有两个这样的词作为素材。

作名词使用时,purport 的意思为"意旨""目的"。但这种用法并非法律上的用法。作为动词,purport 的主要意思为"声称""据称""意指"或"看起来是",词义上与另一个英文词"allege"颇为相似(用法上大不相同)。作为该词的衍生词,还有 purported,purporting 以及 purportedly 等。该词在普通英语中的功用无足轻重,可以完全忽略,因为在以英语为母语的国家中,受过高等教育的普通人士一般都不会使用该词,即使学者也不会在著作中使用该词。但在法律英语中,虽然其实际意义含糊,用途飘忽,但时常被滥用。

事实上该词是某些法律条文写手的风格用词,没有任何特别的法律概念或实质意义,英译中时通常都可以忽略。在权威的双语法律(如香港法律的真确版中)的中文版中,通常找不到其相应的或对等的译文。例如:

例 1. For the purpose of this Part—

(a) an instrument is false if it purports to have been—

(i) made in the form in which it is made by a person who did not in fact make it that form;

(ii) made in the form in which it is made on the authority of a person who did not in fact authorize its making in that form;

就本部而言——

(a) 任何文书如有以下情况,即属虚假——

(i) 该文书是以某种式样制成,并看来是由某人以该式样制成,但事实上该人并无以该式样制造该文书;

(ii) 该文书是以某种式样制成,并看来是获某人授权以该式样制造,但事实上该人并无授权以该式样制造该文书;①

如果要使译文达到完全忠实的程度,译文势必是这样的:"(a) 如任何文书据称已被(i)制成这么一种形式,即它看起来是由某人以该式样制成,但事实上该人并无以该式样制造该文书;(ii)……即属虚假。"这样的译文,不但会使读者莫名其妙,而且译文本身也有逻辑上的矛盾:制成这么一种形式不过是"据称的",事实上可能并非如此,那怎么可以被认定"即属虚假"呢?

例 2. As to the drafts or acceptances under or purporting to be under the Credit, which are payable in United States Dollars, we agree:

---

① 香港《刑事罪行条例》,第 69 条(真确本)。

对于本信用证项下的用美元支付的汇票或承兑汇票,我们同意:(宋雷:445)

例 3. If at our special request the Credit is issued in transferable form, it is understood and agreed that you are under no duty to determine the proper identity of a one appearing in the draft or documents as transferee, nor shall you be charged with responsibility of any nature or character for the validity or correctness of any transfer or successive transfers, and payment by you to any <u>purported transferee or transferees</u> as determined by you hereby authorized and approved…

如应我方特别要求,此信用证以可转让形式开立时,我们同意贵行不负担鉴定任何汇票或单据受让人身份的责任,贵行则无须负担任何性质的转让或连续转让的合法性或真实性的责任,在此特准许贵行支付给由贵行认定的任何<u>受让人</u>……(同上)

例 4. In absence of written instructions expressly to the contrary, we agree that you or any of your correspondents may receive and accept as "bills of lading" under the Credit, any document issued or <u>purporting to be issued</u> by or on behalf of any carrier, which acknowledges receipt of property for transportation, whatever the other specific provisions of such document(s),…

如无相反的书面文件明确规定,我们同意贵行或贵代理银行接受任何承运人或其代理人签发或<u>旨在签发的</u>,承认收到财产准备付运的一切单据,并将其视为本信用证的"提单",不论此种单据有无其他任何具体规定……(同上)

以上例1,选自香港刑法的《刑事罪行条例》,英文版中的 purporting 在中文版中被完全忽略。其他几例选自一本经贸法律教科书。其中例 2 和例 3 中的 purporting 和 purported 在译本中同样被完全忽略。如果我们字字对译,在例 2 中将译文变作:"对于本信用证项下或旨在(据称)纳入本信用证项下的用美元支付的汇票或承兑汇票……",我们会发现不但中文译文非常累赘,而且有关该词的译文也没有任何实质意义。不译,该条款的文义未受任何改变,其可操作性不受丝毫影响。在例 3 的译文中,"purported transferee or transferees"仅仅被译成"受让人",汉语里受让人可以是单数也可以是复数,所以汉语里"受让人"一个顶俩。而本文主题讨论的 purported,在译文里完全没有位置,但译文条款仍然没有半点歧义。如果要忠实地把这个短语译成中文,必然是"支付给由贵行认定的任何<u>据称的(打算成为之)受让人</u>"。事实上,这样"细致入微"的译文只能是画蛇添足之笔:既然受让人是贵行认定的(determined by you),那么其身份已确定,再添上"据称的受让人"或"打算成为之受让人",岂非多此一举或自相矛盾?

例 4 中的 purporting to be issued 被译成"旨在签发",在原文用法和译法上似乎比例2、例 3 较为合理一些。"我们同意接受由承运人或其代理人签发的或旨在签发的、承认收到的……一切单据。"在这一句中,"旨在签发"换句话说就是"打算签发"。在实际操作上,如果单据实际上没有被签发,那么其所接受的完全是空洞的、摸不着、看不见或意念上的东西。这样的文字游戏与务实的商业行为是格格不入的,也是毫无意义的。作为译者,是否需要忠实地翻译这种毫无意义的风格化词语呢(而且又是属于律师专用的不良风格的词语),笔者认为没有必要。

以上援引四例只是想说明 purporting 有各种译法。但其中最合理、最简洁而又不会造成任何法律歧义的译法往往是不译。

作为法律文本的译者,为了追求精确的对等,有时我们很无奈,唯一能做的是"如法炮制"这类恶劣的文风,不可以将 purport 一概去除,把译文改得也像前面的段落那样"干净利落"、简明扼要。所以,在上文,我们将 purporting 和 purported 均翻译成"打算"。

四、合同违约条款写作涉及的几个要素

合同违约的情形可以五花八门。在合同违约条款写作中,一定要订明什么样的情形属于合同违约行为;以及违约后如何补救。

最常见的合同违约行为

1. failure to perform any of its material obligations/ material breach of this Agreement(未能履行协议规定的主要义务);
2. failure to perform the obligations required herein, in whole or in part(未能全部或部分履行合同规定的义务);
3. a representation or warranty made by a Party is untrue or materially inconsistent with the fact(一方所做的陈述或保证不真实或与事实有重大出入);
4. any violation of any terms or provisions herein (hereof) by either Party B or Party A(甲方或乙方违反本协议任何条款);
5. any incomplete or mistaken performance of any obligation provided hereunder(未完全履行或错误履行合同义务);
6. any misrepresentation made hereunder(在合同中做出虚假陈述);
7. any material nondisclosure(重要资料不予披露);
8. omission of any material fact(忽略重要事实)

构成是否违约的表述

1. such Party is deemed to have breached this Contract/ violated or caused a default(该方即被视为违约);
2. become a default or event of default(构成违约或违约事件);
3. constitute breach of contract, or cause a default(构成违约或违约事件);
4. is not alleged to be in breach or default/ shall not have any obligation/ there exists no default or event of default(不被视为违约/无需负责);

违约的补救措施

1. The breaching party is not assuming nor shall it be responsible for any Liabilities of the non-breaching party(违约方无需对未违约方的任何债务负责任——属于霸王条款);
2. Remedy of this agreement in respect of any material breach hereof(by Consultant) shall be to terminate this Agreement(对本协议的重大违约的补救是终止本协议——最轻的补救措施);
3. The breaching Party shall compensate the non-breaching Party for the losses or damages incurred(由违约方补偿未违约方遭受的损失或损害);
4. The breaching Party shall be liable to the non-breaching party for all liabilities, obligations, damages, losses, costs and expenses (including reasonable attorneys fees and court costs) arising as a direct or consequential result of...(违约方须负责未违约方的所有债务、义务、损害、损失、包括合理的律师费和诉讼费(香港称之为"堂费")在内的各种开

支——属最严格违约赔偿条款之一）；

5. The breaching Party shall hold the non-breaching Party harmless from and against any and all losses, damages, penalties, costs, expenses (including reasonable attorneys fees) and liabilities (including product liabilities) incurred by its breaching conduct（违约方须防止对未违约方造成各种损失、损害……）；

6. to indemnify or reimburse the non-breaching party for...（由违约方补偿未违约方某方面的损失）；

7. to give the non-breaching party the right to exercise any remedy, or the right to any rebate, chargeback, penalty or change in...（给予未违约方行使各种救济措施的权利……）。

所以，一条内容较为笼统简约的违约条款可以这样写：

Any violation of any provision hereof, any incomplete or mistaken performance of any obligation provided hereunder, or any failure to perform any covenants provided hereunder by any Party shall constitute a breach of this Agreement. The breaching Party shall be liable for any such breach pursuant to the applicable laws.

任何一方违反本协议的任何条款，或未完全或错误地履行本协议的任何义务，或未履行本协议规定的条款，即构成违约。违约方须依有关法律对其违约行为负责。

五、通用示范条款

根据上文提供的语料以及违约条款的要素要求，一条内容面面俱到、语言简明简约的违约条款可以这样写：

If a Party fails to perform or has mistakenly performed any of its material obligations under this Contract, or if a representation or warranty made by a Party is untrue or materially inconsistent with the fact, such Party is deemed to have breached this Contract. The breaching Party shall compensate or be liable to the non-breaching Party for all liabilities, obligations, damages, losses, costs and expenses (including reasonable attorneys fees and court costs) arising as a direct or consequential result of such a breach.

如果一方未能履行或错误履行本合同的重要义务，或者一方做出的陈述或保证不真实或与事实有重大出入，则视该方已违反本合同。违约方须就该违约行为的直接或间接后果而产生的所有债务、义务、损害、损失、法律费用（包括合理的律师费及诉讼费）向未违约方做出赔偿或对其负责。

第十六章 仲裁条款的写作、翻译和研究(上)

一、引言

(一) 仲裁的概念

仲裁是一种争议解决机制,它是除法庭诉讼以外,解决民商事争议重要的方法之一。双方当事人在争议发生前或后达成协议,自愿将争议提交给双方同意的第三方(该第三方可以是一个仲裁员、数个仲裁员或是仲裁庭),由其做出对双方都有约束力的裁决。

仲裁(arbitration)一词出自法语 arbitrator [同 arbiter,源于拉丁语,意为"one goes to see"(去看的人)](Mo, 2001:8)。仲裁正式发源于古希腊罗马时代,伴随当时各城邦、港口的贸易往来的增多,商事海事纠纷也相应增加。为了解决纠纷,商人纷纷约请第三人居中裁决。在雅典,人们经常聘请私人仲裁员以减轻法院的压力。于是便产生了现代意义的仲裁雏形。近代以来,仲裁作为处理国际贸易和商事纠纷的惯用方法,进而扩展到各个领域的纠纷解决过程中(如劳动纠纷、消费者纠纷等),已成为现代 ADR[①] 的一种基本方法(曾青、邓建尼,2005:5)。

(二) 仲裁程序简述

仲裁程序在许多方面和法庭诉讼相似。仲裁和诉讼都遵循"原告—被告—裁判"的三角架构(如下图所示):

```
Arbitration Clause 仲裁条款
         ↓
Submission of a Claim 提交仲裁申请
         ↓
Admission of a Claim and Appointment of Arbitrator(s)
接受仲裁申请,组建仲裁庭
         ↓
Arbitration Proceedings 仲裁程序
         ↓
Arbitration Reward and Enforcement 仲裁的裁决与执行
```

[①] 所谓 ADR(alternative dispute resolution),即"替代纠纷解决程序",广义上是法庭诉讼以外解决纠纷的方法的总称,包括谈判、调解、仲裁等。之所以将仲裁划入广义的 ADR,是因为它们具备许多共同的特点:争议双方的自愿性、程序的灵活性、经济性等。但因为仲裁(尤其是正式型仲裁)的程序受到法律程序规则的制约,有时候不一定"经济快捷",因此仲裁有时并不像"调解""调停"等被视作纯粹的 ADR(Cane & Joanne, 2008:29、44)。

一方当事人凭仲裁协议和仲裁申请书以启动仲裁程序;仲裁员和法官一样,听取双方当事人主张并审查其提交的书面材料和证据,做出与法院判决具有同等效力的仲裁裁决;裁决对双方当事人均有约束力。如果义务方不执行裁决,权利方可以向有管辖权的法院提出强制执行申请。当然,仲裁的终局性和强制执行力不是绝对的,必须接受法院的监督:如英国法律允许就仲裁裁决中的法律问题向高等法院上诉,受诉法院可以对被上诉的裁决予以变更、撤销或退回复裁;我国允许当事人向法院申请撤销或不予执行仲裁裁决。

(三)仲裁的特点和优越性

商场如战场,世界经济贸易的发展必然产生大量的纠纷。就我国而言,仲裁制度经过近半个世纪的发展,已成为解决国际商务、航运、贸易等纠纷的主要手段。那么,究竟是哪些特点决定了仲裁的优越性?香港国际仲裁中心主席杨良宜先生将其概括为(杨良宜,1997:26—68):国际性,秘密性(privacy),非正式性(informality)与灵活性(flexible),快速、经济性,以及专业性。

仲裁的国际性主要归功于1958年的《纽约公约》[①],截至2013年4月,联合国193个成员国里已有146个加入了该公约,几乎可以说每一个重要的国际贸易国家都已签署了这份公约(我国在1986年签署加入)。根据国际公约高于国内法的司法效力原则,各缔约国普遍承认和认可外国的仲裁裁决;且裁决可以更多地参照国际有关公约、条约、甚至行业惯例,这一优势是法庭判决难以拥有的。

仲裁的秘密性与其民间性不无关系。与法庭诉讼不同,仲裁解决的是当事人之间的私人事项,没有对公众公开的义务。尤其是涉及商业秘密、当事人声誉或双方当事人的人情关系时,仲裁起到了保密作用。

非正式性和灵活性是指仲裁在程序上不像诉讼那么严格。基于意思自治原则,当事人可以选择仲裁庭的组成形式、开庭方式以及仲裁规则等。因此,仲裁在许多环节上可以简化,文书格式和裁决书的内容、形式也可以灵活处理。此外,仲裁在期限、法律适用和代理制度方面也存在很大的弹性和灵活性(张建华,2002:16)。只有相应的灵活、不受正式诉讼形式的束缚,才使得当事人约定的事项不受过于严格的拘束,使得权威人士、专家在处理纠纷时有较大的自由,从而达到快速、经济的目的。

仲裁的专业性主要体现在仲裁员的专业水准上。由于仲裁的对象大多是民事、商事纠纷,纠纷常常涉及专业性极强的经济、贸易和技术问题;复杂的商事仲裁与普通刑事案件不同,后者一般可以让大众用常识来判断。因此,各仲裁机构都备有仲裁员名册,仲裁员都是由专业精通、公正而有权威的人士担当,由当事人选择(仲裁员的具体约定方式将在下文中详述)。

由于仲裁便利、高效的特点,以及裁决跨境执行力的日益增强,仲裁已经成为涉外合同中最受欢迎的解决机制之一。尽管如此,由于不同国家或地区的法律对于仲裁协议的效力和执行力存在不同的要求,在某些情况下,尽管当事人在合同中已经明确表述将争议提交仲裁的意愿,但仲裁条款的效力仍存在争议,需要提交法院进行进一步判定,造成当事人时间、成本和精力的不必要的损耗;有些时候,已经做出仲裁裁决的案子因为仲裁协议的效力存在争议,最终甚至无法执行。所以在起草或翻译涉外合同时,对仲裁条款的效力应给予特别

[①] 《纽约公约》,即1958年6月10日在纽约召开的联合国国际商业仲裁会议上签署的《承认及执行外国仲裁裁决公约》。该公约处理的是对外国仲裁裁决的承认和仲裁条款的执行问题。

关注。

由于仲裁条款在合同通用条款的核心地位,而本文的不少内容完全是研究性质的,故这一部分的篇幅较长。为了方便读者,本专题分为上下两篇,上篇主要作为从事普通翻译和写作人员的参考;下篇为有心专门研究该课题的人员提供进一步探讨的素材。

二、仲裁条款的起草和翻译

(一) 仲裁条款与仲裁协议

仲裁协议有三种形式:(1)包含在主合同中的<u>仲裁条款</u>;(2)有关当事人专门订立的<u>仲裁协议书</u>;(3)援引双方当事人协议项下所指引的文件中有通过仲裁方式解决纠纷的<u>规定</u>。

仲裁条款是指双方当事人在所签订合同中表示愿意将他们之间将来可能发生的争议提交仲裁解决的条款,是实践中最普遍的一种仲裁协议,也是本文的研究主题。仲裁条款是可分割性条款,即主合同的变更、解除、终止或者无效不会影响仲裁条款的效力。

本文对仲裁条款的研究意在为中外经济贸易与合作的合同的起草、翻译提供规范的模板。因此,本文仅讨论国际仲裁条款的起草与翻译,而不会涉及国内仲裁条款。国际仲裁条款主要见于以下领域的合同:国际货物买卖、货物运输、国际保险、国际贸易、支付结算、国际投资、技术贸易;合资、合作经营、补偿贸易、来料加工;国际租赁、国际合作开发自然资源、国际工程承包,国际知识产权保护等等。

(二) 如何起草完善的仲裁条款

现在的国际大趋势是法院对仲裁条款的解释越来越宽松。简单说,只要当事人双方仲裁条款中明确表明了仲裁意愿,即使是一条简陋的仲裁条款,也可以得到完整的仲裁法的补充解释,经过法院的支持补救,双方当事人经过协商、妥协,最终得以有效执行。例如在1995年"Petr Shmidt"[①]案中,法院判定"Arbitration in London"(在伦敦仲裁)是有效的仲裁条款[英国法对仲裁条文的解释非常宽松,只要有"仲裁"一词便够了(杨良宜,1997:157)]。那在中国的涉外仲裁中,有无类似的简单条款呢?中国海事仲裁委员会的示范仲裁条款内,有一条简明仲裁条款:"若有争议,提交中国海事仲裁委员会裁决。"("In case of disputes, they shall be submitted to the China Maritime Arbitration Commission for arbitration.")[②]

以上两个简单的仲裁条款,放入合同中,看上去简明扼要,只要将来不出事,谁也不会在意,何况后者还是仲裁机构的示范条款。但一旦有争议发生时,双方当事人还得另行签订补充的仲裁协议,这个过程中双方当事人相互"扯皮"很常见。在未订明仲裁规则,仲裁员要几人、如何指定,仲裁语言等等的情况下,各当事人一定会争取对自己有利的条件,协商的过程已经拖延了争议案件的解决、耗费双方的时间精力,若协商不成那往往是对簿公堂,劳民伤财。

因此,根据仲裁的实际需要,完善的仲裁条款一般应包括仲裁范围、仲裁地点、仲裁方式(临时仲裁还是机构仲裁)、仲裁规则、适用法律、仲裁员、仲裁效力等几个方面。下例就是一

---

① 参见杨良宜:《国际商务仲裁》,北京:中国政法大学出版社,1997年,第109页。
② 参见中国海事仲裁委员会网站 http://www.cmac-sh.org/tk/tiaokuan.htm。

个简洁而完善的仲裁条款,读者可以轻松辨认出前文所述的所有仲裁条款的要素:

例 1. All controversies and claims arising under or relating to this Agreement are to be resolved by arbitration in accordance with the rules of the American Arbitration Association before a panel of three arbitrators selected in accordance with those rules. The arbitration is to be conducted in [venue]. The arbitrators are to apply (applicable law), without regard to its choice of law principles. Each party shall submit to any court of competent jurisdiction for purposes of the enforcement of any award, order or judgment. Any award, order or judgment pursuant to the arbitration is final and may be entered and enforced in any court of competent jurisdiction. (Stark, 2003:201)	凡因本合同引起的或与本合同有关的任何争执或索偿,均应按照美国仲裁协会的仲裁规则在(地名)进行仲裁。仲裁庭由三名仲裁员组成,根据仲裁规则进行委任。仲裁庭适用(适用的法律),而不适用其自行选择的法律。任何仲裁的裁决的执行,须由一方当事人向具有合法管辖权的法院提交申请。任何仲裁的裁决是终局的,任何一间具有合法管辖权的法院均可对其进行认定与执行。(作者译)

以下将分别对这些要素的内涵、句型和表达进行分析,对现有的条款加以评注,并给出范例供读者参考。

1. 仲裁条款的范围 (Scope)

几乎所有仲裁条款的开头都会述明仲裁条款的范围,即可提交仲裁的合同范畴,在我国《仲裁法》中的表述是"仲裁事项"。除非当事人希望将部分合同争议提交仲裁,部分合同争议诉上法院(这种情况非常少),一般来说仲裁条款的范畴要尽量广泛,以免将来某个争议出现时,别有心机的一方再指称这个争议不在约定仲裁的范围之内。

如何表达广泛的仲裁范围呢?一是对"争议"的表述,二是对"范围"的描述。"争议"一词,常见的表述有 claims/controversies/differences/disputes。1996 年英国仲裁法在第六条说明 dispute 包含 difference,但也有不少司法制度将这两个词界定为同义词。至于"范围"的描述,arising out of/in connection with/in relation to (this contract)都是广泛用字——使得只要是和合同扯得上关系的争议,都包含在了仲裁条款范围之内。还有一常见的表达是 under this contract,就不是那么广泛。因为"under"只约定了在合同"下"的范围,如果单独使用,合同本身的问题就变得不明朗。因此 under 常常会和前述的广泛用字连用,如此一来对仲裁条款范围的约定就密不透风了。如例 1 中:"All controversies and claims arising under or relating to this Agreement are to be resolved by arbitration…",用"controversies and claims"表示"争议",用 "arising under or relating to"(因本合同引起的或与本合同有关的)表述争议"范围"。以下有关仲裁范围的表述选自一些仲裁机构给出的示范仲裁条款:

例 2. Any dispute arising from or in connection with this Contract shall be…	凡因本合同引起的或与本合同有关的任何争议,均应……(中国国际经济贸易仲裁委员会,以下简称"CIETAC")
例 3. All disputes arising out of or in connection with the present contract shall be…	凡产生于本合同或与本合同有关的一切争议均应……(国际商会仲裁院,以下简称"ICC")

例 4. Any dispute, controversy or claim arising out of or relating to this contract, including the validity, invalidity, breach or termination thereof...	凡因本合同产生或与本合同有关的争议、争执或索偿，或违约、合同的终止或有效无效，均应……（香港国际仲裁中心，以下简称"HKIAC"）
例 5. Any dispute, controversy or claim arising out of or in connection with this contract, or the breach, termination or invalidity thereof, shall be...	任何因本合同而产生的或与本合同有关的争议、纠纷或索赔，或者有关违约、终止合同或合同无效的争议，均应……（斯德哥尔摩商会仲裁院，以下简称"SCC"）

例2和例3对"争议"的表述几乎相同，唯一的区别是单复数而已。对争议"范围"的界定是最常用的 arising from (out of) or in connection with。这两款写法用字简洁，且恰当地给出了仲裁条款的范围。

而例4和例5的写法体现的是旧式法律文书的不良文风：表达"争议"的概念用了 dispute, controversy or claim，这是法律文书中典型的三联词，事实上一个 dispute 足矣。在约定"范围"时，用 arising out of or relating to/ in connection with 还不够，还要再加上长长的 including the validity, invalidity, breach or termination thereof 或是 the breach, termination or invalidity thereof，表示即使合同本身存在终止、违约或无效的问题，也不影响前述的仲裁条款问题。虽然这么做是为了将"范围"包罗得更加广泛、全面，但笔者认为没有必要。首先，仲裁条款本身就是可分割性条款，不受主合同影响；其次，relating to/in connection with 已经将此因素包含在内，无需再重复。

以上四例均来自权威性的仲裁机构，其示范条款更是广为流传。通过对其文风的分析，考虑到现代法律英语的潮流也是提倡"简明英语"，建议舍弃例4、例5的写法。下例中的原文乃至翻译都属于典型的"师爷文风"（legalese）。

例 6. All disputes, controversies or differences which may arise between the Sellers and the Buyers, out of or in relation to or in connection with this contract, or the breach thereof, shall be....	出自本合约、或与它有关、或与它有联系的、或不履行该合约而在卖方和买方之间可能产生的一切纠纷、争论或不和，须……（薛华业，1989:15）

更加简洁、现代的写法和翻译应该是：

All disputes out of or in relation to this contract, shall be...	买卖双方之间因本合同产生或与本合同有关（包括因违约产生）的任何争议，应/须……

2. 仲裁方式和仲裁规则

（1）机构仲裁与临时仲裁

仲裁可笼统地分为机构仲裁（Institutional arbitration）和临时仲裁（*ad hoc* arbitration）。机构仲裁是当今世界最主要的仲裁方式。机构仲裁又称作制度仲裁、常设仲裁，指的是有固定的机构，提供仲裁员名单供当事人选定进行仲裁的仲裁类型。仲裁机构是固定的社团法人,每个机构都有自己制定的仲裁规则和收费规定,其仲裁员也都具有一定的专业素质和法律素养。当事人选择了某个仲裁机构后,也可以根据自身需要对其仲裁规则、仲裁程序进行修改。

临时仲裁又称作个别仲裁、随意仲裁,由当事双方在合同中约定将可能发生的争议交给现在约定的或未来争议发生时再确定的仲裁人。临时仲裁不依赖于固定的仲裁机构,随着争议产生由当事人授权成立仲裁庭,一旦争议解决即予以解散。临时仲裁程序上较为灵活,速度较快,费用一般也较低,它对于标的较小、但结案时间要求非常快且十分紧迫的案件有重要意义。在国际实践上,特别是在一些海事案件中,临时仲裁庭大量存在。

仲裁条款中区分机构仲裁和临时仲裁非常简单。仲裁条款中没有写明"将争议提交某仲裁机构仲裁"的,往往就是临时仲裁。如例1中,只说明了使用"the rules of American Arbitration Association"(美国仲裁协会的规则),没有写明将仲裁提交美国仲裁协会,因此例1的情况属于临时仲裁。但无论是机构仲裁还是临时仲裁,必须要按照一套特定的仲裁规则①进行。仲裁方式和仲裁规则也常常一起出现在仲裁的范围之后,于同一句话中进行表述。例7是一则机构仲裁条款,例8、例9属于临时仲裁条款,例10看似机构仲裁条款,其实不一定:如果休斯敦市只有一个仲裁机构,那么该条款指的是机构仲裁,如果有一个以上的仲裁机构,则该条款也是临时仲裁条款,与其他条款不同之处,只是指定了仲裁地点和规则而已。

例7. Any dispute arising from or in connection with this Contract shall be submitted to China International Economic and Trade Arbitration Commission (CIETAC) (venue) Sub-Commission (Arbitration Center) for arbitration which shall be conducted in accordance with the CIETAC's arbitration rules in effect at the time of applying for arbitration...	凡因本合同引起的或与本合同有关的任何争议,均应提交中国国际经济贸易仲裁委员会____分会(仲裁中心)②,按照仲裁申请时中国国际经济贸易仲裁委员会现行有效的仲裁规则进行仲裁。(节选自 CIETAC 示范仲裁条款)
例8. Any dispute, controversy or claim arising out of or relating to this contract, including the validity, invalidity, breach or termination thereof, shall be settled by arbitration in Hong Kong under the Hong Kong International Arbitration Centre Administered Arbitration Rules in force when the Notice of Arbitration is submitted in accordance with these Rules.	凡因本合同产生或与本合同有关的争议、争执或索偿,或违约、合同的终止或有效无效,均应根据提交仲裁通知时有效的《香港国际仲裁中心机构仲裁规则》,在香港仲裁解决。(节选自 HKIAC 示范仲裁条款)

---

① 当事人如果选择了机构仲裁,往往会使用该仲裁机构的仲裁规则,也可以对其规则进行修改,甚至选用其他适用的仲裁规则;如果选择临时仲裁,可以选择某家仲裁机构的规则,也可以选择国际组织制定的用于临时仲裁的规则(如《联合国国际贸易法委员会仲裁规则》),或自行制定法律适用的仲裁规则。

② CIETAC 的总部在北京,并在深圳、上海、天津和重庆分别设有贸仲委华南分会、上海分会、天津国际经济金融仲裁中心(天津分会)和西南分会,在香港特别行政区设立贸仲委香港仲裁中心。在参考示范条款时,只需按照仲裁地将其分支机构对号入座即可。

例 9. Any dispute, controversy or claim arising out of or in connection with this contract, or the breach, termination or invalidity thereof, shall be finally settled by <u>arbitration in accordance with the Arbitration Rules of the Arbitration Institute of the Stockholm Chamber of Commerce</u>.	任何因本合同而产生的或与本合同有关的争议、纠纷或索赔,或者有关违约、终止合同或合同无效的争议,均应当根据斯德哥尔摩商会仲裁院仲裁规则通过仲裁的方式最终予以解决。(节选自 SCC 示范仲裁条款)
例 10. Arbitration. If a dispute <u>should</u> arise regarding this Agreement, the parties agree that all claims, disputes, controversies, differences or other matters in question arising out of this relationship shall be settled finally, completely and conclusively by arbitration in Houston, Texas in accordance with the Commercial Arbitration Rules of the American Arbitration Association (the "Rules")①.	仲裁。假如由于本协议而发生分歧,各方同意所有由于这一关系而产生的索赔、分歧、纠纷、争执或其他有关事项,应在德州休斯敦根据美国仲裁协会的商业仲裁规则(简称"规则")做最后、完全和终局的解决。(作者译)

(2) 相关表述

在理解了这一部分的结构与写作原理之后,我们可以将仲裁方式与仲裁规则的句型结构和关键用词做如下归纳:

仲裁方式:

shall be submitted to [organization] for arbitration (机构仲裁)

shall be resolved/settled/arbitrated by [organization] (机构仲裁)

shall be resolved/settled by arbitration (临时仲裁)

值得一提的是,许多现有的(包括权威的)仲裁条款都会在 settled 或 arbitrated 前加上修饰语 finally 或 finally and exclusively (文风更差的甚至再加一个 completely,如例 10),以强调仲裁裁决效力的终局性。虽然双方当事人在订立仲裁条款时,已经暗示自己接受仲裁裁决是终局的、不可复审的(Stark,2003:197),但因为仲裁裁决的终局性是相对的②,所以只要当事人有明确意愿接受仲裁裁决的终局性,最好还是用白纸黑字写入条款中,这也是国际通行的做法。

仲裁规则:

in accordance with / under [rule] (in effect/in force...)

法律英语中表示"根据、依照"的词或短语,最规范、最常用的是 in accordance with,其他常见的包括:under,according to,pursuant to,in pursuance of,subject to。其中,under 属于法律专用;according to 太口语化、语域较低;pursuant to 和 in pursuance of 太古旧;subject to 的确切意思或译法须根据其在法律条文中的位置来确定——放在句首的作为前提,一般

---

① http://contracts.onecle.com/rick/langan.emp.1998.08.shtml.

② 仲裁的终局性只是相对于司法审查范围的有限性而言,审查范围越大,终局性就越低。而且许多国家和地区的仲裁法都未将仲裁裁决的终局性当作仲裁的一项基本原则加以规定。而且有的国际仲裁机构或组织的规则中设有内部上诉程序,除非仲裁条款中有相反约定,任何一方当事人如对仲裁裁决不服,可以提出二次仲裁上诉。(石现明,2009)

译成"遵照""依从";放在句尾的作"但书"(proviso),译成"但须符合……"。

(3) 仲裁机构在临时仲裁中的身份

上文中提到,仲裁条款中约定"将争议提交某仲裁机构仲裁"的,一定属于机构仲裁。然而,在临时仲裁中,当事人有可能会约定让某家仲裁机构担任"指定机构"(appointing authority)①和"管理机构"(administered authority)②,这和机构仲裁中的仲裁机构(arbitral institution)是不一样的。例如:

例 11. Any dispute, controversy, or claim arising out of or relating to this contract, or the breach, termination, or invalidity thereof, shall be settled by arbitration in accordance with the UNCITRAL Arbitration Rules in effect on the date of this contract. The appointing authority shall be the China International Economic and Trade Arbitration Commission.	任何争议、争执或索赔,凡由于本合同引起的或与之有关的,或由于本合同的违反、终止或无效而引起的或与之有关的,均应按照当时有效的《联合国国际贸易法委员会仲裁规则》③仲裁解决。 指定机构是中国国际经济贸易仲裁委员会。(刘净、刘美邦,2012)

有的译者可能一见到有仲裁机构的名称,如例 11 中的 China International Economic and Trade Arbitration Commission,就以为当事人约定了机构仲裁,进而将"appointing authority"译成"仲裁机构",这么一来,这条临时仲裁条款就变成了机构仲裁条款。所以在分析原文时一定要留意 appoint 和 administer 二字。一家仲裁机构也有可能因为担任"指定机构"或"管理机构"而出现在临时仲裁条款中,相关的表述如下:

> The appointing authority/administered authority shall be [organization].
> The arbitration shall be administered by [organization].

3. 仲裁地 (Venue)

仲裁条款通常都规定仲裁地,一是以地点状语形式插入句中(如前文中的例 7);也有单独成句的(如前文中的例 1、例 8),一律翻译成"仲裁地为……"或"在……仲裁"。

> The arbitration is to be conducted in [city].
> The seat of arbitration shall be [city].

需要注意的是,当仲裁地约定为中国内地时(不包括中国的港澳台地区),当事人必须指定一家仲裁机构,选择机构仲裁。根据我国现行法律,如果当事人在仲裁协议中未能就仲

---

① 当事人无法就独任仲裁员的约定达成一致或者经当事人指定的两名仲裁员无法就首席仲裁员人选达成一致时,由"指定机构"指定独任仲裁员或首席仲裁员。
② "管理机构"主要是为仲裁庭提供管理上或者行政上的服务,具体的服务内容大体包括:通讯联络、文件转递、预订开庭室(会议室)、速记、口译、仲裁费用托管以及仲裁庭提出的其他服务要求等。当事人只约定了管理机构,没有约定指定机构时,管理机构同时履行指定机构职能。
③ 《联合国国际贸易法委员会仲裁规则》(UNCITRAL Arbitration Rules)于 1976 年被建议采用,并于 2010 年被修改,规则虽然供临时仲裁时使用,但当事人也可在书面协议中指定一个常设仲裁机构,负责关于仲裁的行政管理工作。

机构做出约定,且当事人未能进一步做出补充约定,仲裁协议即为无效[1]。不过,当仲裁地在中国境外时(包括中国的港澳台地区),只要当事人选择的法律或者仲裁地的法律是有效的[2],即使仲裁条款内没有约定机构仲裁,换句话说,即使当事人订立的是临时仲裁,中国法院很可能会承认该仲裁协议的效力。因为我国根据《纽约公约》承担了承认与执行外国仲裁裁决的义务,而外国裁决也包括临时仲裁庭做出的裁决。

一言以蔽之,中国目前对临时仲裁采取的是境内境外"两种态度":在仲裁地被约定为中国内地时,如果当事人订立了临时仲裁协议,该协议往往被认定为无效;仲裁地在中国境外的情况下,临时仲裁协议的效力能够得到中国法院认可。

4. 适用法律(Applicable law/Governing law)

仲裁的适用法律一般指的是实体法。实体法,简单说来,就是判断谁对谁错、损失如何计算等等的法律。在国际商事实践中,如果当事人双方未事先约定仲裁的适用法律,发生了争议,双方当事人对适用法律无法达成一致意见的,会交给仲裁庭决定。仲裁庭在选择适用仲裁条款的适用法时,往往会对仲裁庭所在地的强制性法律和公共秩序以及裁决的有效性、承认和执行等相关问题一并做出考虑,最后有可能选择双方在主合同的法律选择条款中约定的适用法律来支配仲裁,也有可能选择其他法律。为了降低这种不确定性,当事人双方有必要约定仲裁的适用法律,一般的做法是在主合同的法律选择条款中约定"对争议的处理受XX法律管辖"(见本书最后几章),也有少数是在仲裁条款中单独进行约定。在国际商事仲裁中,当事人除了可以自主选择某国的实体法,还可以选择国际法与在国际上反复使用的国际贸易惯例。

斯德哥尔摩商会仲裁院公布的2010年国际仲裁调查结果显示,其国际仲裁案的当事人对仲裁地和适用法的选择主要有以下几种组合:

以瑞典为仲裁法定地点与瑞典实体法律的传统组合;

法国与联合国国际货物销售合同公约;

瑞典与英国法、中国法、俄罗斯法、瑞士法或纽约法[3]。

在仲裁条款中单独约定适用法律时,常见的表达句型如下:

The arbitration shall be <u>governed and construed</u> by the substantive law of [state].

仲裁的<u>管辖与解释</u>应适用[某国家]实体法。

The arbitration shall <u>apply</u> [state] law[4].

仲裁应<u>适用</u>[某国家]法。

In rendering an award, the arbitrator is to determine the rights and obligations of

---

[1] 《中华人民共和国仲裁法》第十六条规定:仲裁协议应当具有下列内容:(一)请求仲裁的意思表示;(二)仲裁事项;(三)选定的仲裁委员会。第十八条 仲裁协议对仲裁事项或者仲裁委员会没有约定或者约定不明确的,当事人可以补充协议;达不成补充协议的,仲裁协议无效。

[2] 根据2005年12月26日公布的《最高人民法院关于适用〈中华人民共和国仲裁法〉若干问题的解释》,对于国际仲裁和涉外仲裁中仲裁协议或条款的效力的确定,所适用的法律顺序如下:(1)当事人约定的法律;(2)当事人约定的仲裁地的法律;(3)当事人申请确认仲裁协议或条款效力的法院地法律。

[3] 详见斯德哥尔摩商会仲裁院中文网站,http://www.sccinstitute.se/?id=26742&newsid=38269。

[4] 在仲裁条款中约定使用某国法律,都会被认定是指的实体法。比如说"适用中国法",那便是适用中国的实体法,而不是中国的程序法。因此在写作条款时,用"law"或是"substantive law"都可以。

the parties according to the substantive and procedural laws of [state]. (Stark, 2003: 198)

仲裁员应根据[某国家]的实体法和程序法对当事人各方的权利和义务做出裁决。

Internationally accepted rules of commercial law govern all disputes arising out of or relating to this Agreement, except that the law of [the United States] governs all disputes arising out of or relating to [patent rights]. (Stark, 2003:198)

所有因本合同产生或与本合同相关的争议应受国际公认的商业规则管辖,但因专利权产生或与专利权有关的争议应受美国法律管辖。

5. 仲裁员 (Arbitrator)

对仲裁员的约定和适用法有关建议。在仲裁协议中至少约定仲裁员的人数和指定仲裁员的方式,否则争议发生后双方当事人无法达成一致的,会由相关的仲裁规则和仲裁法补救。国际仲裁中,大多情况下仲裁庭的人数是一人、两人或三人。一般来说,仲裁庭人数不能是双数,但英国的仲裁法说明了两个仲裁员意见不能统一时,由一位公断人(umpire)接手解决,这在英国仲裁中比较多见。

例 12.	If arbitration is necessary, the parties shall request [name of the specific arbitrator] to act as the arbitrator.	若有仲裁必要,双方须指定[特定仲裁员姓名]担任仲裁员。
例 13.	The arbitration is to be conducted before a single arbitrator whom the parties shall jointly select. If the parties are unable to agree upon the arbitrator, either party may request [organization] to select the arbitrator.	双方应共同指定一名仲裁员进行仲裁。若双方无法对仲裁员的人选达成一致,任意一方可要求[机构]代为选定。
例 14.	The arbitration is to be conducted before a panel of three arbitrators. Within 15 days after commencement of the arbitration, each party shall select an arbitrator. The two selected arbitrators are to select a third neutral arbitrator within 10 days of the appointment of the last selected arbitrator. If the arbitrators selected by the parties are unable or fail to agree upon the third arbitrator, either party may request the [organization] to select the third arbitrator. (Stark, 2003:190)	仲裁庭由三名仲裁员组成。仲裁开始后的15天内,每一方当事人应各指定一名仲裁员。第三名仲裁员应在第二名仲裁员获得委任后的10天内,由已被指定的两名仲裁员选定。若已被指定的两名仲裁员对第三名仲裁员的人选无法达成一致,任意一方可要求[机构]代为选定。(作者译)

例12中指定的是一名仲裁员,而且是独任仲裁员。这种情况其实不少。有的经验丰富、声誉卓著的仲裁员,受到双方当事人的信赖,可以在仲裁条款中明写。不过,最好能在条款后多加一句,如果这名仲裁员到时不能如约接受委任,双方应该怎么做。例13和例14就比较完善,约定了各种可能的情况。此外,需要指出,这里的"organization"指的不一定是执行仲裁的"仲裁机构",更有可能是"指定机构"或"管理机构"。

国际仲裁中,双方当事人在选择仲裁员时会考虑诸多因素,如仲裁员的法律专业水准、行业水准、仲裁经验、国籍、沟通管理水平等等,其中非常重要的因素,当事人往往会事先在仲裁条款中提出。比如:

The arbitrator must be a practicing attorney / a retired judge / a certified accountant...

The arbitration is to be conducted before a panel of three arbitrators, each of whom must be a member of LMAA①, and actively engaged in the business of ... for at least ... years.

6. 仲裁裁决的终局性（Finality of arbitration award）

在前文我们已经提到过，双方当事人在订立仲裁条款的同时就意味着接受了仲裁条款的终局性。但因为终局性是相对的，所以还是要明确地用语言表达出来。如果已经在字里行间穿插了 finally arbitrated 之类的表述，那就不需要再重申裁决的终局性。如果没有，一般会这么写：

The arbitral award is final and binding upon both parties.
仲裁裁决是终局的，对双方均有约束力。

细心的读者会发现例1中相关的规定除了说明裁决的终局性，还特别说明了法院对裁决的认可和执行的问题：Each party shall submit to any court of competent jurisdiction for purposes of the enforcement of any award, order or judgment. <u>Any award, order or judgment pursuant to the arbitration is final</u> and may be entered and enforced in any court of competent jurisdiction. 当然了，法院不会因为合同中没有写到这一条就对仲裁裁决不予认可或不予执行。所以这样的表述不是必要的。

7. 对其他争议解决方式的约定（On other dispute resolution solutions）

发生争议后，当事人之间的协商其实是解决问题的第一步，也是最经济、直接的争议解决方式。除了协商，调解也很常见。但协商和调解都属于无约束力的争议解决方式，其处理结果不具有强制执行力。许多合同里包含了一个"几步走"的争议解决机制，概括起来就是：协商—仲裁，调解—仲裁，协商—调解—仲裁。例如：

| 例15. Should a dispute arise out of or be in relation to this Agreement, the parties shall attempt in good faith to resolve the dispute promptly by negotiation (between executives who have the authority to settle the controversy and who are at a higher level of management than the persons with direct responsibility for administration of this contract). If the dispute remains unresolved (after 45 days since the disputing party's notice is received by the other party), the parties may then resort to arbitration. | 如果有任何因本合同产生或与本合同有关的争议，合同双方应通过友好协商解决。（参与协商的应是各合同方内部的高层，其权限应高于直接负责合同的实施的人员且对争议的解决有决定权）。（从提出争议的一方发给另一方通知的45天后，）争议仍无法解决的，双方可以将争议提交仲裁。 |

注：括号中的内容可根据实际需要修改或省略。

---

① London Marine Arbitrators Association 伦敦海事仲裁协会

例 16. The parties shall first try in good faith to settle by mediation any dispute arising out of or relating to this Agreement or its breach. The mediation is to be administered by ＿＿＿＿. If the mediation is unsuccessful, the parties may then resort to arbitration. (Stark, 2003:200)	任何因本合同产生或与本合同有关的争议,合同双方应首先尝试通过友好调解解决。调解由＿＿＿＿管理。如果调解不成,双方可选择仲裁。(作者译)

对争议的终极解决方式是法庭诉讼。但是笔者不建议将法庭诉讼放入"几步走"的争议解决机制中。首先,法庭诉讼本身是最终的争议解决方式,合同方约定与否,都不影响它的地位。其次,各国法律对法院的司法审查的范围规定也不同。比如在中国国内,当事人约定争议可以向仲裁机构申请仲裁也可以向人民法院提起诉讼,仲裁协议无效(除非一方向仲裁机构申请仲裁,另一方未在规定期间内提出异议),这么规定是为了维护仲裁裁决的终局性。当事人对仲裁裁决不服,可以向法院申请撤销或不执行裁决。只有判定裁决是无效的情况下,才能选择重新仲裁或法庭诉讼。

8. 其他

(1) 仲裁时效(time limitation)

既然仲裁条款中规定了仲裁适用的法律,那么仲裁的时效也受到适用法的约束。各国法律对时效规定不同,当事人要留心法律规定的仲裁时效来保护自己。比如滞期费的追偿,英国是 6 年,但法国、希腊、日本、荷兰、瑞士、巴西等多国时效期只有 1 年,德国、波兰等为 2 年,印度、挪威等为 3 年,也有长至 10 年的芬兰与 20 年的葡萄牙(杨良宜,1997:283)。

当事人可以在法律允许的范围内(一般允许当事人缩短仲裁时效,但往往有最低限制,也有特殊情况可以延长时效),在合同中自行约定仲裁时效,通用的写法是:

> Any arbitration proceeding under this Agreement must be commenced no later than ＿＿＿＿ after the controversy or claim arises. Failure timely to commence an arbitration proceeding is both an absolute bar to the commencement of arbitration proceedings with respect to the controversy or claim and a waiver of the controversy or claim. (Stark, 2003:194)

本协议下的任何仲裁程序必须在争议或索赔出现后的＿＿＿＿天内启动,否则等同于放弃该争议或索赔的权利,相关的仲裁程序也不得再启动。(作者译)

类似这样的约定,可以避免双方当事人在对争议的处理上拖泥带水,让争议尽早得到解决。但时效太短会让索赔人处于不利的位置,所以对时效的约定应合情合理。

(2) 仲裁语言(language)

国际仲裁中,仲裁语言多为英文,意味着递交的仲裁文书(包括当事人递交的证据、答辩等)、开庭时的语言、仲裁裁决书都会使用英文。在进入具体的仲裁程序后,当事人可以选择变更仲裁语言。我国的企业在参与国际仲裁时,有评论说是"十案九败",仲裁人才的缺乏、经验不足、语言障碍等是主要原因。所以中国企业应尽量要求在国内的国际仲裁机构进行仲裁,仲裁语言使用中文。约定仲裁语言使用的句型为:

> The language to be used in the arbitral proceedings shall be [...]
> 仲裁程序中应当使用的语言为_____。／仲裁语言为_____。

当然,仲裁语言并不只能是一种。当事人也可以约定双语仲裁,比如同时使用中文和英文。只是这么一来,所有文书需用双语写成,开庭时的陈词、作供、盘问等都要配备口译员,一句话说两遍,还要双语记录,增加了当事人的成本,也拖慢了仲裁进度,这与仲裁快速经济的优点背道而驰。所以仲裁中往往只规定使用一种语言。

（3）仲裁费用（arbitration costs）

广义的仲裁费包括机构费用（申请仲裁费、调查取证费等）、仲裁员的报酬和开销以及当事人费用（律师费、差旅费等）。原则上仲裁费用是由败诉方承担的；当事人部分胜诉、部分败诉的,由仲裁庭根据当事人各方责任大小确定其各自应当承担的比例。但即使当事人在协议中写明"仲裁费用全部由败诉方承担",仲裁庭还是会有一定的裁量权。对此我国的法律没有明确规定,英国1996年仲裁法第65条规定:除非当事人另有约定,仲裁庭有权直接对仲裁或者仲裁程序任何一部分发生的补偿费用限定在一定金额内。对仲裁费用的约定,常见的表述有以下几种：

> All arbitration expense shall be borne by the losing party unless otherwise awarded by the arbitration tribunal.
> 除仲裁庭另有裁定,否则仲裁费用应全部由败诉方承担。
> Each party shall bear its own costs of arbitration and attorney's fees, irrespective of the outcome of the arbitration.
> 无论仲裁结果如何,合同方应承担各自的仲裁开销与律师费。
> Each party shall bear its own costs of discovery, attorney and witness fees but the arbitrator shall be empowered to make a different allocation of such fees and costs in the award.
> 合同方应承担各自的仲裁调查费、律师费和证人费,但仲裁员有权在裁决中对这些费用的分配给出不同判定。

9. 汇总

以上便是仲裁条款中的主要"零部件",读者不妨将它们组合起来,在实际操作时可以根据需要对部件进行"组装、升级或简配"。主合同中的仲裁条款往往比较简短,读者可以参考以下写法,但针对未阐明的事项当事人一定要谨慎,不能让自己在未来可能发生的仲裁中陷入不利的地位。

仲裁范围	Any dispute arising out of or relating to this Agreement shall be resolved by arbitration.
仲裁方式	The arbitration shall be submitted to [organization] and
仲裁规则	shall be conducted in accordance with [rule].
仲裁地	The arbitration shall be conducted in [venue].

仲裁员	The arbitration shall be held before a panel of three arbitrators. No later than 15 days after the arbitration begins, each party shall select an arbitrator and request the two selected arbitrators to select a third neutral arbitrator. If the two arbitrators fail to select a third on or before the 10th day after the second arbitrator was selected, either party is entitled to request the [organization] to appoint the third neutral arbitrator in accordance with its rules.
仲裁时效	Any arbitration under this agreement must be commenced no later than one year after the dispute arose. Failure to timely commence an arbitration proceeding constitutes both an absolute bar to the commencement of an arbitration proceeding with respect to the dispute, and a waiver of the dispute.
适用法律	The arbitrators shall interpret all disputes arising under or relating to this Agreement in accordance with [governing law], without regard to their own choice of laws principles.
仲裁的终局性	The arbitration award shall be final and binding upon the parties.
仲裁费用	All arbitration expense shall be borne by the losing party unless otherwise awarded by the arbitration tribunal.

当然,更完整的仲裁条款可能还包括语言条款。但一般来说,仲裁地和适用法律的选定已经决定语言的使用,不可能让斯德哥尔摩商会仲裁院用中文开展仲裁,因此语言子条款一般可以省略。至此,我们再将本节开头的第一个例子拿过来,与作者提供的以上这个通用模板进行对比。例1的范本相对简洁,可以作为通用仲裁条款的一个"精华版"。除此之外,两者之间一个很大的区别就是情态动词 shall 的使用。

>All controversies and claims arising under or relating to this Agreement are to be resolved by arbitration in accordance with the rules of the American Arbitration Association before a panel of three arbitrators selected in accordance with those rules. The arbitration is to be conducted in [venue]. The arbitrators are to apply (applicable law), without regard to its choice of law principles. Each party shall submit to any court of competent jurisdiction for purposes of the enforcement of any award, order or judgment. Any award, order or judgment pursuant to the arbitration is final and may be entered and enforced in any court of competent jurisdiction. (Stark, 2003:201)

在法律英语中,shall 是使用频率最高的情态动词。笔者提供的模板中也使用了大量的 shall。仲裁条款本身就是当事人意愿的体现,签订合同的双方总是要共同遵守的。shall 在法律英语中主要表达当事人需要履行的法律义务,其强制性次于"must",所以仲裁条款中使用 shall 来表述法律义务和温和的命令都是合适的。不过,很多行内人士受师爷文风的影响,使得 shall 被滥用的情况也很多[①]。当前,以英语为母语的国家兴起的"简明英语运动"已

---

① 参见李克兴:《法律翻译理论与实践》,北京:北京大学出版社,2007年,第104—117页。

经取得了巨大的进展,当今的法律英语已经越来越接近普通英语。例1的仲裁条款是由一位教授法律英语写作的美国大学老师所拟,其行文充分体现了"简明英语"精神,其中将所有的情态动词 shall 用一般将来时 is/are to be 代替,不但不影响原文意思,原文的"强制"意味也没有减弱。文中只有一个地方使用了 shall,因为在美国,法律规定当事人应当将仲裁裁决提交法院进行司法认可及执行,需要将"责任""强制"的意味加重一些。作者并不反对适度、适当地使用 shall,况且这早已是行内人士的写作习惯,不用刻意改变,读者可以根据具体情况自行斟酌。

10. 与仲裁相关的解决争议的概念及其辨析

以下均为与仲裁相关的解决争议的概念:solve, resolve, mediation, reconciliation, arbitration, consultation, negotiation, adjudication(adjudge), judgment (judge)。其意思分别是(1) solve(解决),(2) resolve(解决),(3) mediate/mediation(调解): to settle by friendly intervention;(4) reconcile(和解): to make friendly again, reconciliation 指的是已经获得成功的 mediation,等于一种 settlement 或 resolution;(5) arbitrate(仲裁): to decide a dispute by an arbitrator or in an arbitration tribunal;(6) consult(协商): to talk things over;(7) negotiate(商谈/谈判): to discuss a matter with a view to reaching an agreement;(8) adjudicate(裁定): to hear and decide;(9) adjudge(裁决): to order or award by law;(10) judge(判决): to hear and pass a judgment in a court。在这一系列按序排列的概念中,我们可以清楚地看到"仲裁"在争议解决中的位置。还须注意的是:虽然这最后三个词都作"裁决"解释,是司法机构做出决定的关键词,但低层法官,如裁判官,做出决定时,一般用 adjudicate;而高层法官、大法官、高等法院或终审法院的法官断案或做出决定时应该用 adjudge 或 judge。

不通过司法途径对合同纠纷做出解决,一般都用 mediation, reconciliation, arbitration, consultation, negotiation 以及 resolve, settle(解决)等一系列相关词。但 resolve 与 settle 又有本质上的差别:"resolve" may not arrive at a settlement;"resolve" focuses on the process of reaching a decision 解决是一种手段,强调的是过程,但未必会有"最终的解决方案";"settle" means to reach an agreement or decision。以下是一本解决争议的 Do-it-self 的英文书 *Settle it Out of Court*:*How to Resolve Business and Personal Disputes Using Mediation, Arbitration, and Negotiation*。从这本书的书名中,我们可以很清楚看出 settle 与 resolve 以及 mediation 与 arbitration 和 negotiation 这几个词之间的关系。

特别需要指出的是上述第1个词 solve。在日常英语中,solve 是个最常用的词,但它跟 work out 一样,都不登"大雅之堂",在正式的法律文本中,几乎看不到它的踪影,表达同一概念的 resolve 似乎语域更高,因此被广泛使用,在笔者另一本对比研究"适用法律和争议的解决"的著作中,在其所引用的例文中,resolve 被使用了十次以上,而 solve 居然未被使用过一次[①],但在口语中人人都用该词来"解决"问题。正因为如此,在法律或合同的正式文体中,建议避免使用;况且,solve 在法律上还有"清偿"债务,"解除"义务的用法,如 solvency 指的是清偿债务的能力;而 insolvency 则是指"破产的"或"资不抵债"的状况。

---

① 李克兴:《英汉法律翻译案例讲评》,北京:外文出版社,2011年。

第十七章 仲裁条款的写作、翻译和研究(下)

三、对现有仲裁条款及其译文的评注

(一) 保险单中的仲裁条款

All differences arising out of this Policy shall be referred to the decision of an Arbitrator to be appointed by both parties, or, if they cannot agree upon a single Arbitrator, to the decision of two Arbitrators, one to be appointed in writing by each party, and in case of disagreement between the Arbitrators, to the decision of an Umpire who shall have been appointed in writing by the Arbitrators <u>before</u> <u>entering on the reference</u>, and an Award shall be a condition precedent to any liability of the Insurer or any right of action against the Insurer. If the Insurer shall disclaim liability to the Insured for any claim <u>hereunder</u> and such claim shall not within twelve calendar months from the date of such disclaimer have been referred to arbitration under the provisions <u>herein</u> contained then the claim shall for all purposes be deemed to have been abandoned and shall not <u>thereafter</u> be recoverable <u>hereunder</u>.	本合约中出现的一切争论须交付由双方任命的一名仲裁人决定。如果他们无法同意一位仲裁人,那就交付两位仲裁人决定,两方各书面任命一位。而万一仲裁人之间无法取得一致,<u>在开始咨询之前</u>交付由仲裁人书面任命的<u>裁定人</u>决定。裁定应是承保人所负义务或对承保人采取行动的任何权利的先决条件。如果承保人拒绝对被保人<u>凭本合约</u>索偿的赔偿责任,而这种索偿没有在这种拒绝之后十二个月内按<u>本条所包含</u>的规定交付仲裁,那么索偿则被认为是已被放弃,而且按照本单其后不可取得赔偿。(薛华业,1989:103)

上例的仲裁条款在内容上体现了仲裁意愿、仲裁的范围、仲裁员人数和任命方式、仲裁期限,但未规定仲裁规则和适用的法律。我们假定真有争议发生时,当事人会签订补充仲裁协议。但从语言上分析,该条款原文中的"师爷文风"根深蒂固。

首先,长达155词的英文只分成了两句话。第一句话表述仲裁意愿、仲裁范围、仲裁员的委任和仲裁效力,而约定仲裁员的委任时还有两种假设情况。一句话包含了太多信息量,层次不清,使得外行人读来非常吃力。译者对这句话的层次处理得也不太理想:"而万一仲裁人之间无法取得一致,在开始咨询之前交付由仲裁人书面任命的裁定人决定",更合理的语序应该是:万一两名仲裁人裁决时无法取得一致,这两名仲裁员在做出裁定前(译者将"enter on reference"解释为"在开始咨询前"是错误的)应书面指定一名公断人(原译文"裁定人"也可以),由公断人做出裁决。

原文的第二句也很冗长,但更大的问题在于其中的古旧词(archaic words)。一句话里用了四个古旧词 hereunder,herein,thereafter,hereunder,实属罕见。这样的文本正是普通民众所深恶痛绝的。hereunder 即 under this Policy,herein 即 in this Policy,thereafter 即

after such disclaimer,如此滥用古旧词,非但没有节省多少字,还迫使读者思考文字本身的内涵,四个古旧词一起连用更是叫人摸不着头脑。译者对这四个古旧词的理解基本是正确的,除了 herein,不应是"本条所包含的",而是"本保险单所包含的"。另外,译者对"the Policy"的翻译前后不一致,有时译成"本合约",有时译成"本单",应遵循法律翻译"一致性和同一性"的原则,统一译成"本保险单"或"本单"。

(二) 国际民用工程合同中的仲裁条款

If at any time, any question, disputes or differences whatsoever shall arise between the Purchaser and the Contractor, upon or in relation to, or in connection with this Contract, either party may forthwith give to the other, notice in writing of the existence of such question, dispute or difference and same shall be referred to the arbitration of, three arbitrators, one to be nominated by the Purchaser, the other by the Contractor and the third by the President of the International Chamber of Commerce, in the case of foreign Contractors and Secretary-General of The Engineering Institute of [country], in the case of local contractors. If either of the parties fails to appoint its arbitrator within sixty (60) days after receipt of notice of appointment of its arbitrator, then the President of the International Chamber of Commerce or the President of the Engineers Institution of [country] as the case may be, shall have the power, at the request of either of the parties to appoint an arbitrator. A certified copy of the President making such an appointment shall be furnished to both parties. The arbitration shall be conducted in accordance with the Rules and Procedures for Arbitration of the International Chamber of Commerce, Paris in the case of Foreign Contractors and provisions of Arbitration Act of [local country] or any statutory modification thereof in the case of local contractors, and shall be held at such place and time in [local country] as the arbitrators may determine. The decision of the majority of arbitrators shall be final and binding upon the parties hereto and the expense of the arbitration shall be paid as may be determined by the arbitrators. Performance under the Contract shall, if reasonably possible, continue during the arbitration proceedings and payments due to the Contractor by the Purchaser shall not be withheld unless they are the subject matter of the arbitration proceedings. (韦箐,2005:537、556)	发包方和承包方之间在任何时候发生与合同有关的一切问题、争议或异议,任何一方应当立即以书面形式告知另一方这种问题、争议或异议的存在,同时应提交仲裁。三名仲裁员,一名由发包方指定,另一名由承包方指定,如果承包方为外国人,则第三名由国际商会主席指定;如果承包方为本地的,则第三名由工程协会的主席指定。如果任何一方没能在收到指定仲裁员的通知后 60 日内指定其仲裁员,则国际商会主席或工程技术协会的主席有权根据任何一方请求指定一个仲裁员。主席做出的这种任命的已证实的副本应向双方提供。仲裁在涉及外国承包方时应根据巴黎商会的仲裁规则和程序进行,在仅涉及本地承包商时应当根据本地仲裁法的规定或其修正条款进行仲裁,并且在仲裁员同意而做出的仲裁裁决是终局的,并且对双方都有约束力,并且仲裁应支付的费用由仲裁员决定。如果有合理的可能,在仲裁期间合同项下的执行应继续进行,并且发包方向承包方支付的到期款项也不能扣留,除非上述是仲裁程序中的主要事项。

对原文内容的评注:这是国际工程合同中的仲裁条款。条款的内容比较全面:除了约定仲裁范围、仲裁员的人数和指定方式、仲裁规则、适用法、仲裁费用之外,还结合实际,表示仲

裁不应影响工程的进度和发包方向承包方按时付款。

说到发包方和承包方,大多数读者对承包方(Contractor)的概念比较熟悉,对发包方的概念比较陌生,因为该词的英文是(Purchaser)。在商务英语中后者与 Buyer 是同义词。之所以译成发包商是因为他们购买承包商的服务,把项目发给承包商施行。这个名称在工程或劳务承包领域更为常见。以楼盘开发为例:业主是建筑物的拥有者或使用者。建设方,有可能是业主,但也可能是开发商,或是代理人。施工方,就是施工单位。发包方,就是建设方,俗称甲方。承包方,就是施工方,俗称乙方。比方说,如果北京大学要建一座办公楼,但是出于某种原因,北京大学将此项工作交给万科来进行建设,建成了仍然归北京大学使用。经过招投标,最后是中建三局中标。那么,业主是北京大学,建设方是万科,施工方是中建三局,发包方是万科,承包方是中建三局。如果没有交给万科来开发,建设方和发包方就变成了北京大学。①

从逻辑上讲,原文写得太具体:第三名仲裁员要由 the President of the International Chamber of Commerce in the case of foreign Contractors, or by the President of the Engineers Institution of [country] in the case of local Contractors 指定。这就是说,该国必须有 the Engineers Institution 这么一个机构,否则仲裁无法进行。另外,条件句(If either of the parties fails to appoint its arbitrator within sixty (60) days after receipt of notice of appointment of its arbitrator)中规定的时间也不太切合实际:收到要求各方选出仲裁员的通知后 60 天内如各方仍未采取行动,则该国的工程师协会主席才有权因各方要求来帮忙选定仲裁员。如此下来,没有四个月时间连仲裁庭都休想建立。这与订立仲裁条款以快速解决纠纷的初衷完全背道而驰。所以,该条款的内在逻辑是不够严谨的。

此外,这样的规定在民用工程承包合同中也是不合适的:The arbitration <u>shall</u> be conducted in accordance with the Rules and Procedures for Arbitration of the International Chamber of Commerce, Paris <u>in the case of</u> Foreign Contractors and provisions of Arbitration Act of [local country](仲裁在<u>涉</u>及外国承包方时<u>应</u>根据巴黎商会的仲裁规则和程序进行)。据此规定:仲裁涉及外国承包方就得按照巴黎(国际)商会的仲裁规则和程序进行。这一规定本身也缺乏逻辑和可行性:凡是外国的承包商都得接受或去巴黎仲裁?这样规定似乎太武断。其实,这类规定作为法律条款或仲裁机构本身的规定,可以;作为民间合同的内容,越界。按照什么规定或程序办事是对仲裁机构而言的,民用合同做出如此规定,范围肯定太宽,实际上也无法执行。

再从语言角度分析,原文文风也不是很健康:有个别滥用情态动词 shall 的现象:<u>If at any time, any question, disputes or differences whatsoever <u>shall</u> arise between the Purchaser and the Contractor.</u>其中的 shall 没有必要,用一般现在时态即可。其次,语篇中使用了大量的近义词(any question, disputes or differences whatsoever; upon or in relation to, or in connection with; such question, dispute or difference)和古旧词(forthwith, thereto, hereto)。再次,原文对长句似乎情有独钟,第一句话包含 104 词,其弊病与前一例类似,不再赘述,现代简明的表达应该是:

If any dispute arises upon or in relation to this Contract, either party may

---

① http://zhidao.baidu.com/question/93641463.html? qbl=relate_question_0 promptly give the other party notice in writing and the dispute shall be referred to a panel of three arbitrators. Each party shall nominate one arbitrator, and the third arbitrator shall be nominated by the President of the International Chamber of Commerce in the case of foreign Contractors, or by the President of the Engineers Institution of France in the case of local Contractors.

就翻译而言,第一段总体上比较忠实,对原文的表述也较清楚。只是有个别词语、短语的翻译不太准确。一是第二段中的"in the case of",译成"涉及",这里应当与第一段中的"in the case of"采取一样的处理方法,翻译成"如果……"。二是 withheld,译成"扣留"。试问如何自己扣留自己要付给对方的款项呢?所以这里的 withheld 不能按字面意思翻译,应该按照上下文译成"停止支付"或"不如期支付"。

另外,原文中使用了大量的情态动词 shall。译者大部分时候的处理是正确的。如"The decision...shall be final and binding...","...shall have the power...",shall 后面接表示权利、义务和责任的动词短语时,不能将 shall 译成"应当",而是应选择不译①,译者的处理是正确的。但是条款开头的"if...shall..."是典型的条件句,译文应该使用条件句的句式"如果……"。另外,法律英语中情态动词的否定形式 shall not,must not,may not 等应一律翻译成"不得",译者将本条款的 shall not 译成"不能",使得译文的语域降低、禁令的语气减弱。"能"与"不能"在法律语篇中主要表示行为者能力的问题,用 can/can not,be able/unable to,或 fail to(未能)表述更为恰当。除了 shall,原文中还是用了一个情态动词 may,应译成"可"或"可以",表示行为者的权利,他可以这样做,也可以不做,而不应译成带有强制性的"应该"或"应当"②。

最后,原文中用"have the power"表示国际商会主席或工程技术协会的主席"有权……"。不过 have the power 往往表示纯粹的"权力"或职能方面的"权力",且比较张扬。本条款中,"主席"的权力其实来自于当事人的"授权",属于一种授予的(authorized)权力。因此,应当用 have the authority to 更为恰当。③

上述语篇的第二段存在的翻译问题较大,不宜也不便一一评注,作者将该段相关句子重新翻译,供有志琢磨法律翻译人士对比以决定取舍:

原文	原译文	改译
The arbitration shall be conducted in accordance with the Rules and Procedures for Arbitration of the International Chamber of Commerce, Paris in the case of Foreign Contractors and provisions of Arbitration Act of [local country] or any statutory modification thereof in the case of local contractors, and shall be held at such place and time in [local country] as the arbitrators may determine. The decision of the majority of arbitrators shall be final	仲裁在涉及外国承包方时应根据巴黎商会的仲裁规则和程序进行,在仅涉及本地承包商时应当根据本地仲裁法的规定或其修正条款进行仲裁,并且在仲裁员同意而做	如仲裁涉及外国承包方,仲裁应根据《巴黎国际商会的仲裁规则和程序》进行;如仲裁只涉及本国承包商,仲裁应根据其本国仲裁法的规定、在仲裁庭指定的本国地点及

---

① 李克兴:《法律翻译理论与实践》,北京:北京大学出版社,2007年,第113—115页。
② 李克兴:《英语法律文本中主要情态动词的作用及其翻译》,《中国翻译》2007年第6期。
③ 李克兴:《高级法律翻译与写作》,北京:北京大学出版社,2013年,第130—145页。

原文	原译文	改译
and binding upon the parties hereto and the expense of the arbitration shall be paid as may be determined by the arbitrators. Performance under the Contract <u>shall</u>, if reasonably possible, continue during the arbitration proceedings and payments due to the Contractor by the Purchaser <u>shall not be</u> withheld unless they are the subject matter of the arbitration proceedings.	出的仲裁裁决是终局的，并且对双方都有约束力，并且仲裁应支付的费用由仲裁员决定。 如果有合理的可能，在仲裁期间合同项下的执行应继续进行，并且发包方向承包方支付的到期款项也不能扣留，除非上述是仲裁程序中的主要事项。	时间进行仲裁。仲裁庭的多数裁决是终局的，对双方都有约束力。仲裁费用根据仲裁庭的裁决支付。 在合理可能的情况下，仲裁期间双方应继续履行合同。发包方不得停止向承包方支付到期款项，除非该款项就是仲裁程序的主题。

（三）日本买家和中国工厂间的货物销售合同

一切因执行本合同所引起的争议，均应由双方友好协商解决。如协商不能得到解决，则应提交仲裁。仲裁应在被告所在国进行。如仲裁在中国，应提交北京或上海，或深圳中国国际贸易促进委员会对外贸易仲裁委员会，按照其仲裁规则进行仲裁。如仲裁在日本，应提交东京或大阪日本商事仲裁协会，按照其仲裁规则进行仲裁。该仲裁委员会的裁决为终局性的，对双方均有约束力，仲裁费用，除非仲裁委员会另有裁定，概由败诉方承担。	All disputes arising from the performance of this Contract, shall be settled through friendly negotiation. Should no settlement be reached through negotiation, the case shall then be submitted for arbitration in the country where the defendant resides. If the arbitration takes place in China, the case shall be submitted to China International Economic and Trade Arbitration Commission Beijing, or Shanghai, or Shenzhen and the arbitration rules of this Commission shall be applied. If the arbitration takes place in Japan, the case shall be submitted to the Japan Commercial Arbitration Association Tokyo, or Osaka and the arbitration rules of this arbitration organization shall be applied. The award to the arbitration shall be final and binding upon both parties. The arbitration fee shall be borne by the losing party unless otherwise awarded by the arbitration organization. （庞广廉、袁宪军，1997：163、171）

与前两例不同，这则条款约定的是机构仲裁，其中对仲裁地的规定是，"仲裁应在被告所在国进行"。所以双方当事人中，如果是"中国工厂"成为"被告"，那么仲裁地就是在中国。而中国内地是不承认临时仲裁的，所以仲裁条款中必须指定一家仲裁机构进行机构仲裁，本条约定的是贸仲在北京、上海或深圳的仲裁委员会，并使用选定机构的仲裁规则。如果是"日本买家"成为"被告"，仲裁地是日本，仲裁机构为东京或大阪的日本商事仲裁协会，并使用选定机构的仲裁规则。最后，条款对仲裁的终局性、仲裁费用都做了规定。总的来说，这则条款从内容到文字表达都十分的清晰、完整，但有一处不足：虽然根据"被告"所在国可以确定仲裁地，但在"中国"和"日本"两地又分别约定了两三个城市的仲裁机构。根据我国最

高人民法院关于适用《中华人民共和国仲裁法》若干问题的解释第五条:仲裁协议约定两个以上仲裁机构的,当事人可以协议选择其中的一个仲裁机构申请仲裁;当事人不能就仲裁机构选择达成一致的,仲裁协议无效。假设"中国工厂"成为"被告",若有意逃避仲裁,"中国工厂"就可以向法院上诉,提出这则仲裁条款是无效的条款。虽然这种情况发生的几率很低,但不怕一万,只怕万一,选择在中国内地仲裁时,最好就只约定一家仲裁机构。

最后值得一提的是,仲裁在目前的中国法律体系中起着越来越重要的作用。它与调解机制一样,是当前中国司法系统解决争议金额数目并非十分巨大,案情并非十分复杂的民事案件的法律手段,法庭也不肯对这类案子做出判决,担心判决之后会成为后人或下级法院判案的裁量依据。故各级法庭都尽可能规劝当事人采取仲裁或调解手段解决争议。

本章附录一：

仲裁条款

附1：BIMCO[①] 2013年争议解决示范条款——伦敦仲裁，适用英国法

This Contract shall be governed by and construed in accordance with English law and any dispute arising out of or in connection with this Contract shall be referred to arbitration in London in accordance with the Arbitration Act 1996 or any statutory modification or re-enactment thereof save to the extent necessary to give effect to the provisions of this Clause.

The arbitration shall be conducted in accordance with the London Maritime Arbitrators Association (LMAA) Terms current at the time when the arbitration proceedings are commenced.

The reference shall be to three arbitrators. A party wishing to refer a dispute to arbitration shall appoint its arbitrator and send notice of such appointment in writing to the other party requiring the other party to appoint its own arbitrator within fourteen (14) calendar days of that notice and stating that it will appoint its arbitrator as sole arbitrator unless the other party appoints its own arbitrator and gives notice that it has done so within the fourteen (14) days specified. If the other party does not appoint its own arbitrator and give notice that it has done so within the fourteen (14) days specified, the party referring a dispute to arbitration may, without the requirement of any further prior notice to the other party, appoint its arbitrator as sole arbitrator and shall advise the other party accordingly. The award of a sole arbitrator shall be binding on both parties as if he had been appointed by agreement.

Nothing herein shall prevent the parties agreeing in writing to vary these provisions to provide for the appointment of a sole arbitrator.

In cases where neither the claim nor any counterclaim exceeds the sum of USD 100,000 (or such other sum as the parties may agree) the arbitration shall be conducted in accordance with the LMAA Small Claims Procedure current at the time when the arbitration proceedings are commenced.

In cases where the claim or any counterclaim exceeds the sum agreed for the LMAA Small Claims Procedure and neither the claim nor any counterclaim exceeds the sum of USD 400,000 (or such other sum as the parties may agree) the arbitration shall be conducted in accordance with the LMAA Intermediate Claims Procedure current at the time when the

---

① BIMCO(The Baitic and International Maritime Conference,波罗的海国际航运公会)具有100多年历史且目前被公认为世界上最大的、运营最多样化的国际航运组织。它被认为是具有半官方性质的非政府组织。一方面，BIMCO提供大量实用工具，如标准合同、电子版租船契约编辑体系及其他实时或深度分析报告。另一方面，BIMCO代表整个航运业，并影响国际海事组织的立法及其规定的实施。目前国际海运和相关行业中有将近3/4的交易采用了BIMCO的标准合同和条款。BIMCO拥有来自123个国家的2500多个会员,约占世界海运业总运力的65%以上。

arbitration proceedings are commenced.

附2：世界主要常设仲裁机构与国内涉外仲裁机构简介（来源：法律教育网 http://www.chinalawedu.com/new/18500_186/2009_10_15_ji131935740151019002l0176.shtml）

1. 伦敦国际仲裁院。伦敦国际仲裁院（LCIA）成立于1892年，是世界上最古老的仲裁机构，原称伦敦仲裁会，1903年起使用现名，1986年起改组成为有限责任公司，董事会管理其仲裁活动。仲裁院在仲裁中的主要作用是指定仲裁员和对案件进行一些辅助性管理，也设有可以适应各种类型仲裁案件需要的仲裁员名册。

2. 瑞士苏黎世商会仲裁院。瑞士苏黎世商会仲裁院（ZCC）成立于1911年，是瑞士苏黎世商会下属的仲裁机构。由于瑞士在政治上处于中立地位，因而其仲裁的公正性比较容易为其他国家和当事人所接受，许多国家的当事人都愿意选择该机构来解决纠纷。

3. 国际商会仲裁院。国际商会1919年成立于法国巴黎，是一个国家间商会，现有国家会员60多个；国际商会仲裁院（ICC）成立于1923年，与任何国家没有关系，隶属于国际商会，其总部和秘书局设在巴黎，委员来自40多个国家，工作人员也来自不同的国家；其仲裁的一个主要特点，是可以在世界的任何地方进行仲裁程序。

4. 美国仲裁协会。美国仲裁协会（AAA）成立于1926年，是一个非盈利性的仲裁服务机构；其总部设在纽约，在美国一些州共设有38个办事处，另外在爱尔兰都柏林设有1个办事处。美国仲裁协会的仲裁员来自很多国家，数量达数千人之多，当事人可以在其仲裁员名册之外指定仲裁员；在没有约定的情况下，所有案件只有一名仲裁员，但如果仲裁协会认为该案件复杂时，可以决定由三名仲裁员组成仲裁庭；该仲裁协会的受案范围很广，从国际经济贸易纠纷到劳动争议、消费者争议乃至证券纠纷等无所不包，但均有相应规则。

5. 德国仲裁协会。德国仲裁协会（DIS）是经注册的社团，其宗旨是促进德国国内的国际仲裁。1920年，德国一些工商业协会建议成立了"德国仲裁委员会"（DAS）；1947年，德国一些经济协会、学术机构和仲裁实务界共同建立了"德国仲裁院"（DIS）；1992年1月，德国仲裁院与德国仲裁委员会合并成为"德国仲裁协会"；实际上有资料证明，是德国仲裁院接管了德国仲裁委员会之后，改名为"德国仲裁协会"，但其简称仍然沿用德国仲裁院的简称DIS。

6. 斯德哥尔摩商会仲裁院。斯德哥尔摩商会成立于1917年，其仲裁院（SCC）成立于1949年，总部设在瑞典首都斯德哥尔摩，包括秘书局和三名成员组成的委员会，委员任期三年、由商会任命，其中一名须具有解决工商争议的经验、一名须为有实践经验的律师、一名须具备与商业组织沟通的能力。该仲裁院主要解决工业、贸易和运输领域的国际争议，尤以解决涉及远东或中国的争议而著称。

7. 荷兰仲裁协会。荷兰仲裁协会（NAI）成立于1949年，是独立的非营利性组织，以基金会的形式存在，与政府没有任何关系，也不接受资助；其总部设在鹿特丹，管理机关成员包括商业联合会、阿姆斯特丹商会、国际商会组织、工商协会的代表和其他相关人士等。

8. 日本商事仲裁协会。日本商事仲裁协会（JCAA）成立于1950年3月，是日本工商联合会和其他一些全国性的工商组织根据《日本民法典》设立的社团法人，总会设在东京，横滨等大城市设有分会。

9. 中国国际经济贸易仲裁委员会。贸仲（CIETAC）成立于1956年，从1994年起步入世界主要仲裁机构行列,其受案量一直排在世界各仲裁机构前列。现在的贸仲不仅仅是一个国际商事仲裁机构,因为它也同时受理纯中国国内性质的各类具备仲裁要件的纠纷案件。

10. 意大利仲裁协会。意大利仲裁协会(AIA)是在学者以及工商业界、不同经济领域的组织和外国事务部的代表支持下,于1958年10月在罗马成立的,其总部设在罗马,下设处理紧急措施常设委员会,在仲裁庭组成之前根据其仲裁规则的规定发布指令。

11. 解决国际投资争端中心。解决国际投资争端中心(ICSID)成立于1965年,总部设在美国华盛顿,是一个国际性法人组织。因为该中心是根据《华盛顿公约》成立的,所以它要求申请仲裁的争议双方必须是华盛顿公约的成员国,争议主体为国家或国家机构或代理机构,解决的争议必须是直接由投资引起的法律争议,审理案件的仲裁员和调解时的调解员必须从其仲裁员名册和调解员名册中选定。

12. 印度仲裁协会。印度仲裁协会(ICA)成立于1965年,成员有印度政府、重要商会、贸易组织、出口促进会、公共部门企业等。

13. 中国香港国际仲裁中心。香港国际仲裁中心(HKIAC)成立于1985年,是依据香港公司法注册的(有限保证责任)非营利性公司。中心受到香港商界和香港政府的资助,但完全独立,财政上自给自足,不受政府或其他任何官员的影响或控制。中心的管理机构是理事会,由不同国籍的商界、法律界和其他相关人士组成;中心的首席行政人员和登记主管是秘书长,由一名律师担任;中心的行政工作,由理事会下属的管理委员会通过秘书长进行。

14. 新加坡国际仲裁中心。新加坡国际仲裁中心(SIAC)于1990年3月经新加坡政府经济委员会提议成立。该中心是依据新加坡公司法设立的担保公司,以解决建筑工程、航运、银行和保险等方面的争议见长,并致力于培养熟悉国际仲裁法律和实践的仲裁员和专家。

15. 世界知识产权组织仲裁与调解中心。世界知识产权组织是根据1967年在瑞典斯德哥尔摩签署的《关于成立世界知识产权公约》成立的政府组织,负责监管知识产权事务,其总部设在瑞士首都日内瓦,1974年成为联合国的一个专门机构,是迄今为止联合国的最大的国际组织。世界知识产权组织仲裁与调解中心,是1993年9月在世界知识产权组织全体会议上正式获准成立的,属世界知识产权组织的国际局,1994年10月在日内瓦开始工作。

16. 中国北京仲裁委员会。北京仲裁委员会(BAC)是依据我国《仲裁法》和国务院关于重新组建仲裁机构的相关规定,经北京市人民政府批准,于1995年9月28日成立的;是《仲裁法》施行之后重新组建仲裁机构以来,我国发展最好的、具有一定国际知名度的仲裁机构。

本章附录二：

仲裁案例样本及译文

附3：CIETAC某案裁决书

CIETAC规定,当事人约定了仲裁语言的,从其约定。当事人没有约定的,仲裁程序以中文为正式语言。即使仲裁程序以中文为正式语言,如果当事人要求提供英文或其他语文翻译的,CIETAC应当提供,不过该译本如与中文版本有不一致之处,应以中文版本为准。对于不了解中文的当事人,CIETAC在发送程序函件时,也会提供相应的英文译本。以下裁决书(中英对照)来自CIETAC仲裁的真实案例,双方当事人的真实身份被隐去,且因篇幅有限,只选取裁决书的主体部分。

一、案情

申诉人和被申诉人于1988年1月7日签订了88QH-407B85CK合同。合同规定：被申诉人向申诉人购买高密度低压聚乙烯225吨,总货款292 275美元；付款条件为买方于1988年1月12日开出不可撤销的即期信用证。

申诉人及时备妥货物,预订船位准备发货。但被申诉人未能依合同按时开出信用证,并于1月13日通知申诉人要求改用D/P付款。申诉人对此付款方式表示不能接受。被申诉人遂于1月18日通知申诉人准备于1月19日开出信用证。申诉人表示接受,并承诺把1月27日到港的货物售于被申诉人,以履行合同义务。但事后被申诉人仍未能按时开出信用证。申诉人于1月25日正式宣告终止合同,对被申诉人提出索赔要求,把1月27日到港的货物存入公用仓库。以后申诉人在香港就地将货物陆续分批出售处理。

申诉人要求被申诉人赔偿损失,经协商未获结果,遂于1988年6月21日提出仲裁申请。

1. 关于违约责任问题

申诉人提出,被申诉人不能在合同规定的期限内开出信用证,构成根本违约,应承担违约责任,赔偿申诉人由此遭受的各项损失。

2. 关于索赔金额问题

申诉人要求被申诉人赔偿包括差旅费、通讯费、差价损失等8个项目的损失,共计241 893.91港元。

申诉人向仲裁庭提交了在香港出售该批货物的发票和银行对账单,以及有关仓储费用的发票。

被申诉人提出,针对第一点而言,信用证无法开出,是由于国家对外汇管理做出调整,被申诉人无法动用外汇,事属不可抗力的因素,而非被申诉人的过错。被申诉人为此向仲裁庭提交了这方面的有关证据。

被申诉人对申诉人的8项索赔要求中的有些项目提出质疑。关于差旅费、通讯费,被申诉人认为,属于申诉人的正常业务开支,要被申诉人承担这些损失是没有道理的。

被申诉人提出,申诉人提供的售货发票和银行对账单,不能证明出售该合同货物的价格,不具有证据的效力,不能说明其实际损失。

二、仲裁庭的意见

仲裁庭审阅了双方当事人提交的仲裁申请书、答辩书和有关文件,听取了双方当事人的陈述,一致认为:

(一) 关于违约责任问题

被申诉人提交的文件,不能说明当时国家政策对被申诉人履行开立信用证的合同义务造成直接障碍。被申诉人提出的不可抗力的理由不能成立,应承担违约责任。

(二) 关于索赔金额问题

1. 根据申诉人提供的售货发票和银行对账单计算,该批货物的差价损失共计124 052.19港元。仲裁庭并不认为申诉人提供的售货发票和银行对账单可以作为确定该批货物处理价格的充分证据。但鉴于当时货物实市价趋向下跌,同时参照国际贸易惯例和香港的商业环境,按发票价计算的差价金额约为原合同的5.5%,这一幅度是合理的。因此,仲裁庭认为,申诉人的该项索赔要求可以予以满足。

2. 申诉人计算仓储费的方法及由此得出的仓储费的金额不尽合理。申诉人先后分6单卖出合同项下的该批货物,仓储费应按货物吨数的实存仓天数计算,合计12 746.67港元。

3. 货款利息按年利率7%自2月11日起算,至每单卖出止的实际天数计算,合计14 837.12元。申诉人在索赔请求中提出的银行利息一项不能成立,应予驳回。

4. 申诉人提出的差旅费、电话费、传真费、拖头费、公司开支、货柜码头停放费等几项费用,均属申诉人的成本支出,其索赔请求不能成立,应予驳回。

三、裁决

1. 被申诉人应赔偿申诉人的损失(包括差价损失、仓储费损失和货款利息损失)151 635.98港元,并加计从1988年4月18日至1989年12月13日止按年利率7%计算的利息17 593.93港元,共计169 230港元。

2. 被申诉人应在本裁决作出之日起30日内向申诉人支付上述款项。如逾期支付,应加计到实际支付之日止的利息。

3. 本案仲裁手续费由被申诉人承担。

本裁决为终局裁决。

The_____Arbitration
Decision_____

Ⅰ. Facts of the Case

On 7 January 1988, the claimant and the respondent signed a contract No. 88QH-407B85CK for the purchase of 225 tonnes of high-density low-pressure polyethylene by the respondent from the claimant at a total price of US＄292,275. The buyer was to issue an irrevocable L/C payable on sight on 12 January 1988 for the contracted amount.

The claimant prepared the goods for shipping, booked the shipping space and prepared for the delivery of the goods. However, the respondent did not issue the L/C within the time stipulated in the contract, and on 13 January 1988 asked the claimant to change the payment terms to D/P (documents against payment). The claimant found this unacceptable. On 18 January 1988, the respondent informed the claimant that it would issue an L/C on 19 January 1988. The claimant accepted this and promised to sell the respondent the goods that were to arrive on 27 January 1988 in order to fulfill its obligation under the contract. However, the respondent failed to issue the L/C as promised. On 25 January 1988, the claimant declared its termination of the contract and claimed damages from the respondent. The claimant stored the goods, which arrived on 27 January 1988, in the common godown. Thereafter, the claimant sold the goods by batches in Hong Kong.

The claimant requested that the respondent compensate the claimant for losses. After fruitless negotiation, the claimant applied for arbitration on 21 June 1988, stating:

1. The claimant claimed that the failure on the part of the respondent to issue the L/C within the period stipulated in the contract was a fundamental breach of the contract. The respondent should be held liable and should compensate the claimant for all losses suffered as a result of this breach.

2. The claimant requested that the respondent compensate the claimant for a total of HK\$ 241,893.91 representing eight items where losses were incurred, including travelling expenses, communication expenses and price difference.

The claimant presented to the arbitration tribunal the invoices and confirmations from its bank that related to the sale of the goods in Hong Kong and the invoices for storage fees.

Regarding the first issue raised by the claimant, the respondent claimed that the respondent was not able to open an L/C because the State had adjusted its foreign exchange control policy and the respondent could not draw on its foreign exchange account. This was a matter of *force majeure* and was not the fault of the respondent. The respondent submitted supporting evidence to this effect to the arbitration tribunal.

The respondent queried some of the eight items for which the claimant had issued its claim. The respondent was of the opinion that travelling expenses and communication expenses were normal business expenses of the claimant and that it was unreasonable for the claimant to request that the respondent bear these losses.

The respondent submitted that the sales invoices and bank confirmations produced by the claimant did not prove the price at which the goods under the contract were sold and could not be submitted as evidence as they did not reflect the claimant's actual losses.

II. Views of the Arbitration Tribunal

After examining the application for arbitration, the defence and other documents submitted and listening to the presentations of the parties, the arbitration tribunal held that:

1. The documents submitted by the respondent could not prove that State policy at the relevant time directly prevented the respondent from performing its obligation under the contract to issue an L/C. The attribution to the *force majeure* by the respondent should be held responsible for the breach.

2. On the basis of the sales invoices and bank confirmations produced by the claimant, the total loss that the claimant claimed it incurred due to the price difference of the batch of goods when sold equaled HK＄124,052.19. The arbitration tribunal did not consider that the sale invoices and bank confirmations presented by the claimant were sufficient to determine the actual price at which the goods were sold. However, having taken into consideration the falling market price of the goods, international trade practice and the business environment of Hong Kong, the invoiced amount, which reflected a price difference of 5.5 percent from the original contract, was reasonable. Therefore the arbitration tribunal considered that the claim could be awarded.

3. The method by which the claimant calculated the storage fees and the amount of storage fees that the claimant arrived at were not entirely reasonable. The claimant sold the goods under contract in six batches. The storage fees should be calculated according to the actual amount of goods that remained in the godown. The total should therefore be HK＄12,746.67.

4. The interest on the amount owed under the contract should be calculated at the rate of seven per cent per annum from 11 February 1988 onwards until the actual date of sale of each batch of goods. Calculated on this basis the interest owed according to the contract should total HK＄14,837.12. The claimant's claim for bank interest, however, did not have sufficient documentary evidence to support it and should therefore be dismissed.

5. The travelling expenses, telephone and fax expenses, towing fees, company expenses and berthage claimed by the claimant were the claimant's own costs. These claims were not justified and should be dismissed.

Ⅲ. The Decision

1. The respondent shall compensate the claimant for HK＄151,635.98 (including losses incurred due to price difference, storage fees and interest on the contract price of the goods) plus interest of HK＄17,593.93 calculated at seven per cent per annum for the period from 18 April 1988 to 13 December 1989, amounting to a total of HK＄169,230.

2. The respondent shall pay the above amount to the claimant within 30 days of the date of this award. Interest shall be calculated until the actual date of payment on any overdue amount.

3. The arbitration fees for this case shall be borne by the respondent.

This decision shall be final.

第十八章
诉讼地选择条款的写作、翻译和研究

一、引言

前面两章详细讨论解决合同争议的最佳选择——仲裁的方方面面。但在不少状况下,合同各方也不得不走到最后一步:公堂对簿。不过,打官司得首先选择诉讼地以及法庭。本章讨论诉讼地选择条款的写作。

(一) 为何要订立诉讼地选择条款

当事人如果决定将诉讼作为解决合同争议的手段,则要面对一个非常现实的问题——将诉讼提交给哪个法院审理。事实上每个国家都有可被用来解决纠纷的法院,人们的任务只是辨认出恰当的法院并在该法院提起诉讼即可(Fox, 2009:366)。

对没有任何涉外因素的国内案件来说,这不算是难题。如我国法院以纵向的级别管辖、横向的地域管辖以及专属管辖等划分。根据案件的性质,如金额大小、争议类型、原告与被告所在地等等,参照本国(地区)法对号入座,最后得出的结论大多是:对案件具有管辖权的法院往往只有一个。例如,我国《民事诉讼法》规定,因不动产纠纷提起的诉讼,由不动产所在地人民法院管辖;而第一审民事诉讼案件往往由基层人民法院管辖。因此,争议金额较小的普通不动产纠纷只能在不动产所在城市的基层人民法院提起诉讼;争议金额较大的(在500万到1亿元之间的)可在该市中级人民法院提起诉讼;争议金额特大的(1亿元以上的)在该省(直辖市、自治区)的高级人民法院提起诉讼。

但对于跨国(地区)的商业合同引起的争议,至少可以在两个国家(地区)①的法院进行诉讼,法院选择的问题就复杂起来。合同双方来自不同国家,在任何一国进行诉讼,对异国的另一方都意味着更高的诉讼费用与不便。更重要的是,不同国家的法院制度、审判程序亦不相同,双方都希望选择自己最熟悉、或是对自己较有利的诉讼地。倘若一方在本国法院提起诉讼,不愿意配合的另一方,可能不予应诉,并以各种理由对起诉予以回击。还有一种可能的情况是,法院认为本地并非案件最恰当的诉讼地,从而驳回原告的起诉,原告不得不尝试向他国法院提起诉讼。种种不确定性,不仅延误了争议的解决,并对当事人造成诸多不便以及沉重的经济损失。

与其如此,事先约定诉讼地,可以大大降低不确定性。合同内订明将争议提交某(些)国家或地区的法院审理的条款,便是"诉讼地选择条款"(Choice of Forum Clause),或称"管辖

---

① 运用诉讼解决国际商业纠纷时,并没有适用的国际法庭制度;即使设在海牙的国际法院偶尔处理一些商业纠纷,通常也只是出于各国政府的请求。国际法院的主要精力花费在处理国际公法问题上。所以本文所述的诉讼地的选择,指的是当事人选择某一个国家(地区)内的法院对争议提起诉讼。

权条款"(Jurisdiction Clause)。当事人并无权授予法院管辖权,只能从具有管辖权的法院中进行选择;而因为具有管辖权的法院可能有多个,所以当事人需要提前选择并指定法院。当事人在合同中明确表示将争议提交某(些)国家或地区的法院之后,便很难在诉讼发生时再对审理法院的管辖权提出异议。

(二) 诉讼地选择条款与法律选择条款

通常当事人对诉讼地的选择和对合同适用法律的选择应该是一致的。例如,选择适用中国法律,则选择在中国的法院进行诉讼;选择适用美国法律,则在美国某个州的法院(或联邦法院)进行诉讼。否则,适用中国法律,却跑到美国去打官司,美国的法官不懂中国法律,必定要请专家"出席作证",还要参考中美两国条约。如此大费周章,还不能保证美国法院能对中国法律进行正确的解释与运用。所以,一般是约定适用某国法律就在该国的法院诉讼,法律选择条款与诉讼地选择条款也是一前一后的出现在合同中,有的合同中甚至将二者合二为一,例如:This Agreement shall be governed and construed in accordance with English Law and each party agrees to submit to the jurisdiction of the English courts as regards any claim or matter arising under this Agreement. (Christou,2002:209)(本合同受英国法律管辖并根据英国法律予以解释。合同各方均同意就任何因合同产生的索赔或事宜服从英国法院的管辖)(笔者译)。

不过,适用法律和诉讼地的选择是两个不同的概念,不提倡将两者合并为一则条款进行表述。

二、诉讼地选择条款的句型、内容和语用特征分析

(一) 诉讼地选择条款的基本句型

笔者观察了欧美大量的包括诉讼地选择条款的合同,对诉讼地的选择主要有以下几类句型:

1. XXX courts have jurisdiction

(The parties agree that) the courts of country/district have jurisdiction to [settle dispute/ hear and decide proceeding].

(合同各方同意)某国/地区法院对[争议的解决/诉讼的审理和判决]具有管辖权。

2. the venue is XXX courts

(The parties agree that) the venue of [proceeding] is the courts of country/district.

(合同各方同意)[诉讼]地为某国/地区法院。

3. proceeding in XXX courts

The parties agree that [proceeding] shall be instituted /brought in/submitted to the courts of country/district.

合同各方同意诉讼应提交至某国/地区法院。

(The parties agree that) any party bringing [proceeding] against any other party may bring the [proceeding] in the courts of country/district.

任一合同方对另一方提起的诉讼可提交至某国/地区法院。

4. submit to the jurisdiction of XXX courts

The parties (agree to/consent to) submit to the jurisdiction of courts of country/district [as regards dispute/for the purpose of proceeding].

合同各方(同意)服从某国/地区法院[对争议/对诉讼]的管辖。

句型1、2直接叙述某法院具有管辖权或某地法院为诉讼地点,属于直抒胸臆的表达;句型3中强调合同方作为"原告"时在所选择的法院地提起诉讼的权利;句型4中强调合同方成为"被告"时需要服从法院的管辖。一般说来,这四类句型可以单独使用。但也有很多条款将这些句型组合使用以增强表述严密性,尤其是句型3与4的组合最为多见。

就该条款的语言表达而言,此处的部分例句并非无懈可击:首先,被动语态并不值得推荐;其次,The parties (agree to/consent to) submit 是一种累赘的表达方式,该条款本身就是合同条款,所谓合同指的是双方已经约定要做合同规定的事项,所以就没有必要每次都The parties agree to/consent to (do sth.),只要简单陈述 The parties shall do sth. 即可。

(二) 诉讼地选择条款的主要内容

虽然对诉讼地的选择表达方式各式各样,但构成这些句型的主要内容是一致的,包括① 双方"合意"的表达,②是哪国/地区的法院,③争议(的解决)/诉讼(的审判),④管辖权。

① 双方"合意"的表达:在以上四个句型中,几乎每一句都以 The parties agrees that 或 The parties agree to/consent to 开头。诉讼地选择条款是当事人意思自治原则的体现,许多合同起草人业已习惯了在条款开头述明诉讼地是当事人协商一致的选择。在句子比较冗长的情况下,这样的开场白可以省略。

② 是哪国/地区的法院:在跨国合同中,约定在某国/地区的法院进行诉讼是比较稳妥的做法。因为争议是多样的,不同性质、不同金额的争议或案件在哪一个城市的何种级别的法院审理须符合该国/地区法律规定。即使跨国合同事先选择了某个具体的城市作为诉讼地,该城市往往是国际性都市,具备完善的法院系统和国际声誉,如伦敦。需要注意的是,美国是多法域国家,应当约定某个州(如纽约州)的法院(或联邦法院)具有管辖权,而不能笼统地约定"美国法院"具有管辖权。国外一些律师也特别强调,选择中国香港为诉讼地时,应该写明是"中国香港法院"具有管辖权,与"中国法院"进行区分。

③ 争议(的解决)/诉讼(的审判):为了让以上例句的句型结构更加直观,"争议""诉讼"等表述均被简化,并特别用[方括号]标示。但实际上,对争议/诉讼的范围约定应当尽量广泛,这与其他争议相关条款如"仲裁条款""法律选择条款"中的争议范围的约定如出一辙①。例如,

将句型1中的 [settle dispute/ hear and decide proceeding] 补充完整,可以得出:

a. (The parties agree that) the courts of country/district have jurisdiction to

---

① 详见本书的《仲裁条款的写作、翻译和研究》以及《法律选择条款的起草、翻译和研究》的相关内容。

[settle all disputes that may arise out of or in connection with this Agreement；或者

b.（The parties agree that）the courts of country/district may hear and decide any proceeding arising out of or in connection with this Agreement.

但事实上，省去括号中内容的写法更加简明，更符合用简明英文写作的要求，因为合同条款本身就是双方同意做的事项。

将句型 3 中的 [proceeding] 补充完整，可以得出：

The parties agree that [any legal action or proceeding① arising out of or relating to this Agreement] shall be instituted (brought) in /submitted to the courts of country/district.

The parties agree that any party bringing [a legal action or proceeding] against any other party [arising out of or relating to this Agreement] may bring the [legal action or proceeding] in the courts of country/district.

④ jurisdiction 的翻译：jurisdiction 在中文中常常译为司法权、管辖权、审判权，但在中国的法律制度下，这些中文词汇之间存在着一定差异：在我国，司法权包含了法院、检察院、甚至公安部门和司法行政管理机关所行使的权利；管辖权是指法院与法院之间管辖第一审案件的分工；审判权是指审判具体案件的特定法庭所行使的审理和裁判能力②。在英美司法制度中，judiciary（司法机关）仅指法院，不包括检察机关，因此司法权不包含检察权；所以，在英美司法制度中，jurisdiction 无论翻译为司法权、管辖权或审判权，都是指经过法律的授权或许可，法院或法官对案件进行审判的权力；另外，jurisdiction 还可表示该权力覆盖的地理区域，此时可译为"法域"。

笔者认为，诉讼地选择条款的作用是调整法院之间受理案件的权限范围，因此，诉讼地选择条款中，在表达 XX courts have jurisdiction 时，此 jurisdiction 指司法权或管辖权，最合适的译文应是"管辖权"；在其他情况下，作为与当事人"诉权"相对应的概念，jurisdiction 可译为"审判权"或"司法权"。但不是所有的诉讼地选择条款中的 jurisdiction 都要机械地译为"管辖权"，例如 submit proceeding to the jurisdiction of XX courts，在翻译时应将英语名词 jurisdiction 转换为汉语的动词，译为"管辖"，全句可译为"将诉讼提交 XX 法院管辖"；另外，因为原句中含有当事人"提交诉讼"的内容，jurisdiction 还可以对应地译为"审判"，全句还能译为"将诉讼提交 XX 法院审判"。

（三）诉讼地选择条款的分类和语用特征分析

根据当事人的选择，诉讼地选择条款的起草可以分为三类：专属管辖条款、非专属管辖条款、对合同某一方有利的混合型条款。

1. 专属管辖条款（Exclusive/Mandatory）

专属管辖条款（Exclusive jurisdiction clause），又称强制性（Mandatory）条款，规定诉讼

---

① 一般说来，action 与 proceeding 都是指的诉讼，可以互相替代使用。但因为美国一些州未将 action 与 proceeding 等同起来，如 a special proceeding，指的是处理某种争议的特殊诉讼程序，与一般意义上的 action 不同（见 2012 年纽约民事诉讼法则 103 [NY CPLR § 103 (2012)] 条）。所以一些合同起草者选择将 action and proceeding 作为配对词，或者三联词（suit, action and proceeding），以尽量扩大诉讼地选择条款的覆盖范围。

② 见傅郁林：美国民事诉讼法译序，http://article.chinalawinfo.com/Article_Detail.asp? ArticleID=27005.

只能在条款中所列的诉讼地进行。如果某一方向其他国家(地区)的法院提起诉讼,该国法院在面对强制性条款时,往往会驳回诉讼。

专属管辖条款特别适用于在多国签署的合同,以保证统一性。例如,某大型企业在与不同国家(地区)的供应商签订的类似的供货合同时,会比较倾向使用专属管辖条款,尽量将诉讼限制在同一个国家(地区)。

例 1. The parties irrevocably agree that the courts of Austria have exclusive jurisdiction to settle all disputes that may arise out of or in connection with this Agreement and, accordingly, any proceeding arising out of or in connection with this Agreement is to be brought in these courts. (Daigneault, 2005:118)

协议各方不可撤销地同意,奥地利法院对所有因本协议产生或与本协议相关的争议的解决具有专属管辖权,任何因本协议产生或与本合同相关的诉讼均应向奥地利法院提起。(笔者译)

例 2. All disputes, disagreements or claims between the parties shall be submitted to the exclusive jurisdiction of the state and federal courts of the State of Nevada, with venue in the County of Washoe. The parties hereto waive any defense of lack of personal jurisdiction[①] in said court(s)[②].

合同方之间所有的纠纷、争执或索赔均应提交给内华达州的州法院或联邦法院作专属审判,审判地点位于瓦肖县。以上法院缺乏对人管辖权,各方放弃以此为由的任何辩护。(笔者译)

由以上两例我们可以看出,专属管辖条款的标志是特定用词 exclusive。另外,情态动词应当使用带有强制性的 shall。例 1 中虽然未使用 shall,但使用 is to be 是简明英语的用法,也达到了同等的强制的效果;不过大部分合同草拟者仍然习惯于用 shall 表达合同中的义务和一般性的强制要求。

需要说明的是,例 2 中最后一句 The parties hereto waive any defense of lack of personal jurisdiction in said court(s)的作用是确保合同某一方成为被告之后,不会再试图以法院对其不具备对人管辖权为借口摆脱当地的诉讼或否认法院的裁定。在本章的引言部分我们讨论过,有意逃避、拖延诉讼的被告总会找出各种理由对起诉予以回击。在英美法普通法系国家,被告有可能以"不方便法院"[③](*forum non conveniens*)为由,要求法院驳回原告起诉或是将案件移交至另一司法系统里的更为适合的法院。因此,为了保证被告能遵守专属管辖条款中做出的承诺,防止其利用"不方便法院"原则拖延诉讼或将诉讼地转移,有的专

---

① personal jurisdiction(国内最常见的译法是"对人管辖权")是美国司法管辖权制度中的概念,指法院具有对诉讼中涉及的当事人做出影响其权利义务的裁决的权力。

② 选自 Randall K. Edwards 法律事务所网站,http://www.randallkedwards.com/article7.htm。

③ "不方便法院原则"是英美法系中的一个特有的概念,指某一涉外民事案件具有管辖权的法院,由于其审理此案将给当事人及司法带来种种不便,或者无法保障司法公正,而此时如果存在对该诉讼同样有管辖权的更为方便和更加适合的可替代法院,则该法院根据被告的请求,可以"不方便法院"为由自由裁量而拒绝行使管辖权。"不方便法院原则"盛行于英美普通法系国家,其主要被美国、英国、加拿大、澳大利亚、新西兰、爱尔兰、以色列等国家所采纳。一些混合法制地区以及少数大陆法国家也有与"不方便法院原则"相类似的立法与实践,如美国的路易斯安那州、加拿大的魁北克省以及日本。而大部分大陆法系国家,因法理基础和立法体系与英美法系的不同,一般不倾向使用该原则。我国民事诉讼法没有规定该原则,但在实践中,满足一定条件的情况下法院可以适用该原则放弃行使司法管辖权,驳回上诉。

属管辖条款后会接一条弃权条款(contractual waiver),这在英美法系国家比较常见,现举一例如下:

例 3. In relation to any legal action or proceedings① arising out of or in connection with this Agreement, each of the Parties irrevocably submits to the exclusive jurisdiction of the English courts and <u>waives any objection to the proceedings in such courts on the grounds of venue or on the grounds that proceedings have been brought in an inappropriate forum</u>.

因本协议或与本协议相关的任何法律诉讼有关问题,各方都只能不可撤销地提交英国法院审判,<u>且无权对基于诉讼地点或诉讼管辖不当缘故而反对该诉讼</u>。(范文祥,2007:185)

如以上几例所示,一般的专属管辖条款中,拥有专属管辖权的诉讼地有且仅有一个。但也有例外的情况,有一种做法是规定在甲方起诉乙方时,X 地法院拥有专属管辖权,在乙方起诉甲方时,Y 地法院拥有专属管辖权。如下例:

例 4. Any legal proceedings instituted against the Distributor by the Principal <u>shall</u> be brought <u>in the courts of the Distributor's country of domicile</u> and any legal proceedings against the Principal by the Distributor <u>shall</u> be brought in <u>the courts of the Principal's country of domicile</u> and for the purpose of such proceedings the law governing this Agreement shall in each case be deemed to be the law of the country in which the relevant proceedings have been instituted in accordance with this Clause. For the purpose of proceedings brought against it by the other party under this Clause each party agrees to submit to the <u>exclusive</u> jurisdiction of the courts of the other party's country of domicile. (Christou,2002: 210)

任何由委托人向经销商提起的诉讼<u>应</u>在<u>经销商居住国的法院</u>提起,任何由经销商向委托人提起的诉讼<u>应</u>在<u>委托人居住国的法院</u>提起。就该诉讼而言,在依照本条款向某国法院提起诉讼时,本合同的适用法即被认定为该国法律。就其他方根据本条款一方提起诉讼而言,各方同意将诉讼提交给提起诉讼的其他方居住国法院作<u>专属</u>审判。(笔者译)

尽管以上一段出处并不含糊,但内容似乎互相冲突。首先,第一句规定你要告我,到我的城市来告。这很合理,否则我不是被你拖垮了:你要告我,在你自己的城市或国家的法庭提交一纸诉状,我得迢迢千里来应诉。但本段最后一句的内容与上文有冲突。前面一句涉及的当事人是委托人和经销商,最后一句中的当事人变成了难以捉摸的一方或其他方(the other party)与指代不清的 it,而且诉讼地原则也发生了变化:原告地的法院居然有了专属司法管辖权(the exclusive jurisdiction)。如此一来,一个条款里并存了两个互相矛盾的陈述。所以,对专家的阐述也要用批判的眼光加以审察。为了克服该条款的内在矛盾或含混,笔者将原文做如下修订:For the purpose of proceedings brought against one of the parties to this Agreement by any third party under this Clause, each party agrees to submit to the

---

① proceeding 在法律英语中常以复数形式出现,意思与单数形式时相同。

exclusive jurisdiction of the courts of that third party's country of domicile. (就其他方根据本条款向本合同的一方提起诉讼而言，各方同意将诉讼提交给提起诉讼的其他方居住国法院作专属审判。)

2. 非专属管辖条款（Non-exclusive/Permissive）

非专属管辖条款(Non-exclusive jurisdiction clause)，又称可选择性(Permissive)管辖条款，明确地规定诉讼地在某一个国家(地区)，但不会限制合同方在合适的情况下在别国提起诉讼的权利。

与专属管辖条款相比，非专属管辖条款显得更有弹性。很多情况下，我们无法提前预知所有争议的最佳诉讼地。拿银行与其借款人签订的借款合同来说，银行一般会倾向在其所在国(地区)的法院进行诉讼，但少数情况下银行有可能会选择在借款人所在国(地区)的法院进行诉讼，因为那是借款人的财产所在，若是借款人输了官司，就可以由当地法院执行判决：变卖其资产还债或对其实行清盘。所以，非专属管辖条款保留了在非一般情况下当事人选择诉讼地的权力，让当事人能更好地应对变化的环境。所以，在实力或地位悬殊的合同方之间(如银行与借款人，担保人与被担保人)签署的合同中，非专属管辖条款较专属管辖条款更加常见。

例 5. (a) Any party bringing a legal action or proceeding against any other party arising out of or relating to this Agreement or the transactions it contemplates may bring the legal action or proceeding in the United States District Court for the Northern District of Illinois or in any court of the State of Illinois sitting in Chicago①.

(b) Each party to this Agreement submits to the nonexclusive jurisdiction of (i) the United States District Court for the Northern District of Illinois and its appellate courts, and

(ii) any court of the State of Illinois sitting in Chicago and its appellate courts,

for the purpose of all legal actions and proceedings arising out of or relating to this Agreement. (Stark, 2003:138)

(a) 任何因本协议或本协议之预期交易产生或与之相关的诉讼，由任一合同方向另一方提起时，可提交至美国伊利诺斯州北部地区联邦法院或位于芝加哥市的任一伊利诺斯州州法院。

(b) 就因本合同产生或与本合同相关的所有法律诉讼，合同各方服从

(i) 美国伊利诺斯州北部地区联邦法院或其上诉法院，和

(ii) 位于芝加哥市的任一伊利诺斯州州法院或其上诉法院的非专属管辖。（笔者译）

例 5 的句型强调合同方作为"原告"在所选择的诉讼地起诉的权利及其作为"被告"时服从该法院管辖的责任。由例 5 我们可以看出，一如 exclusive 代表了专属管辖条款，nonexclusive 是非专属管辖条款的标志性词汇；再加上不具备强制性的情态动词 may，例 5 的这一条款毫无疑问是非专属管辖条款。

---

① 美国的五十个州各有两套不同的法院系统：联邦法院系统和州法院系统。两套法院系统都受理民事案件，这条诉讼地选择条款包含了两个法院系统内的法院。

需要说明的是,如果诉讼地选择条款对"专属"与否保持沉默,换句话说,如果在该条款中找不到 exclusive 或 nonexclusive 这样的标志性词汇或任何的近义词,该条款往往被认定为非专属管辖条款。如例 6 对法院的管辖权是否专属就没有任何特定的修饰词:

例 6. Any claim or dispute arising out of or related to this agreement or its interpretation shall be brought in a court of competent jurisdiction sitting within the State of Delaware.

因本协议或与本协议解释有关的任何索赔或争议应向位于特拉华州境内有管辖权的法院提起诉讼。(范文祥,2007:185)

例 6 中虽然使用了具有明确强制语气的情态动词 shall,但因为没有任何标志"专属"管辖权的词汇,该条款属于非专属管辖条款,也就是说,在实际发生纠纷时,当事人仍有权选择位于特拉华州之外的有管辖权的法院提起诉讼。

3. 对合同一方有利的混合型条款 (Unilateral hybrid clause)

这样的条款显示了合同双方悬殊的谈判力——甲方可以在任一具有管辖权的法院起诉乙方,而乙方只能在某一个国家的法院起诉甲方。显然,有争议或诉讼发生时,甲方将比乙方处于更加有利的地位。如下例:

例 7. 就本协议有关的任何起诉、诉讼或其他法律程序(以下统称"法律程序"),以及为了银行的利益,对方应不可撤销地:

第一,服从香港法院的管辖;

第二,放弃其在任何时间对将任何该等法院(就在任何此等法院所提起的任何法律程序而言)作为审判地可能提出的任何反对意见,并放弃声称该等法律程序已经在不便的诉讼地提出或该法院对其不拥有司法管辖权;

第三,本协议不(能)排除银行在其他任何有管辖权的法院提起诉讼,在一个或多个有管辖权的法院提起的诉讼不(能)排除在其他任何有管辖权的法院提起。

For the purpose of any suit, action or legal proceeding in connection with this Agreement ("Proceeding") and for the interests of the Bank, the other party irrevocably agrees

(1) to submit to the exclusive jurisdiction of the courts of Hong Kong;

(2) to waive any objection it may have to the proceeding in such courts on the grounds of venue or on the grounds that the proceeding has been instituted in an inappropriate forum, and waive any defense of lack of jurisdiction in such courts.

(3) that this Agreement does not preclude the Bank taking the proceeding to any other courts of competent jurisdiction, or taking the proceeding to one or more courts of competent jurisdiction does not preclude the Bank to take the proceeding to any other court of competent jurisdiction. (笔者译)

例 7 的条款出自 2010 年一起真实的民事案件[①],因只能找到中文条款的原文,英文条款

---

① 详情参见张远忠金融网博客,http://zhangyuanzhongblog.blog.163.com/blog/static/11487565220098815111244/及北大法意——中国裁判文书库,http://www.lawyee.org/Case/Case_Data.asp?ChannelID=2010102&KeyWord=&RID=1094348

由笔者译出。此案中,中国人赖某在购买了某国外银行的一项理财产品后承受了数千万元的巨额亏损。赖某将银行告上法庭,但上海市中级法院驳回上诉;赖某不服判决,告上了上海市高级人民法院,结果仍是不予受理。正是因为例7中这条诉讼地选择条款,法院认定当事人之间就司法管辖权有明确的约定,根据约定,中国内地法院对诉讼没有管辖权,赖某只能向香港法院起诉该银行。对于不熟悉香港法律和诉讼程序的赖某来说,这可谓是雪上加霜。实际上,这种条款在国际市场上被诸多银行作为标准条款写入合同。但在某些国家,该类条款也有可能会被认定为缺乏公平性或"一边倒"而被判无效。无独有偶,2012年一名法国人也因为其购买的某国外银行的理财产品业绩不佳而决定在巴黎起诉该银行[①]。但此案中的诉讼地选择条款(见例8)被法国最高法院判为无效,法国人可以不受该条款中"服从卢森堡法院专属管辖"的限制,在本国的法院起诉银行。所以,如果合同与法国有联系,银行在使用这类对自身有益的条款时应多加注意了,至少法国的法院很可能会受理另一方的上诉。

例8. Potential disputes between the client and the Bank shall be subject to the exclusive jurisdiction of the Courts of Luxembourg. In the event the Bank does not rely on such jurisdiction the Bank reserves the right to bring an action before the Courts of the client's domicile or any other court of competent jurisdiction.

客户与银行之间的争议应服从卢森堡法院的专属管辖。万一银行未依赖该管辖,银行保留在客户居住国的法院或任何其他具有管辖权的法院提起诉讼的权利。(笔者译)

三、诉讼地选择条款写作范例

上文给出的例子已是经过作者精挑细选,在遣词构句上都具有示范性的例句。现总结出一组具有通用价值的条款,供读者参考:

(一) 专属管辖条款/非专属管辖条款

(a) Any party bringing a suit, action or proceeding ("Proceeding") against any other party arising out of or relating to this Agreement shall take the Proceeding in the courts of _____.

(b) Both parties agree to submit to the exclusive/non-exclusive jurisdiction of the courts of _____.

(a) 合同一方向另一方提起的任何因本协议产生或与本协议相关的诉讼应提交至_____法院。

(b) 合同双方同意服从_____法院的专属/非专属管辖。

(二) 对一方有利的混合型条款

(a) Subject to clause (b) the parties irrevocably agree that the courts of _____

---

① 此案的原告是一位定居于西班牙的法国人,被告是卢森堡的一家私人银行,原告不满被告在替其理财过程中业绩下滑,故在法国巴黎提起上诉。被告称原告无权在巴黎起诉,因为双方理财合同中的诉讼地条款中规定被告仅有权在卢森堡上诉。最终法国最高法院将此条款判为无效,原告得以在巴黎起诉被告。

shall have exclusive jurisdiction for the purpose of hearing and determining any suit, action or proceeding arising out of or relating to this Agreement ("Proceeding").

(b) Nothing in this clause shall limit the right of Party A to take Proceeding against Party B in any other court of competent jurisdiction.

（a）在符合本条（b）款的前提下，合同双方不可撤销地同意，对于任何因本合同产生或与合同相关的诉讼（简称"诉讼"），_____法院具有专属管辖权。

（b）甲方有权在任何其他具有管辖权的法院起诉乙方而不受本条中的任何内容限制。

四、结语

在草拟跨国合同中，诉讼地选择是一个必须置于专家手中的问题。在选择法院时除了经济性、便利性的考虑，更要注意法院所在国（地区）的司法制度，以及该法院做出的判决在执行地（若与诉讼地不在同一国家或地区）是否得到承认或有效执行的问题。对合同的起草者和译者而言，必须清楚地将当事人的意图用文字表达出来，尤其要注意关键词 exclusive/non-exclusive 和情态动词 shall/may 的使用。

第十九章 转让条款的写作、翻译和研究

一、引言：转让条款的定义及基本内涵

转让条款订明合同中规定的权利（rights）、利益（benefits）、责任（duties）以及义务（obligations）是否可以全部转让或部分转让，以及在什么情况下可以转让。该条款有时跟"继承人及转让"（"successors and assign"）的通用条款合并在一起或置放在其名下。大多数国家的法律都允许合同权利和义务的转让，但转让的条件会因合同性质不同和各方特殊的利益需要而有所差异。

根据 common law is common sense 的基本原理，人有生老病死，公司（法人）有兴盛衰败，因此，尚未完全履行或只有部分履行的合同应允许转让。如果某份合同一定要签署人本人完全自行履行，那世间恐怕很少有人敢签订合同。但任何合同也不都是可以随便转让的。合同当事人一般都希望跟自己熟悉的或几经磨合才达成共识的"原配"合作；在不得不转让的情况下，转让必须得到非转让方的同意，并且还要求转让方满足一定的条件。合同中具体可转让的内容包括合同本身或其项下的权利、利益、责任以及义务。在多数情况下，这一部分的内容置放在不得转让（NO ASSIGNMENT）的小标题之下，这是把丑话说在前。其实，还有不少转让条款是放在合同转让（ASSIGNMENT）小标题之下的，但其内容往往"名不符实"：转让条款仍然会包含不可转让的规定。以下是转让条款写作的基本句型以及关键用词：

二、转让条款的基本句型和关键用词/语

（一）转让或不得转让的句式

1. Party A (shall) be free to assign its rights hereof to the third party.

2. The parties may not assign this Agreement.

3. Neither this Agreement nor any of the rights, interests or obligations... shall be assigned, in whole or in part.

4. Neither party shall have the right to assign or transfer any duties, rights or obligations.

5. <u>Any purported transfer, assignment or delegation</u> by either party without the appropriate prior written approval shall <u>be null and void and of no force or effect</u>.

6. This Agreement is personal to... who may not assign or delegate any of Employee's rights or obligations hereunder.

(二) 转让条件

1. If Party A's assignee assumes all the obligations of Party A hereunder and sends written notice of the assignment to attesting.

2. ... continues to be liable for the performance of its obligations.

3. ... except that the Company may assign the Agreement to its successor.

4. ... without prior written consent of the other party.

5. ... shall not be unreasonably withheld.

6. Subject to the foregoing/Notwithstanding the foregoing.

(三) 转让方法及其他

1. by operation of law or otherwise, by way of merger or consolidation or the acquisition of substantially all of the business and assets of the assigning party relating to the Agreement.

2. this Agreement shall inure to the benefit of the respective Parties, their heirs, executors, administrators, successors and assignees.

3. to execute a general release of Party from claims or liabilities of Party A under this Agreement.

有一定经验的作者或译者，利用这些"零部件"就可以"组装"出各种转让条款；但他们往往很难确定哪些写法是流行的、哪些是过时的、哪些在语言风格上是得体的、哪些已经迂腐。以下我们来看一些完整的转让条款语段，以便在再下一节分析各种写法的风格。

三、传统转让条款的主要表达方式

1. Assignment. The parties may not assign this Agreement or any rights or obligations hereunder, by operation of law or otherwise [without prior written consent of the party],[which shall not be unreasonably withheld].

2. No Assignment. Neither this Agreement nor any of the rights, interests or obligations under this Agreement shall be assigned, in whole or in part, by operation of law or otherwise by either of the parties hereto without the prior written consent of the other party.

3. It is agreed that neither party shall have the right to assign or transfer any duties, rights or obligations due hereunder without the express written consent of the other party, except that the Company may assign the Agreement to its successor or any entity acquiring all or substantially all of the assets of the Company.

就雇佣合约而言，该不许转让条款可以这样写：

4. This Agreement is personal to Employee and Employee may not assign or delegate any of Employee's rights or obligations hereunder. Subject to the foregoing, this Agreement shall be binding upon and inure to the benefit of the respective

Parties, their heirs, executors, administrators, successors and assigns.①

标准的可转让条款一般是这样的：

5. This Agreement shall inure to the benefit of the successors and assigns of Party A. Party A shall have the right to transfer or assign its interest in this Agreement to any person, persons, partnership, association, or corporation. If Party A's assignees assumes all the obligations of Party A hereunder and sends written notice of the assignment to attesting, Developer agrees promptly to execute a general release of Party A, and any affiliates of Party A, from claims or liabilities of Party A under this Agreement.

6. The Party shall be free to assign its rights hereof to the third party without containing a prior consent from the other Party. Notwithstanding, the assigning Party shall deliver a notice of the same to the other Party within 10 days after such assignment.

不过，从本质上讲，签订合同的双方都是不愿意对方将合同转让给第三方的。因此，该条款往往以 NO ASSIGNMENT 作为合同的小标题。但考虑到万一情况，较合理的写法如下：

7. NO ASSIGNMENT. Neither party shall transfer or assign any rights *or* delegate any obligations hereunder, in whole or in part, whether voluntarily or by operation of law, without the prior written consent of the other party. Any purported transfer, assignment or delegation by either party without the appropriate prior written approval shall be null and void and of no force or effect. Notwithstanding the foregoing, without securing such prior consent, each party shall have the right to assign this Agreement or any of its rights or obligations to an Affiliate *provided* that such party continues to be liable for the performance of its obligations and either party shall have the right to assign this Agreement and the obligations hereunder to any successor of such party by way of merger or consolidation or the acquisition of substantially all of the business and assets of the assigning party relating to the Agreement.

不得转让。未经对方事先书面同意，无论出于自愿还是以法律途径，任何一方都不得转让本合同项下的任何（全部或部分）权利或义务。任何未经适当手续事先书面获准的所谓转让一概无效。尽管有前述规定，即使未获得该事先同意的，任何一方都有权转让本合同或本合同的任何权利或义务给其关联公司，但该关联公司一方将继续对其义务的履行承担法律责任，并且任何一方均有权将本协议及其下的义务转让给该方通过

---

① 即使是母语读者一般都会认为 assignees 才是与前述 successors 等词般配的词语，并且往往会将该词（assign）仅仅当作动词使用。其实，这样解读是错误的。assigns 用在此处不但指受让人，还指受让人之受让人或受让人之继承人（有子子孙孙无穷尽继承的寓意）。根据有关法律网站解释：The term assigns comprises not merely a single person, but a line or succession of persons. The word assigns includes the assignee of an assignee in perpetuum and the heir of an assignee or the assignee of a heir. Additionally, the term includes the assignee of an assignee's executor and a devisee. (http://assignments.uslegal.com/assigns/; accessed on March 21, 2013)

<u>实质兼并、合并或并购</u>本协议有关的转让方业务和资产的方式而产生的继承方。

四、对传统转让条款语用特征的分析

我们从写作风格角度对以上第 7 条转让条款的内容做重点详细分析。就该条款的语言而言,有几个非常明显的特征值得注意:

1. 大量使用法律配对词:如 transfer, assign, delegate 及其名词形式 transfer, assignment, delegation;该三词在本条款中本来只有一个意思,就是"转让"。但事实上,delegate 与前两者是有区别的,后者主要指委托他人行使责任或义务。

2. 另一组相同性质的词汇是 null and void and of no force or effect。这四个短语,并不互补,只有一个意思;所以,该段译文的处理手法是"合四为一",即译作"无效"。就中译英而言,建议译者不必模仿这种写作风格,因为已经过时,甚至迂腐,在较新的合同写作中,坚持使用这类重言词的律师人数也已急剧减少,用简洁、简明的当代语言写作合同条款是大势所趋。

3. 还要注意的是 merger or consolidation, acquisition—— 虽然看似法律同义词,都是"合并",其实三者在法律上是有区别的。merger 指"兼并",即其中一个公司继续存在,另一个被消灭;consolidation 在美英各国的公司法中,指两公司合并后成立一个新公司;而后者 acquisition,指用任何方法(但主要通过购买)获得别家公司的财产,所以"并购"更合该词的实义。在对待风格型的同义词[即配对词(legal pair/doublet)和三联词(legal triplet)]时,我们可以合二为一或合三为一;而对待法律近义词时,必须尽可能以概念有明确差别的对等词汇译出,以准确反映作者的写作意图。

4. *Notwithstanding* the foregoing—— 这样的写法比较简洁,尽管表达方式过于"法律",相当于 Except as specifically set forth in the preceding sentences 或者 Although the above provision exists,用了 notwithstanding+名词短语,一个让步状语从句立刻简化为一个短语,但需要注意的是:普通英文不接受这样的表达方式。在法律文本中另外有一个表达方式与此短语非常相似,即 Subject to (noun),如 Subject the foregoing 或 Subject to the proceeding paragraph。但两短语的相似只局限在形式上,实质意义几乎是完全相反的。直接跟随 *Notwithstanding* 之后的内容是被否定的,所以该短语的内容相当于一个让步状语从句的内容,在该短语之后的主句中提出的内容往往是更宽容的条件;而跟随 Subject to 之后的内容却是前提性的条件,即必须符合或满足前面所述的条件后,主句中提出的新条件或法律行为才能成立或可以着手实施。例如:<u>Subject to this section</u>, where an order is made under section 12AA in respect of pecuniary resources or property held by a person other than the person convicted, that other person may, within 28 days after the date of making the order, appeal against the order of the Court of Appeal. [①] (<u>在符合本条的规定下</u>,凡法庭根据第 12AA 条对并非被定罪的人持有的金钱资源或财产作出命令,该人可在命令做出的日期后 28 天内就该命令向上诉法院提出上诉。)

---

① Laws of Hong Kong, Cap. 201, *Prevention of Bribery Ordinance*, Art. 12AB[1]

5. *provided* that是又一个英文法律文本专用的表达方式。由于其处于句子的后端,根据法律写作的惯例,显然是个"但书"(proviso,即例外条件),其作用相当于普通英文中的but,however或if。但根据法律翻译惯例,该短语译作"但",而不是"但是"。

6. 本条款中最后一个值得注意的短语是be liable for:虽然大多数内地的法律译本将该词简单地译作"负责"或"承担责任",但在绝大多数香港立法文本中该词被译作"承担法律责任"——这是比较到位的译法,因为它的确与be responsible for (to)、be accountable to是有差别的,它所蕴含的是民事赔偿责任,因此由该词衍生出来的就是"债务"(liabilities)。

五、标准转让条款的写作及说明

鉴于以上传统转让条款中语言上存在的种种问题,建议对其做如下修改,并可视之为这一通用条款的标准写作模式:

Assignment. The parties may not assign this Agreement or any rights or obligations under it to any third party, by operation of law or otherwise without prior written consent of the other party.

Neither party may withhold or delay such consent unreasonably. But either party may withhold consent on any of the following grounds: The other party is in default of an obligation under this Agreement when consent is requested; the proposed assignee cannot financially perform the other party's remaining obligations under this Agreement; or the proposed assignee refused to assume all of the party's remaining obligations under this Agreement.

Notwithstanding the foregoing, without securing such prior consent, each party shall have the right to assign this Agreement or any of its rights or obligations to an affiliate or any successor of such party by way of merger or consolidation, or the acquisition of substantially all of the business and assets of the assigning party relating to the Agreement, if such party will continue to be liable for the performance of its obligations under this agreement.

转让。未经对方事先书面同意,无论是通过法律或其他途径,任何一方都不得将本合同项下的任何权利或义务转让给第三方。任何一方也不得无理拒绝或拖延同意。但任何一方均可因以下理由拒绝转让:对方在要求同意转让时履行义务违约;拟受让方在财力上不能按照本协议要求履行对方的义务;或拟受让方拒绝承担对方在本协议下所有未履行之义务。

尽管有前述规定,即使未经事先获准,任何一方均有权将本协议或其项下的任何权利或义务转让给该方通过兼并、合并,或并购本协议有关的转让方的实质上的全部业务和资产的方式而产生的关联公司或继承方——如果该关联公司或继承方愿意继续对本合同义务的履行承担法律责任。

修改说明:

显而易见,以上建议的标准转让条款是在上节第7条基础上改编的。之所以做如下修改,原因如下:

1. 加上 which shall not be unreasonably withheld or delayed 这一定语从句，是为了让各方在转让问题上不要故意刁难对方；上文原文中有 in whole or in part, whether voluntarily or by operation of law，其实，一个修饰词 any（rights or obligation）已经包括 in whole or in part，没有必要多此一举；另外一个副词 or otherwise，也已经把原文的 whether voluntarily 的意思包括在内，而且还更周全。大部分这类条款都没有"不得拖延"这个字眼，这是必要的添加，有些存心欠良的生意伙伴，最终还是会同意转让，但会拖死对方。加上这样的字眼，可以起到预防作用。

2. 原文第二句 Any <u>purported transfer, assignment or delegation</u> by either party without the appropriate prior written approval shall be <u>null and void and of no force or effect</u> 的意图是为了维持履行合同环境的稳定，也从法律层面要求签约双方互相尊重：不要轻易转让合同，确实需要转让必须得到彼此的同意。但原文所用的谓语动词（shall be null and void and of no force or effect）是最典型的、最累赘的"师爷"用语，即使要用，改为 Any proposed assignment by either party without the appropriate prior written consent shall be void 即可，这样的表达更加简洁。另外，把原文的 Any purported transfer, assignment or delegation 改作 Any proposed assignment，可以剔除毫无实质意义的内容，摈弃会让律师以外的读者倍感困惑的"师爷"文风：在普通英文中根本无人使用 purported，很多英美律师自己也搞不清该词确切意思究竟是什么，用 proposed 这个普通词取而代之，不但可以让任何签约方（尤其是普通生意人）明白自己在做什么，而且该合同言语也更富有现代气息。

但是，在笔者建议的标准条款中，这一部分的内容还是被完全删除了。如果读者从语篇而不是从语句的角度去理解，就会明白个中原因：该句之前已经明确规定：The parties may not assign... without prior written consent of the other party.（没有对方书面同意，不得转让。）紧接着再来一句 Any proposed assignment... without the appropriate prior written consent shall be void（没有对方书面同意而提出的转让属无效），岂非与前句的意思完全重复？故此句可以予以删除。

3. 在一般情况下合同终究是可以转让的，任何一方都不得无理拒绝同意。但也有例外，即 a. 乙方在要求同意转让时履行义务违约；b. 拟受让方在财力上不能按照本合同要求履行乙方的义务；或 c. 拟受让方拒绝承担乙方在本合同下所有未履行之义务。这三条构成拒绝转让的理由是合情合理的，否则，公理何在？合同约束力何以体现？违约方可以借此转让逃避法律责任。

4. 不过，有一种情况的转让，对方是必须无条件同意的，即将合同或合同项下的权利或义务，转让给关联公司或继承方，只要他们同意继续履行合同义务，这是任何一方都期盼的、也是合情合理的；否则，谁敢签订合同？月有阴晴圆缺，人有生老病死，生意也有兴有衰，任何公司业务都可能被继承，被售卖，被并购……，而买方或继承方肯定不可能只买下利益或获得利益而不承担利益让予方必须承担的义务。所以，只要关联公司或继承方愿意承担合同的义务，就应该允许转让；而加上 without securing such prior consent，目的是为了给予双方充分的经商自由，否则因为签了这份合同，搞个关联公司，进行公司合并、兼并或售卖公司，就会受到太多的限制。

六、转让条款不同写法

现实的商业世界是复杂的。虽然合同或协议的性质可以大同小异,但具体内容或细则可以有千差万别。所以,有关的转让条款的写法可以五花八门。为了配合各行各业合同制作人士的不同需求或提供更多的参考,以下将过去三十多年间在国内外主要合同文本有关该转让条款的不同写法及其中文翻译表列如下:

Transfer of Contracts	合同的转让
Neither Party hereto <u>shall</u> assign this Agreement or any of its rights and interests hereunder without the other Party's prior written consent, which <u>shall not</u> be unreasonably withheld.	本协议的任何一方未经另一方事先书面同意(该另一方<u>不得无理拒绝同意</u>),<u>不得</u>转让本协定或其在本协定项下的任何权利和权益。(孙万彪,2002:10-19)
Neither Party <u>may</u> assign this Agreement, in whole or in part, without the other Party's prior written consent, except to (i) any corporation resulting from any merger, consolidation or other reorganization involving the assigning Party...	任何一方未经另一方事先同意,<u>不得</u>转让本协定的全部或部分,除非转让给(i)涉及转让方的因兼并、合并或其他重组而产生的任何公司……(孙万彪,2002:10-18)
(a) No assignments. No party may assign any of its rights under this Agreement, voluntarily or involuntarily, whether by merger, consolidation, dissolution, operation of law, or any other manner. (b) Specific Assignments Prohibited. Assignments prohibited under subsection (a) include, without limitation, assignment of (i) any claim for damages arising out of the non-assigning party's breach of the whole contract; and (ii) any right arising out of the assignor's full performance of this Agreement. (乔焕然,2008:154)	(a)不得转让。任一方都不得转让其本协议下之权利,无论自愿、非自愿,无论以兼并、合并、解散、按照法律要求还是以其他方式。 (b)具体的转让禁止。(a)项所禁止的转让包括但不限于:(i)对非转让方违反整个合同而提出赔偿请求的转让;以及(ii)因转让方全面履行协议而产生的任何权利的转让。
1. Transfer by Party A. This Agreement shall <u>inure to the benefit of</u> the successors and assignees of Party A. Party A shall have the right to transfer or assign its interest in this Agreement to <u>any person, persons, partnership, association, or corporation.</u> If Party A's assignee <u>assumes all the obligations of</u> Party A hereunder and sends written notice of the assignment to attest thereto, Developer agrees promptly to execute a general release of Party A, and any affiliates of Party A, from claims or liabilities of Party A under this Agreement. 2. Transfer by Developer. Developer understands and acknowledges	1. 甲方的转让。本协议应为甲方的继承者和受让人之利益生效。甲方有权将其在本协议中的利益转让给任何个人、数人、合伙人、联合体或法人公司。若甲方的受让人承担甲方在本协议下的所有义务,并发出证明受让的书面通知,开发商同意立即全面豁免甲方,以及甲方的任何关联公司,使其不再承担本协议下的任何责任或债务。 2. 开发商的转让。开发商知晓并确认:

续表

Transfer of Contracts	合同的转让
that the rights and duties set forth in this Agreement are personal to Developer, and that Party A has granted this <u>Agreement in reliance on</u> Developer's business skill and financial capacity. Accordingly, neither (i) Developer, nor (ii) any immediate or remote successor to Developer, nor (iii) any individual, partnership, corporation or other legal entity which directly or indirectly owns any interest in the Developer or in this Development Agreement, shall <u>sell, assign, transfer, convey, donate, pledge, mortgage, or otherwise encumber</u> any direct or indirect interest in this Agreement or in Developer without the prior written consent of Party A. Any purported assignment or transfer, by operation of law or otherwise, not having the written consent of Party A, shall be null and void, and shall constitute a material breach of this Agreement, for which Party A may then terminate without opportunity to cure pursuant to Section 5.03 of this Agreement. <u>Notwithstanding anything in this Agreement to the contrary</u>, Developer understands and acknowledges that individual development rights to obtain franchises to establish and operate Franchised Units may not be transferred except in connection with a transfer of this Development Agreement, together with all remaining development options due to be developed under this Agreement, in accordance with the conditions set forth herein. (乔焕然,2008:229)	本协议规定的权利和义务须由开发商亲自承担,且甲方签订了本协议是基于对开发商的商业技能和财政能力的信赖。因此,不论(i)开发商,还是(ii)开发商的任何直接或间接继承人,还是(iii)直接或间接地在开发商或本开发协议中拥有任何利益的任何个人、合伙人、公司或其他法人,在未取得甲方的事先书面同意之前,都不得将本协议的或开发商的任何直接或间接利益出卖、转让、让与、转移、捐赠、质押、抵押或施加其他权利负担。任何声称的转让或让予,不论是通过法律途径还是其他手段,若无甲方的书面同意,均为无效,并构成对本协议的实质违约,甲方可就此终止本协议,而无需根据第5.03条给予补救机会。尽管本协议中可能有相反规定,开发商知晓并确认:除非与本开发协议之转让相关,并按照本协议规定的条件,与所有根据本协议尚应开发的剩余的开发选择权的转让一起进行,否则不得转让为组建和运行特许机构取得的个人开发权。
Any <u>purported</u> assignment without the written approval of the other party shall be absolutely void against the non-assigning party. In such event, the non-assigning party shall have no obligation whatsoever to the <u>purported</u> assignee. Any such <u>purported</u> assignment shall not release or relieve the party attempting to make an assignment of any of its obligations under the Purchase Order. (范文祥,2007:217)	任何未经对方书面同意的所谓转让订单对非转让方绝对无效。在这种情况下,非转让方对所谓受让方不承担任何义务。任何这类所谓转让并不解除或减轻试图进行转让一方的在该订单项下的义务。
The Purchaser shall not be entitled to assign its rights, benefits and claims under this Agreement (including the benefits of warranties, undertakings and indemnities herein contained) without the prior written consent of the Vendor, which consent shall not be unreasonably withheld or delayed.	买方未经销售商书面同意,无权转让其合同项下的权利、利益或索赔权(包括本协议约定的保证、承诺和赔偿利益),但销售商不得无故拒绝或拖延买方的转让请求。

续表

Transfer of Contracts	合同的转让
Either Party hereto may at any time, with the prior written consent of the other party, such consent not to be unreasonably withheld or delayed, assign all or any part of the benefit or its rights under this Agreement, except that no consent shall be required in the case of an assignment of rights or benefits to an Affiliate. (范文祥,2007:216)	协议任何一方可在任何时候,在事先获得对方书面同意后转让其在本协议项下的全部或部分利益或权利,对方不得无故拒绝或拖延不予同意,但如向关联公司做这样的转让则无须对方同意。
The Party shall be free to assign its rights hereof to the third party without obtaining a prior consent from the other Party. Notwithstanding, the assigning Party shall deliver a notice of the same to the other Party within 10 days after such assignment. (范文祥,2007:215)	合同方可以未经对方事先同意而将其在本合同项下的权利转让给第三方,不过转让方应在转让后10日内向对方发送该转让事宜的通知。
NO ASSIGNMENT. Neither party shall <u>transfer or assign</u> any rights or delegate any obligations hereunder, in whole or in part, whether voluntarily or by operation of law, without the prior written consent of the other party. Any <u>purported transfer, assignment or delegation</u> by either party without the appropriate prior written approval shall be null and void and of no force or effect. Notwithstanding the foregoing, without securing such prior consent, each party shall have the right to assign this Agreement or any of its rights or obligations to an Affiliate <u>provided that</u> such party continues to <u>be liable for</u> the performance of its obligations and either party shall have the right to assign this Agreement and the obligations hereunder to any successor of such party by way of <u>merger or consolidation or the acquisition</u> of substantially all of the business and assets of the assigning party relating to the Agreement. (王辉,2007:78)	不得转让。未经对方事先书面同意,无论出于自愿还是以法律途径,任何一方都不得转让本合同项下的任何(全部或部分)权利或义务。任何未经适当手续事先书面获准的所谓转让一概无效。尽管有前述规定,即使未获得事先同意的,任何一方都有权转让本合同或本合同的任何权利或义务给其关联公司,但该关联公司一方将继续对其义务的履行承担法律责任,并且任何一方均有权将本协议及其下的义务转让给该方通过实质兼并、合并或并购本协议有关的转让方业务和资产的方式而产生的继承方。
ASSIGNMENT. Neither party's rights, duties or responsibilities under this Agreement may be assigned, delegated or otherwise transferred in any manner, without the prior written consent of the other party. Notwithstanding the foregoing, no such consent shall be required in connection with the assignment, delegation or other transfer of any such rights, duties or responsibilities (a) by a party to any affiliate which directly or indirectly controls, is controlled by or is under common control with such party, where such control is by more than fifty percent (50%) of the relevant voting power, or (b) in connection with any transaction, regardless of its form, in which all or substantially all of the assets of Lycos are acquired. (王辉,2007:78)	转让。未经他方事先的书面同意,任何一方不得以转让、让予或其他任何方式转让其合同项下的权利、义务或责任。尽管有上述规定,以下的有关上述权利、义务或责任转让、变更或其他转移无须取得对方书面同意:(a)由一方转让给任何直接或间接控制该方,该方受其控制或受该方共同控制的关联公司(如果该控制不小于有关投票权的50%),或(b)不论形式,与任何Lycos全部或实质全部资产遭收购的交易有关。

续表

Transfer of Contracts	合同的转让
Subject to Article 2.2, no Party shall be entitled to assign or transfer any of its interests, rights or obligations under this Contract without the written permission of the other. In the event that Seller assigns or transfers its interests, rights or obligations under the Petroleum Contract, then it shall be deemed that Buyer has consented to an assignment or transfer of Sellers' interests, rights or obligations under this Contract. (范文祥, 2007:218)	协议任何一方未经另一方书面同意, 无权转让或转移其在本合同项下的利益、权利或义务, 但 2.2 款另有规定的除外。 如果卖方转让其在石油合同项下的利益、权利或义务, 应视为买方已经同意卖方转让本合同项下的利益、权利或义务。
The Seller shall not assign the whole or any part of Purchase Order or any benefit or interest under it without the prior written approval of the Buyer. The Buyer shall be entitled to assign the whole or any part of the Purchase Order or any benefit or interest under it at any time without the approval of the Seller provided that the Buyer notifies the Seller of such an assignment. (范文祥, 2007:218)	卖方未经买方事先书面同意, 不得转让全部或部分采购订单, 也不得转让其在本采购订单下的任何权益或利益。买方有权在任何时候不经卖方同意转让全部或部分采购订单或本采购订单项下的任何权益或利益, 但买方应将有关转让通知卖方。
5.1 The parties may <u>modify (amend, alter, change, revise)</u> their contract upon agreement reached through consultation. Where laws and administrative regulations <u>provided</u> that the modification of a contract shall go through the procedures of approval and registration, such <u>provision</u> shall <u>govern</u>. 5.2 Party B shall not assign or subcontract the whole or any part of the Contract nor any benefit or interest under it without the prior written approval of Party A. Party A shall not be entitled to assign the whole or any part of the Contract or any benefit or interest hereunder at any time without the approval of Party B provided that Party A notifies Party B of such an assignment. 5.3 The creditor may assign all or part of his rights under the contract to a third person, except in any of the following circumstances: (1) by nature of the contract such rights are not assignable; (2) the parties have agreed that such rights may not be assigned; or (3) the law provides that such rights may not be assigned. 5.3.1 If the creditor <u>assigns</u> his rights, it shall notify the debtor. Such <u>assignment</u> without notification shall be invalid as far as the debtor is concerned. The creditor may not <u>revoke</u> the notification of the assignment of his rights, unless otherwise agreed by the assignee. 5.3.2 <u>When</u> the creditor assigns his rights, the assignee shall also acquire the <u>incidental</u> rights <u>in connection with</u> the claim, unless	5.1 合同方可通过协商对签订的合同进行修改。凡法律和行政法规规定合同修改应经过审批与登记程序的, 该规定方可适用。 5.2 未经甲方事先书面同意, 乙方不得转让或分包全部合同或合同的任何部分, 以及本合同项下的任何权益或利益。未经乙方同意, 甲方在任何时候不得转让全部合同或合同的任何部分, 以及本合同项下的任何权益或利益, 但如甲方通知乙方该转让则属例外。 5.3 债权人可向第三方转让本合同规定的其全部或部分权利, 但下列情况则属例外: (1) 根据合同性质, 该权利不得转让; (2) 合同双方同意该权利不得转让; 或 (3) 法律规定该权利不得转让。 5.3.1 如债权人转让其权利, 应通知债务人。未通知债务人的转让应视为无效。债权人不得撤销转让其权利的通知, 除受让人同意者外。 5.3.2 如债权人转让其权利, 受让人也应获取与该主张相关的附属权利,

续表

Transfer of Contracts	合同的转让
such incidental rights are exclusive to the creditor. 5.3.3 If the debtor intends to transfer all or part of his obligations under the contract to a third person, such transfer shall be subject to the consent of the creditor. 5.3.4 Either party may, with the consent of the other party, assign all of his rights and obligations under the contract to a third person.	除该权利为债权人独有。 5.3.3 如债务人打算向第三方转让其在本合同项下的全部或部分义务,该转让必须得到债权人同意。 5.3.4 经另一方同意后,任何一方可向第三方转让其在本合同项下的所有权利和义务。
Party A may not assign, transfer or subcontract any part of the Contract without the prior written consent of Party B, and any assignment in violation of this provision shall be null and void. Distributor shall not assign any of its rights under this agreement, except with the prior written consent of the other party. The preceding sentence applies to all assignments of rights, whether they are voluntary or involuntary, by merger, consolidation, dissolution, operation of law or any other manner. Any purported assignment of rights or delegation of performance in violation of this Section is void.	未经乙方事先书面同意,甲方不得转让、转移或分包合同的任何部分,且违反本规定的转让应视为无效。 未经另一方事先书面同意,经销商不得转让其在本协议项下的任何权利。前一句适用于所有的权利转让,不论是自愿还是非自愿,或是通过合并、兼并、解散、以法律途径或其他任何方式进行的权利转让。任何违反本条款声称的权利转让或执行委托均属无效。

第二十章 法律选择条款的起草、翻译和研究

一、引言

(一) 法律选择条款的作用与意义

法律选择条款(governing law/choice-of-law clause)载明了合同当事人一致同意的、对合同进行解释与管辖的适用法律(applicable law of contract)。从起草合同的角度来讲,起草人无法完全预测当事人之间可能发生的所有争议,针对合同条款的每一个细节的问题逐一做出详细的解释或为其分别制定规则,即使假设所有的问题都可以用合同中的文字进行表述,倘若如此,双方当事人的谈判也会举步维艰(甚至因此导致谈判破裂),同时合同本身会因此而浩瀚冗长。因此,在实践中,当事人会尽量规定合同的重大事项与基本细节,在合同的尾部写入法律选择条款,即选择一个法律体系或一系列的法律规则,以"填补"合同最终未能述及的"空白"。例如:This Agreement shall be governed and construed by the laws of People's Republic of China. 该法律选择条款规定中华人民共和国法律为合同的适用法律,对合同进行解释与管辖。国际商务合同往往会涉及多个国家和地区的法律。例如买卖双方来自两个不同的国家,合同的履行地在第三个国家——此时多个国家或地区的法律都与合同相关,因而不可避免地遇到适用法律的选择问题。买方与卖方可能会同时要求选择自己国家(地区)的法律体系,若双方都不同意选择对方国家(地区)的法律体系,往往会选择中立的第三国的法律体系,但此国应具备相当发达的商法体系和政治上相对稳定的国家法律制度,如瑞士法律,以此消除巨大的国际政治不稳定性(Fox,2009:132—133)。

合同各方如此重视合同的适用法律,是因为它关系到"合同的有效性、成立的时间、内容和解释、合同的履行、违约责任,以及对合同的变更、中止、转让、解除、终止的解释"(王相国,2008:129);尤其是在有争议发生时,适用法律成为裁决争议的依据。每一方都想选择自己更熟悉,或是对自己更有利的"游戏规则"。例如美国的大企业往往要求选择特拉华州法律[1],因为该州的法律对企业发展更加重视,有更完备的利于企业发展的法律制度,在一些争议的处理上更倾向于做出对企业有利的判决,从而增加了企业对争议解决结果的可预见性[2]。这个道理就如同大型合资或外资企业在一定时期喜欢在深圳特区和上海的自贸区设立分支机构一样,因为相对而言那里的法规对他们的经营会更有利。

---

[1] 美国存在多个法域:联邦和各州自成法律体系,联邦和各州有独立的立法机关和司法系统。在联邦和各州分享立法权的模式下,商法范畴的法律大多属于州法。虽然美国以统一法律为目标制定了《统一商法典》,且已为大多数州所采用,但《统一商法典》只有在美国某一特定州采纳之后才具有效力。因此,如果合同方希望采用美国《统一商法典》作为合同的适用法律,则必须约定是某一个州,如"纽约州"或"特拉华州"的法律制度,而不是"美国"法律。

[2] 参见 Ashurst Quickguides-Governing Law Clauses. http://www.ashurst.com

(二) 合同适用法律的多样性及相关表述

传统意义上的合同适用法律指的是某个特定的法律体系(a system of law),如中国法律、中国香港法律①、英国法律。伴随国际商务的发展,合同适用法律的选择不再局限于某个法律体系。英美普通法系允许当事人在同一合同中用不同的法律体系分别管辖不同的条款;在国际仲裁中,当事人选择国际公约、商业惯例作为合同适用法的也很常见,如货物买卖合同选择适用《联合国国际货物销售合同公约》。这时,将适用法律限制为某一个法律体系已太狭隘,更贴切的形容应该是法律规则(rules of law)(Maniruzzaman,1999:143)。

"适用法律"在各语言中有不同的表达。英语中的说法,除了在前文使用过的 applicable law,还有 proper law,governing law。proper law 出现得最早,在英国普通法系中以及基于英国法的法系中使用较多。proper law 有其特殊的内涵,它对应的是某一个国家或地区的法律体系(a system of law)。而 applicable law,governing law 没有这样的限制,可以对应我们前文所述的法律规则(rules of law),显然更适合在国际环境下使用,也因此渐渐取代了传统古板的 proper law。

在中国,对适用法律的翻译五花八门。本文中使用的"适用法律",是香港对 applicable law 的译法。由于国内的国际私法学者对 the proper law 的理解各不相同,以致出现了形形色色的译名。例如,李浩培、唐表明、刘慧珊译为"准据法";朱学山译为"宜用法";肖永平、吕岩峰译为"适当法";李双元译为"特有法";卢峻译为"关系法";韩德培、肖永平译为"自体法"②。在所有的翻译中,"准据法"是最被国内法学界认可的。"准据法"其实是19世纪末20世纪初随着国际司法学经从日本传入我国的。在日语中,"准据"写法为"準據"或"準拠",同古汉语,作"依据""根据""标准"解。自20世纪80年代初以来,国内绝大部分国际私法教材使用的都是"准据法"的表述③。随着人们越来越频繁地使用更现代、更中性的 applicable law 和 governing law,更直白的翻译如"适用法""管辖法"逐渐流行。笔者认为"准据法"对外行人来说不易理解,不像"适用法""管辖法"那样平实简朴,让人一目了然。另外,法律选择条款的基本句型不外乎是"本合同适用……法律"或"本合同……受 XX 法律管辖",根本不会有"准据"二字出现。随着时代的发展,proper law 已渐渐被 governing law,applicable law 所取代,以此类推,"准据法"是否也该让贤于"适用法"或"管辖法"呢?

(三) 选择适用法律的限制

在意思自治的原则下④,当事人对适用法律的选择得到了各国立法的尊重与支持,但同时也伴随着不同程度的限制。大多数传统贸易国家的法律选择原则均要求被选择的法律制度与合同本身之间有某种联系。

另外,在一些情况下,即使当事人通过法律选择条款规定了合同的适用法律,也不能避免合同履行地法律的强制适用。比如在我国境内履行的中外合资企业合同、中外合作企业

---

① 中国香港的法律制度以普通法为根基,与内地截然不同。回归后,在"一国两制"的前提下,香港的法律基本不变,法律制度和司法独立,和中华人民共和国的法律制度是两种体系。
② 参见陈卫佐:《论准据法与适当准据法》,《清华法学》2009年第3期,第125页。
③ 参见刘慧珊:《"Proper Law"问题研究》,《国际经济法学刊》2010年第9期,第2,5页。
④ 意思自治原则是指合同当事人可以自由选择处理合同争议所适用的法律原则,它是确定合同准据法的最普遍的原则,*baike.baidu.com/view/183028.htm*。

合同、中外合作勘探开发自然资源合同,自动适用中华人民共和国的法律①,当事人不得自行选择其他适用法律。

当然,对适用法律的选择应该在合同当事人的谈判中解决,并听从专业意见;一旦做出选择,就进入本文的主题——法律选择条款的起草与翻译。

二、法律选择条款的内容、句型及语用特征分析

(一) 典型法律选择条款的句型

典型的法律选择条款的表述,可分为狭义和广义两类。

狭义的法律选择条款如:

① The laws of Switzerland govern this Agreement. 本合同受瑞士法律管辖。

② This Agreement shall be governed by and construed in accordance with the laws of the State of New York, United States of America. 本合同受美国纽约州法律管辖并根据该州法律予以解释。

③ The applicable law of this Agreement shall be English law. 本合同适用英国法。

商业诉讼往往牵涉合同内索赔(contractual claim)与合同外索赔(extra-contractual claim)。对侵权行为中诸如干涉合同、商业欺诈等的申诉都属于合同外索赔。一般来说,当合同双方约定某适用法律对合同进行管辖时,其本意都是希望适用法律能够管辖与合同相关的任何争议,包括合同外索赔。然而,如果法律选择条款按照上述的三种句型写成,往往会被法庭认为是狭义的法律选择条款,而无法管辖合同外索赔②。

所以,尽管以上列出的句型在实践中被频繁使用,若当事人的原意是让适用法律管辖所有与合同相关的争议,合同起草者就应当将当事人的这一意图体现在文字中,许多评论家、法院也都推荐更加详细、广义的表述。

广义的法律选择条款:

① The laws of Switzerland govern all matters arising out of or relating to this Agreement, including and without limitation, its validity, interpretation, construction, performance, and enforcement. (Stark, 2003: 120)

所有因本合同产生或与本合同相关的事宜,包括但不限于其有效性、解释、履行和强制执行,均受瑞士法律的管辖。(笔者译)

---

① 1993年《中华人民共和国合同法》第126条:涉外合同的当事人可以选择处理合同争议所适用的法律,但法律另有规定的除外。涉外合同的当事人没有选择的,适用与合同有最密切联系的国家的法律。在中华人民共和国境内履行的中外合资企业合同、中外合作经营企业合同、中外合作勘探开发自然资源合同,适用中华人民共和国法律。

② 如2005年 Finance One Public Co. Ltd. 诉 Lehman Bros. Special Financing 一案中,联邦上诉法院认为合同的法律选择条款——"Agreement shall be governed by, and construed in accordance with, the internal laws of the State of New York..."未能描述出合同双方的全部关系,适用法律的管辖仅局限在合同中规定的合同方关系,而无法管辖合同规定之外的合同方关系,属于"狭义"的法律选择条款。更多案例详见 Timothy Murray: Drafting Choice of Law Clauses. http://www.mhandl.com/content/draftingchoiceoflawclauses.

② This Agreement and all disputes arising out of or in relation to this Agreement shall be governed by, construed, and enforced in accordance with the laws of the State of New York, United States of America.

本合同及所有因本合同产生或与本合同相关的争议均受美国纽约州法律管辖,并根据该州法律予以解释和强制执行。(笔者译)

③ The applicable law of this Agreement shall be English law and English Law shall be used for interpreting the Agreement and for resolving all claims or disputes arising out of or in connection with the Agreement (whether based on contract, tort or any other legal doctrine).

本合同适用英国法,合同的解释、因本合同产生或与本合同有关的索赔或争议的解决都应适用英国法(不论是否基于合同、侵权或其他法律原则)。(范文祥,2007:196,但笔者对译文做了修订)

这三条广义的法律选择条款,实际上是对前述三条狭义条款的补充(画线部分);与狭义的条款相比,它们的广泛性表现为:

(1) 合同受管辖的范围更广:狭义的条款只规定"本合同"受某法律管辖。但在广义的表述中,所有与本合同有关的事宜或争议都将受到适用法律的管辖(句 3 中甚至列出了"tort"——明确规定"侵权"这种合同外责任亦受到管辖),消除了前者的不确定性。

(2) 适用法律的管辖内容更加明确具体:句 1 中,适用法律对合同的管辖被描述为"including and without limitation, its validity, interpretation, construction, performance, and enforcement",包含了合同及所有与合同相关事宜的有效性、解释、履行和执行(其他更细节性的如合同的订立、变更、中止、转让等等,没有必要一一述明,因为"including and without limitation"已经将其囊括在内)。句 1 中的大部分关键词亦可在句 2、句 3 中见到,如:govern, governed, construction, construed, enforcement, enforced。值得一提的是,普通英语中,construction 的动词原形为 construct,然而在法律英语中 construction 的动词原形为 construe(解释)。下面让我们对这些关键词的法律内涵与使用技巧做一些阐述和分析。

(二) 法律选择条款的关键词

1. govern ——管辖

"管辖"是法律选择条款的主题,管辖意味着适用法律对合同完全彻底的引导、控制与制约。笔者所见的每一条法律选择条款中都使用了 govern(管辖)一词,因此,英文对适用法律的表达除了 applicable law,亦惯用 governing law;法律选择条款除了 choice-of-law clause,亦称作 governing law clause。

2. validity——合同的有效性

在不同法律的管辖下,合同的有效性会产生质的差别。比如,两个公司签约成立合伙公司(partnership),如果该合同适用意大利法律,则该合同自始无效,因为根据意大利法律,公司不能成为合伙成员之一。(范文祥,2007:190)

历史上,美国的法院曾持有一种观点,认为当事人自主选择适用法律是对立法职能的篡夺,所以法院曾将合同的适用法律的作用局限于对合同条款的"解释",而不能作为合同条款"有效性"的判定依据。当然,如今这种观点已被摒弃,当事人选择的适用法律作为判定合同有效性的依据已是不争的事实,即使在法律选择条款中将 validity 这一项省略,也不会产生任何争议;但因为历史上有过相关的辩论,许多合同起草者还是"小心驶得万年船",特别将 validity 写入法律选择条款,以强调适用法律对合同有效性的决定性管辖作用。

3. interpretation & construction——合同(条款)的解释

对合同条款的"解释",毫无疑问,是法律选择条款的基本作用。如有任何一条条款订得不清楚或有漏洞,都需要依靠合同的适用法律做出最终的解释。细心的读者会留意到笔者在广义的示范条款 1 中用了两个近义词 interpretation 和 construction 来表示"解释"。这两个词已经被视为同义词,大多数法律选择条款中也只取其一。

但根据传统的观点,interpret 与 construe 是有区别的:interpret 指对合同方用词背后的"意图"的理解,而 construe 表示对词语的"法律内涵"的判定。比方说,"chicken"一词,若是按更具 common sense 的"interpret"解释,应该是不分大小重量的"鸡";而要是按照"construe"解释,参照相关行业法规,"chicken"专指饲育不足一定时间的"小鸡"(Stark 2003:123)。所以,现在仍有一些合同条款延续传统的写作习惯,将两个词并列使用,例如:This Agreement shall be <u>construed and interpreted</u> in accordance with [applicable law] and the laws of [applicable law] shall govern the dispute。在翻译实践中,这两个词一般被当作配对词(doublets/legal pairs)处理,合二为一地译为"解释"。

4. performance——合同(权利与义务)的履行

选择了合同的适用法律,合同方对合同的履行可做到心中有数。换句话说,若合同方对其在合同下具体的权利与义务存在疑问或争议时,可在合同的适用法律中找到答案,依法履行合同。法律英语中除了用 performance 表达合同的"履行",常见的还有 execution、fulfillment,或是直接表述为 rights and obligations of the parties。但值得注意的是,就合同而言,execution 还是个多义词,出现在合同之首,通常指签署、盖章、交付合同而使之生效,the successful execution of the contract 可以指合同的成功履行,也可以指成功地使合同生效。所以该词的确切词义还要根据上下文而定。但为了避免不必要的误解,笔者还是建议用 perform/performance 一词来表达履行合同的意思。

5. enforcement(dispute resolution)——合同的执行(争议的解决)

如果说 performance(合同的履行)是合同方的主动行为,那么 enforcement(合同的执行)就是合同方依靠法律强制手段的被动行为。在什么情况下合同需要被强制执行? 在当事人之间出现争议、但无法达成一致之时。解决争议有诸多手段——协商、调解、仲裁、诉讼等,其中能保证争议解决结果执行力的只有仲裁与诉讼:仲裁裁决具有终局性,若一方当事人拒绝执行,另一方可以上诉法庭,要求对仲裁裁决予以强制执行;法庭诉讼是争议的终端解决方式,法庭判决具有绝对的终局性和强制执行力。所以,在法律选择条款中规定合同的执行受到适用法律管辖,等同于约定了当事人的仲裁或诉讼程序受到适用法律中相关规则的管辖。

(三) 示范条款

以下是几则法律选择条款的示范条款,这些条款对法律管辖范围的表述均十分广泛,读者可留意画线的关键词的使用。

1. The [applicable law] shall govern <u>all matters arising out of or relating to this Agreement</u>, including but without limitation to its (validity), <u>construction</u>, <u>performance</u>, and <u>enforcement/resolution of disputes</u>.

所有因本协议产生或与本协议相关的事宜,包括但不限于其(有效性)解释、履行以及执行/争议的解决,均受[适用法律]的管辖。

或以被动语态的形式表述:

2. This Agreement and all matters arising out of or relating to this Agreement shall be governed by, construed, performed and enforced in accordance with [applicable law].

本协议以及所有因本协议产生或与之相关事宜,包括其解释、履行和执行/争议的解决,均受[适用法律]的管辖。

3. This Agreement and the resolution of all disputes arising out of or in connection to this Agreement shall be governed by and construed in accordance with [applicable law].

本协议以及所有因本协议产生或与本协议相关的争议解决都受[适用法律]的解释与管辖。

值得注意的是:不论英文条款使用主动语态还是被动语态,翻译成汉语时一般都使用被动语态"受……管辖"。

三、法律选择条款的翻译

经过前一部分对法律选择条款的关键词以及句型的分析,结合笔者给出的示范条款和译文,相信读者对此类条款的翻译已经有了足够的认识。法律选择条款的起草与翻译并不难,以下几例各选自中外合作、合资经营和贸易合同,其中有一些不起眼的小毛病,但却是我国的合同起草人或译者经常忽略的错误或通病。

例1. 本合同的订立、效力、解释、履行和争议的解决均受中华人民共和国法律的保护和管辖。	The conclusion, effect, interpretation, execution and the dispute settlement of this contract shall be under the protection and jurisdiction of the laws of the People's Republic of China. (刘国柱、吴树君,1990:170、183)
例2. 本合同的订立、生效、解释和履行及有关争议的解决,均按中华人民共和国颁布的法律来管辖和解释。	The establishment, effectiveness, interpretation, performance of this Contract and the resolution of disputes hereunder shall be governed by and construed in accordance with the published laws of the People's Republic of China. (刘国柱、吴树君,1990:218、251)
例3. The validity, construction and performance of this Agreement shall be governed and construed in all respects by the laws of Hong Kong.	本合约的有效性、构成和执行须在各方面受香港法律管辖和解释。(薛华业,1989:44)

对以上例句的分析：

1. 适用法律的管辖范围

例 1 和例 2 分别选自中外合作合同与中外合资经营合同，根据我国《合同法》，这两种合同都必须适用中国法律，当事人不得自行选择合同的适用法律。两条条款均是狭义的法律选择条款，未涉及合同外义务的法律管辖问题。尤其是例 2，原中文条款的叙述中包含"本合同有关的争议"，已经说明当事人的意图是让适用法律的管辖范围尽可能地宽泛；但翻译成英文时，"相关"被译成"hereunder"，变成了"under the contract"，范围被局限在本合同之下，与当事人的本意恰恰相反！再一次证明，古旧词不可滥用。

例 3 中"in all respects"，与我们反复论述的 "arising out of or in relation to"类似，同属于广泛用词。但该条款中并未论及对"争议的处理"是否也受到香港法律管辖。除非当事人的本意是让争议的处理适用除香港法律以外的其他法律，否则，应当将"争议的处理"这一重要的因素写入条款。或者干脆将 "validity, construction and performance"也省略，直接表述为：This Agreement shall be governed and construed in all respects by the laws of Hong Kong，与原句相比反而不显得那么狭隘。

2. validity 的译法

validity 在译成中文时，常常被翻译成"效力""生效"，作者认为这些译法是不准确的，因为这些词语在英语中还对应其他的意思，如效力 effect（binding effects），生效 come into effect，若将"效力""生效"进行回译（back-translation），很可能出现其他版本。

例 1 中的"效力"，单单从字面意思分析，很难讲究竟指的是 validity 还是 effect。不过，作者浏览了大量英美合同的法律选择条款，其中有许多包含了 validity，却从未见过哪一条使用 effect 一词。另一方面，从句子的逻辑分析，合同"订立、效力、解释、履行和争议的解决"显然存在时间上的先后顺序。若将"效力"理解为 effect①，与同句中的 performance（履行）的内涵②产生了重叠，这明显打乱了句子的逻辑。所以，例 1 中的"效力"所指的应是合同依法生效、在法律上成立，即 validity。

例 2 中的"生效"被译为 effectiveness，这是译者的英语语言功底不佳或是粗心造成的。实际上，effectiveness 指的是"效果""效能"，译者不能想当然地将其与 come into effect 划为同义。所以将"生效"翻译成 effectiveness 是错误的，对"生效"正确的理解和翻译仍应是 validity。

综上所述，合同起草者与译者应注意区分 validity 和 effect 的法律内涵，一份合同要先有了自身的 validity，才会对合同方产生 effect。在翻译过程中，最好将 validity 与"有效性"相对应，将"effect"与"效力"对应，以免混淆。

3. construction 不是指"建设"或"构成"

例 3 中，译者将 construction 理解为合同的构成。实际上，这里的 construction 的原形是 construe。即使在相隔了九个单词之后，construe 以动词的被动形式 construed 又出现了一次，译者也未能意识到这一点。所以，该条款正确的译文应是：本合约的有效性、<u>解释</u>和执行须在各方面受香港法律管辖和<u>解释</u>。可见英文原文也不是十全十美，construe 以名词和

---

① 布莱克法律大辞典和元照英美法词典对 effect(n.)的解释是合同方签订的法律文本对合同方的相关权利造成的结果。在法律选择条款的语境下，effect 指的就是合同方签署的合同对各自权利带来的影响。

② 合同的"履行"指的就是合同方在合同约束下的具体的权利和义务。

动词的被动形式先后出现了两次,正确的做法是将后面出现的 construed 删去。

专业从事法律翻译的译者应区分一些英语单词在普通英语环境与法律英语环境中迥然不同的意义,如:award(奖励—裁决),presents(文件—法律文本),save(节省—除……外),等等[①]。

4. jurisdiction 的误用

govern 一般被译成"管辖",jurisdiction 可以被译成"管辖权",这也许是译者选择将"管辖"译为 jurisdiction 的原因。但 jurisdiction 指的是法院或法官的审判权或行使司法权力的地域限制[②];与之相关的英文表述一般有 sth. is under jurisdiction of the courts of a country/district 或是 a country/district has jurisdiction over sth.。但例 1 中的"... under jurisdiction of the laws of the People's Republic of China",经过回译,就变成"中国法律对合同有管辖的'权力'"。显然,该条款的译者将"管辖"误译成 jurisdiction 是欠缺法律专业知识、滥用同义词所导致。

5. protection 的文化内涵

许多中外合资、合作合同的法律选择条款的句型一律是"合同……受中华人民共和国法律的保护和管辖"(如例 1)。与国际上通行的法律选择条款相比,"保护"一词无疑是"中国特色"。改革开放以来,引进外资成为中国经济增长的重要方式。作为外商投资的东道国,我国在强调对外资企业进行法律管辖的同时,在相关政策、法规中亦频频使用"保护"一词以增加外商的投资信心。法律选择条款中的"保护"一词是受到了国家改革开放政策大环境的影响的特殊用词,并非是写作该条款的典型用词。任何个人或企业的合法行为,即使在没有特别规定的情形下,也都受到所在国的法律的"保护",而不需要特别提出"保护",倘若如此,那就是特权式的保护,体现不出法律面前人人(包括法人)平等的司法理念。

四、非典型的法律选择条款

(一) 排除冲突法的法律选择条款

冲突法(或称"国际私法")是一系列的程序性规则,决定着一项民商事争议的适用法律及管辖权。尤其是争议涉及国际因素时,例如当事人来自不同国家(或同一个国家内的不同法域,如美国、加拿大、澳大利亚都是多法域国家)。即使当事人在法律选择条款中规定了合同适用某国法律,也不排除在该国的冲突法原则下,法院将某个争议的适用法律判为其他法律。(但如果当事人选择的法律为欧盟国家的法律,就不涉及冲突法的问题。因为 1980 年《罗马公约》第 15 条规定:"凡适用依本公约确定的任何国家的法律,意即适用该国现行的法律规则而非适用其国际私法规则。")

因为冲突法涉及很多不确定的因素,令合同双方很难把握。所以,有的合同会排除有潜在冲突的法律、国际惯例或国际条款的适用。举个例子,我国加入的《联合国国际货物销售公约》(以下简称"CISG"),适用于营业地在不同国家当事人之间所订立的货物买卖合同(但这种适用不具有强制性)。假设当事人在货物买卖合同中明确规定适用中国法律,公约仍可

---

① 参见李克兴:《法律翻译理论与实践》,北京:北京大学出版社,2007 年,第 28、29 页。
② 参见 L.B. 科尔森:《朗文法律词典》(第六版)或《布莱克法律大辞典》(第九版)。

以作为中国法律的补充;除非双方当事人在法律选择条款中明确规定不适用该公约,方能完全排除该公约的适用①,具体的表述如:

CISG <u>shall not apply</u> to this Agreement or any disputes...

本协议以及任何……争议<u>不适用</u>《联合国国际货物销售公约》。

This Agreement and all matters... shall be governed and construed by..., <u>without any applicability of CISG</u>.

本协议以及所有……事宜的解释与管辖适用 XX 法律,但<u>不适用</u>《联合国国际货物销售公约》。

还有一种常见的情况是当事人直接在法律选择条款中约定排除冲突法原则,如:

This Agreement shall be governed by and construed in accordance with the domestic laws of the People's Republic of China.

本协议受中华人民共和国法律管辖与解释。

a) <u>without giving effect to</u> principles of conflicts of law.

冲突法原则<u>无效</u>。

或:b) <u>without giving effect to</u> any choice or conflict of law provision or rule that would cause the application of the laws of any jurisdictions other than the People's Republic of China.

导致合同适用除中华人民共和国之外的其他法域之法律的选择或冲突法规则<u>无效</u>。

或:c) <u>regardless of</u> the laws that might otherwise govern under applicable principles of conflicts of laws.

不得适用冲突法原则之下的其他法律。②

综上所述,在法律选择条款中将冲突法原则"一棒子打死"的表述是不可取的。在选择适用法律时,尽量选择合同签订地或与合同标的的执行有关联的法域的法律,这么一来,有争议发生时,法律选择条款无论如何是不会被法院判为"无效"的。既然是有效的法律选择条款,法院就不会再用冲突法原则来寻找其他适用法律。当事人切忌"标新立异"或"崇洋媚外"地选择一个与合同无密切联系的国家法律。以合同双方分别是中国公司与美国加州公司为例,适用法律最好选择中国法律(若合同在中国签订)或加州法律(若合同在加州签订)。

---

① 参见杜新立:《国际司法实务中的法律问题》,北京:中信出版社,2005年,第141页。
② 这种排除冲突法原则的表述在美国最为常见,而且有相当一部分律师都习惯了在法律选择条款中这么写,甚至把这种写法作为格式条款加以推广。但是笔者认为,这样的表述可以说是"画蛇添足"。首先,诉讼地的法院要运用本地的冲突法规则来判断当事人的适用法律选择是否有效,如果排除了冲突法的适用,法律选择条款本身的有效性便无从判定。其次,如果在本地的冲突法规则下,当事人选择的适用法是有效的,法院就不会运用冲突规则来选择其他法律,当事人对适用法律的选择会得到法院的尊重和采纳;但如果当事人的选择在本地的冲突法规则下是无效的,即使事先在法律选择条款中约定"排除冲突法的适用",也无法把无效的选择变得有效。第三,有的起草人在条款中写入"排除冲突法的适用",有可能是想排除诉讼地冲突法中的"强制规则",在强制规则下,当事人选择的法律会被其他法律替代。强制规则例如外国破产法律程序,国家行为原则等等,这些原则下强制适用的法律不容得当事人"排除"。第四,有的起草人的目的可能是要排除冲突法中的"反致学说"。但诉讼地的法院会如何解读,是否会尊重当事人的意思不接受"反致",目前还没有定论。

（二）结语：同一个合同由多个适用法律管辖

有的合同当事人选择不同的法域管辖合同的不同部分，或是约定不同的情况适用不同的法律。当有纠纷发生时，这可能会导致巨大的混乱，但往往法院仍会尊重当事人合法合理的选择。下例选自 Adobe 系统终端用户软件许可证协议[①]，兹录于此，既作为本章的结语，也提供给读者参考和思考：

> This Agreement, each transaction entered into hereunder, and all matters arising from or related to this Agreement (including its validity and interpretation), will be governed and enforced by and construed in accordance with the substantive laws in force in:
>
> (a) the State of California, if a license to the Materials is purchased when you are in the United States, Canada, or Mexico;
>
> or (b) Japan, if a license to the Materials is purchased when you are in Japan, China, Korea, or other Southeast Asian country where all official languages are written in either an ideographic script (e. g., hanzi, kanji, orhanja), and/or other script based upon or similar in structure to an ideographic script, such as hangul or kana;
>
> or (c) England, if a license to the Materials is purchased when you are in any other jurisdiction not described above.

> 本协议、本协议下订立的所有交易以及所有因本协议产生或与本协议相关的事宜（包括其有效性与解释）均根据以下各国现行有效的实体法予以管辖和执行：
>
> （a）如果资料的许可协议是用户在美国、加拿大或墨西哥境内购得，则适用美国加利福尼亚州法律；
>
> 或（b）如果资料的许可协议是用户在官方语言为象形文字（如汉字、日本汉字、韩文汉字）或与象形文字结构相似的文字（如韩文、日语假名）的国家购得，包括中国、日本、韩国或其他东南亚国家，则适用日本法律；
>
> 或（c）如果资料的许可协议是用户在除上述国家以外的其他法域购得，则适用英国法律。（笔者译）

从以上条款的行文中，读者可以观察到，合同适用多个法域，情形该有多混乱，写法该有多啰嗦和武断，因为世界上司法独立的国家目前有 224 个[②]，我们不可能去穷尽所有的适用的法域，如果只列出以上提到的几个国家，凭什么？所以，这类形式主义的条文，不能照搬照抄，人云亦云。关于这一条，最简洁、最有逻辑、最公平的写法应该是：

> This Agreement, each transaction entered into under it, and all matters arising from or related to this Agreement (including its validity and interpretation), shall be governed and enforced by and construed in accordance with the substantive laws in force in the country or territory where a license to the Materials is purchased. （笔者改写）

---

① 参见 Adobe 公司官方网站，http://www.adobe.com/cn/devnet/livecycle/licenseagreement.html.
② wenwen.soso.com/z/q84312938.htm.

第二十一章 通知条款的写作、翻译和研究

一、引言

(一) 一般通知条款与具体通知条款

通知条款(Notice Clause)规定了在合同期间双方相互传递信息的方式。通知条款分一般通知条款和具体通知条款。一般通知条款出现在合同的格式条款中,规定合同下所有通知的一般程序;具体通知条款散落在合同各处,约定在某个"事件"出现时或需要达到某个"目的"时发送通知。一般通知条款统领具体通知条款并与之共同发挥作用。比方说,当事人在合同中约定要行使优先购买权,或是向对方提出违约的抗议,或是声明获得某项赔偿的权利,都需要以通知的方式提出,这些条款属于具体通知条款。而通知的格式、如何寄出、何时生效等问题,都是在一般通知条款中做统一规定的。本文研究的是格式条款中的一般通知条款。

某些人以为一般通知条款的起草只是一种"例行公事",从而忽略了其重要性。但一般通知条款是与合同中相当一部分具体通知条款协同作用的,那些条款得以实现的前提是当事人根据一般通知条款正确地履行通知义务。一则通知究竟是有效还是无效,得对照通知条款中的标准判定。通知条款拟得不好,会给当事人带来一定的麻烦和风险,甚至还可能造成合同的无法执行。

(二) 投邮主义与到达主义

通知条款源于英美法系的投邮主义(Mail-box Rule)[①]。投邮主义指以书信、电报做出的承诺,一经投邮即发生法律效力。按此原则,受要约人只要将做出承诺的书信投入邮箱或电报交邮局发出,承诺即生效。即使邮局疏忽,使承诺在传递中遗失,也不妨碍承诺的效力,从这个角度讲,接收方须承担风险。但另一方面,如果接收方接受了发送方的承诺,再以相同的途径回复给发送方,接收方便获得了相应的权利,而万一接收方不知情的话,风险便转嫁给了发送方。可以说,投邮主义是一种风险分配机制(Risk Allocation Mechanism)。

将投邮主义的概念应用到现代的通知条款中,举个例子:某借款人用其持有的股票作抵押向银行借款,在他逾期未还款时,银行通知他立刻还款,否则在邮寄出通知的五天后仍未

[①] "投邮主义"(或"发信主义")是从 Mail-box Rule 翻译而来,并已为国内普遍使用。中国人好讲"主义",这种偏好亦被带入了翻译中。一个 Mail-box Rule 是否真的够得上"主义"的高度? 笔者认为,若非表示一种理念或有完整体系的思想和信念,最好避开"主义"一词,结合原文的法律内涵,恰当的翻译应当是"投邮生效规则"。同理,下文的 Effectiveness upon Receipt,国内普遍译为"到达主义"(或"收信主义")。但因为"投邮主义"和"到达主义"已经成一种"约定俗成"的译文,本文也尊重并沿用这种为大众所接受的译法。

能还款的话,借款人即是违约,银行会取消他赎回抵押品的权利。于是,银行以邮寄的方式将通知发送给了借款人。但不幸的是,这封信偏偏在递送过程中弄丢了,最终借款人的股票被银行没收。可以说,借款人无计可施,因为在他签订借款合同时,即同意了合同中基于"投邮主义"的通知条款(Stark,2003:464)。

当然,这种风险分配机制是可以修改的。与"投邮主义"相对立的,是大陆法系中的"收信主义",又称"到达主义"(Effectiveness upon Receipt),主张发送方的承诺要到达接收人时承诺才生效。所谓到达,并不指接收方亲自收到电报、信函,而仅以到达接收方支配范围以内为必要,例如,邮差将信交于接收方的信箱或指定的收件人,均认定为到达。如果把到达主义的概念运用到上例中,借款人可以在和银行签订合同时指出:通知必须要在送达接收方时方才生效。这么一来,借款人便成功将部分风险转移给银行,如果通知没有成功递送给他,银行无权没收他的股票。

曾经,信件被认作是除专人递送以外最可靠的沟通方式,投邮主义也相应地得以广泛应用。在现代,更多人认为快递、传真和电子邮件更为可靠,导致这类通知"发送不成功"的因素更多来源于发送方;另一方面,通知的目的主要是交流信息,如果通知无法送达到接收方的话,便失去了意义,所以越来越多的通知条款主张"到达"生效。无论是"投邮主义"或"到达主义",都是为了平衡当事人之间的利益和风险。在起草通知条款时,合同起草者应平衡合同双方的风险,结合通知的实际目的以制定出一条公平、可行的通知条款。

二、一般通知条款的主要内容、句型和语用特征分析

一般通知条款应包括以下几个方面的内容:1)通知的形式(What),包括通知的范围、书面要求、签署要求;2)发送方式(How),一般有专人递送、传统的邮件(如航空信、挂号信)、快递、传真、电传①、电子邮件;3)接收方及其地址(Where);以及 4)生效时间(When),是"投邮生效"还是"到达生效"。这样的顺序也反映了现实中一条通知从起草、发出、送达、生效的程序。

(一) 通知的形式(What)

几乎所有的通知条款都会在一开头就约定通知的形式,包括①通知的范围、②书面形式的要求、③用什么语言、④签署要求,其句型可归纳如下:

    All notices, requests, claims, demands and other communications hereunder ① shall be in writing② [in the XXX language③] [and shall be signed by XXX to provide such notice]. ④

① 因为要适用于合同中规定的各种情况,所以通知的范围越广泛越好。上例中,所有的合同约定范围内的沟通(包括最基本的通知、请求、索赔、要求)都在通知范围之内。hereunder 即 under this Agreement,两种表达相比之下,后者更符合法律语言现代、简明的发展趋势;相同效果的表达还有: in accordance with the Agreement;更广泛的用词是 in

---

① 电传是对电报技术进行技术革新后的一种通讯手段,是国际信用证交易中所使用的传统通讯方式。如今,绝大多数企业或个人更加依赖电邮、传真和快递的通知发送手段;除非合同涉及国际贸易,否则没有必要规定将电传作为一种通知发送方式写入合同。尽管如此,不少合同样本的通知条款中依然包含了电传,这是起草人未独立思考、照搬过时样本的表现。

connection to/in relation to the Agreement，表示凡是与本合同有关系的沟通，都在可通知的范围之内；这些短语常常和 under 连用，即 under or in connection to the Agreement，或 under or in relation to the Agreement①当然，对传统法律语言风格情有独钟的作者一定会选择 pursuant to 去表达相同的概念。

② 通知应该使用书面形式。书面的通知保障了被传递信息的可靠性，同时也为通知的发送提供了证据。几乎所有通知条款都会要求通知以书面形式。更有不厌其烦者，将通知条款包含的所有通知发送方式都规定为书面形式，如：

  Each party giving any notice or making any request, demand or other communication shall be <u>in writing</u> and shall use one of <u>the following methods of delivery</u>, each of which, for the purpose of this Agreement, <u>is a writing</u>: (i)Personal delivery. (ii)Registered Mail. (iii)Email②...

也有通知条款规定了某些情况下"口头通知"亦有效（如电话通知，但非常少见），这时只要在书面通知的约定之后加上 except for..., in which event oral notice may be given（除非在……情况下，可以做出口头通知）。"书面""口头"搭配的情态动词分别是 shall 和 may，shall 对应的翻译是"应、须"，may 对应的翻译是"可以"。足见书面通知是通知应有的形式，而口头通知只能存在于个别特殊情况。如果要强调"书面形式"是通知有效性的先决条件，只需将 shall 换成 must 即可，因为 must 的强制性高于前者。

③ 在双方当事人使用不同语言时，往往会约定通知的语言：或是使用一种语言（shall be in English/Chinese）；或是使用一种语言并提供翻译作参照（shall be in English/Chinese, accompanied by a translation into Chinese/English）；或是两种语言（shall be made both in English and Chinese, and both language versions shall be equally authentic），这种情况往往是跟从了主合同中"双语同等有效"的规定。

④ 公司高级管理者的行为对外代表着公司行为，所以公司文件的签署人往往是公司董事长/董事/总经理。这样的常识性规定在通知条款中往往被省略。当然也可以特别规定由固定的联络人或担任某职务的人签署通知。另外，在信息技术高度发展的今天，"签署"已不仅仅指用笔签名或公司盖章，广义的署名指的是"一方当事人为了证实其书面文件的真实性而在当时采用的任何符号"③。随着当事人越来越依赖电子邮件发送通知，"数字签名"技术也应运而生。如果双方当事人希望通过邮件方式通知对方，而不使用传统的签名的话，也可以使用数字签名④或其他身份识别代码，以验证通知的真实性。

综上所述，在"通知的形式"部分，通知的范围和书面要求是必要的，而语言要求和署名要求则根据具体情况加以约定。以下几例是对"通知的形式"的比较完整的表达，其主要内

---

 ① 对范围的广泛的表达方式，详见本书"仲裁条款"相关章节。
 ② 各国法律上已经确认了包括电子邮件在内的书面形式地位。我国《合同法》第 11 条规定：合同的书面形式是指合同书、信件和数据电文（包括电报、电传、传真、电子数据交换和电子邮件）等可以有形地表现所在内容的形式。
 ③ 见《美国统一商法典》§1201.(38) Signed includes any symbol executed or adopted by a party with present intention to authenticate a writing.
 ④ 通过对电子邮件进行数字签名，可将唯一数字标记应用于邮件。数字签名包括证书和公钥，它们源自数字标识。经过数字签名的邮件可向收件人证明该邮件的内容是经您签名的而非冒名，而且内容在传输过程中未被修改。为了更好地保护隐私，还可以对电子邮件进行加密。摘自微软办公软件官方网站，http://office.microsoft.com/zh-cn/outlook-help/HP010355563.aspx.

容不外乎以上四点。

例 1. Any notice or communication under or in connection with this Agreement① shall be made in English or Chinese③ in writing② and signed by or on behalf of the party giving it④.（范文祥,2007:210）

例 2. 1.1 Any notice given under or in connection with this Agreement① shall only be effective if given in writing② in English③ by one of the methods specified in Clause 1.2.（范文祥,2007:208）

例 3. Each party giving any notice or making any request, demand, or other communication (each, a "Notice")① pursuant to this Agreement shall

(a) give the Notice in writing②; and

(b) cause the Notice to be signed by XXX④. （Stark,2003:473）

以上各段的注释标记,与该段之前的说明相符,例 3)有缺项（即缺第③项）,其实用何种语言并不重要,这是翻译的工作,不管用何种语言,我们译者都可以做好。

（二）发送方式(How)和生效时间(When)

1. 发送方式与生效时间的关系

伴随通知的生效,权利和义务也随之而来。因此通知条款中对生效时间的约定显得尤其重要。前文已经介绍过"投邮主义"和"到达主义",通知的生效时间相应地分为"投邮生效"和"到达生效"。各国法律对通知生效的时间有不同规定,但通常情况下,当事人可以自行约定通知的生效时间。我国法律对于通知采用"到达生效",即通知到达对方时生效,这就要求发送方就接收方是否已经收到通知承担举证责任(能够证明对方已经收到通知的证据,如签收收据、邮件回复)。但在实务当中,有时候根本无法实际送达。要么根本找不到接收方,要么接收方拒绝签收。针对这种情况就要考虑在合同当中双方是否明确约定过采用"投邮生效",以降低举证不能的风险①。

通知的发送方式和生效时间是紧密相连的,一则通知以不同方式发出,这则通知的生效时间也会有所不同。以下两例分别代表了"到达生效"与"投邮生效"的通知条款。

例 4. ... A Notice is deemed to have been received as follows:

a. If a Notice is delivered in person, or sent by Registered or Certified Mail②, or nationally [or internationally] recognized overnight courier③, upon receipt as indicated by the date on the signed receipt.

b. If a Notice is sent by facsimile④, upon receipt by the party giving or making the

---

① 见王荣洲律师:《如何起草合同中的通知条款》,http://blog.sina.com.cn/s/blog_8709f80c0100yrkb.html。

② Register mail 即挂号信,Certified mail 译为"保证邮件"。中国邮政不提供保证邮件业务。两者共同点是邮局会向发送方提供一份交邮收据,若额外付费,发送方还可获得送达回执。两者的区别是,保证邮件走的是普通信件的系统,发送方只能查讯邮件是否已经签收。挂号信走的是独立的系统,途中的每一站都有记录可查(现在中国邮政的挂号信也可以进行网上查询)。

③ 隔夜快递是承诺接件后 24 小时内送达的快递服务。

④ facsimile 有两层意思,一是摹真本或复制品;二是作为现代通讯手段的传真。facsimile 的缩写 fax 专指"传真"。在本文中,fascimile 也是传真的意思。

Notice of an acknowledgement or transmission report generated by the machine from which the facsimile was sent indicating that the facsimile was sent in its entirety to the Addressee's facsimile number.

　　c. If a Notice is sent by e-mail [insert agreed-upon standard].

(Stark, 2003:476)

　　上例是一则典型的"送达生效"的通知条款。送达的方式囊括了专人递送、挂号信或保证邮件、隔夜快递、电传、邮件,且这些方式有一个共同点——都很容易获取对方已收到通知的证据:如果是专人送达或快递送达的通知,可以要求签收人签署回执(receipt);如果是挂号信送达的通知,邮局会保留有邮递记录供发送方查询(另付费用也能获得邮件送达的回执);如果是经传真发送的通知,大多数传真机都会自动插入信息来源、发送与接收的号码和时间,这些信息本身已经可以作为通知已经到达对方的证据;如果是经电子邮件发送的通知,双方可以约定一个确认通知到达接收方的标准,一般有:1)发送方邮件系统显示已发送视为送达,2)发送方邮件系统显示到达对方服务器时视为送达,3)到达对方服务器视为送达①。

　　几种发送方式中,用电子邮件发送通知的方式比较特殊。越来越多的当事人倾向使用电子邮件发送通知。不可否认,电子邮件沟通即时,方便快捷,但现今垃圾邮件泛滥,一封通知很有可能被接收方在无意中忽略或删除。所以除非是当事人坚持,律师一般不会将电子邮件列入发送通知的可行方式②。即使是承认了电子邮件发送通知的有效性,也会要求接收方以电话或其他书面方式回复发送方,以确认收到了通知(有时用传真发送的通知也会有这样的要求)。所以对例4的条款可以做如下补充:

　　If a Notice is sent by e-mail or facsimile, the Addressee [shall confirm the receipt by telephone] [shall provide the Addresser a confirmation copy delivered by facsimile/registered mail/overnight courier].

　　有的通知会给接收方带来不利的后果,接收方会故意逃避或拒绝签收。"投邮主义"排除了这种风险;但"送达生效"的通知,如上例所示,往往需要接收方签署送达的收据或是主动以其他方式向发送方确认通知的收悉。为了防范接收方"拒收"的风险,例4中的通知条款可以再加上一句:

　　A party's failure to confirm the receipt of a Notice does not affect the effectiveness of a Notice.

　　虽然通知条款的"到达生效"已经成为主流,但传统的"投邮生效"也有重要的意义,如银行给客户发送的一般通知往往采用"投邮生效":

　　例 5. 15.4 Any notice:

　　15.4.1 sent by prepaid registered post will be deemed to have been received on the 5th (fifth) business day after posting.

---

　　① 我国《合同法》第16条规定:采用数据电文形式订立合同,收件人指定特定系统接收数据电文的,该数据电文进入该特定系统的时间,视为到达时间;未指定特定系统的,该数据电文进入收件人的任何系统的首次时间,视为到达时间。

　　② 律师 Daniel A. Batterman 建议不将电子邮件作为常规的通知发送方法。详见:http://www.battermanlaw.com/articles/boilerplate-contracts-part1.html。

15.4.2 sent by ordinary mail will be deemed to have been received on the 7th (seventh) business day after posting.

15.4.3 delivered by hand will be deemed to have been received on the day of delivery.

15.4.4 sent by telefax or email will be deemed to have been received on the 1st (first) business day after the date it was sent.

——Standard Bank(渣打银行)信用卡使用条款

例5中,无论是哪种通知发送方式,银行都规定通知在发出的当日或发出一段时间后即视为送达。条款的潜台词是:客户将自行承担通知发送失败的风险。如果银行有1 000万的信用卡客户,每个月单单是信用卡账单就至少有1 000万张。如果将通知条款制定为"到达生效",那么银行需要跟进每个通知的投递进度,甚至向客户索取回执,这不但是时间与成本的巨大消耗,更重要的是增加了银行的风险,如果滞期还款的客户以未收到账单为由拒绝付利息,银行举证时又无法提供通知已经送达客户处的证据,那银行大概是收不回利息了。

2. 表述方式

笔者观察了大量通知条款,将其中对"发送方式"和"生效时间"的表述进行拆解、归纳,将其关键词语与句型总结如下:

发送方式的关键词和句型结构:

——[Notice] shall be delivered/sent/given/addressed by [manner] to [addressee & address].

——[Addresser] shall notify/deliver/send [addressee] [notice] by [manners] to [addressee & address]。

通知生效时间的关键词和句型结构:

——[Notice] shall be (considered/deemed) effective/received/given/served

到达生效 { (confirmed/acknowledged) delivery/transmission...
upon receipt (as confirmed/indicated by...)
conditional clause

投邮生效 { upon the delivery at/to...
at the time of sending or the next business day
upon/on the [ordinal number] (business) day after...
after [number] (business) days
upon/on the earlier of [默认送达之日] or [实际送达之日]
conditional clause

根据以上对句型的分析,我们可以得出以下几点结论:

(1) 表达"生效"不一定用 effective。其他单词如 given,delivered,received,served 虽然字面意思与效力没有半点关系,但它们都是形容词性的动词过去分词,暗示了通知发送成功的状态。在翻译这些词语时,译者应根据其法律内涵,结合动词本身的字面意思译成"送达""收悉"。另一方面,在表示发送的动作时,例如:A Notice shall be given/delivered/sent by...,一模一样的单词,意义却不同,在这里是表示动作的被动语态,正确的翻译应是"发送""递送"。例如:

Any notice required to be given by you to us shall be in writing and shall be deemed to have been so given if addressed to us at the address hereinafter mentioned.

贵行给本公司的任何通知应该是书面的,而且如果按照下述地址给本公司的通知均应被认为已经致送。(薛华业,1989:164)

这则通知条款中 given 出现了两次,第一个表示的是发送的"动作",被译成"给"(更书面的译文可以是"发送");第二个 given 表示的是将通知视为"生效",被译成"致送",可见译者正确理解了原文的法律内涵,当然,也可以更直白地译成"送达""生效"或"送达生效"。

(2) 如果是"到达生效"的通知,发送方往往会要求接收方签署回执、提供确认函。如果是"投邮生效"的通知,或是规定通知一旦发送立刻生效(有时候通知发出时已经是下班时间或正值节假日,这种情况会规定通知在发出后第一个工作日生效),或是规定在发出后默认的某个时间生效。

值得注意的是,在投邮生效的若干种表达方式中,规定通知送出后若干个工作日生效(... after [number] business days 或 upon/on the [ordinal number] (business) day after...)是最不容易引发不必要的商业纠纷的表达方式。如果规定通知发出那一刻即生效,或者某一个日期生效,可能恰好遇上对方的假期,如圣诞、春节等,容易引发双方争执。另外,规定通知送出后若干个工作日视为送达,是发送者对送达所需时间的估计,我们可以称之为"默认送达之日"。但事实上,接收方收到通知的时间很可能早于默认送达之日。比如例 5 中,15.4.1 款规定若使用挂号信发送通知时,通知在寄出后第五个工作日视为送达,但实际上有的客户在第二个工作日就收到了通知。这种情况,应该在"默认送达之日"和"实际送达之日"中认定较早的一个为通知生效的时间。所以 15.4.1 款可以改为:sent by prepaid registered post will be deemed to have been received on the earlier of [5th (fifth) business day after posting] or [receipt].

(3) 现代的合同中往往会约定多种通知发送方式,而且各种方式下通知的生效时间也互不相同,这种情况下最合适的表达方式是用多个条件句分别进行表述。

现将上面几点结论运用到以下几例的分析中:

例 6. 1.1 Any notice given under or in connection with this Agreement shall only be effective if given in writing in English by one of the methods specified in Clause 4.2. Service of notice by telex, e-mail or international airmail shall not be effective.

1.2 A notice shall be addressed as provided in Clause 4.3 and shall be (a) personally delivered, in which case it shall be deemed to have been given upon delivery at the relevant address; or (b) if within the United States, sent by first class pre-paid post[①], in which case it shall be deemed to have been given two Business Days after the date of posting; or (c) if from or to any place outside the United States, sent by courier[②] in which case it shall be deemed to have been given two Business Days after

---

① first class pre-paid post 即"一等邮资预付邮件",是美国邮局的一项服务,由发送方负担邮资,邮局承诺三天内将信件或物品送达;适合商业往来中单据、文件的发送。

② Courier 可译成"快递"或"速递",其特点包括:专人揽件与派件,快捷,安全,可查询寄件状态,需收件方签收等等,因此区别于传统的邮政服务;又因为快递服务只能寄送质量轻、体积小的信件和包裹,所以也不同于快运(express shipping)。另外,courier 本身也可以指快递公司,尤其是大型的国内或跨国快递公司。

delivery to the courier; or (d) sent by facsimile, in which case it shall be deemed to have been given when dispatched, but shall only be effective if its uninterrupted transmission can be confirmed by a transmission report of sender. Any notice given or deemed to have been given after 17:00 on any Business Day or at any time on a day which is not a Business Day shall be deemed to have been given at 09:00 on the next Business Day.

(范文祥,2007:207)

例6中,1.1款规定了通知应当按照本协议第4.2款规定的方法之一递送,且明确规定使用电传、电子邮件和国际航空件发送的通知无效。1.2款中使用多个if条件句说明各个发送方式及该方式下通知的生效时间：(a)如果是专人递送,通知在送到相应地址时视为送达；(b)如果收件地址在美国境内,可使用一等邮资预付邮件,在邮寄之日后的两个工作日后视为寄抵；(c)如果收件地址在美国境外,可使用快递寄送,在快递员取件后的第三到第五个工作日视为寄抵(根据航班频密或路途距离有所差异,如在加拿大或墨西哥境内第三个工作日基本上是有保障的)；(d)如果采用传真,则传真发出时即视为送达,但只有在发送方的传真报告证实传真被完整发送时方才有效。(a)和(d)属于"到达生效",(b)和(c)属于"投邮生效"。该条款最后还有一点补充：任何在工作日17点整后送达或非工作日送达的通知应视为在下一个工作日的上午9点送达。

例7. All notices, demands and other communications to be given hereunder shall be made by registered airmail, or cable or telex followed by a confirmation letter, to [addressee & address*]. All notices, demands and other communications mentioned above shall be deemed to have been given or made at the date of their dispatch. (薛华业,1989:48)

*此处省略,详见第(三)部分——接收方和地址

例7的通知条款选自一个比较老的代理与经销合约。条款规定的通知发送方式有挂号航空件、电报或电传,可以推断出这是一个跨国合约,且当时连传真机和电脑都没有普及。对生效时间的约定是传统的"投邮生效"：规定一切通知在发出时即视为送达,因此也没有必要附带提出其他条件,不跟任何条件句。

(三) 接收方和地址(Where)

1. 合同方及其地址

所有合同方既可能成为发送方,也可能成为接收方。所以接收方理所当然包括所有的合同方。合同方的地址,并非狭义上的住宅或办公地址。现代合同中常见的各合同方的地址应包含邮寄地址、快递地址、传真号码和电子邮箱地址,具体表述如下：

① [Notice] shall be addressed as follows：
  Party A: Name ＿＿＿＿＿ (自然人或法人名称)
    Attention ＿＿＿＿＿ (收件人：接收方为法人时,往往要额外规定一个收件人,否则的话通知很可能无法及时交到负责人手中,或被遗忘在公司的收发室,或被留在传真机上无人问津)

Mailing Address _____（邮寄地址：可能是住宅/办公地址，也可能是邮政信箱；邮寄地址须包含邮编）

Courtier Address _____（快递地址：与邮寄地址不同时须写收件人名）

Telephone No. _____（用快递作为通知方式时须写收件人名；通知条款规定接收方收到通知后用电话予以确认时也须写收件人名）

Facsimile No. _____（传真号码）

E-mail _____（电子邮箱地址）

Party B：同上

这里有必要提一提邮寄地址的排列规矩以及中英文在表述上的不同：

中文表述是由大到小： 香港 九龙旺角 弥敦道 500 号风景阁 一座 10 层 G 室	英文则是由小到大： Flat G, 10th Floor, Tower One, Vista Court, Nathan Street ♯500, Mong Kok, Kowloon, Hong Kong

若合同起草者或是译者将中英文对地址的叙述顺序弄错，可能功亏一篑，让外方认为你不够专业，贻笑大方。

其实，许多合同中的签署页或附件就包含了以上信息。不想通知条款过长的话，可以在通知条款中约定使用签署页或附件中列出的当事人地址，相关的表述如下：

② ——[Notice] shall be delivered to the address on the signature page.
——[Notice] shall be sent to the receiving party/addressee whose address is set forth on Exhibit XX.

另外，合同方的地址有可能会变更，而且在企业或组织内部的管理层也有流动性，所以对地址和收件人的变更情况做出规定是合同通用条款中的标准作法，常见的表述有：

③ ——Any party may change its address by giving notice in writing to the other.
——Any party to this Agreement may notify any other party of any changes to the address or any of the other details specified in this paragraph.
——[Notice] shall be delivered to the address set forth above or to such other address as either party may from time to time specify in writing to the other party.

在①表列形式的地址和②签署页（附件页）地址中择其一，与③变更的地址组合起来，便可以得出一个关于合同方及其地址的完整通用条款，例如：

Each party giving a Notice shall address the Notice to the appropriate person at the receiving party (the "Addressee")
① at the following address / ②at the address set forth on the signature page
③ or to other address(es) as may be notified by a party in writing to the other party.

2. 非合同方及其地址

许多通知条款规定,通知的发送方还包括合同签署方以外的"非合同方"。这些非合同方往往是合同方各自的顾问、律师,或是在合同执行过程中能够起到辅助作用的一方。"非合同方"地址的表述往往置放在"合同方"地址之后。

(1) 对非合同方地址的表述

如果合同方地址是按上文所述①表列形式写入通知条款的,那么可在合同方地址下方注明:"with a copy to XXX"(发送副本至:XXX),再附上"非合同方"的地址:

① Party A: Name _____
    Attention _____
    Mailing Address _____
    Courtier Address _____ (if different)
    Telephone No. _____ (for verification purpose only)
    Facsimile No. _____
    E-mail _____
    [with a copy to: Party A's counsel]
  Party A's counsel: Name _____
      Attention _____
      Mailing Address _____
      Courtier Address _____ (if different)
      Telephone No. _____ (for verification purpose only)
      Facsimile No. _____
      E-mail _____
    Party B: Name _____
      Attention _____
      Mailing Address _____
      Courtier Address _____ (if different)
      Telephone No. _____ (for verification purpose only)
      Facsimile No. _____
      E-mail _____
      [with a copy to: Party B's counsel]
  Party B's counsel: Name _____
      Attention _____
      Mailing Address _____
      Courtier Address _____ (if different)
      Telephone No. _____ (for verification purpose only)
      Facsimile No. _____
      E-mail _____

如果"合同方"的地址并未以表列形式写入通知条款,可以用完整的句子对"非合同方"的地址加以表述:

② The addresser <u>shall</u> also send an <u>informational copy</u> of each Notice to counsel for the Addressee, as follows:...

(2) 通知副本的生效时间

发送通知"副本"给非合同方,往往是因为当事人希望向其律师或顾问咨询通知的内容,又或是降低通知无法送达当事人的风险。一般情况下,发送"副本"仅仅是礼节性或程序性的,即使没有成功发送给非合同方,也不会影响通知的效力。所以许多通知条款在规定要发送通知"副本"时,会对通知的生效时间予以进一步的说明:

③ The addresser's failure to deliver an <u>informational copy</u> of a Notice to counsel does not constitute a breach of this Agreement or affect the effectiveness of the Notice.

(Stark,2003:490)

但是,如果通知的目的在于获得所有合同方与非合同方的反馈,此时的"副本"就不仅仅是 informative(告知性的)。更合理的做法是规定通知被所有接收方(包括非合同方)收悉后方才生效,为此,以上句②和句③应相应地作如下修改:

② → The addresser <u>must</u> also send a <u>copy</u> of each Notice to counsel for the Addressee, as follows:...

[Insert address of the Addressee]

③ →A Notice is only effective when each Person required to receive a <u>copy</u> of the Notice has received the copy.

总的来说,向"非合同方"发送通知的表述不外乎上述的1、2、3三种情况,合同起草者应根据向"非合同方"发送通知的目的,规定通知生效的时间是否受通知"副本"的影响。

(四) 总结及模式句型

通知条款的四大要素 what,how,when,where(通知的形式、发送方式、生效时间、接收方及其地址)已经阐述完毕。尽管在合同起草的实务中,通知条款的内容未必那么复杂。有的规定只使用一两种发送方式,有的只适用"投邮生效",有的不需要向非合同方发送副本……但无论如何,起草者都应从这四个要素的角度考虑,理解各要素的法律内涵并掌握基本用词和句型,拟出一条符合法理、平衡风险、切实可行的通知条款。

对译者来说,除了掌握各要素的词汇和句型,更重要的是理解通知条款的目的以及内容背后的法律内涵。例如 delivered,可用来表述"发送方式"——shall be delivered by courier,也会被用在"生效时间"的表述中——shall be deemed delivered。两个"delivered",一个译成"寄送",一个译成"送达",前者意味着通知尚不具备法律效力,后者象征着通知条款的即刻生效。又如情态动词的使用。如果条款原文中规定 a copy shall be sent to the counsel,那通知的副本"应当"发送给合同方的律师或顾问,但若是没有这样做,也不影响通知效力,发送方也无需承担任何法律责任;但如果条文原文规定 a copy must be sent to the counsel,那通知的副本就"必须"发送给合同方的律师或顾问,否则通知的效力就存在争议。译者翻译中的一字之差,就可能严重影响通知条款的效力。

现将前文中表述通知条款各要素的句型加以汇总，取其合理的内核，组合成一则较为完整的通知条款，可作为该通用条款的写作楷模：

通知的形式 What	(a) All notices, requests, claims, demands and other communications relating to this Agreement shall be made in writing in English accompanied by a translation into Chinese.
发送方式 How	(b) The party sending the Notice (the "Addresser") shall use one of the following methods for delivery of a Notice：(i) registered mail；(ii) courier；(iii) facsimile；(iv) e-mail.
生效时间 When	(c) A Notice is deemed to have been received： (i) if a Notice is delivered by registered mail, upon the fifth business day after posting； (ii) if a Notice is delivered by courier, upon receipt as indicated by the date on the signed receipt； (iii) if a Notice is sent by facsimile, at the time of sending or the next business day if sent outside the business hours of the receiving party (the "Addressee")； (iv) if a Notice is sent by e-mail, upon the Addressee's acknowledgement of receipt by answering the e-mail (excluding auto-reply). If a Notice is sent by e-mail or facsimile, the Addressee shall provide the Addresser a confirmation copy sent by facsimile. A party's failure to confirm the receipt of the Notice does not affect the effectiveness of the Notice.
接收方 及地址 Where	(d) The Addresser shall address the Notice to the appropriate person as the Addressee at the following address or to other address(es) as may be notified by a party in writing to the other party. Party A：Name ＿＿＿＿＿＿＿＿＿ 　　　　Attention ＿＿＿＿＿＿＿＿ 　　　　Mailing Address ＿＿＿＿＿ 　　　　Courtier Address ＿＿＿＿（if different） 　　　　Telephone No. ＿＿＿＿＿（for verification purpose only） 　　　　Facsimile No. ＿＿＿＿＿＿ 　　　　E-mail ＿＿＿＿＿＿＿＿＿ ［with an informational copy to：Party A's counsel］ Party A's counsel：Name ＿＿＿＿＿＿＿＿＿ 　　　　　　　　 Attention ＿＿＿＿＿＿＿＿ 　　　　　　　　 Mailing Address ＿＿＿＿＿ 　　　　　　　　 Courtier Address ＿＿＿＿（if different） 　　　　　　　　 Telephone No. ＿＿＿＿＿（for verification purpose only） 　　　　　　　　 Facsimile No. ＿＿＿＿＿＿ 　　　　　　　　 E-mail ＿＿＿＿＿＿＿＿＿ Party B：(同上，此处省略) The Addresser's failure to deliver an informational copy of a Notice to counsel does not constitute a breach of this Agreement or affect the effectiveness of the Notice.

三、参考条款及译文

当然,涉及的金额不大或合作规模较小的合同,其有关通知条款并无必要都写得如楷模条款那样面面俱到。以下几例是笔者在其他有关合同写作的专著中挑选出的具有一定参考价值的通知条款。其译文原文存在少许瑕疵,故笔者做了适当订正或修改,作为备用的通用通知条款,附录于此,供读者参考。

Notice	通知
All notices required or permitted by this agreement shall be in writing and shall be deemed sufficient where sent by certified mail to the receiving party at the address set forth above or at such other address as that party may have designated in writing.(王辉,2007:97)	本协议所要求或允许的通知应采取书面形式,通过保证邮件发至上文列明的地址或双方以书面形式指定的其他地址,通知一经发出即视为有效。
All notices authorized or required between the Parties shall be in writing and addressed to the persons as designated below. If notice is given by an international courier service it shall be deemed received three (3) days after sending and if sent by facsimile it shall be deemed received at the time of sending or next business day if sent outside business hours of the recipient, subject to confirmation of success of transmission by proof of machine answerback.(范文祥,2007:211)	所有合同方授权或要求的通知应采用书面形式并发送至下方指定的接收人。如果通知以国际快件的方式寄出,在寄出后第3日视为收悉;如果采用传真方式发送,则在传真发出之时视为收悉(如果发送时间并非接收方的常规工作日,则在发出后的下一个工作日视为收悉),但前提是有对方机器应答的证明以确认发送成功。
11.1 All the notices (including any invoice or report) authorized or required by and between Seller and Buyer as set out in any of the articles herein shall be made in writing in Chinese and English, and delivered by hand, courier, or registered mail to the following address or other address informed by both Parties in writing. Party A: Address for Notices: Attention: Telephone: Facsimile: Party B: Address for Notices: Attention: Telephone: Facsimile: 11.2 Notices are effective when received by the recipient during the recipient's regular business hours. Notices shall be deemed to have been received: (1) upon confirmed receipt of delivery if delivered by hand; (2) upon confirmed transmission if sent by fax; (3) upon	11.1 本合同所有条款规定的买卖双方授权或要求的所有通知(包括发票和报告)均须采取中英文书面形式,并且采用专人递送、快递或挂号信送至下方地址或双方书面通知的其他地址。 甲方: 地址: 接收人: 电话: 传真: 乙方: 地址: 接收人: 电话: 传真: 11.2 通知只有在接收方于其正常工作时段内收到方才有效。通知在以下情形视作收悉:(1)如果由专人递送,于确认收到之时;(2)如果经传真发出,于确认传送成功之时;(3)如果以挂号信

Notice	通知
acknowledgement of receipt if sent by registered mail or courier; (4) upon acknowledgement of receipt of contents of email (other than auto-reply) if sent by email. 11.3 If the time of such deemed receipt is not during customary hours of business, notice shall be deemed to have been received at 8:00 a.m. on the first day of business thereafter. (范文祥,2007:110)	或快递方式发出,于确认收到之时;(4)如果经电子邮件发出,于电子邮件内容确认收到之时(但不包括自动回复)。 11.3 如果通知视为收悉的时间不在日常工作期间,则该通知应视为在随后第一个工作日的早晨8点收悉。

四、特定通知条款及参考译文

特定或具体通知条款,都是根据合同的特殊性质定制的,因为太具特殊性或太具体而无法做一般性的介绍和归纳,故不在本文的探讨范畴。但为了让读者更直观地了解具体通知条款与一般性通知条款之间的差异以及各自的功用,以下罗列几例,以供读者参考:

| 国际贷款与担保合同中的通知条款 | Unless otherwise provided in this Agreement, all notices or demands by any party relating to this Agreement or any other agreement entered into in connection herewith shall be in writing and (except for financial statements and other informational documents which may be sent by first-class mail, postage prepaid) shall be personally delivered or sent by certified mail, postage prepaid, return receipt requested, or by telefacsimile to Borrower or to Bank, as the case may be, at the address set forth below:

If to Bank: _____
_____
_____
Attn: _____
Fax: _____
If to Borrower: _____
_____
_____
Attn: _____
Fax: _____
The parties hereto may change the address at which they are to receive notices hereunder, by notice in writing in the foregoing manner given to the other. (韦箐,2005:879) | 除非本合同另有约定,本合同下的或与本合同有关而签订的其他合同下的所有的通知和要求都应采取书面形式,由专人递送、保证邮件或传真的方式发给借款人或银行,前两种方式由发送方预付邮资并索要收件回执(但不包括财务报表与其他告知性的文件,这类文件以一等邮资预付邮件寄出)。对应不同的发送方式,借款人和银行的收件地址如下方所示:

银行:_____
_____
_____
收件人:_____
传真号:_____

借款人:_____
_____
_____
收件人:_____
传真号:_____
合同双方若要更改收件地址,可以前述方式,书面告知对方。 |

		续表
解除性通知	DISTRIBUTOR shall immediately advise its VARs and each shall advise all of its respective employees, agents, and consultants (collectively, "Persons") of the termination of this Agreement and the termination of its rights to market and distribute the Products, and provide Services. In addition, DISTRIBUTOR shall: (i) obtain the return from each such Person of all copies of all materials described in Section 14.6 hereof; (ii) cease all training of such Persons in the use and features of the Product; and (iii) advise such Persons in writing of their continued duty to hold in confidence and not to use, reproduce, disclose, transfer or transmit, in whole or in part, in any manner, any Product, or any information which would permit the duplication, recreation or other utilization of any Confidential Information.	本协议终止时,经销商应立即通知其分销商,且各方应通知其所有雇员、代理和顾问(总称"人员")关于终止本协议的情况以及终止相关产品和服务的销售和分销权利。此外,经销商应:(i)从该等人员处取回本协议第14.6条描述的所有材料的影印件;(ii)终止一切该等"人员"就产品使用和特性的培训;以及(iii)书面通知该等"人员"仍有义务保密且不得以任何方式使用、复制、泄露、转让、传输或传送任何以往允许复制、重制或作其他用途的任何产品或信息的全部或部分内容。
请示性通知	The Contractor shall give written notice to the Employer whenever planning or progress of the Works is likely to be delayed or disrupted unless any further drawing or order, including a direction, instruction or approval, is issued by the Employer within a reasonable time. The notice shall include details of the drawing or order required and of why and by when it is required and of any delay or disruption likely to be suffered if it is late. (韦箐,2005:541)	无论何时,当工程计划或进展有较大可能被拖延或中断时,承包方应当向发包方发出书面通知,除非发包方在合理的时间内发出任何进一步的图纸或命令,包括指示、指令或认可。通知的内容须详细,应包括对图纸或命令的要求,解释为何提出要求,要求何时须满足以及未及时满足的情况下可能会造成的任何延误或中断。
确认性通知	The Borrower agrees to repay the principal amount of the Loan on the installment Payment Dates in eight equal installments and to pay interest on each interest Payment Date on the outstanding principal balance of the Loan at the Interest Rate. The Borrower shall give notice to the Bank not less than five Business Days prior to the commencement of each interest Period (other than the first Interest Period) whether it has elected an Interested Period of three months or six months. (韦箐,2005:823)	借款人同意分八期偿还贷款本金;且依照协议规定的利息率,就未偿还的贷款本金支付利息。本金和利息分别在本金偿付日和利息偿付日支付。借款人须选择三个月或六个月的利息期,并将其选择在利息期起计前的至少五个营业日(第一个利息期除外)通知银行。

第二十二章
弃权条款的写作、翻译和研究

一、引言：弃权条款的内涵

在法律上，waiver 有两个意思，一指证明放弃某种权利的弃权书。二指当事人或合同的一方自愿放弃合同、法令或法律中规定的其所拥有的某种权利，并且是一个单方面的行为。如果该放弃是自愿的，则该放弃是明示的（an express waiver），是有效的，是受法庭保护的。

如根据美国宪法《第五修正案》，美国的刑法就有这样的规定：在警察逮捕疑犯时，警察必须告诉疑犯，他可以对警察讯问保持缄默，或要求在有其律师在场的情况下回答警察的问题；但他也可以放弃这一权利，自愿招供。但警察必须向法庭证明，疑犯是知道自己有这两项权利的，他是在自愿而不是在受威胁、胁迫或被欺骗的情况下放弃这一权利的（称作：Miranda rights）。不过，本文的焦点是通用合同条款中的权利放弃，不讨论司法程序中的权利放弃。

合同中的权利放弃，通常指乙方违约而甲方放弃行使追究其责任的权利。例如，租客违反租约（如拖欠房租），根据原租约的规定，业主本来是可以终止租约、让租客搬离出租屋的，但考虑到租务市场的不景气或租客违约性质的严重程度，或者其他客观因素，业主接受了租客新交来的租金（即便是在下达"逐客令"后），这样一来，业主就以暗示的方式放弃（an implied waiver）了他可以终止其租约的权利，从而使租约继续有效。

在合同中，弃权或权利放弃条款中经常涉及的、可能会被放弃的权利一般包括以下几项：权利（right）、权力（power）、特权（authority/privilege）、裁量权/酌情权（discretion）、索赔权（claim）、救济权（remedy）；以及放弃对违约或违反合同（breach or default of the contract）或违反合同条款（breach or default of the term of the contract）、条件（condition）、规定（provision），以及错误行为（wrongful conduct）的追究。

但在写作合约中弃权这一通用条款时，需要考虑的因素并非就如上例（有关租务纠纷的处理）那么简单。例如，业主这次放弃追究租客责任、不采取任何法律行动，是不是意味着下次出现类似情况也不予以追究？如果不是，那么在合同中如何明确告诉租客如何"下不为例"？还有，未违约方是否可以放弃其一部分权利、而选择性行使另一部分权利？放弃权利应以何种方式进行？这些都是草拟这条合同条款时必须考虑和写清楚的。

二、权利放弃条款的基本句型和关键用语/词

主要例句：

<u>No provision in this Agreement may be waived</u>, except pursuant to a writing executed by the party against whom the waiver is sought to be enforced.

No waiver of any term, provision or condition of this Agreement, the breach or default thereof, shall be deemed to be either a continuing waiver or a waiver of a subsequent breach or default of any such term, provision or condition of this Agreement.

The failure of either party to this Agreement to object to or to take affirmation action with respect to any conduct of the other which is in violation of the terms of this Agreement shall not be construed as a waiver of the violation or breach, or of any future violation, breach or wrongful conduct.

Either Party's failure to exercise or delay in exercising any right, power or privilege under this Contract shall not operate as a waiver thereof, and any single or partial exercise of any right, power or privilege shall not preclude the exercise of any other right, power or privilege.

The failure or for bearance of... shall in no way be construed to be a waiver of... and shall not in any way affect the validity or effectiveness of this Agreement or any part thereof, nor the right of... to thereafter enforce each and every provision.

The failure of either party at any time or times to require performance of any provision hereof shall in no manner affect its right at a later time to enforce the same. No waiver by either party of any condition or any breach of any of the terms, covenants or conditions contained in this Agreement shall be effective unless in writing, and no waiver in any one or more instances shall be construed as a further or continuing waiver of any other condition or any breach of any other terms, covenants or conditions.

The single or partial exercise of any right, power or remedy provided by law or under this Agreement shall not preclude any further exercise of it or the exercise of any other right, power or remedy.

句型基本结构和关键用词：

1. ... partial exercise of or delay in exercising any right, power or remedy provided by law or under this Agreement shall not affect/preclude any other right, power or remedy.

2. (No waiver...) shall operate as/be construed as...

3. (Failure to exercise its right) shall not be deemed as.../shall not constitute...;/shall not preclude...;(A failure or delay in exercise, or partial exercise, of...) does not result in a waiver of...

4. (Waiver by either party of any condition or any breach of any of the terms) shall be/become effective /shall take effect...

5. (Failure)... shall not affect the validity or effectiveness of...

由以上基本句型可以看出,弃权条款基本上都是由否定形式构成的:要么 sth. shall not affect/preclude sth.；要么 No waiver shall operate as/be construed as....。

三、权利放弃条款的内容和句型分析

一般来说,合同中较完整的权利放弃条款包括以下五个方面的内容:

1. 某一方 a. 没有行使(b. 延期行使, c. 疏忽行使, 或 d. 部分行使)自己的某项权利, 或对对方的违约行为没有追究, 或没有强制对方履约, 不得看作是对其这方面权利的放弃, 也不影响其这方面的权利。

a. Failure to exercise its right or take any action against the other Party for any breach of Contract shall not be deemed as a waiver of such breach. / Failure by any party to enforce the performance by the other parties of any of the provisions of this Agreement shall not be deemed as a waiver by it of its rights hereunder.

b. & c. No delay or omission by either Party in exercising any right, power or remedy provided by law or under this Agreement shall: (1) affect the right, power or remedy; or (2) operate as a waiver of it.

d. The single or partial exercise of any right, power or remedy provided by law or under this Agreement shall not preclude any further exercise of it or the exercise of any other right, power or remedy.

2. 对某项权利的放弃不得视为对其他权利的放弃。

No waiver of any Party to any right shall be deemed as a waiver to any other rights under this contract.

3. 本次的放弃权利不等于今后也会放弃, 也不影响今后对其这方面权利或其他方面的权利的行使。

Any waiver by a party for a breach of any provision of this Agreement on the part of the other parties shall not constitute a precedent to any subsequent breach of such provision of a waiver of the provisions itself.

No waiver in any one or more instances shall be construed as a further or continuing waiver of any other condition or any breach of any other terms, covenants or conditions.

The failure of either party at any time or times to require performance of any provision hereof shall in no manner affect its right at a later time to enforce the same.

The single or partial exercise of any right, power or remedy provided by law or under this Agreement shall not preclude any further exercise of it or the exercise of any other right, power or remedy.

4. 放弃某项权利须以书面方式通知对方。

Waiver of any Party to any of its right shall be sent to the other Party in writing.

No waiver by either party of any condition or any breach of any of the terms, covenants or conditions contained in this Agreement shall be effective unless in writing.

No waiver of any right, power or remedy provided by law or under this Agreement shall take effect unless it is in writing and signed by authorized representative of the Party giving the waiver.

5. 某一方没有行使自己的权利(如要求对方履行合同义务的权利)不影响合同的效力。

Failure by any party to enforce the performance by the other parties of any of the provisions of this Agreement shall not affect the validity of this Agreement...

从上文的句式用词可以观察到,写作该条款的句型非常单调、有规律;所用的词组和单词非常简单而清晰。几乎毫无例外,该条款的主要内容都用否定的形式来表达,或者用否定词前置(倒装形式)的否定句,如 No waiver... shall be effective; No waiver ... shall take effect...; No delay or omission... shall (1) affect the right, power or remedy; or (2) operate as a waiver of it...;或者在谓语部分用否定的形式(但主语必须是肯定的),如:Any waiver... shall not constitute...; Failure to do sth.... shall not be deemed as...;以及 The single or partial exercise of... shall not preclude...。

虽然笔者研读过大量的包含这一条款的合同,但从以上两种句式比例上还是看不出哪一种更占优势。所以,笔者不对句式优胜妄加判断,或做出特别推荐。但就谓语部分所用的动词而言,笔者更倾向选用接近普通英文用法的"shall not be deemed as",虽然其他三者(shall operate/be construed as; shall not constitute;不包括 shall not preclude)用法也并不冷僻,但毕竟前者最简明易懂。后三者中的 shall be construed as(应解释为……)用在合同或法律的释义部分更为恰当;而 shall not constitute 更常用于违约条款(如某种行为"构成"违约)。

四、权利放弃条款写作模板及原理说明

由上文条款的内容分析可见,如果有现成的、能够包括以上五方面(或尽可能多的)内容的权利放弃条款,可考虑作为该条款的写作模块(template)。通过对大量现成条款的对比分析,以下两例比较接近这一要求:

例 1. No waiver of any term, provision or condition of this Agreement, the breach or default thereof, shall be deemed to be either a continuing waiver or a waiver of a subsequent breach or default of any such term, provision or condition of this Agreement.

例 2. 1.1 No delay or omission by either Party in exercising any right, power or remedy provided by law or under this Agreement shall: (a) affect the right, power or remedy; or (b) operate as a waiver of it.

1.2 The single or partial exercise of any right, power or remedy provided by law or under this Agreement shall not preclude any further exercise of it or the exercise of any other right, power or remedy.

1.3 No waiver of any right, power or remedy provided by law or under this Agreement shall take effect unless it is in writing and signed by authorized representative of the Party giving the waiver.

1.1 任何一方延迟或没有行使任何法律或本协议规定的权利、权力或补救权并不(a)影响该权利、权力或补救权;或(b)构成对该权利(力)的放弃。

1.2 单独行使或部分行使任何法律或本协议规定的权利、权力或补救权并不阻止其进一步行使这些权利(力)或行使其他的权利、权力或补救权。

1.3 放弃任何法律或本协议规定的权利、权力或补救权须采用书面形式并经弃权方授权代表签字后方才生效。(范文祥、吴怡,2008:212;译文经笔者修订)

以上例1的合理性是由于语段含糊地包括了该类条款应当包括的主要内容；而例2的合理性则是由于语段的清晰性和内容的周详性，故更可视作写作这一条款的楷模。具体而言：1)内容完整，面面俱到。不但把各类合同一般都会提到的各种常见权(权利、权力或补救权)都包括在内，而且把权利放弃须采用何种方式(in writing)，以及具体由谁来行使(signed by authorized representative...)都写得清清楚楚；2)句型规范，符合绝大部分该类条款的主流表达方式；3)语言风格简明，与时俱进，没有滥用或偏执使用古旧词的现象，尽管文内有多处是可以使用的。对比以下一段的写法，我们更可以看出上文写作风格上的难能可贵：

> No failure on the part of either party to exercise, and no delay in exercising, any right or remedy <u>hereunder</u> shall operate as a waiver <u>thereof</u>; nor shall any single or partial waiver of a breach of any provision of this Agreement operate or be construed as a waiver of any subsequent breach; nor shall any single or partial exercise of any right or remedy <u>hereunder</u> preclude any other or further exercise <u>thereof</u> or the exercise of any other right or remedy granted <u>hereby</u> or by law.

该段用了五个冷僻的古旧词(见画线部分)，虽然这些古旧词使语段看上去有点"古色古香"，但实际上给读者增添的只是阅读的难度和解读的负担。

但以上推荐的例2模式条款并非无改进的余地，如第一段中的"(b) operate as a waiver of it"，以改写成"(b) be deemed as a waiver of it"更加通俗易懂。可能会有挑剔的作/读者认为其中的"of it"是个失误，应该写成"thereof"。当然，要是追求"复古"风格，这是不错的选择，因为"thereof"这个古旧词等于"of any right, power or remedy provided by law or under this Agreement"，它十分准确地反映了原义，也省却了不少笔墨。但是，这仍然是个古旧而啰唆的写法，原文"of it"并没有错，因为其前面的短语是"the right, power or remedy"，其中所用连词是表示可以"任选"其一的"or"而不是可将单数名词合成为复数的"and"；所以，此处的"it"可以指代其中的任何一项。

也许还有作/读者认为以上条款内容不够全面，没有将违反合同中应有的"term, provision or condition"等处置权包括在内。其实"权利、权力、补救权"包含的范围更加宽泛，因为这种"权利、权力、补救权"可以由该合同产生，也可以由违反合同或合同条款而引发(a right, power, authority, discretion or remedy created or arising upon default under this contract)。不过，有些合同权利放弃条款的侧重点仅仅是其中的条款，即 term, condition, provision，而不是权利。故在此不妨再提供另一条可供选择的范例条款：

> No waiver of any term, provision or condition of this Agreement, the breach or default of it, shall be deemed to be either a continuing waiver or a waiver of a subsequent breach or default of any such term, provision or condition of this Agreement. Any waiver by either party of any term, provision or condition of this Agreement, or of the breach or default of it, shall be effective unless it is authorized in writing by an authorized representative of the Party giving the waiver.

> 对本协议任何条款、规定或条件的放弃，或对违反或不履行该等条款、规定或条件行为的放弃，不得视为对本协议该等条款、规定或条件的持续性放弃，不得视为对其后续该等条款、规定或条件行为的放弃。任何对本协议条款、规定或条件的放弃，或对违反或不履行该等条款、规定或条件行为的放弃，须以书面形式、并由弃权方授权代表签

字后方才生效。

五、Waiver 翻译的差异

Waiver 这个词的翻译，在内地与香港有很大的不同。在香港，该词被翻译成"豁免"。例如，香港银行业的服务条款中都有这么一条：

WAIVER In the event that any party fails, or delays, to exercise a right under these Terms, that party may still exercise that right later. Any waiver or any right shall be in writing and limited to the specific circumstances. …… No failure to exercise or delay in exercising the same shall operate as a waiver thereof, nor shall any single or partial exercise thereof preclude any other or further exercise thereof.

豁免 倘任何人士未能获延迟行使此等条款下的权利，该人士其后仍可行使该权利。任何豁免或任何权利将须以书面形式做出，并局限于特定的情况。……未能行使或延迟行使该等权利或补偿概不等于对该等权利或补偿的放弃或豁免，任何单一或部分行使该等权利或补偿亦不影响任何其他或进一步行使该等权利或补偿。①

但根据语义逻辑和对条款内容的分析，弃权更贴近该条款用词的原意。

六、权利放弃参考条款及译文

以下供对比的双语条款选自目前中国市场上仅有的若干本与合同或法律写作或翻译相关的专著。但原文以及原译文中都存在各种瑕疵。故笔者在以下附文中对其原文和译文都作了适当的订正和修改。如未注明出处者，译文由笔者提供。

Waivers	权利放弃
No failure or delay by GTA toinsist upon the strict performance of any term, condition, covenant or agreement set forth in this, or to exercise any right, power or remedy consequent upon a breach thereof, shall constitute a waiver of such term, condition, covenant or agreement or of any such breach, or preclude GTA from exercising any such right, power or remedy at any later time or times. （闫洋，2013）	GTA 未能或延迟坚持供货商严格履行本合同所订的任何条款、条件、契诺或协定，或者在供货商违反该等条款、条件、契诺或协定后而未能或延迟行使 GTA 所拥有的任何权利、权力或补救权，并不构成 GTA 对该等条款、条件、契诺或协定的放弃；也不构成对供货商任何这类违约的弃权；也并不影响 GTA 在以后任何时候再行使任何该等权利、权力或补救权。
No provision in this Agreement may be waived, except pursuant to a writing executed by the party against whom the waiver is sought to be enforced. （乔焕然，2008：158）	协议方不得放弃本协议中的任何条款，除非由该种放弃根据所试图针对的一方当事人签署的书面文件进行。

---

① 该条文的英文和译文见香港恒生银行 2014 年 8 月给其客户的《业务关系条款》。

续表

Waivers	权利放弃
The failure of either party to this Agreement to object to or to take affirmation action with respect to any conduct of the other which is in violation of the terms of this Agreement shall not be construed as a waiver of the violation or breach, or of any future violation, breach or wrongful conduct. (王辉,2007:141)	本协议任一方未就其他一方违反本协议条款的行为提出反对或提起积极诉讼的,不得解释为对该违反、违约或任何将来的违反、违约或不正当行为做出弃权。①
No waiver of any term, provision or condition of this Agreement, the breach or default thereof, shall be deemed to be either a continuing waiver or a waiver of a subsequent breach or default of any such term, provision or condition of this Agreement.	对本协议任何条款、规定或条件的放弃,或对违反或不履行该等条款、规定或条件行为的放弃,不得视为对本协议该等条款、规定或条件的持续性放弃,不得视为对其后续该等条款、规定或条件行为的放弃。
Either Party's failure to exercise or delay in exercising any right, power or privilege under this Contract shall not operate as a waiver thereof, and any single or partial exercise of any right, power or privilege shall not preclude the exercise of any other right, power or privilege. (乔焕然,2008:117)	如果一方未行使或延迟行使其在本合同项下的任何权利、权力或特权,不构成该方对此项权利、权力或特权的放弃,如果该方已经行使或部分行使某项权利、权力或特权,并不妨碍其行使其他权利、权力或特权。
Failure of any Party to exercise its right or take any action against the other Party for any breach of Contract shall not be deemed as a waiver of such breach. No waiver of any Party to any right shall be deemed as a waiver to any other rights. Waiver of any Party to any of its right shall be sent to the other Party in writing. (范文祥,2008:110)	任何一方对另一方的违约行为没有行使其权利或未采取任何法律行动,不得视为放弃追究违约方的责任。任何一方对任何权利的放弃,不得视为是对任何其他权利的放弃。任何一方对任何权利的放弃,均应以书面形式通知对方。②
(a) The failure or forbearance of the Manufacturer to enforce at anytime any of the provisions of this Agreement or to exercise any option or right which is herein provided including the right to terminate under Section 34 or to require at any time performance by the Distributor of any of the provisions hereof shall in no way be construed to be a waiver of its rights under such provision and shall not in any way affect the validity or effectiveness of this Agreement or any part thereof (hereof) nor the right of the Manufacturer to thereafter enforce each and every provision. (b) The exercise of one right or remedy shall not constitute an election to preclude the Manufacturer from exercising all the rights and remedies available to it by law or under this Agreement. (王相国,2008:364)	(a)制造商任何时候未能履行或迟延履行本协议任何规定或行使本协议规定的任何选择权或权利(包括依据第34条终止协议的权利),或未能或迟延要求分销商履行本协议任何规定,无论如何都不得解释为放弃依该等规定所享有之权利,且无论如何也不影响本协议或本协议任何部分的有效性或效力,亦无论如何不影响制造商此后执行任何一条款规定的权利。 (b)某项权利之行使或某种救济之采取,不得妨碍制造商行使和采取其依据法律或本协议享有之所有权利和救济。

---

① 原译"不正当行为"属于欠额翻译,倘若以回译方法检验,一定不会是"wrongful conduct",所以译成"错误行为"为妥。

② 笔者对原译文做了三处修正。

续表

Waivers	权利放弃
Failure by any party to enforce the performance by the other parties of any of the provisions of this Agreement shall neither be deemed a waiver by it of its rights hereunder, nor shall it affect the validity of this Agreement in any way. Any waiver by a party for a breach of any provision of this Agreement on the part of the other parties shall not constitute a precedent to any subsequent breach of such provision of a waiver of the provisions itself.	任何一方没有要求其他方履行本协议中的任何规定，不得视为该方放弃其在本协议下的权利，也无论如何不影响本协议的效力。一方对于其他方违反本协议的任何规定或规定之一部分放弃行使权利，并不构成对其他方以后违反本规定而放弃行使权利的先例。
The Guarantor shall have no right of subrogation, reimbursement, exoneration, contribution or any other rights that would result in the Guarantor being deemed a creditor of Seller under the United States Bankruptcy Code or any other law or for any other purpose and the Guarantor hereby irrevocably waives all such rights, the right to assert any such rights and any right to enforce any remedy which Guarantor may now or hereafter have against Seller and hereby irrevocably waives any benefit of and any right to participate in, any security now or hereafter held by Buyer, whether any of the foregoing rights arise in equity, at law or by contract.（范文祥、吴怡，2008：213）	担保人不具有代位权、求偿权、免除权、补偿权或其他任何根据美国破产法典或任何其他法律或为任何其他目的会导致担保人被视为卖方债权人的权利，担保人据此不可撤销地放弃上述权利、主张上述权利的权利以及强制执行担保人现在或今后可能针对卖方采取的任何救济措施的权利。担保人据此不可撤销地放弃由买方现在或今后持有的任何担保物所带来的利益并放弃任何分享该担保物的权利，不论上述任何一种权利源于衡平法、普通法或合同。
B represents and warrants that this Agreement is the commercial rather than public or governmental act and that B waives its right to claim immunity from legal proceedings with respect to itself or any of its assets on the ground of sovereignty or otherwise under any law or in any jurisdiction whether an action may be brought for the enforcement of any of the obligations arising under this Agreement.（范文祥、吴怡，2008：214）	B声明并保证：本协议是商业行为而不是公共或政府行为，B放弃就其本身或其任何资产由于主权或根据任何法律的其他理由或在任何管辖范围内要求免予提起诉讼（该诉讼可能是为了强制实施根据本协议产生的义务而提起的）的权力。①
The failure of either party at any time or times to require performance of any provision hereof shall in no manner affect its right at a later time to enforce the same. No waiver by either party of any condition or any breach of any of the terms, covenants or conditions contained in this Agreement shall be effective unless in writing, and no waiver in any one or more instances shall be construed as a further or continuing waiver of any other condition or any breach of any other terms, covenants or conditions.（乔焕然，2008：117）	任何一方在任何时候未要求另一方履行本协议任一条款，并不影响其以后强制执行该条款的权利。任何一方放弃本协议的任何条件或放弃追究另一方违反本协议中的任何条款、规定或条件的行为，只有做出书面弃权方为有效。一方一次或多次放弃该等权利，不应被视为该方进一步或继续放弃任何其他条件或进一步或继续放弃追究另一方违反任何其他条款、规定或条件的行为。

---

① 该条款在合同中采用时一定要非常谨慎：B方需要放弃的是对于"其任何资产……要求免予提起诉讼的权利"。这就是说，由于签订此合同，B方的全部家当都押上了。

Waivers	权利放弃
1.1 No delay or omission by either Party in exercising any right, power or remedy provided by law or under this Agreement shall: (a) affect the right, power or remedy; or (b) operate as a waiver of it. 1.2 The single or partial exercise of any right, power or provided by law or under this Agreement shall not preclude any further exercise of it or the exercise of any other right, power or remedy. 1.3 No waiver of any right, power or remedy provided by law or under this Agreement shall take effect unless it is in writing and signed by authorized representative of the Party giving the waiver.	1.1 任何一方延迟或没有行使任何法律或本协议规定的权利、权力或救济权并不(a)影响该权利、权力或救济权;或(b)构成对该权利(力)的弃权。 1.2 单独行使或部分行使任何法律或本协议规定的权利、权力或救济权并不阻止其进一步行使这些权利或行使其他的权利、权力或救济权。 1.3 放弃任何法律或本协议规定的权利、权力或救济权必须采用书面形式并经弃权方授权代表签字后方才生效。(范文祥、吴怡,2008:212,经修订)
No failure on the part of either party to exercise, and no delay in exercising, any right or remedy hereunder shall operate as a waiver thereof; nor shall any single or partial waiver of a breach of any provision of this Agreement operate or be construed as a waiver of any subsequent breach; nor shall any single or partial exercise of any right or remedy hereunder preclude any other or further exercise thereof or the exercise of any other right or remedy granted hereby or by law.	任何一方未能行使或延迟行使本协议项下的任何权利或救济权并不构成对该等权利或救济权的放弃;任何单独放弃或部分放弃对违反本协议任何规定行为的追究不得视为或解释为放弃对以后违反本协议行为的追究;任何单独行使或部分行使本协议规定的权利或救济权不得阻止任何其他或进一步行使这些权利或行使本协议或法律许可的其他权利或救济权。
No failure by Manager or Owner to insist upon the strict performances of any covenant, agreement, term or condition of this Agreement, or to exercise any right or remedy consequent upon the breach thereof, shall constitute a waiver of any such breach or any subsequent breach of such covenant, agreement, term or condition. No covenant, agreement, term or condition of this Agreement shall be waived, altered or modified except by written instrument. No waiver of any breach shall affect or alter this Agreement, but each and every covenant, agreement, term and condition of this Agreement shall continue in full force and effect with respect to any other then existing or subsequent breach thereof.	经理人或业主未能坚持严格履行本协议的任何契诺、协定、条款或条件,或未能在继后的违反本协议的该等契诺、协定、条款或条件时行使任何权利或采取补救措施,不构成对该违反或继后违反契诺、协定、条款或条件的弃权。除以书面形式做出规定外,不得对本协议的任何契诺、协定、条款或条件做出弃权、修改或变更。对任何违约的弃权并不影响或改变本协议,但本协议的每个契诺、协定、条款或条件对于任何其他既有的或随后的违反而言应继续完全有效。

续表

Waivers	权利放弃
Any term or provision of this Agreement may be waived, or the time for its performance may be extended, by the party or parties entitled to the benefit thereof. Any such waiver shall be validly and sufficiently authorized for the purposes of this Agreement if, as to any party, it is authorized in writing by an authorized representative of such party. The failure of any party hereto to enforce at any time any provision of this Agreement shall not be construed to be a waiver of such provision, nor in any way to affect the validity of this Agreement or any part hereof or the right of any party thereafter to enforce each and every such provision. No waiver of any breach of this Agreement shall be held to constitute a waiver of any other or subsequent breach.	有权根据本协议规定获益的协议方可放弃本协议的任何条款或规定，或延长本协议的履行时间。如任何一方由其授权代表以书面形式授权，任何弃权应视为出于本协议考虑的合理充分的授权。本协议任何一方未能在任何时间履行本协议的任何规定，不得解释为放弃该规定，也不影响之后的本协议的有效性，且不影响本协议或其任何部分或任何一方的权利以履行该等规定。对违反本协议的任何弃权不得视作对其他的或后续违约的弃权。
(a) Waiver of any right arising from a breach of this Deed or of any right, power, authority, discretion or remedy arising upon default under this Deed must be in writing and signed by the party granting the waiver. (b) A failure or delay in exercise, or partial exercise, of (i) a right arising from a breach of this Deed; or (ii) a right, power, authority, discretion or remedy created or arising upon default under this Deed, does not result in a waiver of that right, power, authority, discretion or remedy. (c) A party is not entitled to rely on a delay in the exercise or non-exercise of a right, power, authority, discretion or remedy arising from a breach of this Deed or on a default under this Deed as constituting a waiver of that right, power, authority, discretion or remedy. (d) A party may not rely on any conduct of another party as a defence to exercise of a right, power, authority, discretion or remedy by that other party. (e) This clause may not itself be waived except by writing. (f) No waiver by a party of a failure or failures by the other party to perform any provision of this Deed shall operate or be construed as a waiver in respect of any other or further failure whether of alike or different character.	(a)放弃由于违反本契约而产生的任何权利或由于不履行本契约而产生的任何权利、权力、特权、裁量权或救济权必须以书面形式做出，并由同意该弃权的一方签署。(b)未能或迟延行使或部分行使(i)由于违反本契约而产生的权利；或(ii)由于不履行本契约而产生的任何权利、权力、特权、裁量权或救济权，并不导致放弃该权利、权力、特权、裁量权或救济权。(c)一方无权依赖延迟行使或不行使由于违反本契约或不履行本契约而产生的权利、权力、特权、裁量权或救济权，而该延迟行使或不履行行为则构成对该等权利、权力、特权、裁量权或救济权的放弃。(d)一方不得依赖另一方的任何行为作为该另一方行使权利、权力、特权、裁量权或救济权的辩护。(e)除以书面行使，不得放弃该条款本身。(f)如另一方未能履行本契约的任何规定造成一方弃权，则该弃权行为不得当作或解释为该方放弃任何其他或进一步的权利(不论性质是否相同)。

续表

Waivers	权利放弃
<u>The failure</u> of the Landlord to insist in any one or more instances upon the strict and literal performance of any of the agreements, terms, or conditions of this lease or to exercise any option of the Landlord herein contained, shall not be construed as a waiver for the future of such term, condition, agreement or option. The receipt by the Landlord of rent with knowledge of the breach of any term, condition, or agreement shall not be deemed to be a waiver of such breach. The receipt by the Landlord of rent after the giving of any notice required to be given to the Tenant by law or by the terms of this lease shall not in any way affect the operation of such notice.	业主未能在任何一种或多种情况下坚持严格履行本租约的任何协定条款或条件或行使本租约所包括的业主的任何选择权,不得解释为将来对该等条款、条件、协定或选择权的弃权。业主知悉租客违反任何条款、条件或协定而继续收取租金不得视作对该等违反的弃权。根据法律规定或本租约的条款,业主在给予租客通知之后收取租金并不影响该通知的执行。
<u>No waiver</u> by Lessor of the Default or Breach of any term, covenant or condition hereof by Lessee, shall be deemed a waiver of any other term, covenant or condition hereof, or of any subsequent Default or Breach by Lessee of the same or of any other term, covenant or condition hereof. Lessor's consent to, or approval of, any act shall not be deemed to render unnecessary the obtaining of Lessor's consent to, or approval of, any subsequent or similar act by Lessee, or be construed as the basis of an Estoppel to enforce the provision or provisions of this Lease requiring such consent. The acceptance of Rent by Lessor shall not be a waiver of any Default or Breach by Lessee. Any payment by Lessee may be accepted by Lessor on account of moneys or damages due, notwithstanding any qualifying statements or conditions made by Lessee. In connection therewith, which such statements and/or conditions shall be of no force or effect whatsoever unless specifically agreed to in writing by Lessor at or before the time of deposit of such payment.	出租人放弃对承租人违反本租约的任何条款、契诺或条件的追究不得视为是对本租约的任何其他条款、契诺或条件的放弃,也不得视为放弃对承租人继后的违约或违反该等条款、契诺或条件的追究。出租人同意或批准任何行为不得视为承租人在采取继后或类似行为时无必要获得出租人的同意或批准,也不得解释为这是禁止实施本租约要求取得该类同意之规定的依据。出租人接受租金不得视为对承租人任何不履行或违约行为的弃权。尽管承租人提出合理的声明或条件,出租人仍可接受承租人欠负的任何到期的款项或赔偿金。有鉴于此,除出租人在存入该款项之时或之前做出书面同意,否则承租人的该类声明和/或条件均属无效。①

---

① 该条款写法啰嗦,内容隐晦,其中"禁止实施本租约要求取得该类同意之规定的依据"语焉不详;而最后部分有关承租人所付的究竟是什么款项(拖欠的租金?),做出什么声明或提出什么条件,均含混其词。所以,该条款的写法值得商榷,不宜作为现代租约写法的楷模。

…

第二十三章 可分割性条款的写作、翻译和研究

一、引言

Severability(可分割性或可分性)一词源于拉丁词 salvatorius,以该词冠名的条款跟 saving clause 同属一个概念。但如今的合同或法律中一般都称之为 severability clause,指的是合同或法律文件中某个部分或某一条款或条文成为非法或不再具有可执行性时,其他部分、条款或条文不受影响。不过,该条款有时也会订明:如合同或法律中的某些核心条款成为非法或无法执行时,则整个合同宣告无效或有关法律作废。这类条款叫作不可分割性条款(inseverability clause)。例如,美国新罕布什尔州的一条法律就是这样写的:

> This act is to be construed as a whole, and all parts of it are to be read and construed together. If any part of this act shall be adjudged by any court of competent jurisdiction to be invalid, the remainder of this act shall be invalidated. Nothing herein shall be construed to affect the parties' right to appeal the matter.[①]

但就本文的主题(合同通用条款)而言,绝大部分合同中只有"可分割性"条款,而没有"不可分割性"条款。要是从法理上讲,这一条款与普通法中的"蓝笔原则"(Blue-Pencil Doctrine)密切关联。在实施普通法的国家,法庭有一项特别的权力:如果发现合同中存在无效或无法实施的内容,法庭可命令合同的各有关方只执行可实施的条款,法庭可用"蓝笔"将合同中的无效部分画线删除。在实际操作中,法律也允许合同的任何一方在执行合同过程中遇到该种情况时,请求法庭将有关条款删除。[②]

不少律师在草拟合同、写作该条款时都有一个没有言明的意图,即将合同的"灰色地带"最大化,因为有些合同项目或合同各方可以做的事项当时的法律可能没有明确规定,不一定非法,也不能确切预见该有关条款将来不可实施或无法实施,所以订合同时先把这类操作条款(operative clause)写进去再说;将来出了问题,才按本文讨论的这一通用条款去处理。[③]解决的方法除了请求法庭按"蓝笔原则"删除某些条款之外,一般还会包括其他一些补救措施,有关措施内容及其写法,会在下一节中做较详细的叙述和分析。

---

① New Hampshire statute:http://en.wikipedia.org/wiki/Severability http://www.contractstandards.com/contract-structure/.
② http://en.wikipedia.org/wiki/Blue_pencil_doctrine.
③ general-provisions/severability:有关内容如下:The severability clause is frequently one of the most variable (or inconsistent) clauses in an agreement as lawyers creatively attempt to maximize the scope of restrictive covenants. It is also interesting to note that virtually all executive employments contain savings clause language, but surprisingly few contain reformation language.

二、可分割性条款的内涵、句型和关键用词

(一) 可分割条款的内容介绍和句型分析

完整的可分割条款通常都由两部分内容构成——虽然这两部分内容可以是一个语段，也可以明确分为两个、甚至三个语段。第一部分的内容阐述在部分条款无效的情况下，合同的其余条款不受影响；第二部分讲述相关的补救措施。例如：

例 1. If any term or other provision of this Agreement is determined to be invalid, illegal or incapable of being enforced by any rule or law, or public policy, all other conditions and provisions of this Agreement shall nevertheless remain in full force and effect so long as the economic or legal substance of the transactions contemplated hereby is not affected in any manner materially adverse to any party.

如本合同的任何条款或其他条件根据任何规定或法律或公共政策被判定无效、非法或无法实施，本合同的所有其他条件或规定——只要本合同计划执行的交易的经济或法律主体不对任何一方有重大的不利影响，仍然完全有效。

Upon such determination that any term or other provision is invalid, illegal or incapable of being enforced, the parties hereto shall negotiate in good faith to modify this Agreement so as to effect the original intent of the parties as closely as possible in an acceptable manner to the end that transactions contemplated hereby is fulfilled to the extent possible.

在任何条款或其他条件被判定无效、非法或无法实施后，合同各方应真诚协商、修订合同，以各方都可以接受的方式在修订中尽可能地反映出各方签订此合同的原意，从而使原合同计划进行的交易得以圆满完成。①

例 2. If any provision, or part of a provision of this Agreement is invalidated by operation of law, the provision or part will to that extent be deemed omitted and the remainder of this Agreement will remain in full force and effect so long as the economic or legal substance of the transactions contemplated hereby is not affected in any manner adverse to any party. Upon such determination that any term or other provision is invalid, illegal or incapable of being enforced, the parties hereto shall negotiate in good faith to modify this Agreement so as to effect the original intent of the parties as closely as possible in a mutually acceptable manner in order that the transactions contemplated hereby be consummated as originally contemplated to the fullest extent possible.

如本协议的任何条款或任何条款之一部分依照法律无效，该条款或条款之一部分将被忽略，而本协议的剩余内容将继续有效——只要根据本协议打算进行的交易的经济或法律内容不对任何一方产生不利的影响。在任何条件或其他条款被判定无效、违

---

① http://www.sec.gov/Archives/edgar/data/777001/000091412108

法或不可执行后,协议方应真诚协商修改本协议,以双方都可接受的方式尽可能使之接近协议方的本意,从而保证本协议打算进行的交易与最初的打算最大限度的吻合。

以上两例的共同点是部分条款出现"状况"时,其余条款(在法律允许的范围)仍然有效。其主句均用肯定的句式写成:(the remainder) shall nevertheless remain in full force and effect / will remain in full force and effect。第二句中所用的情态动词(will)还是不够规范,虽然在传意上没有问题,并且更加接近普通英文,但规范的语言是大众的选择。在法律领域,当绝大多数写手还是用 shall + verb 去表达法律上的带强制性的行为("应当"或"须"的概念)时,用在此处的 will 仍然是非规范的小众用语。

综上所述的可分割条款(尤其是例2)在写法上都略嫌冗长啰唆,也有些晦涩难懂。以下一条简短易明,并且包括了该条款应有的两层主要意思:

例3. Each term and provision of this agreement shall be valid and enforceable to the fullest extent permitted by law and any invalid, illegal or unenforceable term or provision shall be replaced by a term or provision that is valid and enforceable and that comes closest to expressing the intention of the invalid, illegal or unenforceable term or provision.

这一条款语段总共不到60字,但法律上所需的该条款核心概念还是基本具备的,把例1中总共128字的内容都基本包括在内。除了言简意赅的特点外,该语段还有其他一些特点:文风上不带"师爷"习气,无重言词,无古旧词;不像传统的可分割性条款那样,必须由一个条件句加一个主句构成;它实质上由两个平行的陈述句组成。第一句讲"本协议的每一个条款或规定只要法律允许就完全有效";第二句讲"无效、非法或不可执行的条款或规定应由最接近的能够表达该无效、非法或不可执行条款或规定意旨的有效的、可实行的条款来替代"。至于有关条款为何无效、非法或不可执行,该由谁来确定,则不加具体限定,因为不可行的原因基本上都是由于国家有关的政策法规变了;而条款被认定无效、非法或不可执行,除了法庭判定之外,也可以是协议双方的共识,如果双方对有争议的条款能达成共识,未必一定要劳民伤财闹到法庭去由法官判定,双方可以自己坐下来重新协商,修订有关条款,而且这种解决的可能性更大,因为这类可分割条款在各类合同(尤其是标的物金额较小的合同)中基本上都是众所周知的形式主义条款。

在审察该可分割条款时,读者必然都会注意到,表达该通用条款更常用的句式还是由条件句加否定形式的主句构成的(本章附表提供的双语对照语段中有更多的例证):If...(或其他类型的条件句), legal subject + shall not affect (be effected)。例如:

例4. If any provision of this Agreement (shall be) is invalid or unenforceable in any jurisdiction, such invalidity or unenforceability shall not affect the validity or enforceability of the remainder of this Agreement or the validity or enforceability of this Agreement in any other jurisdiction. (如本协议的任何条款在任何司法管辖区域内无效或不可执行,该无效性或不可执行性并不影响本协议其他条款的有效性或可执行性,也不影响本协议在任何其他司法管辖区域内的有效性或可执行性。)

例5. a. If any provision or provisions of this Agreement (shall be) are held to be invalid, illegal, unenforceable or in conflict with the law of any jurisdiction, the validity, legality and enforceability of the remaining provisions shall not in any way be affected or impaired thereby. b. Invalidity or unenforceability of one or more

provisions of this Agreement <u>shall not affect</u> any other provision of this Agreement.
c. In the event that any one or more of the provisions contained herein <u>shall</u>, for any reason, be held to be invalid, illegal or unenforceable in any respect, such invalidity, illegality or unenforceability <u>shall not affect</u> any other provisions of this agreement, but this agreement shall be construed as if such invalid, illegal or unenforceable provisions had never been contained herein, unless the deletion of such provision or provisions would result in such a material change so as to cause completion of the transactions contemplated herein to be unreasonable. ①

例 5 的三段可分割条款虽然是由英国律师拟订的,但在其中的两个条件句(由 If 和 In the event that 引导)部分,情态动词 shall 仍然被滥用。众所周知,shall 在法律文本中表示义务,而在这两个条件句中,所要表达的均为一种状态或条件,主句部分才包含需要用 shall 表达的强制成分。所以读者或译者在阅读法律文本时要有鉴别的目光,分清"是非",不可全单照收,更不可在中译英的过程中人云亦云,将错就错。

就可分割条款的内容而言,在一些大型的项目或复杂的合同中,该条款往往还包括一系列各方应当采取的"善后"或补救措施,其中有:a. 双方同意只执行法律允许及可以实施的合同条款(be limited only to the extent required by applicable law and enforced as so limited);b. 缩小合同实施范围、缩短合同执行期限(reduce the scope, duration, area or applicability of the term or provision,);c. 自行(而不是一定由法庭根据"蓝笔原理")取消合同中不合适的词句(to delete specific words or phrases,);d. 用有效条款取代无效条款(to replace any invalid, void or unenforceable term or provision with a term or provision that is valid...)。例如:

例 6. To the extent that any provision of this Agreement is adjudicated to be invalid or unenforceable because it is overbroad, that provision <u>shall not be void but rather shall be limited only to the extent required by applicable law and enforced as so limited</u>.

If the final judgment of such court or arbitrator declares that any term or provision hereof is invalid, void or unenforceable, the parties agree to <u>reduce the scope, duration, area or applicability of the term or provision</u>, <u>to delete specific words or phrases</u>, or <u>to replace any invalid, void or unenforceable term or provision with a term or provision that is valid</u> and enforceable and that comes closest to expressing the original intention of the invalid or unenforceable term or provision. ②

在本文下一节笔者将介绍合同中最流行的、语言风格上更加言简意赅的标准语段。但在此我们不妨先将撰写该条款的常用句型和关键用词做一梳理:

---

① http://liblicense.ukoln.ac.uk/sevcls.shtml.
② http://www.techagreements.com/agreement: AGREEMENT AND PLAN OF MERGER, DATED AS OF MARCH 2, 2009, BY AND AMONG FIRST SOLAR, INC., FIRST SOLAR ACQUISITION CORP., OPTISOLAR INC. AND OPTISOLAR HOLDINGS, LLC (Law Firms: Cravath, Swaine & Moore; Covington & Burling).

(二) 句型和关键用词

- shall be declared or adjudged to be illegal, invalid or unenforceable
- is determined to be invalid and contrary to, or in conflict with
- shall be deemed not to be a part of this agreement
- such invalidity or unenforceability shall not affect the validity or enforceability of the remainder of this Agreement
- replace each invalid, illegal or unenforceable provision with a valid, legal and enforceable provision
- does not in substance have any material adverse effect on
- shall not be affected, and shall be implemented to the maximum extent
- illegal, invalid, unenforceable or void, contrary to, or in conflict with
- be declared or adjudged to, is determined to, is held to, is invalidated by operation of law

affected vs <u>vitiate</u>, impair the operation or affect
contemplated vs <u>purported</u>
complete vs <u>consummate</u>
<u>enumeration</u> of the provisions listed

（以上画线部分为冷僻词，即使在法律英文中也须慎用。）

三、对现有条款的评注

在现有的几本有关英文合同写作及翻译的著作中①，几乎都能找到该可分割性条款及中文译本，但其条文的英文原文和译文质量参差，最遗憾的是其作者从未从语言的角度对其引用的英文条文做出任何分析或提出批评意见。因此，如果读者或文本使用者本人不善于对文本的语言进行分析或做出适当的鉴别，就有可能在不知其优劣的情况全盘照搬，其结果是对不良文风一脉相承，甚至在自己的写作中将错就错、以讹传讹。在下文，笔者除了对译文做出必要的订正外，主要从写作角度对这类原文做些评注。

例 7. If any one or more of the provisions of this Contract or any part or parts <u>thereof</u> <u>shall</u> be declared or adjudged to be illegal, invalid or unenforceable under any applicable law, such illegality, invalidity or unenforceability shall not <u>vitiate</u> any other provisions <u>hereof</u> and this Contract shall be construed as if such illegal, invalid or unenforceable provisions were not contained <u>herein</u>. （范文祥、吴怡，2008：109）

如果本合同任何条款或者任何部分根据适用法律被宣告或判决违反法律、无效或不可执行，则该违反法律、无效或不可执行并不影响合同其他条款的效力，合同解释就好像没有包含这些违反法律、无效或不可执行的条款一样。

---

① 国内近年出版的有关合同的著作参见参考文献部分。

这个范例中的内容还是相当全面的,可分割性条款中的基本要素几乎应有尽有。但语言风格上有一些瑕疵。正如上文别处提到的,本文也有滥用古旧词的习惯:短短一段之中用了三个古旧词和一个冷僻词(见画线部分)。从事法律写作和翻译的人士的确应该掌握古旧词的准确用法,否则可能"失之毫厘,谬之千里"。应该知道:法律文本中使用这类古旧词的主要目的是为了避免用词重复。其使用规矩是:以 here 为词根的古旧词跟该主题(subject-matter)文件有关,以 there 为词根的古旧词跟该词之前曾经出现过的某事物有关。就本例而言,hereof 就是"of this Contract",herein 就是"in this Contract";而 thereof 则指"of any one or more of the provisions of this Contract",并非是"of this Contract"(即主题文件)。所以严格说来,原译"如果本合同任何条款或者任何部分根据适用法律被宣告或判决违反法律、无效或不可执行"是"欠额翻译",确切一点,应该译为"如果本合同任何条款或者该类条款中的任何部分根据适用法律被宣告或判决违反法律、无效或不可执行"。如果不是这样表述,说明对原文的古旧词的意思并没有真正理解。此外,在该条款的条件中,情态动词 shall 仍然被滥用:shall be declared or adjudged 等于说被法庭强制宣布或判决。该句正确的、现代的表达应该是:If any of the provisions of this Contract or any part of the such provision is declared or adjudged to be illegal, invalid or unenforceable under any applicable law, such illegality, invalidity or unenforceability shall not impair any other provisions of the contract and this Contract shall be construed as if such illegal, invalid or unenforceable provisions were not contained in the contract.

另外,我们也可以将以上的可分割性条款与另一著作中的相关条款加以比较:①

例 8. If any provision of this Agreement is held invalid, illegal or unenforceable, the parties shall negotiate in good faith so as to replace each invalid, illegal or unenforceable provision with a valid, legal and enforceable provision which will, in effect, from an economic viewpoint, most nearly and fairly approach the effect of the invalid, illegal or unenforceable provision and the intent of the parties in entering into this Agreement. (乔焕然,2008:231)

如本协议之任何条款被(管辖法庭)认定为无效、非法或不可执行,各方应诚信协商,以有效、合法和可执行的条款来替代每一无效、非法或不可执行的条款,用来替代的条款从经济上应能最接近和最公平地取代该无效、非法或不可执行的条款之效力,并最接近和最公平地反映当事人签订本协议时的意图。

读者会发现乔本中的条款更为合理。原因如下:以上两条的内容相似,但就语言风格而言,该条款简明清晰,避免了任何古旧词的使用,而所有需要表达的内容又毫无遗漏,且语体也非常得体。上例(范本)足足用了三个古旧词(thereof, hereof, herein),其实 thereof 的内涵用 any provisions of this Contract(本协议之任何条款)来表示,已经非常清楚到位,如硬要写成范本的 any one or more of the provisions of this Contract or any part or parts thereof,并不会给这个条件句主语增添任何实质性的内容,只能让读者感知这是"师爷们"的啰唆写法(lawyerism)而已。此外,乔本中提出以"诚信协商"的态度,用"有效、合法和可执行的条款来替代……",比范本的"这条无效,其他条款继续有效"的写法更加富有建设性,更加"有济于事"。

---

① 乔本即乔焕然:《英文合同阅读指南》。

四、可分割性条款写作原理及范例

可分割条款的核心是"如有部分条款无效或无法执行,合同的其他部分不受影响"。所以,不管"戏法"怎么变,只要包含这一层意思,这一条款就可成立,当然更完善的条款可包括"用有效的、可执行的条款取而代之"。至于合同中的某些条款是否有效、合法、可执行,则须由相关的主管机构决定。这类机构是否一定是法庭?未必,可以是某规管机构或行政部门,如中国的工商管理部门、政府环保机构,美国的 FDA(食品药品管理局)等。所以,这类机构的名称在条款中还是不明言更有回旋余地。如果内容太明确,条款的无效、非法、不可执行,要由法庭宣布(is declared by a court of competent jurisdiction to be illegal, unenforceable or void),这样会使该条款的实用性大大降低。以下提供一条详尽的标准条款:

例 9. If any provision, or part of a provision of this Agreement is determined to be invalid, illegal or unenforceable by any rule or law, or public policy of any jurisdiction, all other provisions, or other parts of the provision of this Agreement shall nevertheless remain in full force and effect so long as such invalidity, illegality or unenforceability does not in essence have any material adverse effect on the economic or legal substance of the subject-matter contemplated in the agreement.

如本协议的任何条款或条款之一部分依照有关司法管辖区的法庭裁决、法律或公共政策而被确定无效、违法或不可执行,本协议的其余款或条款之其余部分仍将继续完全有效,只要本协议拟执行的标的物的经济或法律内容没有受到任何实质性的不利影响。

Upon such determination all parties shall negotiate in good faith to modify this Agreement so as to effect the original intent of the parties as closely as possible in a mutually acceptable manner. The parties may 1) reduce the scope, duration, area or applicability of the provision or the part, 2) delete the specific words or phrases in the provision, or 3) replace any invalid, illegal or unenforceable provision or part with provision or part that is valid, legal or enforceable and that comes closest to expressing the original intention of the invalid, illegal or unenforceable provision or part.

在确定本协议任何条款或条款之一部分无效、违法或不可执行后,各协议方应真诚协商修订本协议,以双方都可接受的方式尽可能使修订接近协议方的本意。各方可以 1)缩窄协议条款或条款之一部分的实施范围、适用性或实施期限;2)删除条款中的特定词语;或 3)用最接近无效、违法或不可执行条款或条款之一部分原意的有效、合法、可执行的条款取而代之。

与常见的可分割性条款比较,以上范例有以下若干项改进:

1) 判定条款无效的动词选用 is determined,而不是 be declared or adjudged,是为了扩大权威机构的范围:如果用了 be adjudged,那么这项决定一定是由法庭机构做出的;其实仲裁机构、权威部门(如工商管理部门或其他政府职能机构)都有可能判定或认定合同条款无效、违法或不可实施,如中国政府临时发布的"限制稀土出口令",中国各省市或地方政府为调控房地产出台的各种新政策或新规定,中国香港政府因为当地婴儿奶粉供应紧张而临时采取的"限奶令",美国奥巴马总统基于所谓国土安全理由而下达的不准中国某企业收购美国风电项目的行政命令……,均可使原有签订的合同条款无法执行(而未必要等到法庭的最后判决)。所以,将一般条款中常用的、使部分合同无效的司法机构("... by a court of competent jurisdiction")改为"any rule or law, or public policy"更为妥当。

2) 该 any rule or law, or public policy of any jurisdiction 短语中添加"司法管辖区"一词是有必要的(绝大部分这类条款没有这一限定),这有助于解决跨国合同发生的争拗。合同条款出现无效、违法或不可实施的状况,不一定是合同签订国的原因,也可以是任何一个对合同拥有司法管辖权的地区或国家之规定、法律或公共政策的原因。

3) 为了使该条款达到通用目的,受影响的以合同"标的物"(subject-matter)称谓之更为合适,因为未必所有合同都是围绕一桩"买卖"(transaction——这几乎是大多数现有合同的标准写法)而进行的。如果是成立一家合资企业,或双方合作开发一个房地产项目,其中因条款无效而可能受影响的主题就不是单纯的"买卖",所以用较模糊但概括范围更广的"the subject-matter"一词来表达合同的核心内容,可以让该条款更具通用性。顺便值得一提的是 contemplated 一词:这在普通英文中是个冷僻词,但在法律英文中,尤其是在合同条款中确实是个常用词,而且几乎是个不可替代的热门词,如果用来修饰 transaction 或 subject-matter(如 the transaction contemplated in the agreement)指的是一宗经过"深思熟虑的"买卖或合同标的物——任何合同订立之前都有这个过程。①

4) 由于法律概念的复杂性,或作者为了达到表达精确以使文本不留任何歧义(其实是不可能的),法律条文中的句子往往写得啰唆冗长,大量使用近义词,重复的内容多之又多。以上语段几乎把 invalid, illegal or unenforceable(近义词)重复了五次。当然使用一些以 there-为词根的古旧词可以避免部分重复。但那样会增加文本使用者解读文意的难度。所以,本范例并没有使用任何古旧词。

笔者认为,在可能的情况下,还是应当避免太多的用词重复。例如,在写作该条款的第二段时一般都会这样开头:"Upon such determination that any term or other provision is invalid, illegal or incapable of being enforced"。其实省却修饰 determination 的 that any term or other provision is invalid, illegal or incapable of being enforced 这个冗长的定语从句,是不会让文意产生歧义的,任何词语的意思都是根据上下文来理解的,上文刚刚说过"is determined to be invalid, illegal or unenforceable",那么这个"determination"绝对不可能指代其他内容。所以,在不造成歧义的前提下,法律语言也应尽可能简洁,避免不必要的重复。

众所周知,可分割性条款是以防万一用的,在实际操作中几乎都用不到。所以,不必写得太啰唆,各种可能的或假设的状况无需面面俱到。最简单的写法分别是:

例 9. a. If any provision of this Agreement becomes invalid or unenforceable in any jurisdiction, such invalidity or unenforceability shall not affect the validity or enforceability of the remainder of this Agreement.

b. If any of the provision of this Contract is held to be invalid or unenforceable, this Contract shall be construed as if it did not contain such invalid or unenforceable provision and the remaining provisions of this Contract shall remain in full force.

---

① 该词的定义是: you thought about something seriously or considered something carefully and at length. If you thought for about 10 minutes about taking a nap but then decided not to, this is an example of when you contemplated a nap. 见 http://www.yourdictionary.com/contemplated

这些变成无效的内容可以是协议或合同的条款、条件、条文、规定、段落、部分或规定之全部或一部分(Each section, part, any section, part, term, or provision of this agreement, terms and conditions, any provision, or part of a provision, in whole or in part, any part or parts thereof)。而使这些条款变成无效、违法或无法执行的方式可以是被有关司法部门的宣布、判决、或根据法律运作，或因与现有的、将来的法律或规定相冲突而造成的(be declared or adjudged to be illegal, invalid or unenforceable, <u>by operation of law, is determined to be invalid, is held invalid, illegal or unenforceable (by any competent judicial organization)</u>, is determined to be invalid and contrary to, or in conflict with any existing or future law or regulation of a court or agency having valid jurisdiction)。以上说法五花八门，没有统一措辞，有些简单，有些详细，有些甚至啰唆，但就该条款的内容而言，无太多实质性差异。所以，这些内容均可简化，甚至省略。为了给起草不同性质的可分性条款提供更多的参考，以下辑录来自不同合同的相关条款及其译文。

五、可分割性参考条款及译文

3. Severability	可分性/可分割性
Each provision of these Terms is severable and if any provision is or becomes illegal, invalid or unenforceable in any jurisdiction, that provision is severed only in that particular jurisdiction. All other provisions shall continue to have effect.①	此等条款中的每项条款为可分割，如任何条文在任何司法权区为或可能为不合法、无效或不可依法执行，将只在该特定司法权区内分割该条文。所有其他条文将继续生效。
If any one or more of the <u>provisions of this Contract or any part or parts thereof shall be declared or adjudged to be illegal, invalid or unenforceable under any applicable law</u>, such illegality, invalidity or unenforceability shall not vitiate any other provisions hereof and this Contract shall be construed as if such illegal, invalid or unenforceable provisions were not contained herein.（范文祥、吴怡，2008:109）	如果本合同任何条款或者任何部分根据适用法律被宣告或判决违反法律、无效或不可执行，则该违反法律、无效或不可执行并不影响合同其他条款的效力，合同解释就好像没有包含这些违反法律、无效或不可执行的条款一样。
It *shall* be acknowledged by both Parties that this Contract shall be implemented in accordance with and only to such extent as permitted by all the applicable laws, regulations, and rules. If any provision of this Contract, or the application of this Contract to any Party or any circumstances, is invalid and unenforceable for whatever reason or to any extent, and such invalidity or unenforceability <u>does not in substance have any material adverse effect on</u> the economy or law for the transaction <u>contemplated</u> in this contract, then the remaining provisions in this contract or the application of these provisions to any Party or any circumstances in question <u>shall not be affected</u>, and shall be implemented to the Each	双方知道：本合同应遵照所有适用法律、法规和规则并仅可在上述法律、法规和规则许可的范围内执行。如果由于任何原因或在任何范围内本合同的任何条款或本合同对任何一方或任何情形的适用无效或不具有可执行性，且该无效或不可执行性实质上对于本合同中规定的交易的经济或法律内容不会造成任何重大不利影响，则本合同的其余条款或这些条款对于任何一方或任何相关情形的适用性不受影响，

---

① 该条文的译文属于典型的香港式译文。见香港恒生银行2014年8月给其客户的《业务关系条款》。

3. Severability	可分性/可分割性
maximum extent as provided by law.（范文祥、吴怡，2008:224）	并应在法律所规定的最大限度内执行这些条款。
Section, part, term, and provision of this agreement <u>shall be considered severable</u>. If, for any reason, any section, part, term, or provision of this agreement <u>is determined to be invalid and contrary to</u>, or <u>in conflict with</u>, any existing or future law or regulation of a court or agency having valid jurisdiction, such determination <u>shall not impair the operation or affect the remaining</u> portions, sections, parts, terms, or <u>provisions</u> of this agreement, and the latter *will* continue to be given full force and effect and bind the parties to this agreement. The invalid section, part, term, or provision <u>shall be deemed not to be a part of this agreement</u>.（王辉，2007:97）	本协议每章、节、条、款应被认为是可分开的。如出于某种原因，本协议任何一章、节、条、款被认定为无效或与有管辖权法院或机构的现行或将来的法律法规发生矛盾或冲突，则该裁决不损害或影响本协议其余部分、章、节、条、款的适用性，且后者继续完全有效，对本协议双方均有约束力。无效的章、节、条、款应视为不再是本协议之一部分。
If any provision of this Agreement shall be invalid or unenforceable in any jurisdiction, such invalidity or unenforceability <u>shall not affect</u> the validity or enforceability of the remainder of this Agreement or the validity or enforceability of this Agreement in any other jurisdiction.	如本协议的任何条款在任何司法管辖区域内无效或不可执行，则该无效或不可执行不影响本协议其他条款的有效性或可执行性，也不影响本协议在任何其他司法管辖区域内的有效性或可执行性。
If any of the provisions of this Contract are held to be invalid or unenforceable, this Contract shall be construed <u>as if</u> it did not contain such invalid or unenforceable provision and the remaining provisions of this Contract shall <u>remain in full force and effect</u>.	如本合同的任何条款无效或不可执行，本合同解释就如未包含这些无效或不可执行的条款一样，且本合同其他条款继续有效。
If any provision, or part of a provision of this Agreement is invalidated by operation of law, the provision or part will to that extent be deemed omitted and the remainder of this Agreement will remain <u>in full force and effect</u> so long as the economic or legal substance of the transactions <u>contemplated</u> hereby are not <u>affected</u> in any manner adverse to any party. Upon such determination that any term or other provision is invalid, illegal or incapable of being enforced, the parties hereto shall negotiate in good faith to modify this Agreement so as to effect the original intent of the parties as closely as possible in a mutually acceptable manner in order that the transactions contemplated hereby be consummated as originally contemplated to the fullest extent possible.	如本协议的任何条款或任何条款之一部分依照法律无效，该条款或条款之一部分将被忽略，而本协议的剩余内容将继续有效——只要根据本协议打算交易的经济或法律内容不对任何一方产生不利的影响。在决定任何条件或其他条款无效、违法或不可执行时，协议方应真诚协商修改本协议，以双方都可接受的方式尽可能使之接近协议方的本意，从而保证本协议打算进行的交易与最初的打算最大限度的吻合。

3. Severability	可分性/可分割性
A judicial determination that any provision of this agreement is invalid, in whole or in part, shall not affect the enforceability of those provisions unaffected by the finding of inability. (乔焕然, 2008:116)	如本协议中任何条款之一部分或整条被法院判决无效, 则其他未受影响部分条款的可执行性不受影响。
The invalidity, in whole or in part, of any term of this agreement does not affect the validity of the remainder of the agreement. (乔焕然, 2008:116)	本协议任何条款之一部分或全部内容无效不影响协议剩余部分内容的有效性。
If any provision of this Agreement <u>is held invalid, illegal or unenforceable</u> (by any competent judicial organization), the parties shall negotiate in good faith so as to <u>replace each invalid, illegal or unenforceable provision with a valid, legal and enforceable provision</u> which will, in effect, from an economic viewpoint, most nearly and fairly approach the effect of the <u>invalid, illegal or unenforceable provision</u> and the intent of the parties in entering into this Agreement. (乔焕然, 2008:231)	如本协议之任何条款被(管辖法庭)认定为无效、非法或不可执行, 各方应诚信协商, 以有效、合法和可执行的条款来替代每一无效、非法或不可执行的条款, 用来替代的条款从经济上应能最接近和最公平地取得该无效、非法或不可执行的条款之效力, 并最接近和最公平地反映当事人签订本协议时的意图。
If any provision of this Agreement is determined to <u>be invalid, illegal or unenforceable</u>, the remaining provisions of this Agreement <u>remain in full force and effect</u>, if the essential terms and conditions of this Agreement for both parties remain valid, legal and enforceable. Without limiting the previous sentence, the parties acknowledge and agree that the provisions of Sections 1 and 2 constitute essential elements of the agreed exchange that is the subject matter of this Agreement. Accordingly, if any of these provisions is determined to <u>be invalid, illegal or unenforceable</u> in any material respect, the remainder of this Agreement is not enforceable against either of the parties. The specific enumeration of the provisions listed does not mean or imply that no other provisions of this Agreement constitutes an essential element of the agreed exchange that is the subject matter of this Agreement. (乔焕然, 2008:231)	如本协议之任何条款被认定为无效、非法或不可执行, 本协议的其他条款仍将保持全部效力, 但前提是本协议的基本条款和条件对双方而言仍然有效、合法和可执行。双方当事人承认并同意第1和第2条构成本协议标的即双方同意的交换之基本要素(该种承认和同意不构成对上一句的限制)。相应的, 如这些条款的任何实质方面被认定为无效、非法或不可执行, 本协议的其他部分对任何一方都不可执行。上述具体列举的条款并不意味着也不暗示本协议的其他条款都不构成本协议的标的即双方同意的交换之基本要素。
<u>In the event</u> that any provision of this Agreement becomes or is declared by a court of competent jurisdiction to <u>be illegal, unenforceable or void</u>, this Agreement shall continue <u>in full force and effect</u> without said provision; provided that no such severability shall be effective if it materially changes the economic benefit of this Agreement to any party. (乔焕然, 2008:231)	万一本协议之任何条款成为或被有管辖权的法院宣布为非法、不可执行或无效, 本协议之其余部分应继续完全有效; 但该条款分开实质改变了任一方本协议下的经济利益的除外。

第二十四章 合同变更条款的写作和翻译

一、引言：合同变更条款的定义及基本内涵

合同变更指对合同已有内容做出改变。虽然英文合同中有时会用 change 或 alteration，但更常用的词是 modification。使用标准格式的合同的，如租约，对其中条款所做的细小变更，往往采用简单的涂改或添加的方式，不过，在每个涂改或添加处，双方（尤其是非合同起草方）一定要草签（sign initials），即签上全名的缩略形式，以证明该处变更经过双方确认。但本文不讨论这类细微的在合同准备阶段的变更，而是讨论合同生效之后因情况有变而不得不采取的条款变更问题，也就是要探索如何写作合同变更条款，这是合同通用条款之一。

就合同的更变内容而言，通常不外乎以下几方面：1) 延长合同履行的期限；2) 扩充合同涉及的业务范围；3) 更改合同所订的货品数量；4) 改变付款条件，等等。

变更合同的常规程序是就需要变更的条款或事宜与对方协商，如果对方同意，就请求原先草拟合同的人士打印一份经过修改的合同，各合同方重新审核经修订的合同，再由原有合同当事人在经修订或变更的合同上签字。如果变更内容是以附加条款（rider）形式出现的，在其上签署的也必须是原合同的签署人。

就合同变更的有关法律而言，各国的法律基本上是相同的：只要合同各方同意，就可以变更原合同的内容，且变更部分亦受法律保护。变更合同的形式有两种：可以是口头的，也可以是书面的；但如果合同本身规定任何变更须以书面形式做出的，则口头形式的变更属无效。在美国，为了提高效率以及减少开支，如变更会使合同的价值增加或减少 500 美元，才需要以书面形式做出。（Legal-dictionary）的确，这是很好的法典规定，否则为了区区小变，所付出的律师费用可能远远不止此数，更何况在合同执行期间根据具体情况需要做出的这类"微调"有时可能是很频繁的。但较重要或重大的变更一定要双方协商、以附加条款或附件（a rider, additional section）的书面形式做出，并且双方必须在附加条款或附件上签字。特别重要的变更（如合资企业注册资本的增减/经营范围的变更）还须将有关的变更内容送交当地主管部门备案、甚至审批。

任何合同的变更内容都要合情合理、符合行业规矩，否则法庭仍然有权剔除其认为在胁迫（duress）或欺诈（bad faith）情况下所做的任何变更。

二、变更条款的基本句型和关键用词/语

（一）有关变更合同程序的规定和写法

1. MODIFICATION. This agreement may not be amended, changed or modified except

by a writing duly executed by both parties, and it is expressly understood that in the case of Party A, any such writing shall be executed by an authorized representative of Party A.

2. Either party may propose to modify the contract. If Party A requests a modification, its business office must submit a signed request to Party B's contracting officer explaining the modification and its anticipated effect on the contract.

3. Only contracting officers acting within their delegated authority may modify a contract or change a contractual commitment on behalf.

4. Any modification of this Contract must be discussed by both parties with the written agreement to be reached.

5. This agreement may be amended during the duration of this Agreement by the Parties, provided that such amendment shall be in writing and signed by both Parties and shall be approved by the competent government agency.

6. This Contact and its appendixes may be modified only after Party A and Party B have held consultations and executed a supplementary agreement on the modification.

7. The party proposing such modification shall notify in writing the other party two (2) months in advance, explaining the reason thereof.

8. The modification shall go through the procedures of approval and registration.

9. The amendment hereto has been approved by the Examination and Approval Authority.

10. Modification of any article hereof shall be modification of this Contract.

11. If any modification of a Purchase Order causes... shall notify OMP prior to enacting such change and the change,... shall become effective immediately upon the date of such notification.

12. Amendment to this Contract shall become effective only after a written agreement to amend the Contract signed by Party A and Party B.

13. The modifications made pursuant to such Change Order shall be effective upon Company's issuance of a Change Order with respect thereto.

14. The Parties may not modify a Purchase Order except in writing and upon obtaining the signature of an authorized representative of each Party.

15. The Lender and the Borrower agreed to modify the contents of the Main Contract as follows:

16. The following changes are hereby made to the contract:

17. Supplies or Services and Prices/Costs are amended as follows:

18. Paragraph B. XX (x) is modified to add the following:

19. The detailed description of the work is contained in the attachments to this modification identified as Attachment XX of the contract.

20. The parties may modify(amend, alter, change, revise)their contract...

(二) 关键词辨析

在合同变更条款中,常用的动词除了 modify 之外,还有 amend, alter, change, revise。

这些词的意思都指对法律文本的修改，但如果小标题称作"合同变更"条款，一般只用 Modifications。如果用 Amendments，通常称作"合同修订"。amend 所做改动，一般都以附件形式，附加在主合同或现行合同（或法律文本）之后。如美国的宪法，虽然是几百年前颁布的，至今仍然在施行，就是因为它有无数个 Amendments（修正案）。amendments 主要包括三项：添加（addition）、纠正（correction）和删除（deletion）。由于它们是附加性质的，所以常跟介词 to 连用，成为主文件的附件。例如：The editors made few amendments to the manuscript. 而其他的 alteration, modification, revision, change，往往指对原有条文的直接修订或增删，原合同未必有错。但更变或修订的内容比较多的也会写成一个单独的附加条款，法律英文中称这类文件为 Rider 或 Amendment。要使之生效，合同各方（一般同为主合同的签字人）必须在附加条款上签字。

在这些词中，尽可能避免使用 revise，该词指的是较大的改动，尤其是改正错误，或加工改造，这往往是在主合同起草过程中发生的事情；而合同中的更变一般都是主合同生效后的"小打小闹"，做些小的改动或修正，尤其是在 Modification 这个条款中。

三、标准通用变更条款的写作及说明

从现有的英文合同语料来看，该通用条款在语言上是最接近普通英文的。也就是说，合同起草者在撰写这一条款的语段时，较少使用那些迂腐的、具有"师爷"语言特征的词语。我们可以将典型的写法分作三段总结如下：

Modifications: This Contact (and its appendixes) may be modified only after Party A and Party B have held consultations and executed a supplementary agreement on the modifications.

甲乙双方经过磋商、签署有关变更事宜的补充协议后才可对本合同（及其附件）进行变更。

The party proposing such modification shall notify in writing the other party one (1) month in advance, explaining the reason of such modifications.

提出这类变更的一方应提前一个月以书面形式通知对方，解释变更的因由。

Modifications to this Contract shall become effective only after they are signed by Party A and Party B, and have been approved by the competent government organization if the law requires.

只有甲乙双方在本合同的变更文件上签字，变更才生效；如法律有规定，还须得到有关政府主管部门的批准。

第一段规定合同可以变更或修订，但必须在合同双方经过协商、签署有关变更事项的补充协议之后进行。

第二段讲述如何着手合同的变更。这类变更一般都是由其中一方提出的，所以第二段规定：拟修订合同的一方须提前一个月以书面形式向另一方提出要求，并说明修订的理由。当然，在这一句的写作上，很多合同会用上一个古旧词，写成"explaining the reason thereof"。其实，没有必要，使用这类古旧词的主要目的是为了简约，节省用词，避免重复，不提及前面刚刚提到的内容（当然也有风格上的考虑）。但是，此处实质上只省去一个词（of such modifications vs thereof),因为后者这个古旧词本身也是由两个单词(there+of)合并构成的。用了一个难懂的古旧词节省的不过是一个 such,可谓得不偿失。

第三段规定修订内容何时生效:双方在有关的修订内容上签字之后即可生效。不过,有些修订或变更(如合资企业的经营范围、注册资本等)的生效还需得到政府主管部门的批准。在中国,主要是得到相应级别的工商管理部门的批准。此外,如合同涉及一些具体细节上的更变,一般都会用一句诸如此类的"引言":

1) Party A and Party B agree to modify the contents of the Main Contract as follows:

甲乙双方同意对主合同的内容作如下变更:

2) The following changes (amendments) are hereby made to the contract:

特此对本合同做如下改变(修订):

3) The detailed description of the work is contained in the Attachment to this modification identified as Attachment XX of the contract # between XXX Ltd. & YYY Ltd.

本合同附件,即 XXX 有限公司与 YYY 有限公司所订的第#合同的第 xx 号附件,包括了对本工程的详细描述。

这三个引导句不属于主合同内的通用变更条款用语,是具体变更内容的引语。其中最后一句更为常用,也更加灵活,尤其适合以附件形式出现的变更。

四、霸王式变更条款的写作

Amendments: You agree that from time to time we may alter (including adding or eliminating all or parts of provisions) these Terms, including but not limited to the Privacy Policy ("Amendments"). Amended versions of these Terms will take effect on the date specified for the amended version ("Effective Date") and will apply to all information that was collected before or after the Effective Date, including information in databases. You have no continuing right to use the Sites——it is like a store and each time you visit you will be subject to the version of the Terms in effect on your visit. Like terms on the door to a store, those terms will change from time to time and the changes will be effective when they appear in a replacement version of these Terms as posted by us on the Sites. No other Amendments will be valid unless they are in a paper writing signed by us and by you.

这类"修订条款"在网站合同、商业服务、银行服务合同中非常普遍。虽然这也是合同中的修订条款,但实际上并非是平等的条款,你要使用它们的服务,你就得接受。你不接受,你就离开。他们所订的条款是单边的,而且经常更变,就像银行的利息一样,商店中商品的价格一样。所以,我们称之为霸王条款。其中的写法"霸气"十足。这些体现强硬语气的句子如:

Terms will take effect on the date specified for the amended version; You have no continuing right to use the Sites; you will be subject to the version of the Terms in effect on your visit; those terms will change from time to time; the changes will be effective when they appear in a replacement version of these Terms. (修订版的条款将在指定日期生效;贵方无继续使用本网站的权利;贵方必须遵守访问本网站时有效的条款;该类条款不时会有更变;该类更变出现在取代以前版本的条款时即已生效。)(笔者译)

五、其他变更条款及参考译文

Modification of Contracts	合同的变更
The parties may <u>modify</u> their contract upon agreement reached through consultation. <u>Where</u> laws and administrative <u>regulations</u> <u>provide</u> that the modification of a contract shall go through the procedures of approval and registration, such <u>provision</u> shall <u>govern</u>.	合同方可通过协商对签订的合同进行修改。凡法律和行政法规规定合同修改应经过审批与登记程序的,该规定方可适用。
Amendment: This agreement may be amended during the duration of this Agreement by the Parties, provided that such amendment shall be in writing and signed by both Parties and shall be approved by the competent government agency.	修订:本协议在有效期内经双方签署书面协议后,可予以修改,但修订仍须经政府主管部门批准。
(A) Except for the other stipulations made in this Contract, <u>any modification of this Contract must be discussed</u> by the Guarantor and the Lender with the written agreement to be reached. (B) If the Lender legally transfers the creditor's rights under the Main Contract, the Guarantor will continue to undertake the joint guarantee responsibility guaranteed in the scope of this Contract. (C) If the Lender allows the Borrower to transfer the debts under the Main Contract, the written approval should be obtained from the Guarantor, and the Guarantor will not undertake the guarantee responsibility any more for the transferred debts that are not agreed by the Guarantor. (D) In the course of the guarantee, <u>when there are some changes</u> (except for the interest rate of the loan under the Main Contract to be adjusted as per the Peoples Bank of China) for the interest rate of the loan and the loan amount to be made by the Lender and the Borrower, which are not agreed by the Guarantor, if it is for reducing the debts of the Borrower, the Guarantor will still undertake the guarantee responsibility for the modified contract; if it is for increasing the debts of the Borrower, the Guarantor will not undertake the guarantee responsibility for the increased part. <u>If the Lender and the Borrower make some changes for the fulfillment term of the repayment plan</u> stipulated under the Main Contract without the written approval from the Guarantor, the same guarantee term will be the term stipulated in the original contract or the term as regulated by law. The Lender and the Borrower agreed to modify the contents of the Main Contract,	(A)除合同另有规定外,本合同的任何更改必须与担保人和贷方商议并以书面协议形式进行。(B)如果贷方合法转让主合同下的债权,担保人将继续承担对本合同范围内的联保责任。(C)如果贷方允许借方转让主合同下的债务,则应取得担保人的书面许可。对于未经担保人许可而转让的债务,担保人不再承担任何担保责任。(D)在担保期间,当借方与贷方在未经担保人许可的情况下更改贷款利率(除非是本合同项下的贷款利率按照中国人民银行的规定做出调整)及贷款数额时,如果是减少借方的债务,则担保人应继续承担修改后的合同规定的担保责任;如果是增加借方的债务,则担保人对所增加的部分无担保责任。如果借贷双方在未得到担保人书面许可的情况下更改主合同规定的债务偿还计划的履行条款,相同的担保条款应为原有合同规定的条款或法律规定的条款。借贷双方同意修改主合同中并未实施的内容,在此情况下,担保人将继续承担担保责任。(E)万一借贷双

续表

Modification of Contracts	合同的变更
which are not actually carried out, and in this case, the Guarantor will still undertake the guarantee responsibility. (E) In the event that the Lender and the Borrower agree to modify <u>the draw plan</u> stipulated in the Main Contract, the Guarantor will still undertake the guarantee responsibility.	方同意更改主合同规定的提取计划时,则担保人将继续负有担保责任。
<u>Amendment</u> to this Contract shall become effective only after a written agreement to <u>amend</u> the Contract signed by Party A and Party B, the board resolution for <u>amending</u> the Contract and the <u>amendment</u> hereto have been approved by the Examination and Approval Authority.	本合同的修改,只有在甲方和乙方签署的修改合同的书面协议、董事会有关修改合同的决议以及对合同的修改经审批机构批准后方能生效。
Modification of any article <u>hereof</u> shall be modification of this Contract. The party proposing such modification shall notify in writing the other party two (2) months in advance, <u>explaining the reason thereof</u>. This Contact and its appendixes may be modified only after Party A and Party B have held consultations and executed a supplementary agreement on the modification.	本合同任何条款的变更,均为合同本身的变更。提议变更的一方应提前两个月书面通知另一方,说明变更的理由。本合同及其附件只有经甲、乙方协商并签署补充协议后方能变更。

六、订单变更条款写作范例

Other Modifications Of Purchase Order. Each Purchase Order shall constitute a binding agreement between Triax and OMP, and the Parties may not modify a Purchase Order except in writing and upon obtaining the signature of an authorized representative of each Party. If any modification of a Purchase Order <u>causes a decrease or reasonably-supported increase in Triax's manufacturing cost</u>, Triax promptly shall notify OMP prior to enacting such change and the change, which shall be noted in writing on the Purchase Order, shall become effective immediately upon the date of such notification.

<u>If a Change in the Product is initiated</u> under this Article 8, then the Change Order and the modifications made pursuant to such Change Order shall be effective upon Company's issuance of a Change Order with respect thereto. Notwithstanding a dispute regarding any proposed or requested Change Order, or any adjustment of one or more of the Contract Price, the Schedule (including the Guaranteed Substantial Completion Date and the Guaranteed Final Completion Date), or any other such part of this Contract as may be affected with respect to a Change Order, Contractor shall proceed with the performance of such Change Order promptly following Company's execution of the corresponding Change Order.

第二十五章 完整协议/最终协议条款的写作和翻译

一、引言

在合同中包括这一条款的目的是为了保护这个来之不易的最终文本,使之成为有关主题事项(即文内所指的"合同标的")唯一的有效合同文本,不再受以往为达成本协议而签署的各种临时或过渡性文件(如意向书、谅解书、备忘录以及各种口头承诺)的干扰或因其而可能造成的混乱。不过,不同性质的合同表述该条内容的措辞仍然稍有不同。见以下各例:

二、完整协议样本

Entire Agreement/ Final Agreement	完整协议/最终协议	使用说明
1. This Agreement constitutes the entire agreement between the parties and there are no representations, express or implied, statutory or otherwise and no collateral agreements other than as expressly set out or referred to in this Agreement.	本协议构成各方之间的完整协议,除了本协议明确说明或提到的文件外,没有其他明示的或暗含的、合法的或其他形式的陈述,也没有其他的担保协议。	适合简单的无其他附加内容的合同,尤其适合资产购买协议
2. This Security Agreement embodies the entire agreement and understanding between the Debtor and the Agent relating to the Collateral and supersedes all prior agreements and understandings between the Debtor and the Agent relating to the Collateral.	本担保协议包括债务人与代理人就本受担保品达成的完整协议和谅解,取代先前债务人和代理人之间就本担保品达成的所有协议和谅解。	简单担保合同,如信用卡合同
3. This Agreement, including any agreements set forth as an annex to any this Agreement, is the final agreement between the parties and constitutes the entire agreement between the parties hereto and supersedes all prior agreements and understandings, both written and oral, whether signed or unsigned, with respect to the subject matter hereof.	本协议,包括作为本协议之附件的任何协议,是各方之间的最后协议,构成本协议各方之间的完整协议,取代先前就本协议之标的而达成的任何书面的或口头的、签署的或未签署的所有协议及谅解。	适合任何性质(包括有附录的)合同的完整协议条款

Entire Agreement/ Final Agreement	完整协议/最终协议	使用说明
4. This Agreement, including all exhibits, schedules, attachments and any agreements set forth as an annex to any this Agreement, is the final agreement between the parties and constitutes the entire agreement between the parties hereto and supersedes all prior agreements and understandings, both written and oral, whether signed or unsigned, with respect to the subject matter hereof, and specifically supersedes the Letter of Intent between the parties dated (month/day/year).	本协议,包括作为本协议之所有证明、附表、附件以及本协议附录中提及的任何协议,是各方之间的最后协议,构成本协议各方之间的完整协议,取代先前就本协议之标的达成的任何书面的或口头的、签署的或未签署的所有协议及谅解,特别将取代各方于____年__月__日签署的意向书。	适合任何性质(包括有附表、附录以及意向书的)合同,尤其适合有诸多附件的大型合同
5. This Agreement sets forth the entire agreement of the parties hereto in respect of the subject matter contained herein and supersedes all prior agreements, promises, covenants, arrangements, communications, representations or warranties, whether oral or written, by any officer, employee or representative of any party hereto in respect of the subject matter contained herein; and any prior agreement of the parties hereto in respect of the subject matter contained herein is hereby terminated and cancelled.①	本协议是各方就本协议之标的达成的完整协议,取代由本协议任何一方之高级官员、雇员或代表先前做出的关于本协议标的之任何书面的或口头的协议、许诺、契约、安排、通讯、陈述或保证。本协议各方先前就本协议之标的而达成的任何协议特此终止并作废。	适合先前有许多允诺的合同,尤其是雇佣合同;但本条文风陈腐,充满法律术语
6. The terms and conditions herein contained, including the Appendices hereto, constitute the entire agreement between the Parties hereto. This Contract shall supersede all previous communications, either oral or written, between the Parties. Amendments modifying or extending the Contract shall be binding upon both parties only if in writing and signed by a duly authorized officer or representative of each party.	本合同所包含的条款和条件,包括合同附件,构成合同各方的完整协议。本合同取代各方先前所有的口头或书面的通讯。对合同所做的修改或补充条款,只有采取书面形式并经各方正式授权的主管人员或代表签署后,方对各方具有约束力。	适合只包含条款、条件和附件的简单合同,但对补充条款的形成有具体规定

---

① http://www.realdealdocs.com/ClauseSearchResult.aspx

续表

Entire Agreement/ Final Agreement	完整协议/最终协议	使用说明
7. Effective upon the execution of this Agreement, the Confidentiality Agreement shall automatically terminate without any further action by the parties hereto. This Agreement (including the documents and instruments referred to in this Agreement) sets forth the entire understanding and agreement among the parties as to the matters covered in this Agreement and supersedes and replaces any prior understanding, agreement or statement of intent, written or oral, with respect to the Confidentiality Agreement.	在本协议签署生效之日起,各方无需采取任何进一步行动,该保密协议即自动终止。本协议(包括本协议中提及的任何法律文件)阐明各方就本协议包括的事项达成的完整谅解和协议,取代以前的就本保密协议而达成的任何书面的或口头的谅解、协议或意向陈述。	适合保密合同
8. This note and the other loan documents contain the final, entire agreement between the parties hereto relating to the subject matter hereof and thereof and all prior agreements, whether written or oral, relative hereto and thereto which are not contained herein or therein are superseded and terminated hereby, and this note and the other loan documents may not be contradicted or varied by evidence of prior, contemporaneous or subsequent oral agreements or discussions of the parties hereto. There are no unwritten oral agreements among the parties hereto.	本票据或其他贷款文件包含本票据及其他贷款文件各方就本票据以及其他贷款文件之标的而达成的最后及完整的协议,取代所有先前的就本票据及其他贷款文件达成的书面的或口头的协议。本票据及其他贷款文件不得与各方就此而进行的任何口头协议或磋商证据(无论是先前的、同时的或继后的)相抵触或因此而做出改变。各方之间并不存在任何非书面形式的口头协议。	票据及贷款合约,但本条文风陈腐,充满古旧词语
9. All the appendices to this Agreement shall be an integral part of this Agreement. This Agreement and all its appendices shall constitute the entire agreement between the Parties with respect to the subject matter set forth herein and supersede any and all previous oral and written discussions, negotiations, notices, memoranda, documents, agreements, contracts and communications between the Parties relating to such subject matter.	本协议的所有附件都是本协议不可分割的组成部分。本协议及其附件构成双方就本协议规定的标的达成的完整协议,并取代双方先前与该标的有关的一切和所有的口头和书面的洽谈、谈判、通知、备忘录、文件、协议、合同和通讯。(孙万彪,2002)①	适合供货协议的完整协议条款

---

① 又见 http://translation168. lingdi. net/article－4327080－1. html

Entire Agreement/ Final Agreement	完整协议/最终协议	使用说明
10. This Agreement, entered into as of the data written above, <u>constitutes</u> the entire agreement between the Parties relating to the subject matter hereof and shall be in addition to and not in derogation of the provisions of the Supply Agreement. No terms or provisions of this Agreement shall be varied or modified by any prior or subsequent statement, conduct or act of either of the Parties, except that the Parties may amend this Agreement by written instruments referring to and executed in the same manner as this Agreement.	自文首载明的日期签订的本协议,构成各方关于本协议标的的完整协议,是对供应协议的补充而不是减损。任何一方均不得以先前或以后的声明、举动或行为修改或变更本协议的任何条款或规定,但各方可以以本协议中提及的和以本协议相同方式签署的书面文件修改本协议。(同上)	适合供货协议的完整协议条款

三、写作要点及关键词讲解

以上共有 10 条适合不同性质合同的完整协议条款。虽然其所针对的合同性质各异,各条的措辞均有差别,但其写作上有两个共同特点:第一,几乎每一段条文都使用下列的其中两个动词和一个介词短语。该类动词为:be/include/contain/constitutes/embody;supersede/replace;介词短语为:in(with) respect of the subject matter contained hereof / relating to the subject matter hereof。第二,写作该条款的动词,可以一律不用情态动词。因为这一款的句子都是普通陈述句,主语往往是文件而不是人或法人,从逻辑上讲,我们不可以要求或强制文件做某事或赋予其某种权利,所以在法律文本中表示强制的情态动词 shall 和 must,以及表示权利和选择的 may,都不应该在句子中使用,即使有作者使用 shall 或者 may,那也是多余的或是滥用的。

任何性质合同的完整协议条款的基本写作套路如下:

(1) 本合同<u>是/构成</u>(be/include/contain/constitutes)完整协议或最后协议;由于是完整或最后协议,所以:

(2) 本协议<u>取代或代替</u>(supersede/replace)以前为达成本协议所准备的所有文件,无论是书面的还是口头的;

(3) 为了说明取代的是何种性质的文件,须指明有关文件关于什么标的/主题(relating to the subject matter hereof)。其完整的表达方式是:This Agreement constitutes the final and entire agreement between the Parties relating to the subject matter hereof (of the parties hereto in respect of the subject matter contained herein) and supersedes all prior agreements(legal documents, understandings, representation, arrangement, undertaking, discussion, letter of intent, etc.), whether oral or written, (by the officers, representatives, employees, etc.), relating to such subject matter

(in respect of the subject matter contained herein)。复杂一点的、古雅一点的就用括号内的表达方式。

对以上句型中的用词还有一点说明：即合同标的的概念。以上 10 则不同的完整协议条款中几乎都出现过合同标的(subject matter)一词。合同标的究竟是什么意思？纯粹从事翻译工作的人士可能会觉得该词概念抽象。它指的是合同当事人双方权利和义务所共同指向的对象，比如买卖合同，标的就是买卖的物。Subject matter of insurance，就是保险标的，即保险的对象；subject matter of an action or litigation，就是诉讼标的，即诉讼的主体事项。

四、推荐条款

This Agreement, including all exhibits, schedules, attachments and any agreements set forth as an annex to any this Agreement, is the final agreement between the parties and constitutes the entire agreement between the parties hereto and supersedes all prior agreements and understandings, both written and oral, whether signed or unsigned, with respect to the subject matter hereof, and specifically supersedes the Letter of Intent between the parties dated __month __day ____year.

本协议，包括作为本协议之所有证明、附表、附件以及本协议附录中提及的任何协议，是各方之间的最后协议，构成本协议各方之间的完整协议，取代先前就本协议之标的达成的任何书面的或口头的、签署的或未签署的所有协议及谅解，特别将取代各方于____年__月__日签署的意向书。

如前一节说明所示：该段条款适合任何性质的合同，尤其适合包括有附表、附录和意向书等诸多附件的大型合同。

第二十六章 合同附件的写作、翻译和研究

一、引言

合同起草中一个普遍但却不起眼的问题便是合同的附加信息或补充材料。虽然是附加的内容,但其数和量往往超过合同本身,而且这类文件名目繁多。试看以下条款:This Agreement, including all exhibits, schedules, attachments and any agreements set forth as an annex to any this Agreement, is the final agreement between the parties and constitutes the entire agreement between the parties hereto and supersedes all prior agreements and understandings, both written and oral, whether signed or unsigned, with respect to the subject matter hereof, and specifically supersedes the Letter of Intent between the parties dated ____month ____day _____year.(本协议,包括作为本协议之所有证明、附表、附件以及本协议附录中提及的任何协议,是各方之间的最后协议,构成本协议各方之间的完整协议,取代先前就本协议之标的达成的任何书面的或口头的、签署的或未签署的所有协议及谅解,特别将取代各方于____年____月__日签署的意向书。)

由上可见:中文的主要表述有"附表""附件"或"附录"。英文中更有 schedule, exhibit, annex, appendix, attachment, addendum, rider, postscript 等等。但究竟 which is which? 它们之间有何不同? 中英之间如何对等? 各自如何使用?

在英文中,"附件"虽有表达多样,但业界并没有特别规定必须使用哪一种。虽然前述词汇在内涵和使用上有微妙的差异,但合同起草者选择词汇时,大多是因为个人风格或是受到本国合同起草传统的影响。可以说,以上任选一词来命名附件都不会影响合同的法律效力,关键是要保证附件名称"前后一致""有迹可循"。

何谓"前后一致"? 附件的命名要专一,起草合同时尽量只使用一种附件名称。庞大的合同(如并购合同)有时会有两种附件名称,但同时使用三种附件名称的合同笔者前所未见。在翻译时亦不能"附录"、"附件"信手拈来,同一个英文名称只能对应一个中文译名——用词的一致性是法律文书起草与翻译的基本原则。例如,Schedule A 是一份股东决议,Schedule B 是一份公司董事名录,译者不能因为 Schedule A 是文书、Schedule B 是表单,就将 Schedule A 译为"附件 A"、Schedule B 译为"附录 B",正确的做法是统一地译为"附件 A""附件 B"。

何谓"有迹可循"? 附件是合同不可分割的一部分。然而,附件对合同各方的约束力或是约束范围是由主合同中的条款决定的。例如在一份销售合同中,如果仅仅是将销售的通用条款作为附件 A 放在主合同之后,但在主合同中根本没有提及附件 A,换言之,主合同与附件 A 之间没有文字将两者联系起来,交易便无法依据附件 A 中的条款或细则进行。如何在主合同中提述附件,笔者将会在第三部分进行详细介绍。

本文的目的是对英文中附件的不同表述及其译法进行探讨,并帮助读者对附件进行规范的命名、排序和提述。在合同的起草或翻译中,这看似不起眼的提升,恰能体现出起草者或译者的专业水准。

二、英文对"附件"的不同表述及其特点

(一) 附件的类型

笔者认为,根据附件与合同的关系,"附件"可以大致分为两类——exhibit 与 schedule。

1. Exhibit

在法律英语中,exhibit 更多地被用来表示庭审中的"呈堂证物"。在表示合同附件时,exhibit 代表的是一类独立性更强的文件,它能够独立于合同存在,对合同起到佐证或补充说明的作用,它可以是签约时有效的文件,抑或是由合同方约定在未来某个时刻生效的文件,主要指有佐证作用的文件,因此通常被译成"证明"。

前者如例 1 的企业并购合同中①,HP 公司的财务报表作为附件,被命名为 <u>Exhibit A</u>。财务报表作为公司的组织性文件,先于并购合同存在,它客观地反映了 HP 公司的财务状况,适合用 exhibit 来命名。若是举一反三的话,产品销售合同中的"技术许可证"、贷款合同中"贷款人资信证明"、进出口买卖合同中的"进/出口许可证、装箱单、保险单"等等附件都可冠以 <u>Exhibit X</u> 的标题。

例 1. 并购合同目录

TABLE OF CONTENTS
ARTICLE I.　　THE MERGER
ARTICLE II.　　CONVERSION OF SECURITIES
ARTICLE III.　　REPRESENTATIONS AND WARRANTIES OF MMAX AND HLM PAYMEON
ARTICLE IV.　　REPRESENTATIONS AND WARRANTIES OF HP
ARTICLE V.　　COVENANTS OF MMAX AND HP
ARTICLE VI.　　CONDITIONS TO THE OBLIGATIONS OF MMAX
ARTICLE VII.　　CONDITIONS TO THE OBLIGATIONS OF HP
ARTICLE VIII.　　TERMINATION OF AGREEMENT
ARTICLE IX.　　OMITTED
ARTICLE X.　　MISCELLANEOUS
EXHIBIT A：　HP Financial Statements Closing
SCHEDULES：
SCHEDULE 1.05　　Directors and Executive Officers of MMAX
SCHEDULE 2.01　　Conversion Shares
SCHEDULE 3.02　　Subsidiaries of MMAX

---

① 详细并购合同参见 http://www.sec.gov/Archives/edgar/data/1448705/000135007111000024/ex21agrmrgr.txt

SCHEDULE 3.03　　Capitalization of MMAX
SCHEDULE 3.11　　MMAX Absence of Certain Changes
SCHEDULE 3.16　　MMAX Taxes

由上表目录可见，EXHIBIT A 是个相对独立的文件：HP 公司的财务报告。而 SCHEDULES 从 1.05 到 3.16 都是与该合同密切相关的文件，离开合同就无所依无附，不能独立存在。

exhibit 也可以表示合同方约定在未来某个时刻生效的文件，例如几家公司合资成立一家新公司，需要签署股东合同，合同的附件往往会包含新成立公司的章程——Exhibit A Articles of Association。又如雇佣合同中的"政府退休金计划"、销售合同下的"回购合同"，都属于约定在未来某个时刻生效的附属文件。不过，这类性质的附件并非只能用 exhibit 表示，尤其是内容定制化程度较高、与交易标的、合同方权利义务关联较紧密时，schedule 是更好的选择。所以，上述例子中，"政府退休金计划"是普遍适用的文件，且并非由合同当事人制定，可以作为一种告知性的文件并命名为 Exhibit X；相比之下，公司章程以及销售合同下的"回购合同"则更符合 schedule 的特征。

2. Schedule

schedule 的形式多为目录、表单或详细的描述性文字，一般译为"附表"、"附录"或"附件"。schedule 包含的内容是可以出现在主合同中的，但往往因为主合同交易的复杂性，才作为附件放在主合同之后，以下几种情况较为常见：

（1）交易下包含子交易：主合同中的交易包含或牵涉多个不同的子交易。例如合资企业合同中往往包含很多不同的业务安排以及典型的出资合同（子合同），均可放入 schedule 中。

（2）合同内容牵涉不同的规范，需要多方的参与：例如在典型的产品开发合同中，对开发工作会有一份陈述，光是这个陈述就包含了方方面面的信息，如产品参数、检测标准、验收程序、交付条件与时间表、预算分配、不同阶段的相关人员等等。对这些高度"自定义"的内容，合同起草者无法越俎代庖，往往是将合同的标准条款完成，大框架建好，合同方"自定义"的内容作为一系列独立的文档，由各个相关人员负责编制，如此分工合作、有条不紊。这一现象反映了现代合同起草的模块化——许多合同的起草都是基于现成的合同模板，将标准化的内容与定制的内容分割开来，对律师、对客户来说都是省时省力，亦大大增加了合同的可读性[①]。

（3）将事实与义务分开：强烈建议将说明、解释性的语言，或是技术参数、客观事实放入 schedule，因为这些内容一来不需要合同起草者投入精力，其次在未来发生变化的可能性也很高。例如合资企业合同中，对合资企业的业务范围往往会有很详细的描述，签约前在双方的谈判过程中，关于业务范围的描述往往需要润色、修改，不如作为附件单独处理。又如在"通知"条款中，合同方约定在一定范围内以特定的形式向对方履行"通知"义务，而通知的接收方地址属于客观的信息，适合放入 schedule 内。

（4）合同包含可更新的文件：比较典型的有销售合同中产品的价格表、工程项目合同中的工作说明（项目的初步工作或许已经有很细致的说明、但未来的工作与服务无法准确预

---

① 见 Willem Wiggers：*Drafting contracts*-techniques, best practices and recommendations related to contract drafting, published by Kluwer. http://www.weagree.com/book/144-Schedules%2C+annexes+and+exhibits.html.

料,所以后期还是会根据主合同中的原则进行补充修改)。

（5）保护敏感信息：对外披露合同时,往往只是公布主合同,向美国证监会递交合同时往往也是指递交合同主体部分。所以敏感信息通常被放入 schedule,避免被广泛披露。

对比 exhibit 与 schedule,我们可以总结以下几点特征：

> exhibit 往往是能够独立于合同存在的文件,作为合同附件起到"参照、参考、佐证"的作用；而 schedule "定制"程度较高,其形式包括表格、文字说明或文件,往往是基于合同而产生或与合同联系非常紧密。exhibit 往往先于合同存在,且内容一般不能因合同而改变,而 schedule 的内容可以改变。

（二）英文中对附件的其他表述及特征

鉴于 exhibit 与 schedule 鲜明的特征,笔者建议,如果附件的数量不多,仅需一个英文名称来表示,又或者对 exhibit 与 schedule 的选择没有把握时,最好是使用较笼统的 appendix。

1. Appendix

appendix 置于合同最后时,译为"附录"或"附件"均可。在出版界 appendix 被广泛地用来指代书籍尾部的附加材料(通常是以列表形式出现,并统一地译为"附录"),例如 appendix glossary——附录词汇表。大量的例证显示,许多人在翻译合同时也习惯性地将 appendix 译为"附录",它可以指代合同附件,也可以指代"列表"。但究竟是译为"附件"还是"附录"还是"附表",要根据实际情况来定——如果合同附件的确只有两张表格,那么 Appendix 1 与 Appendix 2 分别译为"附表 1"和"附表 2"是再好不过的。若附件有一个文件和一张表格,那么 Appendix1 和 Appendix 2 就不能译为"附件 1"与"附表 2",应统一译为"附件 1"与"附件 2"——虽然"附件 2"的内容可能的确是一张表,但附件译名要统一、要专一,不能将同一个 Appendix 一个译成"附件"一个译成"附表",有关这一点笔者已在本书的第三章强调过。

2. Attachment

attachment 指附加于主文件之后的项目或文件。它可能是最具有大众缘的附件,因为人们习惯用它表示电子邮件的附件。毕竟这是一个普通人用惯了的普通词,用来指代法律文件中附件有点勉强。

3. Annex（Annexure）

annex(annexure)在表示国际公约(或类似的具有国际效力的文件)的附加材料时,annex(annexure)是最多见的。该词比较冷僻,不建议在普通合同中使用。

不同的英语国家对表示附件的词亦是各有所爱：美国的合同附件偏爱用 exhibit,澳洲人较喜欢使用 annex(annexure),而在英国一般使用 appendix 和 schedule；但各国都有人用 attachment,不过并不普遍—笔者建议随大流,用 appendix 和 exhibit 指代合同附件。

必须再次强调的是,无论选择 schedule, exhibit, appendix, attachment 还是 annex 作为附件名称都不会对附件的法律效力有影响。在实践中,你可能看到也有英国律师用起 attachment,又或者 exhibit 与 schedule "张冠李戴"—— 这些不符合附件命名传统或规律的情况,并不少见,我们不必介意,更不必去矫正。

（三）不建议使用的英文"附件"名称：

1. Enclosure(信件或包裹的附件)

上文说到 attachment，我们自然会联想起它的同义词 enclosure。笔者曾见过有合同的附件被命名为"Enclosure X"（极为少见）。虽然 enclosure 在电子邮件中也能指代附件，与 attachment 不同的是，enclosure 可以指与电邮正文不相干的独立存在的文件，而 attachment 则指对电邮正文起到解释说明作用的附件。况且，enclosure 更恰当的用法是指传统邮政信件或包裹中的实物附件。所以，用 enclosure 来指代合同的附件并不恰当，不能因为字面意思相同而混为一谈。

2. Supplement & Attendum（补充附件/补充条款/补充合同）

虽然 supplement 的字面意思是"增加、补充"，也常常被译为"附录"，但它是在合同已经签订完成后，当事人对合同内容进行解释或补充时增加的一部分内容，它可以是文件、或是几条增补的条款、或是一份补充合同（supplement agreement）。在合同英语范畴内，supplement 与 attendum 是同义词。可以说"附件"的大家族包含了 supplement 和 attendum，但 supplement 与 attendum 无法用来表示广义上的"附件"。

3. 其他用词

最后需要提及的是：前言中所列的另外三个同义词 addendum，rider，postscript，虽然也偶尔作为附件的名称在使用，但实际上并不流行，毕竟其含义与普通合同的附件稍有区别：addendum 主要指"补遗/增编"——放在文件或书籍末尾，提供额外的补充资料，在出版物中更常见；rider 通常指合同或法律的附加条款或但书，因此就单位而言，比前者更细微，如保单里的附加条款/附加险（又如在标准的房屋保险中补充一条，将受保人的手提电脑也纳入受保范围——这类附加险就称作 rider）；postscript 是写作普通信函时的一个常用词，指"附言/附笔/又及"，一般简称为 P.S.，与较为正式的合同文体是格格不入的，所以该词通常不作合同附件名称用词。

三、附件的位置与格式

（一）附件的位置

合同起草者或将附件置于签字页之前（英国做法），或将其置于签字页之后（美国做法）。为了防止某一方在合同签署后，增加或删减页数，当事人有时会在合同的每一页加盖印章或由代表签名（或盖骑缝章）。

（二）附件的顺序和编号

附件一般是按照在主合同中被提到的先后顺序依次排列的。也有少数起草者会将附件按其重要性排序，比如销售合同将产品价格表作为第一份附件，也是很合理的。

附件的编号一般使用阿拉伯数字（Exhibit 1,2,3...）、罗马数字（Schedule I,II,III...）或英文字母（Appendix A,B,C...）。

另一种常用的附件编号方式是与主合同中首次提到该附件的条款使用相同的编号。如下例：

例 2. Article I Status of the Premises for Lease

Section 1.1 The Premises to be leased to Party B by Party A is located at (address). The measured construction area of said Premises is ____ square meters, the

Land on which the Premises are located is used for industrial purposes, which allows for office building, R&D and CRO usage. The Premises are factory buildings, and the construction is Frame Construction. See *Appendix* 1.1 of this Contract for the floor plan of said Premises and any CRO Zoning permit/document.

一　出租房屋情况

1.1 甲方出租给乙方的房屋坐落在＿＿＿（地址）＿＿。该房屋出租（实测）建筑面积为＿＿＿平方米，房屋所占据的土地用途为工业用途，该工业用途允许办公楼、研发以及服务外包企业所用。房屋类型为厂房、结构为框架剪力墙。该房屋的平面图以及任何服务外包企业区域许可/文件见本合同附件1.1。

这样的编号方式让整个合同显得更加有序，对主合同与附件进行比照时非常方便，但需要注意一些特殊情况：如例2的Section1.1中，如果同时有两个附件都是第一次被提到，我们的第一反应是将两个附件分别命名为Appendix 1.1(a)与Appendix 1.1(b)，以保证附件序号与主合同条款序号的一致性。但如果Section1.1下还包含子项，子项的编号就要避免用Section 1.1(a), 1.1(b), 1.1(c)…，而是应该用Section 1.1.1, 1.1.2, 1.1.3…，以免与附件的编号混淆。

（三）附件的附件

在引言中笔者提到，有的较庞大的合同会有两种附件名称，原因是合同附件中还含有附件。这种情况尤见于包含子合同的伞状合同，如例3中，合资企业合同包含子合同——出资合同、技术转让合同等，虽被列入附件，但这些子合同下还会包含数个附件。若子合同被命名为"附件X"，那子合同下的附件应作不同命名——"附录Y"。相应地，译为英文时我们可以分别使用Appendix与Annex，以清楚区分不同层级的附件。

例3. 合资企业合同

附件1. 业务范围＿＿＿附件2. 出资合同＿＿＿附件3. 技术转让合同＿＿＿……其他附件（Appendix）X

附录1. 资产项目＿＿＿附录2. 技术内容＿＿＿附录3. 质量标准＿＿＿附录4. 培训人员……附录（Annex）Y

（四）如何在正文中提述附件

引言中笔者也提出了附件名称"有迹可循"的原则，即主合同的条款中必须有文字将附件与主合同联系起来。试看以下几例：

例4. Section 6.1 Constitution. The Constitution, a copy of which *is attached as Annex A*, is hereby adopted for the governance of Amex and is incorporated by reference herein, as amended from time to time by its terms.

6.1 章程. Amex的管理依据章程。章程以附件A的形式附于合同后且通过在合同中被提及的方式成为合同的一部分。章程会依据其自身条款进行不时的修订。

例5. Section 6.2 Management by Board of Governors. (d) The Board of Governors as of the Effective Date (the "Initial Governors") *shall be as set forth on attached Schedule II*.

6.2 理事会的管理.(d)随合同生效而产生的理事("首任理事")应记述于附表 II 中。

例 6.2.4 In providing the Services to the University, the Contractor may apply his own method of work and shall comply with the reasonable requests of the University Representative *named in Annex 1*.

2.4 在向大学提供服务过程中,承包人可以实施自己的工作方式,并遵守附件 1 中所列的大学代表人提出的合理要求。

例 7.1.1 "Major Decision" refers to the decisions *listed in Schedule 2* that require a two-thirds majority of the votes cast at a meeting of the Board of Directors;

1.1 "重大决定"是指附件表 2 中所列的需要在董事会会议中以三分之二大选票通过的决定。

例 8. Article 3 The Contractor and the Partner shall perform and complete their share of the work under the present Contract in accordance with the requirements *set out in Appendix A, E and F of the present Contract*.

第三条 承包商及合伙人应按照本合同的附录 A、E 与 F 中所述要求执行并完成本合同所规定的各自的工作份额。

由以上几例可以看出,条款中带出附件的方式多种多样,主要有 be set out/listed/named in...,be attached as...这样几种句型。虽然表述方法很多,但在同一份合同中最好是选用一种表达,坚持使用统一的句型。如果是在同一份合同中用了若干不同英文名称(如 schedule,annex,appendix),译文一定要有可区分的、对应的译名(如附表、附件、附录)——尽管它们在本质上并无差别,要不然读者或文件的使用者会不知所云或感到困惑。

另外,一些人在提述附件时喜欢添加诸如 hereto 或 to this agreement 之类的附件,例如 be listed in Appendix II *hereto/to this agreement*(列于本合同的附件 II),唯恐 Appendix II 被误会成别的什么地方的附件。这种表述完全是多此一举,所以例 8 中的 *of the present Contract*(本合同的)应该删去。例 4 也存在类似的问题。如果把例 4 中的 *and is incorporated by reference herein*(通过在合同中被提及的方式成为合同的一部分)删去,对原条款的意思和效力没有任何影响。因为已经有文字表明章程载于附件(The Constitution, a copy of which *is attached as Annex A*),而附件只要在主合同中被提及,就等于被认定是合同不可分割的一部分,无须再重复说明。

四、结语

本章比较分析了英语中常用的"附件"名称,包括 exhibit,schedule,appendix,annex 及 attachment,并介绍了附件的格式与提述的技巧。

虽然在名称的选择上我们可以"随心所欲",但在使用时必须保证做到前后一致、有迹可循。前后一致,即保证名称的一致性,尽量只使用一个名称,并有统一的对应一个(而不是多个不同的)译名。在庞大的合同中会出现多层附件,建议每个层级的附件对应同一个附件名称。有迹可循,即所有附在主合同之后的附件,其名称(名称与编号,如 Exhibit A, Schedule B, Attachment II,)必须要在主合同条款及目录(如有)中被提到,如此才能建立主合同与附件的联系;而在同一份合同中,尽量只使用一种句型对附件名称进行提述。

本书虽然讨论合同的写作,但并非合同,也不具备合同的文体特征,所以不妨来几段附文,简称为 P.S.,作为本章的收尾。

又及:

以下表达方式虽然在合同中并不罕见,但文风不健康,因为每一句都用了一组累赘的配对词。

The <u>exhibits and schedules</u> hereto are an integral part of this agreement and are deemed incorporated by reference herein.

本合同的<u>附件</u>是本合同的组成部分,且通过在合同中提及的方式被纳入合同。

All <u>exhibits and schedules</u> annexed hereto are expressly made a part of this agreement as though fully set forth herein.

本合同附加的所有<u>附件</u>,虽只提及名称,但其全部内容都在此被明确纳入合同的一部分。

This agreement (including any <u>exhibits and schedules</u> hereto) constitutes the entire agreement among the parties hereto.

本合同(包括本合同的任何<u>附件</u>)都构成合同各方之间的完整合同。

其他附件条款及表达方式:

还要指出的是,合同正文里的"完整合同条款"中也经常包含上述最后一例的表述,我们姑且称这类表述为"附件条款"。不过,"附件条款"是多余的:任何一个附件都必然会在合同的正文中被提及,一旦在正文中被提到,就等于是认可该附件是合同的一部分。除此之外,"附件条款"和"完整合同条款"重复的情况亦非鲜见。所以,许多合同起草专家都认为"附件条款"是画蛇添足。

不过,"附件条款"经年累月,已经成为合同的固定模式,很难剔除。

第二十七章 标准通用合同条款汇总

引 言

"上穷扉页下封底,两处茫茫皆不见。"近320页的书,共有二十七章的内容,且有大量的与写作关系不甚密切的研究性质的论述,要在应急之时从中找到一条比较标准、可以作为范例的通用条款,实非易事。所以,本章将值得推荐的通用条款汇集一处,目的是:"踏破铁鞋无觅处,得来全不费工夫。"

本章各条款的顺序安排,如同本书各章内容的安排一样,与一般合同通用条款的安排顺序类似:先出现在合同中的条款,排列在先。其实,不少比较简易务实的合同将"转让条款"(包括"转让条款")以后的所有条款(如"适用法律/准据法""通知""权利放弃""可分割性""合同变更""完整合同"等等)均置于"其他条款"(Miscellaneous)的标题之下。当然,对于小型或简易合同而言,这无可厚非。如果合同本身只有十来个条款,而让通用条款占去其中的三分之二或一半以上,从合同的结构上看也显得不甚合理。笔者建议,如果属于中型或复杂合同,总条款数目一般在20条以上的,不妨让个各个通用条款"独立"。除少数通用条款可以按照其相关性,穿插在各操作条款(Operative Clauses)之间、以使合同内容更具连贯性和逻辑性之外,我们不妨遵循行内不成文的规矩,按照本书各章内容的顺序安排通用条款在合同中的顺序。

(一) 通用合同序言条款

This Contract, is made and entered into in (place of signature (签约地)) on 26 January, 2015, by and between (name of a party), a corporation duly organized and existing under the laws of (name of country) with its registered office at (address) (referred to as "Party A"), and (name of the other party), a company incorporated and existing under the laws of (name of country) with its registered office (address) (referred to as "Party B").

WHEREAS, the parties desire to do sth... (or Party A is desirous of doing sth...; And WHEREAS, Party B is desirous of doing sth...),

NOW, THEREFORE, in consideration of the mutual promises and undertakings contained in this Agreement, the Parties agree as follows:

本合同由_____公司(称为"甲方"),一家依(国家名称)法律正式组建并存续的公司,其注册的营业所在地位于:(公司地址),和_____公司(称为"乙方"),一家依(国家名称)法律正式组建并存续的公司,其营业所在地位于:(公司地址)于_____年__月__日在(签约地点)签署。

鉴于双方欲做某事（或：鉴于甲方欲做某事，而鉴于乙方欲做某事），

考虑到"双方"在本协议中的相互约定和承诺，"双方"协定如下：

IN WITNESS WHEREOF, the parties hereto have caused this Agreement to be executed by their respective officers duly authorized, as of the date first written above.

IN WITNESS WHEREOF, the parties hereto have executed this Agreement the day and year first above written.

Each party is signing this agreement on the date stated opposite that party's signature.

（二）通用定义条款

Unless the context otherwise requires in this AGREEMENT, word denoting the singular includes the plural and vice versa, and word denoting any one gender includes all genders, and word denoting person includes a natural person, body corporate, unincorporated association and partnership.

除本协议文意另有所指,表示单数的词包括复数,反之亦然；表示一个性别的词包括所有性别；表示人的词包括自然人、法人团体、非法人团体以及合伙组织。

（三）通用语言与文本条款

This Agreement and all its appendices (if any) is executed in English, and the Chinese version is a translation. In case of any discrepancy between the English and Chinese versions, the English version shall prevail. All communications, including notices, demands, requests, statements, etc. to be made or given by the parties in performing the Agreement shall also be in the English language. If they are not originally in English, a certified English translation shall be accompanied.

This Agreement may be executed in any number of counterparts and they shall have the same effect as if the signatures on the counterparts were on a single copy of the Agreement.

（四）通用不可抗力条款

1. Neither party shall be liable to the other for any failure to perform or delay in performance of the terms of this Contract, if such a failure or delay is caused by a Force Majeure event.

2. Force Majeure includes earthquakes, typhoons, flood, fire, war, strikes, riots, acts of governments, changes in law during the contracting period or any other instances which cannot be foreseen, prevented or controlled and are accepted as Force Majeure in general international commercial practice.

3. In the event of the occurrence of such an incident, the Party so affected shall immediately notify (via both email and fax) the other Party, stating the period of time the occurrence is expected to continue and shall use diligent efforts to end the failure

or delay and ensure that the effects of such Force Majeure be minimized.

The affected Party shall also, within 15 days after the incident, send to the other party a certificate of the incident issued by the competent government authority which is located at the place where the accident occurred as its evidence.

4. The Parties shall, through consultation, decide whether to terminate this Contract, or release part of the affected Party's responsibilities to perform this Contract, or delay its performance. In case the Force Majeure lasts more than 60 days, the other party shall have the right to cancel the whole or the unperformed part of the Contract by giving a written notice to the non-performing party.

(五) 通用保证条款

1. 一般商品的保证条款

Seller warrants that all Products sold hereunder shall be new and not refurbished or reconditioned, and free from defects in materials and workmanship under normal use for a period of twelve (12) months from the date of original retail purchase. Should a breach of the warranty occur, Buyer's exclusive remedy under this Section shall be, at Seller's option, a full refund of the purchase price of the product, or replacement of the product which is returned to Seller or a Seller's authorized representative with a copy of the receipt. In the case of replacement, the parties shall respectively pay the shipping cost.

卖方保证根据本合同所售的所有产品为全新产品，无翻新或修复品，其用料和做工在正常使用情况下自原零售购买日期起十二(12)个月内均无瑕疵。一旦违反本保证，买方的唯一补偿是根据卖方选择，得到产品购买价的全额退款，或将产品(附上收据)退还给卖方或其授权的代理商后获得替换品。就后者而言，各方自行负责退货或发货的运费。

2. 高科技产品复杂保证条款

Warranties: Seller warrants that all material, work product, and merchandise supplied under the Order (a) shall strictly conform to all specifications, drawings, samples, or other descriptions furnished to and approved by Buyer, (b) shall be fit and serviceable for the purpose intended, as agreed to by Buyer and Seller, (c) shall be of good quality and free from defects in materials and workmanship, (d) shall be new and not refurbished or reconditioned, unless expressly agreed in writing by Buyer, and (e) shall not infringe any patent, copyright, mask work, trademark, trade secret or other intellectual property, proprietary or contractual right of any third party. In addition, Seller warrants that Buyer shall have good and marketable title to all goods (including all components thereof) purchased by Buyer pursuant to the Order, free of all liens and encumbrances and that no licenses are required for Buyer to use such goods. With respect to services, Seller warrants that all services shall be provided in a professional and workmanlike manner, with a degree of skill and care consistent with current, good and sound professional procedures. Neither receipt of material, work product or merchandise nor payment therefor shall constitute a waiver of this provision. If a breach of warranty occurs, Buyer may, in its sole discretion, and without waiving any other rights, return for credit or require prompt correction or replacement of the nonconforming goods or services.

保证:卖方保证本订单下供应的所有原料、制成品和商品(a)须严格符合买方提供和认可的产品规格、图纸、样品或其他说明,(b)均为双方约定的合格产品并符合预期的用途,(c)品质优良,无原料和工艺缺陷,(d)除有买方明确的书面同意者外,为全新产品,无翻新或修复品,(e)无侵犯任何第三方的任何专利权、著作权、掩膜作品权、商标权、商业秘密或者其他的知识产权、专有权或合同权。此外,卖方保证买方拥有根据订单所购全部货物(包括货物的全部零部件)的合法交易权,无任何留置权或抵押权,且买方在使用上述货物时无须任何许可证。就服务而言,卖方保证根据现行适用的行业标准程序,提供技术合格、态度专业的服务。买方接受原料、制成品和商品或者支付其货款并不代表放弃该保证条款。如果违反本保证,买方可在不放弃任何其他权利的情况下单方面决定退货并要求将货款计入贷方账户,或要求立即更正或更换不合格之产品或服务。

3. 服务保证条款

Seller warrants that all services provided by Seller in the operation of the Business shall be in a professional and workmanlike manner, with a degree of skill and care consistent with current, good and sound professional procedures, and in conformity with all applicable contractual commitments. No service provided by Seller is subject to any guaranty, warranty or other indemnity beyond the terms and conditions of service contained in the contract, and the maximum potential liability of Seller under any guaranty, warranty or other indemnity set forth herein is limited to the cost of reprocessing the products (if required) and the manufacturing costs of the Buyer's product being processed.

卖方保证在经营的业务中根据现行适用的行业标准程序,提供技术合格、态度专业的服务,并与所有适合的本合同所承担的保证相符。卖方提供的服务不受本合同包含的服务条款和条件以外的任何保证、担保或其他补偿的限制;卖方根据本合同订明的保证、担保或其他补偿条款所需承担的最大责任仅限于产品再处理(如要求)的成本和正在处理的客户产品的制造成本。

(六) 通用责任及义务条款

雇佣合同中的责任条款:

Employer hereby engages Employee as the full-time Chief Financial Officer of Employer and Employee accepts such employment. Employee shall report to the Chief Executive Officer of Employer and shall perform such duties and responsibilities assigned to him from time to time by the Chief Executive Officer and by the Board of Directors of Employer that are consistent with the titles held by Employee. Employee shall devote all of his business time and best efforts to, and shall perform faithfully, loyally and efficiently, his duties as the Chief Financial Officer of Employer and shall exercise such powers and fulfill such responsibilities as may be duly assigned to or vested in him by the Chief Executive Officer and by the Board of Directors of Employer consistent with the responsibilities of the Chief Financial Officer. If requested by the Board of Directors, Employee shall serve on any committee established by the Board of Directors without additional compensation. Employee shall observe and comply with the Employer's material policies, rules and regulations regarding the performance of his duties. However, Employer's failure to comply therewith shall not relieve him of any of his duties, liabilities or obligations hereunder.

雇主据此协议雇佣雇员为本公司的全职财务总管。雇员接受该职位的雇佣。雇员应当向雇主公司的总执行官报告，并执行总执行官及公司董事会不时下达给他的与其职位相称的职责。雇员应尽其所能，将其全部的上班时间和最大的努力投入其所担任的公司财务总监职务工作中，雇员应忠于职守、勤勉高效地工作，行使公司总执行官及董事会授予其行使的、与其财务总监职位相称的权力和职责。如应董事会要求，雇员应加入董事会设立的各种委员会，但不获额外报酬。雇员应当遵守雇主公司有关其职责行使的各项重要政策及规章制度。但雇员未能遵守有关政策或规章制度，并不免除其根据本合同应尽之职责、责任或义务。

（七）通用知识产权条款

Party B owns or possesses the Intellectual Property which consists its trade marks, trade names, service names, service marks, service mark registrations, patents, patent rights, copyrights, inventions, licenses, approvals, governmental authorizations, trade secrets and rights necessary to conduct its businesses as now conducted. To the knowledge of Party B, there is no claim, action or proceeding being made or brought against Party B regarding any of the foregoing Intellectual Property items.

乙方拥有或享有以满足经营目前业务所需而使用的知识产权，包括其商标、商号、服务名称、服务标记、服务标记注册专利、专利、专利权、版权、发明、许可证、核准书、政府授权书、商业秘密和商业权利。据乙方所知，没有任何一方就上述知识产权项目对乙方提出权利主张或提起诉讼。

Party A may resell, lease, rent or manufacture the Goods only if Party B's Intellectual Property is used in connection with the Goods. Party A is prohibited from using the Party B's Intellectual Property in connection with any Goods that are not furnished or approved by Party B.

只有乙方的知识产权用于与货品相关的目的，甲方才可以转售、租赁或制造货品。甲方不得在销售任何非由乙方提供或批准的货品中使用乙方的知识产权。

Party A's unauthorized use or registration of the Party B's Intellectual Property, or of any intellectual property that is confusingly or deceptively similar to the Party B's Intellectual Property, shall also be deemed an infringement of the Party B's exclusive rights. In such case, Party B may terminate this Agreement upon the giving of thirty (30) days' prior written notice and Party A shall still be liable to Party B for any such infringement under the applicable laws.

甲方如擅自使用或注册乙方知识产权或者与乙方知识产权相混淆的知识产权将构成侵害乙方的专有权。在该种情况下，乙方可提前给予甲方三十天的书面通知而终止本协议。但甲方仍须按照相关法律对其侵害行为负上法律责任。

Party A shall promptly notify Party B of any known infringement or improper use of Party B's Intellectual Property Right in its region or territory. Party A will reasonably cooperate with Party B in any action taken by Party B against such third parties, provided that all expenses of such action shall be borne by Party B and all damages which may be awarded or agreed upon in settlement of such action shall accrue to Party B.

甲方如发现在其区域或地区内有人侵害或不当使用乙方的知识产权，甲方应及时通知乙方，并在乙方对有关的第三方展开法律行动时给予合理的配合；但所有的诉讼花费应由乙方自行负责，而诉讼中所获的赔偿或解决获益亦归乙方所有。

(八) 通用保密条款

1. 高要求保密条款

1.1 Confidentiality. "Confidential Information" means any and all tangible and intangible information (whether written or otherwise recorded or oral) of Party B that: (a) derives independent economic value, actual or potential, from not being generally known to, and not being readily ascertainable by proper means by, other persons who can obtain economic value from its disclosure or use and is the subject of efforts that are reasonable under the circumstances to maintain its secrecy; (b) Party B designates as confidential or, given the nature of the information or the circumstances surrounding its disclosure, reasonably should be considered as confidential. Confidential Information includes, without limitation: (i) nonpublic information relating to Party B's technology, customers, business plans, promotional and marketing activities, finances and other business affairs; (ii) the terms and conditions of this agreement; and (iii) any nonpublic information relating to any activities conducted hereunder. Notwithstanding the above, the term "Confidential Information" does not include any information that is readily discernible from publicly-available products or literature.

1.1 保密条款。"保密资料"指乙方之所有有形或无形的资料（不论是书面的、口头的或以其他方式录制的）：(a)该资料由于一般不为他人所知，他人使用常规方法无法轻易获得，其披露、使用可使该他人从中获得经济价值，因而具有独立的经济价值（实际的或潜在的），并且是要做出合理努力以维持其保密状态的主体；(b)乙方指定其为保密的资料，或根据该资料的性质或围绕其披露状况而应合理地认为是保密的资料，其中包括（但不限于）(i)与乙方的技术、客户、营商计划、促销和营销活动、财务及其他业务有关的非公开的资料；(ii)本合同的条款；以及(iii)与根据本合同开展的活动有关的任何非公开的资料。尽管有以上规定，"保密资料"一词并不包括从已经可以公开得到的产品或文献中获得的任何资料。

1.2 Use of Confidential Information. Party A shall only use Confidential Information solely in furtherance of the activities contemplated by this agreement, and it shall not disclose Confidential Information to third parties without Party B's prior written consent.

1.2 保密资料的使用。甲方应将保密资料只用于促进本合同打算执行的各项活动；没有乙方的书面许可，甲方不得将保密资料披露给第三方。

1.3 Required Disclosures. Party A may disclose Confidential Information as required to comply with binding orders of governmental entities that have jurisdiction over it or as otherwise required by law, provided that Party A (i) gives Party B reasonable written notice to allow it to seek a protective order or other appropriate remedy (except to the extent compliance with the foregoing would cause Distributor to violate a court order or other legal requirement), (ii) discloses only such information as is required by the governmental entity or otherwise required by law, and (iii) and uses its best efforts to obtain confidential treatment for any Confidential Information so disclosed.

1.3 必需的披露。甲方可以根据对机密资料有管辖权的政府部门必须服从的命令或其他法律要求披露机密资料；但甲方(i)要以合理的书面形式通知乙方，以允许乙方寻求保护令或寻求其他适当的补救措施(但如果因此会造成甲方违反法庭命令或其他法律要求则属例外)，(ii)只披露政府部门或其他法律要求而需要披露的资料，以及(iii)尽一切努力对以上方式披露的资料采取保密措施。

1.4 Survival. The parties hereto covenant and agree that this Section 1 shall survive the expiration, termination, or cancellation of this agreement for a period of three (3) years, except for Confidential Information described in Section 1.1(a), which shall survive the expiration, termination, or cancellation of this agreement for so long as such Confidential Information remains a trade secret as defined by relevant laws.

1.4 存续条款。本合同双方兹同意：本合同上述 1 条(Section 1)的保密资料在本合同到期、终止或取消之后的三年内存续有效，但上述 1.1(a)条的保密资料只要仍属于有关法律界定的商业机密、即使在本合同到期、终止或取消之后仍然存续有效。

2. 普通保密条款

Confidentiality. "Confidential Information" means all information obtained by a Party (the "Receiving Party") from the other Party (the "Disclosing Party") in connection with its business activities, products, services, intellectual property rights, technical details and performance and structure of company's management. It shall be deemed to be confidential. But the term does not include any information that is readily discernible from publicly-available products or literature.

保密。"保密资料"指一方("接受方")从另一方("披露方")获得的与披露方生意活动、产品、服务、知识产权、详细技术资料和技术性能以及与其公司管理架构有关的所有资料。该资料应视为保密性质。但该词并不包括从已经可以公开得到的产品或文献中获得的任何资料。

The Receiving Party agrees that it and all of its employees and personnel shall use the Confidential Information only for the purposes specified in this Contract and shall not disclose in anyway whatsoever any of the Confidential Information to any third Party without the prior written consent of the Disclosing Party.

接受方同意其与所有员工和人员仅为本合同规定之用途使用该保密资料,未获披露方事先书面同意,不会以任何方式向任何第三方披露该保密资料。

The Receiving Party also agrees that the Confidential Information shall survive the expiration, termination, or cancellation of this agreement for a period of two (2) years. It shall either be returned to the Disclosing Party, at the Receiving Party's cost, promptly if this Agreement is terminated for any reason, or be destroyed if it is in tangible form.

接受方还同意该保密资料条款在本协议到期、终止或取消之后的两(2)年内存续有效。不管本协议因何种原因而终止,接收方应以自费方式将该保密资料及时还返给披露方,或将以有形形式提供给接收方的保密资料予以销毁。

3. 简易保密条款

Party A acknowledges and agrees that the Technology it will receive from Party B during the term of this Contract shall be kept secret and confidential. Party A agrees that it and all of its employees and personnel shall use the Technology only for the purposes specified in this Contract and shall not disclose in anyway whatsoever any of the Technology to any third Party or Parties without the prior written consent of Party B. Such confidentiality shall be maintained during the terms of this Contract and for a period of two (2) years after the termination of this Contract. (王辉,2007:100)

甲方承认并同意在本合同期间内对将从乙方收到的技术予以保密。甲方同意其与所有员工和人员仅为本合同规定之用途使用该技术,未经乙方事先书面同意,不会以任何方式向任何第三方披露该技术的任何信息。该保密义务在本合同期间以及本合同终止后两(2)年内继续有效。

4. 合资企业保密条款

Confidentiality

12.1 Each of the Parties shall at all times use all reasonable efforts to keep confidential (and to ensure that its employees and agents keep confidential) all commercial and technical information which it may acquire (i) in relation to the JVC or (ii) in relation to the clients, Business or affairs of the other party (or any member of its respective group). Neither party shall use or disclose any such information except with the consent of the other party or, in the case of information relating to the JVC, in the ordinary course of advancing the JVC's Business. The restriction in this Article 12.1 shall not apply to any information that is:

12.1.1 Publicly available through no fault of that party;

12.1.2 Already in the possession of that party prior to its disclosure without any obligation of confidentiality; or

12.1.3 Required to be disclosed by that party pursuant to any law, stock exchange regulation or binding judgment, order or requirement of any court or other competent authority.

12.2 Each party shall use all its respective powers to ensure (so far as it is able) that the JVC and its officers, employees and agents observe a similar obligation of confidence in favour of the Parties to this contract.

12.3 The provisions of this Article 12 shall survive any termination of this contract.

(九) 通用合同期限及终止条款

1. 标准型合同期限及终止条款

This Agreement, including all its attachments if any, shall terminate on an earlier date mutually agreed by both parties or on its Expiration Date. Upon such termination, this Agreement will become void, and both parties and all their employees and other personnel shall have no liability regarding this Agreement, except that they shall still be liable for any willful breach of this Agreement prior to the termination.

Each party may terminate this Agreement by written notice in which the basis for the termination should be set forth. No termination of this Agreement shall affect the parties' rights available under applicable law and their obligations for pending purchases under this Agreement. Both parties shall complete their respective obligations for the pending purchases.

2. 复杂型合同期限及终止条款

Duration. This Agreement shall come into effect on the Commencement Date and shall continue in force until the 5th Anniversary of the Commencement Date. On such date this Agreement shall terminate automatically by expiry, but it may be extended by written agreement between the Parties.

期限。本协议自协议开始日起生效,到第五个周年日一直有效,自该日起自动失效,但双方可通过书面协议使本协议展期。

Early Termination. If the other Party has materially breached this Agreement such as ... and, in case of a remediable breach other than a persistent breach, has failed to remedy that breach within thirty days of the date of service of a written notice from the other Party specifying the breach and requiring that it be remedied; or the other Party ceases to carry on business; or is unable to pay its debts when they fall due, or is to be assigned for the benefit of creditors; or is declared bankrupt, or a court order is made or a resolution of board of directors passed for the winding up of that other Party; or is in a situation of similar nature, the non-default party may immediately terminate this agreement by giving written notice to the other party.

提前终止。如果另一方严重违约,诸如……;如该等违约并非持续行为而是可以补救的、但另一方在对方指出其违约行为并要求其采取补救措施的书面通知送达后的30

天内仍未采取补救措施;或另一方停止其业务;或债务到期而无法偿还;或打算以转让其公司的方式向债权人还债;或被宣布破产、或法庭颁令或公司董事会通过决议决定公司结业;或处于类似性质的状态,未违约一方可书面通知另一方立即终止本协议。

Rights After Termination. The expiry or termination of this Agreement does not affect any rights or obligations of either Party which have arisen or accrued up to and including the date of expiry or termination including the right to payment under this Agreement. In the event of any such expiry or termination, the terms and conditions of this agreement shall continue to be binding upon the parties in connection with the obligations and payment on the part of the default party under this Agreement.

协议终止后的权利。本协议到期或终止并不影响各方直至协议到期或终止日(包括该日)而产生或累积的权利和义务,其中包括获得根据本协议付款的权利。如本协议到期或终止,本协议的条款继续对与本协议违约方根据本协议须履行的义务或支付的款项有关联的各方具有约束力。

3. 雇佣合同终止条款

(1) The Employment Period shall commence on the Effective Date of Employees reporting to duty and shall initially terminate on the third anniversary of the Effective Date. The Employment Period will automatically extend for one year unless either the Employee or the Company gives at least 90 days advance written notice of non-extension.

雇佣期从雇佣合同生效、即雇员述职之日起开始,首个雇佣期至合同生效日的三周年日终止,并会自动延长一年,除非雇员或雇主至少提前90天书面通知对方不做延长。

(2) In the event that the Employees employment is terminated during the Employment Period (i) by the Employee for Good Reason (as defined either in Appendix or a clause hereunder) or (ii) by the Company without Cause (as defined either in Appendix or in a clause hereunder), subject to the Employees execution and delivery of a valid and effective release and waiver in a form satisfactory to the Company, the Company shall pay the Employee a lump sum cash payment equal to one (1) time Employees Base Salary, within thirty (30) days following the effective date of such release and waiver, plus any cash payment of the unused vacation time accrued through the Termination Date on the basis of the daily rate of employees Base Salary.

万一雇员的雇佣在雇佣期内(i)由雇员凭合理的因由(见附录或本合同下文的界定)或(ii)公司无故(见附录或本合同下文的界定)予以终止,公司须向雇员支付相当于雇员一个月基本工资的一次性现金补偿,但雇员必须签署一份有效的、令公司满意的索赔弃权书,公司应当在雇员签署的该弃权书生效日期起的三十(30)天内做出支付,再加上直至雇佣终止日所累积的假期薪金(按照基本工资的日薪计算)。

(3) Upon the termination of the Employees employment for any reason, if the rights of the Employee with respect to any shares of restricted stock of the Company, as of the Termination Date, have not been forfeited, they shall be subject to the applicable rules of the plan or agreement under which such shares of the restricted

stock were granted as they exist from time to time.

不管雇佣的雇佣因何因终止,在雇佣终止时,就雇员原本拥有的购买本公司限制性股票的权利而言,如在雇佣终止日尚未被收回,必须受准许购买该限制性股票的计划或协议不时订定的有关规定的规管。

(4) In addition, upon the termination of the Employees employment for any reason, any vested benefits and other amounts that the Employee is otherwise entitled to receive under any employee benefit plan, policy, practice or program of the Company or any of its affiliates shall be payable in accordance with such employee benefit plan, policy, practice or program as the case may be, provided that the Employee shall not be entitled to receive any other payments or benefits in the nature of severance or termination pay.

此外,在雇员的雇佣因任何因由而终止时,雇员根据公司或其附属公司的任何雇员福利计划、政策、惯例或安排原本有权得到的既得利益或其他款额应按各有关个案的这类雇员福利计划、政策、惯例或安排予以支付,但雇员无权再享有任何属于遣散费或雇佣终止金性质的其他付款或福利。

(十) 通用违约条款

1. Any violation of any provision hereof, any incomplete or mistaken performance of any obligation provided hereunder, or any failure to perform any covenants provided hereunder by any Party shall constitute a breach of this Agreement. The breaching Party shall be liable for any such breach pursuant to the applicable laws.

任何一方违反本协议的任何条款,或未完全或错误地履行本协议的任何义务,或未履行本协议规定的条款,即构成违约。违约方须依有关法律对其违约行为负责。

2. If a Party fails to perform or has mistakenly performed any of its material obligations under this Contract, or if a representation or warranty made by a Party is untrue or materially inconsistent with the fact, such Party is deemed to have breached this Contract. The breaching Party shall compensate or be liable to the non-breaching Party for all liabilities, obligations, damages, losses, costs and expenses (including reasonable attorneys fees and court costs) arising as a direct or consequential result of such a breach.

如果一方未能履行或错误履行本合同的重要义务,或者一方做出的陈述或保证不真实或与事实有重大出入,则视该方已违反本合同。违约方须就该违约行为的直接或间接后果而产生的所有债务、义务、损害、损失、法律费用(包括合理的律师费及诉讼费)向未违约方做出赔偿或对其负责。

(十一) 通用仲裁条款

1. 简易型

a. Any dispute arising from or in connection with this Contract shall be submitted to China International Economic and Trade Arbitration Commission (CIETAC) in

Beijing for arbitration which shall be conducted in accordance with the CIETAC's arbitration rules in effect at the time of applying for arbitration. The arbitrators are to apply laws of the PRC, without regard to its choice of law principles. Each party shall submit to any court of competent jurisdiction for purposes of the enforcement of any award, order or judgment. Any award, order or judgment of the arbitration is final and shall bind upon both parties.

b. All controversies and claims arising under or relating to this Agreement are to be resolved by arbitration in accordance with the rules of the American Arbitration Association before a panel of three arbitrators selected in accordance with those rules. The arbitration is to be conducted in [venue]. The arbitrators are to apply (applicable law), without regard to its choice of law principles. Each party shall submit to any court of competent jurisdiction for purposes of the enforcement of any award, order or judgment. Any award, order or judgment pursuant to the arbitration is final and may be entered and enforced in any court of competent jurisdiction. (Stark, 2003: 201)

2. 标准型(跨国工程项目)

The arbitration shall be conducted in accordance with the Rules and Procedures for Arbitration of the International Chamber of Commerce, Paris in the case of Foreign Contractors and provisions of Arbitration Act of [local country] or any statutory modification thereof in the case of local contractors, and shall be held at such place and time in [local country] as the arbitrators may determine. The decision of the majority of arbitrators shall be final and binding upon the parties hereto and the expense of the arbitration shall be paid as may be determined by the arbitrators.

如仲裁涉及外国承包方,仲裁应根据《巴黎国际商会的仲裁规则和程序》进行;如仲裁只涉及本国承包商,仲裁应根据其本国仲裁法的规定、在仲裁庭指定的本国地点及时间进行仲裁。仲裁庭的多数裁决是终局的,对双方都有约束力。仲裁费用根据仲裁庭的裁决支付。

Performance under the Contract shall, if reasonably possible, continue during the arbitration proceedings and payments due to the Contractor by the Purchaser shall not be withheld unless they are the subject matter of the arbitration proceedings.

在合理可能的情况下,仲裁期间双方应继续履行合同。发包方不得停止向承包方支付到期款项,除非该款项就是仲裁程序的主题。

3. 复杂型

仲裁范围	Any dispute arising out of or relating to this Agreement shall be resolved by arbitration.
仲裁方式	The arbitration shall be submitted to [organization] and…
仲裁规则	…shall be conducted in accordance with [rule].
仲裁地	The arbitration is shall be conducted in [venue].

仲裁员	The arbitration shall be held before a panel of three arbitrators. No later than 15 days after the arbitration begins, each party shall select an arbitrator and request the two selected arbitrators to select a third neutral arbitrator. If the two arbitrators fail to select a third on or before the 10th day after the second arbitrator was selected, either party is entitled to request the [organization] to appoint the third neutral arbitrator in accordance with its rules.
仲裁时效	Any arbitration under this agreement must be commenced no later than one year after the dispute arose. Failure to timely commence an arbitration proceeding constitutes both an absolute bar to the commencement of an arbitration proceeding with respect to the dispute, and a waiver of the dispute.
适用法律	The arbitrators shall interpret all disputes arising under or relating to this Agreement in accordance with [governing law], without regard to their own choice of laws principles.
仲裁的终局性	The arbitration award shall be final and binding upon the parties.
仲裁费用	All arbitration expense shall be borne by the losing party unless otherwise awarded by the arbitration tribunal.

（十二）通用诉讼地选择条款

Any legal proceedings instituted against the Distributor by the Principal shall be brought in the courts of the Distributor's country of domicile and any legal proceedings against the Principal by the Distributor shall be brought in the courts of the Principal's country of domicile and for the purpose of such proceedings the law governing this Agreement shall in each case be deemed to be the law of the country in which the relevant proceedings have been instituted in accordance with this Clause. For the purpose of proceedings brought against one of the parties to this Agreement by any third party under this Clause, each party agrees to submit to the exclusive jurisdiction of the courts of that third party's country of domicile. (Christou, 2002: 210)

任何由委托人向经销商提起的诉讼应在经销商居住国的法院提起，任何由经销商向委托人提起的诉讼应在委托人居住国的法院提起。就该诉讼而言，在依照本条款向某国法院提起诉讼时，本合同的适用法即被认定为该国法律。就其他方根据本条款向本合同的一方提起诉讼而言，各方同意将诉讼提交给提起诉讼的其他方居住国法院作专属审判。（笔者译）

诉讼地为香港的条款

就本协议有关的任何起诉、诉讼或其他法律程序（以下统称"法律程序"），以及为了银行的利益，对方应不可撤销地：

（1）服从香港法院的管辖；

（2）放弃其在任何时间对将任何该等法院（就在任何此等法院所提起的任何法律程序而言）作为审判地可能提出的任何反对意见，并放弃声称该等法律程序已经在不便

的诉讼地提出或该法院对其不拥有司法管辖权;

（3）本协议不(能)排除银行在其他任何有管辖权的法院提起诉讼,在一个或多个有管辖权的法院提起的诉讼不(能)排除在其他任何有管辖权的法院提起。

For the purpose of any suit, action or legal proceeding in connection with this Agreement ("Proceeding") and for the interests of the Bank, the other party irrevocably agrees

(1) to submit to the exclusive jurisdiction of the courts of Hong Kong;

(2) to waive any objection it may have to the proceeding in such courts on the grounds of venue or on the grounds that the proceeding has been instituted in an inappropriate forum, and waive any defense of lack of jurisdiction in such courts.

(3) that this Agreement does not preclude the Bank taking the proceeding to any other courts of competent jurisdiction, or taking the proceeding to one or more courts of competent jurisdiction does not preclude the Bank to take the proceeding to any other court of competent jurisdiction.（笔者译）

（十三）通用转让条款

The parties may not assign this Agreement or any rights or obligations under it to any third party, by operation of law or otherwise without prior written consent of the other party.

未经对方事先书面同意,无论是通过法律或其他途径,任何一方都不得将本合同项下的任何权利或义务转让给第三方。

Neither party may withhold or delay such consent unreasonably. But either party may withhold consent on any of the following grounds: The other party is in default of an obligation under this Agreement when consent is requested; the proposed assignee cannot financially perform the other party's remaining obligations under this Agreement; or the proposed assignee refused to assume all of the party's remaining obligations under this Agreement.

任何一方也不得无理拒绝或拖延同意。但任何一方均可因以下理由方拒绝转让:对方在要求同意转让时履行义务违约;拟受让方在财力上不能按照本协议要求履行对方的义务;或拟受让方拒绝承担对方在本协议下所有未履行之义务。

Notwithstanding the foregoing, without securing such prior consent, each party shall have the right to assign this Agreement or any of its rights or obligations to an affiliate or any successor of such party by way of merger or consolidation, or the acquisition of substantially all of the business and assets of the assigning party relating to the Agreement, if such party will continue to be liable for the performance of its obligations under this agreement.

尽管有前述规定,即使未经事先获准,任何一方均有权将本协议或其项下的任何权利或义务转让给该方通过兼并、合并,或并购本协议有关的转让方的实质上的全部业务和资产的方式而产生的关联公司或继承方——如果该关联公司或继承方愿意继续对本合同义务的履行承担法律责任。

(十四) 通用法律选择/准据法条款

a. The [applicable law] shall govern all matters arising out of or relating to this Agreement, including but without limitation to its (validity), construction, performance, and enforcement/resolution of disputes.

所有因本协议产生或与本协议相关的事宜,包括但不限于其(有效性)解释、履行以及执行/争议的解决,均受(适用法律)的管辖。

b. This Agreement and all matters arising out of or relating to this Agreement shall be governed by, construed, performed and enforced in accordance with [applicable law].

本协议以及所有因本协议产生或与之相关事宜,包括其解释、履行和执行/争议的解决,均受(适用法律)的管辖。

c. This Agreement and the resolution of all disputes arising out of or in connection to this Agreement shall be governed by and construed in accordance with [applicable law].

本协议以及所有因本协议产生或与本协议相关的争议解决都受(适用法律)的解释与管辖。

This Agreement, each transaction entered into under it, and all matters arising from or related to this Agreement (including its validity and interpretation), shall be governed and enforced by and construed in accordance with the substantive laws in force in the country or territory where a license to the products is purchased.

(十五) 通用通知条款

1. 标准型

a. A Notice is deemed to have been received as follows:

a. If a Notice is delivered in person, or sent by Registered or Certified Mail, or nationally [or internationally] recognized overnight courier, upon receipt as indicated by the date on the signed receipt.

b. If a Notice is sent by facsimile, upon receipt by the party giving or making the Notice of an acknowledgement or transmission report generated by the machine from which the facsimile was sent indicating that the facsimile was sent in its entirety to the Addressee's facsimile number.

c. If a Notice is sent by e-mail, the Addressee [shall confirm the receipt by telephone] [shall provide the Addresser a confirmation copy delivered by facsimile/registered mail/overnight courier].

d. A party's failure to confirm the receipt of a Notice does not affect the effectiveness of a Notice.

2. 复杂型

通知的形式 What	(a) All notices, requests, claims, demands and other communications relating to this Agreement shall be made in writing in English accompanied by a translation into Chinese.
发送方式 How	(b) The party sending the Notice (the "Addresser") shall use one of the following methods for delivery of a Notice: (i) registered mail; (ii) courier; (iii) facsimile; (iv) e-mail.
生效时间 When	(c) A Notice is deemed to have been received: (i) if a Notice is delivered by registered mail, upon the fifth business day after posting; (ii) if a Notice is delivered by courier, upon receipt as indicated by the date on the signed receipt; (iii) if a Notice is sent by facsimile, at the time of sending or the next business day if sent outside the business hours of the receiving party (the "Addressee"); (iv) if a Notice is sent by e-mail, upon the Addressee's acknowledgement of receipt by answering the e-mail (excluding auto-reply). If a Notice is sent by e-mail or facsimile, the Addressee shall provide the Addresser a confirmation copy sent by facsimile. A party's failure to confirm the receipt of the Notice does not affect the effectiveness of the Notice.
接收方及地址 Where	(d) The Addresser shall address the Notice to the appropriate person as the Addressee at the following address or to other address(es) as may be notified by a party in writing to the other party. Party A: Name _____ 　　　　 Attention _____ 　　　　 Mailing Address _____ 　　　　 Courtier Address _____ (if different) 　　　　 Telephone No. _____ (for verification purpose only) 　　　　 Facsimile No. _____ 　　　　 E-mail _____ 　　　　 [with an informational copy to: Party A's counsel] Party A's counsel: Name _____ 　　　　　　　　 Attention _____ 　　　　　　　　 Mailing Address _____ 　　　　　　　　 Courtier Address _____ (if different) 　　　　　　　　 Telephone No. _____ (for verification purpose only) 　　　　　　　　 Facsimile No. _____ 　　　　　　　　 E-mail _____ Party B: (同上,此处省略) The Addresser's failure to deliver an informational copy of a Notice to counsel does not constitute a breach of this Agreement or affect the effectiveness of the Notice.

3. 简易型

1.1 Any notice under this contract shall be in writing (which may include e-mail) and may be served by leaving it or sending it to the address of the other party as specified in Article 1.2 below, in a manner that ensures receipt of the notice can be proved.

1.2 For the purposes of Article 1.1, notification details are the following, unless other details have been duly notified in accordance with this Article:

1.1.1 ABC:[specify details];

1.1.2 XYZ:[specify details].

（十六）通用弃权条款

1. 完整型

1.1 No delay or omission by either Party in exercising any right, power or remedy provided by law or under this Agreement shall: (a) affect the right, power or remedy; or (b) operate as a waiver of it.

1.2 The single or partial exercise of any right, power or remedy provided by law or under this Agreement shall not preclude any further exercise of it or the exercise of any other right, power or remedy.

1.3 No waiver of any right, power or remedy provided by law or under this Agreement shall take effect unless it is in writing and signed by authorized representative of the Party giving the waiver.

1.1 任何一方延迟或没有行使任何法律或本协议规定的权利、权力或救济权并不(a)影响该权利、权力或救济权；或(b)构成对该权利(力)的放弃。

1.2 单独行使或部分行使任何法律或本协议规定的权利、权力或救济权并不阻止其进一步行使这些权利(力)或行使其他的权利、权力或救济权。

1.3 放弃任何法律或本协议规定的权利、权力或救济权须采用书面形式并经弃权方授权代表签字后方才生效。(范文祥、吴怡，2008:212；译文经修订)

2. 简易型

No waiver of any term, provision or condition of this Agreement, the breach or default of it, shall be deemed to be either a continuing waiver or a waiver of a subsequent breach or default of any such term, provision or condition of this Agreement. Any waiver by either party of any term, provision or condition of this Agreement, or of the breach or default of it, shall be effective unless it is authorized in writing by an authorized representative of the Party giving the waiver.

对本协议任何条款、规定或条件的放弃，或对违反或不履行该等条款、规定或条件行为的放弃，不得视为对本协议该等条款、规定或条件的持续性放弃，不得视为对其后续该等条款、规定或条件行为的放弃。任何对本协议条款、规定或条件的放弃，或对违反或不履行该等条款、规定或条件行为的放弃，须以书面形式、并由弃权方授权代表签字后方才生效。

(十七) 通用可分割性条款

If any provision, or part of a provision of this Agreement is determined to be invalid, illegal or unenforceable by any rule or law, or public policy of any jurisdiction, all other provisions, or other parts of the provision of this Agreement shall nevertheless remain in full force and effect so long as such invalidity, illegality or unenforceability does not in essence have any material adverse effect on the economic or legal substance of the subject-matter contemplated in the agreement.

如本协议的任何条款或条款之一部分依照有关司法管辖区的法庭裁决、法律或公共政策而被确定无效、违法或不可执行,本协议的其余款或条款之其余部分仍将继续完全有效——只要本协议拟执行的标的物的经济或法律内容没有受到任何实质性的不利影响。

Upon such determination all parties shall negotiate in good faith to modify this Agreement so as to effect the original intent of the parties as closely as possible in a mutually acceptable manner. The parties may 1) reduce the scope, duration, area or applicability of the provision or the part, 2) delete the specific words or phrases in the provision, or 3) replace any invalid, illegal or unenforceable provision or part with provision or part that is valid, legal or enforceable and that comes closest to expressing the original intention of the invalid, illegal or unenforceable provision or part.

在确定本协议任何条款或条款之一部分无效、违法或不可执行后,各协议方应真诚协商修订本协议,以双方都可接受的方式尽可能使修订接近协议方的本意。各方可以1)缩窄协议条款或条款之一部分的实施范围、适用性或实施期限;2)删除条款中的特定词语;或3)用最接近无效、违法或不可执行条款或条款之一部分原意的有效、合法、可执行的条款取而代之。

(十八) 通用合同变更条款

1. 普通合同变更条款

This Contact (and its appendixes) may be modified only after Party A and Party B have held consultations and executed a supplementary agreement on the modifications.

甲乙双方经过磋商、签署有关变更事宜的补充协议后才可对本合同(及其附件)进行变更。

The party proposing such modification shall notify in writing the other party one (1) month in advance, explaining the reason of such modifications.

提出这类变更的一方应提前一个月以书面形式通知对方,解释变更的因由。

Modifications to this Contract shall become effective only after they are signed by Party A and Party B, and have been approved by the competent government organization if the law requires.

只有甲乙双方在本合同的变更文件上签字,变更才生效;如法律有规定,还须得到有关政府主管部门的批准。

2. 霸王式合同变更条款

You agree that from time to time we may alter (including adding or eliminating all or parts of provisions) these Terms, including but not limited to the Privacy Policy ("Amendments"). Amended versions of these Terms will take effect on the date specified for the amended version ("Effective Date") and will apply to all information that was collected before or after the Effective Date, including information in databases. You have no continuing right to use the Sites—it is like a store and each time you visit you will be subject to the version of the Terms in effect on your visit. Like terms on the door to a store, those terms will change from time to time and the changes will be effective when they appear in a replacement version of these Terms as posted by us on the Sites. No other Amendments will be valid unless they are in a paper writing signed by us and by you.

Terms will take effect on the date specified for the amended version; You have no continuing right to use the Sites; you will be subject to the version of the Terms in effect on your visit; those terms will change from time to time; the changes will be effective when they appear in a replacement version of these Terms.

修订版的条款将在指定日期生效;贵方无继续使用本网站的权利;贵方必须遵守访问本网站时有效的条款;该类条款不时会有更变;该类更变出现在取代以前版本的条款时即已生效。(笔者译)

(十九) 通用完整协议条款

1. This Agreement constitutes the final and entire agreement between the Parties relating to the subject matter of this agreement and supersedes all prior agreements (legal documents, understandings, representation, arrangement, undertaking, discussion, letter of intent, etc.), whether oral or written by any officers, representatives, employees, etc., who might had involved in concluding this agreement. There are no representations, warranties, terms, conditions, undertakings or collateral agreements, express, implied, statutory or otherwise between the parties, except as expressly set forth in this Agreement.

2. This Agreement, including all exhibits, schedules, attachments and any agreements set forth as an annex to any this Agreement, is the final agreement between the parties and constitutes the entire agreement between the parties hereto and supersedes all prior agreements and understandings, both written and oral, whether signed or unsigned, with respect to the subject matter hereof, and specifically supersedes the Letter of Intent between the parties dated _____month ____day ____year.

本协议,包括作为本协议之所有证明、附表、附件以及本协议附录中提及的任何协议,是各方之间的最后协议,构成本协议各方之间的完整协议,取代先前就本协议之标的达成的任何书面的或口头的、签署的或未签署的所有协议及谅解,特别将取代各方于_____年____月_____日签署的意向书。

(二十) 与附件相关用语

The exhibits and schedules to this agreement are an integral part of this agreement and are deemed incorporated by reference in the agreement.

本合同的附件是本合同的组成部分,且通过在合同中提及的方式被纳入合同。

All exhibits and schedules annexed hereto are expressly made a part of this agreement as though fully set forth herein.

本合同附加的所有附件,虽只提及名称,但其全部内容都在此被明确纳入合同的一部分。

This agreement (including any exhibits and schedules hereto) constitutes the entire agreement among the parties hereto.

本合同(包括本合同的任何附件)都构成合同各方之间的完整合同。

(二十一) 其他常用辅助条款

Headings. All headings and captions contained herein are for convenience and ease of reference only and are not to be considered in the construction or interpretation of any provision of this Agreement.

标题。本协议中包含的所有标题、题名仅仅是为了参阅方便,不得在解释本协议的任何条款中使用。

Headings. The section titles in these Terms are for convenience only and have no legal or contractual effect.

标题。这些细则中出现的各条款标题仅仅是为了参阅方便,没有任何法律或合同效用。

Paragraph Headings. The headings to the paragraphs to this Agreement are solely for convenience and have no substantive effect on the Agreement nor are they to aid in the interpretation of the Agreement.[①]

各段标题。本协议各段的标题仅仅是为了参阅方便,对本协议无任何实质作用,也无助于解释本协议。

Sections. Numbered or lettered paragraphs, subparagraphs and schedules contained in this Agreement refer to sections, subsections and attachments of this Agreement.

条款。本协议中加了编号或以字母排编的段、节和附表指本协议中的条、款和附件。

Counterparts. This Agreement may be executed in one or more counterparts, each of which will be deemed to be an original copy of this Agreement and all of which, when taken together, will be deemed to constitute one and the same agreement.

文本。本协议可签署为一个或多个文本。每个文本都应视作本协议的正本;所有

---

① http://www.aopa.org/Pilot-Resources/Aircraft-Ownership/Sample-Purchase-Sales-Agreement

文本,作为集合体,应视为构成同一个协议。

Counterparts; Electronic Signatures. This agreement may be signed in one or more counterparts, which together will form a single agreement. This agreement may be signed electronically.

文本;电子签名。本协议可签署为一个或多个文本,集合在一起只构成一份协议。本协议亦可以电子方式签署。

Copies. A printed version of this agreement shall be admissible in judicial or administrative proceedings based upon or relating to this agreement to the same extent and subject to the same conditions as other business documents and records originally generated and maintained in printed form.[1]

副本。本协议的印刷本,如同原本以印刷形式产生和保存的其他商业文件和档案一样,可作为本合同的副本或具有相同作用(受相同的限制)的文本,用于司法或行政程序。(以上一节全部译文均由笔者提供)

---

[1] https://www.sendthisfile.com/policy/terms-of-use.jsp

参考文献

Adams Kenneth A., *Legal Usage in Drafting Corporate Agreements*, Greenwood Publishing Group, 2001.
Black's Law Dictionary, http://www.thelawdictionary.org/.
Bryan A. Garner, *A Dictionary of Modern Legal Usage*, 2nd Edition, 1995.
Cane Peter & Conaghan Joanne, *The New Oxford Companion to Law*, Cornwall: Oxford University Press, 2008.
Chen, Zhongsheng, *Window of Legal Translation*, Beijing: China Foreign Trade Publishing Co., 1992.
Christou Richard, *Boilerplate: Practical Clauses*, London: Sweet & Maxwell, 2002.
Daigneault Edward W., *Drafting International Agreements in Legal English*. Netherland: Kluwer Law International, 2005.
Enne Enquist & Laurel Currie Oates, *Just Writing: Grammar, Punctuation, and Style for the Legal Writer*, 2nd Edition, New York: Aspen Publishers, 2005.
Fox William F., *International Commercial Agreements*, Netherland: Kluwer Law International BV, 2009.
Guo Xiaowen, *Case Studies of China International Economic and Trade Arbitration*, Hong Kong: FT Law & Tax Asia Pacific, 1996.
Henry Weihofen,《法律文体》,北京:法律出版社,2000年。
Maniruzzaman A. F. M., Choice of Law in International Contracts, *Journal of International Arbitration* 16(4): 141—172, 1999.
Martha Faulk & Irving M. Mebler, *The Element of Legal Writing: A Guide to the Principles of Writing Clear, Concise, and Persuasive Legal Documents*, New York: Macmillan Publishing Company, 1996.
Mo, John Shijian, *Arbitration Law in China*, Hong Kong: Sweet & Maxwell Asia, 2001.
Paul Rylance, *Legal Writing and Drafting*, Blackstone Press, 1994.
Robert C. Dick, *Legal Drafting in Plain English*, 3rd Edition, 1995.
Stark Tina L., *Negotiating and Drafting Contract Boilerplate*, New York: ALM Publishing, 2003.
Susan L. Brody, Jane Rutherford, Laurel A. Vietzen & John C. Dernbach, *Legal Drafting*, New York: Aspen Publishers, 1994.
Terri LeClercq, *Legal Writing Style*, New York: Aspen Law and Business, 2000.
Veda R. Charrow, Myra K. Erhardt, *Clear & Effective Legal Writing*, Boston: Little, Brown and Company, 1986.
Dr. Frederic Erbisch, Director (Retired), Office of Intellectual Property, Michigan State University, United Stated, e-mail: erbisch@juno.com.
Kingsley Martin. Contract Analysis and Contract Standards Blog.
http://legal-dictionary.thefreedictionary.com/Force+majeure+clause.
http://www.adamsdrafting.com/during-the-term-of-this-agreement/.
www.weagree.com/weblog? topic=18.

陈建平:《法律文体翻译探索》,杭州:浙江大学出版社,2007年。

法律英语证书(LEC)全国统一考试委员会编:《法律英语翻译教程》,北京:中国法制出版社,2009年。
范文祥、吴怡:《英文合同草拟技巧》,北京:法律出版社,2008年。
范文祥:《英文合同阅读与分析技巧》,北京:法律出版社,2007年。
郭晓文:《中国国际经济贸易仲裁案例分析——第一卷:国际贸易争议》,香港:三联书店有限公司,1995年。
胡庚申、王春晖、申云桢:《国际商务合同起草与翻译》,北京:外文出版社,2002年。
李斐南、黄瑶、曾报春、任崇正编译:《法律英语务实——中外法律文书编译》,广州:中山大学出版社,2005年。
李克兴:《法律翻译理论与实践》,北京:北京大学出版社,2007年。
李克兴:《法律文本与法律翻译》,北京:对外翻译出版社,2006年。
李克兴:《法律英语条件句的写作和翻译》,《中国翻译》2008年第4期。
李克兴:《论英文法律文本中古旧词的使用原则——兼评中国法律译本中滥用古旧词的现象》,《中国翻译》2010年第4期。
李克兴:《英汉法律翻译案例讲评》,北京:外文出版社,2011年。
李克兴:《高级法律翻译与写作》,北京:北京大学出版社,2013年。
李克兴:《英语法律文本中主要情态动词的作用及其翻译》,《中国翻译》2007年第6期。
刘国柱、吴树君:《对外经贸合同大全》,深圳:海天出版社,1990年。
刘净、刘美邦:UNCITRAL仲裁规则在CIETAC的适用。
陆谷孙主编:《英汉大字典》(第四版),上海:上海译文出版社,2009年。
庞广廉、袁宪军:《汉英涉外经济合同大全》,北京:北京大学出版社,1997年。
乔焕然:《英文合同阅读指南》,北京:中国法制出版社,2008年。
石现明:《国际商事仲裁一裁终局的相对性》,《长安大学学报》(社会科学版)2009年。
宋雷主编:《国际经济贸易法律文书格式》(中英文对照),北京:法律出版社,1997年。
孙万彪:《汉英法律翻译教程》,上海:上海外语教育出版社,2004年。
孙万彪:《英汉法律翻译教程》,上海:上海外语教育出版社,2002年。
王辉:《英文合同解读》,北京:法律出版社,2007年。
王相国:《鏖战英文合同》,北京:中国法制出版社,2008年。
韦箐:《对外贸易最新合同范本》,北京:经济贸易出版社,2005年。
文卓主编:《成功签订英文合同》,北京:农村读物出版社,2008年。
吴红云主编:《法庭内外》,北京:中国人民大学出版社,1999年。
香港法律第227章《裁判官条例》:translate.legislation.gov.hk/.
香港法律第32章《公司条例》:http://www.hklii.org/hk/legis/ch/ord/32/.
香港特别行政区《基本法》:http://www.basiclaw.gov.hk/gb/index/.
肖永平:《论冲突法》,武汉:武汉大学出版社,2002年。
薛华业编:《通用英文合约译解》,香港:万里书店有限公司,1989年。
闫洋:*GTA Price Agreement and QDC* (from his working file),2013年。
岩崎一生:《英文合同书制作方法与法理》,北京:外文出版社,2003年。
杨良宜:《国际商务仲裁》,北京:中国政法大学出版社,1997年。
《英汉法律词典》,北京:法律出版社,2005年。
《元照英美法词典》,北京:法律出版社,2008年。
曾青、邓建民:《新编仲裁法学》,成都:电子科技大学出版社,2005年。
张建华:《仲裁新论》,北京:中国法制出版社,2002年。
赵秀文:《国际商事仲裁及其适用法律研究》,北京:北京大学出版社,2002年。